WITTGENSTEIN

A Bibliographical Guide

WITTGENSTEIN

A Bibliographical Guide

Guido Frongia
and Brian McGuinness

Basil Blackwell

Copyright ©Guido Frongia and Brian McGuinness 1990

First published 1990

Basil Blackwell Ltd
108 Cowley Road, Oxford OX4 1JF, UK

Basil Blackwell, Inc.
3 Cambridge Center
Cambridge, Massachusetts 02142, USA

British Library Cataloguing in Publication Data

A CIP catalogue record for this book is available
from the British Library.

Library of Congress Cataloging in Publication Data

Frongia, Guido.
[Guida alla letteratura su Wittgenstein. English]
Wittgenstein: a bibliographical guide/Guido Frongia and Brian
McGuinness.
p. cm.
Rev. and updated translation of: Guida alla letteratura su
Wittgenstein.
ISBN 0-631-13765-3
1. Wittgenstein, Ludwig, 1889–1951—Bibliography. I. McGuinness,
Brian. II. Title.
Z8979.4.F7613 1989
[B3376.W564]
016.192—dc20   89-37725
CIP

Typeset in 11 on 13 point Garamond Book
by Dobbie Typesetting Service
Printed in Great Britain by Billing & Sons Ltd., Worcester

CONTENTS

PREFACE

This volume is designed to provide a summary account of the discussions to which Wittgenstein's philosophy has to date been exposed, an account taking the form of a conspectus, ordered by years, of the critical literature that has been published in the main Western languages. Two purposes are kept in view, that of placing in their historical context the origin and development of certain schools of interpretation, and that of providing the reader with the means of finding his way across a now abundant sea of publications.

Until the early 1950s interest in Wittgenstein's work was restricted to a small academic public and found written expression chiefly in attempts to develop independently some aspect of his thought. Who peruses the first part of the volume will perceive how often brief, apparently marginal, or even merely implicit references to Wittgenstein in what is for us the earlier literature have had great importance in determining the whole course of Wittgenstein criticism and the line of interpretation of his work that has been followed. For this reason, and because the relatively small number of entries involved has permitted it, we have followed rather generous criteria when selecting earlier items of literature, some of which will be found to contain few explicit references to our author.

In the last three decades and a half, since the death of Wittgenstein in fact, his thought has gone out to a much wider public and the type of study devoted to it has altered. For this period it has been necessary to be increasingly selective, lest the reader be overwhelmed by an undigested mass of names and titles. At the same time, whenever a work or article seemed to us to be of particular interest from a theoretical or historical point of view, we have not hesitated to include it. Other choices were less easy. The great variety of the items concerned made it in practice impossible to formulate uniform criteria for inclusion. We have had to decide case by case, always conscious, we can at least claim, of the risks of omission or mistaken evaluation that we were running.

For many of our entries the bibliographical data are followed by short notes, intended to give some indication of the nature of the contribution to criticism made by the work in question, sometimes also what the main themes treated were. In the case of publications in book form these brief indications can be supplemented from reviews, and we have usually indicated some of these, drawn from periodicals that circulate widely. For the reasons stated above and for others that are obvious, our notes are fuller and more analytic for the earliest period and more and more concise as the year under review approaches the present. It is, of course, more than possible that in these notes too, we have fallen into misunderstandings or have, despite a strong contrary intention, allowed ourselves to be influenced by our own interests and preferences. We apologize in particular to any author who may find that the content of his contribution has not been faithfully reproduced in our notes. We can only plead that in work of this kind objectivity and completeness are, necessarily, regulative principles rather than concretely realizable goals.

In both the above respects our book is, as its title indicates, a *guide*. It makes no claim to the comprehensiveness of the bibliography published recently by Croom-Helm (edited by V. A. and S. G. Shanker) though we hope that its selective principles may make it a useful supplement thereto, as indeed that work is, conversely, to those who need or wish to go beyond ours.

Our book, as it stands, is a revision and amplification for the English-speaking reader of a guide first published in Italian by Argalia for the University of Urbino: we gratefully acknowledge here the cession of rights by the publishing house and the university. The earlier volume was entirely the work of one of us (Guido Frongia) and it is proper to repeat here his thanks to former colleagues at the Centro di Storia della Storiografia Filosofica, then at the University of Rome (La Sapienza), where he carried out the basic research in the 1970s, and to the Consiglio Nazionale delle Ricerche of the Republic of Italy, which made possible long stays in England for the collection of material.

The English version has involved a re-sifting of the material, which, in any case, has been brought up to the middle of August 1987. Apart from inevitable errors of judgement or lapses of attention for which we must beg the reader's indulgence there will be omissions even of important works issued near our closing date. Anyone with the least experience of bibliographical work will know that such omissions are inevitable given the slow diffusion of information in this field, the sometimes tardy appearance of numbers of periodicals, and the other delays inseparable from book distribution and library processing. Items of exclusively Italian interest have now been omitted, though for that language, as for all major Western European ones, the earliest contributions, as well as any that are of international interest have been included. The content of the notes has been altered slightly for the present version.

The greater part of the work of preparing this volume has been done in various English libraries, particularly in the University of London Library, where Mrs Margaret Blackburn, the Philosophy Librarian, gave a competent and sensitive response to a large variety of demands; invaluable help was also given by Mrs Monique Mackee, Psychology Librarian, and Miss Sally Herron. Both authors wish to thank very warmly Miss Patricia Lloyd of Queen's College, Oxford, who, over a period now of some years, has typed a complicated text into machine-readable form.

Rome and Oxford, February 1988   G.F. and B.McG.

ARRANGEMENT OF THE *GUIDE*

Part I consists of an historical description of the main periods in the reception of Wittgenstein's work from 1914 to the present.

Part II consists of lists and indexes. First there is a list of Wittgenstein's own writings, giving abbreviations by which they are usually referred to in the rest of the *Guide*. Then follows a list of the most commonly cited periodicals with an indication of the abbreviations normally used for them. (Periodicals cited rarely do not occur in this list and are referred to in the appropriate place by their usual title placed between quotation marks.)

The main list is of books and articles which either as a whole or in part deal with Wittgenstein. These are arranged by year of publication and then alphabetically by author. Periodicals which straddle two years are placed under the earlier. Multi-author volumes are placed under the editor's name when the material contained is reprinted, under the title and before the alphabet of authors when the material is new. This distinction was found to assist cross-reference. Cross-reference is normally by means of author or editor name (or exceptionally volume title) with year of publication. Further details are given when disambiguation requires them. Items are also numbered continuously throughout the *Guide* for purposes of indexing. Reviews to which it is desired to draw attention are listed at the end of the item reviewed. A description of the contents of the item reviewed is frequently also given, as explained in the Preface.

The last list is of reviews of Wittgenstein's own writings. The Wittgenstein writings are again listed in order of composition, but are now numbered, consecutively with the items on Wittgenstein, for purposes of indexing. Under each Wittgenstein title reviews are listed alphabetically by author.

Three indexes conclude the book. The first, thematically arranged, is of subjects touched on in various items. The second is of thinkers from all periods who, in the items given, are referred to as sources, influences, or contrast figures in relation to Wittgenstein. Finally there is an index of authors of items in the main list or of reviews of writings by Wittgenstein (for reasons of space and ease of consultation, other reviews have not been indexed). Here are also shown, at entry end and in italic figures, cross-references, that is to say, references in other items to items by the author in question. (An author may thus figure in both of the last two indexes, but will do so in respect of different writings.)

PART I

HISTORY OF THE RECEPTION OF WITTGENSTEIN'S WORK

PROBLEMS OF THE PAST
AND OF THE PRESENT

Who would consult the vast array of works reviewed in the present volume will find much to assist him in a preliminary consideration of what problems they were that occasioned this literature and what explanation can be conjectured for the great diversity (disharmony even) in the means used over this relatively short period to resolve those problems.

An understanding of palpable changes of direction in scholarship or criticism will more readily be reached if the reader bears in mind the somewhat unusual way in which the corpus wittgensteinianum was given to the world. A first set of problems naturally revolved round *Tractatus*, the sole work that Wittgenstein considered finished enough to be printed. We know from manuscripts written during its preparation (many of which are now available in print) that this work was the fruit of a long and complex gestation (cf. von Wright, 1971). Moreover, when it went into print in 1921, some three years had passed since it received its final form. We shall see that this delay was to affect the reception of the work in Cambridge circles and, in general, the orientation of its first readers, at least throughout the twenties. We must remember too that these years coincided with Wittgenstein's temporary withdrawal from philosophy. At the very time when a debate on his ideas was being set on foot, he refrained from any intervention and even showed on more than one occasion a lack of interest in the reactions of the modest set of readers that he had secured. Small wonder that scholarship, left to its own devices in the face of a strange and hermetic work, finally allowed itself to fall under the sway of outlying influences from neighbouring fields, often far removed from the original intentions of the author.

Wittgenstein's reconciliation with philosophy, followed by his return to Cambridge in 1929, did nothing to ameliorate this situation. Even then those few comments of his that might have served as a guide for those interested in developing the ideas of *Tractatus* remained restricted to a small circle of hearers. To be sure, in such comments he was not slow to express his disappointment at how his work was understood and even exploited; but that was not enough to provide any positive guidance. Besides in the early 1930s he was gradually revising his theoretical position: no longer fully confident about his earlier ideas, he was hardly the person best motivated to defend them.

Even his new ideas, however, remained practically unknown until his death, as far as the learned world was concerned. Only a restricted group of disciples had access to them through attending his lectures. Wittgenstein's new philosophy was the subject of legend and indiscretion: lecture-notes and dictations circulated unofficially. Misunderstandings and difficulties arose from this irregular and provisional divulgation, which have only gradually, and perhaps not completely, been dispelled by the posthumous publication of his actual writings.

These writings are found in manuscripts and typescripts of the most diverse kind, the very ordering and cataloguing of which poses difficult problems, so many are they, so different in date and in level of elaboration: scattered notes and observations made on various occasions, collections of thoughts prepared for ordering, or actually set in order, sometimes even dictated to friends or pupils (cf. von Wright, 1970). In some cases material has been published in the form given to it by Wittgenstein, in others it has been re-arranged, sometimes even made the subject of suppression and selection, by the three literary heirs to whom Wittgenstein gave complete discretion over it. The posthumous publications fall into two main (though unequal) groups: those of 1913–18, antecedent to and preparatory for *Tractatus*, and those subsequent to Wittgenstein's return to philosophy, which date, therefore, from between 1929 and his death in 1951.

Writings of the former group present no insurmountable problems of arrangement or interpretation. We have for them a fixed point of reference in the shape of *Tractatus* itself, which (and which alone) Wittgenstein regarded as a finished work. Their main interest, then, lies in such clarification as they afford of previously obscure features of that work and such light as they throw on its genesis. Some of the questions raised still seem difficult, but there is no reason to doubt that in time a satisfactory solution will be found.

More complex problems confront us when we consider the literary remains dating from 1929 until the philosopher's death. For that period there is no single publication that we can regard as in any sense the definitive result of his researches. Even *Philosophical investigations*, which can fairly be described as the most systematic and exhaustive representation of Wittgenstein's thought among the posthumous publications, is probably in some respects quite far from the completeness that he required for publication. Indeed that is almost true by the very definition of our problem: for it is certainly not an accident that Wittgenstein published nothing in the last twenty years of his life.

The papers from this period give us a complex picture of Wittgenstein's philosophical development. It was by no means linear but testifies rather to indecision and to second thoughts then themselves re-thought. The constant re-ordering of his own remarks that our author carried out in this period bears witness to their lack of superficial unity and to his need to return continually to the same set of problems, attacking them from new points of view and following irregular and unpredictable trains of thought. Variants of a single passage are often to be found in quite different thematic contexts and their true interpretation is hence gravely obscured. It must be added here that, though each of the three literary heirs has displayed great devotion to the task, they have scarcely applied a clear and consistent editorial policy. This has sometimes resulted in confusions and possibilities of misunderstanding even greater than those inherent in the material itself. The first problem for critics and interpreters, therefore, has been that of finding a proper orientation in this tangled web of published and unpublished writings.

It must also be said that Wittgenstein's own style of exposition is of no great help towards the solution of problems of this nature. In his mature writings especially, his continual posing of questions without explicitly answering them and the apparently unsystematic character of his arguments often end up by giving the impression of impenetrable obscurity. Moreover the infrequency with which he refers explicitly to other authors or to works or theories that have an identifiable place in the history of philosophy often makes it difficult to identify his own theoretical aims or the precise views that he is attacking. The further fact that, after 1929, he never engaged in the sort of debate or defence of his own position that is usual in academic journals renders yet more complex the problems of orientation that interpreters have had to face in his regard.

Having no fixed points of reference, it was natural that criticism, interpretation, or scholarship should have had recourse to the most diverse sources of inspiration. It has been found useful, for example, to adopt, and assimilate comments on Wittgenstein to one or other of the theoretical frameworks to be found in secondary or expository literature dealing with philosophical movements that have borrowed or been lent his name – logicism, for example, or logical atomism, neopositivism, analytical philosophy, or the like. Naturally the picture that scholars have had of these movements too has changed and varied over the years, and the accounts or criticisms of Wittgenstein have had to follow course, giving rise to the frequent digressions into exegesis or historiography that we have already noted.

We cannot but be conscious of the possibility that a reader confronted with so complex a panorama may feel disoriented. We shall therefore try to sketch a general picture, with no pretensions to completeness, but giving the main lines of development in the discussion to which our author has from the first been subjected. Four main trends can be identified, which fall into chronological order. The first three are more or less closely associated with the same number of schools of thought in the philosophy of our day.

As a result of the fact already noted that *Tractatus* was practically the only one of Wittgenstein's writings to be known and studied before his death, the first two divisions in our survey of the literature will be concerned with the interpretations of that work that were prevalent in the 1920s and 1930s respectively. The last two divisions, on the other hand, deal with all periods of his thought and reflect the wider diffusion it attained, first within a restricted academic public, but subsequently in ever wider circles. The ordering by years that we have adopted in the body of our guide enables the reader to see at a glance how the acclaim won by our author has grown, and how, *pari passu* with that, the themes treated and the standpoint of their treatment have become ever more diverse, to such an extent that in the later years of our survey they become hard to fit into any traditional set of categories.

LOGICAL ATOMISM AND THE LOGICAL INTERPRETATION OF *TRACTATUS*

We have seen that during the first half of the 1920s *Tractatus* hardly circulated outside Cambridge. This circumstance much favoured the notion, which we shall find still current in later decades, that the book was to be interpreted in the light of the philosophical tendencies prevalent in that university, in particular the work of Moore and of Russell and Whitehead in philosophy and logic. Such a point of view naturally led to the belief that the most important contribution made by the book was its discovery of a way to avoid certain difficulties and paradoxes of that summa of mathematical logic, *Principia mathematica*.

We must here advert to the fact that Russell himself was the first to give currency to this belief, and in an authoritative manner, by a number of references to Wittgenstein in writings published even before *Tractatus* itself was printed. The first such reference is contained in the preface to *Our knowledge of the external world* (Russell, 1914). There Russell stresses his debt to the important discoveries, not yet published, made by 'my friend Ludwig Wittgenstein', as he styles him. The same point of view is given yet more explicit expression in Russell's 'Introduction' to the English edition of *Tractatus* (Russell, 1922), which puts forward a way of reading the book that has influenced more than one generation of readers.

At the very beginning of this 'Introduction' Russell declares that the principal problem faced by Wittgenstein was a logical one and concerned 'the relation which one fact must have to another in order to be capable of being a symbol for that other'. Because it is logical this problem must be distinguished from other questions, psychological, epistemological, or belonging to the special sciences, that can be raised about language. As compared with the central core of doctrine which *Tractatus* contains, which concerns and illuminates the nature of symbolism, all the other theses in it, regarding, say, ethics, religion, or the task of philosophy, are regarded as incidental consequences. Thus, in Russell's account, Wittgenstein's attitude towards the domain of mysticism is a natural development of his doctrine of pure logic, according to which a proposition must have a certain structure in common with the facts, but this structure cannot itself be put into words (ibid., p. 21). On such an account the conclusion of *Tractatus*, that there is a sphere of questions to which we cannot give answers that make sense, is presented rather as a technical difficulty chiefly due to Wittgenstein's excessively rigorous approach to the primary problem of symbolism: an unwelcome consequence, as it were, even if inevitable from the point of view of mere logical consistency, and moreover a consequence that can and should be avoided by the logico-syntactical expedient of a hierarchy of languages (ibid., p .23).

In these pages Russell clearly does not attach much weight to the indications that Wittgenstein himself gave him as to the theoretical goals of *Tractatus*. For example, in a letter written in 1919 from the prisoner-of-war camp at Cassino, Wittgenstein tells Russell that the main point of his work (and even the cardinal question of philosophy as a whole) is 'the theory of what can be expressed (*gesagt*) by propositions – i.e. by language . . . and what cannot be expressed by propositions but only shown (*gezeigt*)'. 'To this contention', he says, 'the whole business of logical propositions is only a corollary' (printed in Russell, 1967, vol. II, p. 118). Yet a grasp of this distinction would have made possible a correct formulation of the point of the book, 'den Sinn des Buches', as Wittgenstein calls it in a letter of about the same date, written to Ficker, the editor of 'Der Brenner', (cf. Engelmann, 1967, p. 144), namely that the book draws a limit to the sphere of the ethical with the aim of making clear that that sphere is quite independent of the sphere of facts.

In the light of these indications a modern reader will readily understand Wittgenstein's discontent with Russell's 'Introduction', a discontent expressed in the judgement that Russell had failed to catch the main thesis of the book (cf. Russell, 1967, pp. 208–9). At the same time it is possible to see why Russell in this period stressed the logical aspects of the book: his judgement was no doubt influenced above all by his personal knowledge of what Wittgenstein had been like during the latter's first sojourn in Cambridge, which was indeed devoted principally to work in the field of logic. After 1913 there was effectively no contact between the two philosophers until Wittgenstein had completed his book, and the manuscript sent from the prison-camp was evidently not enough in itself to convey to Russell the changes in thought and in direction of interest that had overtaken Wittgenstein in the meantime. The two men met for the first time after the war, in late 1919, in The Hague. Russell then saw that Wittgenstein had had a profound change of mind as regarded religion, but seems to have thought that this left the substance of the book untouched.

At all events, as we must here emphasize, Russell's approach was to have a decisive effect on the reading of Wittgenstein's book, an effect only confirmed by the numerous references to *Tractatus*, regarded as a logical tract, in the second edition of *Principia mathematica* (Whitehead and Russell, 1925): in his introduction to that edition Russell acknowledged that in the light of the principle of extensionality enunciated by Wittgenstein he had been obliged to subject to radical review many aspects of his theory of logic with important consequences for certain aspects of the theory of number developed in volumes II and III.

Most of Ramsey's work in this area follows the same lines as Russell's. His review of *Tractatus* in 'Mind' (Ramsey, 1923) already aroused a great deal of interest. He was known to have played a part, perhaps the major part, in translating the work, and subsequently his human and intellectual qualities won him the confidence and esteem of Wittgenstein. Naturally, therefore, he was, rightly or wrongly, regarded as a reliable spokesman. Yet the review had a reductive tendency, not dissimilar to Russell's, and, as Ramsey himself later admitted (cf. Braithwaite, 1931), it contained a number of misunderstandings. To be sure Ramsey at the outset emphasizes that the work is 'of extraordinary interest and deserves the attention of all philosophers', but in what follows he confines his own analysis of it to logical questions, giving only secondary status to the general conclusions about philosophy to be found at the end of the book.

In most of his later writings, too, collected posthumously into the volume *The foundations of mathematics* (1931) Ramsey concentrates above all on those aspects of the theory contained in *Tractatus* that served to overcome the systematic difficulties of *Principia mathematica*. So it is in his 1926 article, whose title was borrowed for the posthumous volume, and which enjoyed a wide diffusion. So also in *Mathematical logic* (1926), where Ramsey stresses the importance of the *Tractatus* analysis of general and existential propositions and the clarification it affords of the tautological nature of the propositions of logic.

With the end of the 1920s this type of interpretation, which saw *Tractatus* principally as an attempt to give a systematic answer to problems in the foundations of logic and mathematics, became progressively rarer, until finally it was to be found only in works of a definitely specialist character, or, of course, in manuals or histories of contemporary logic (cf., e.g., Chadwick, Feys, Langford, 1927; Carnap, Kaufmann, 1930; Jørgensen, 1932; Lazerowitz, 1937; Bochenski, 1956; Broad, 1957). None the less, before we proceed to consider later tendencies in the criticism and interpretation of Wittgenstein, it will be appropriate to take in review another school of interpretation, which also dates back to the 1920s, and which sees a close link, both theoretical and historical, between *Tractatus* and logical atomism. Though appreciably more philosophical in character than the type of interpretation we have just considered, this one has considerable theoretical affinity with it, as might be expected when we observe that Russell was once again the founder of the school. In a series of articles based on lectures and actually entitled *The philosophy of logical atomism*, Russell (1918) presents that philosophy as inspired by Wittgenstein, saying, in an introductory note, that the lectures were 'very largely concerned with explaining certain ideas which I learnt from my friend and former pupil Ludwig Wittgenstein'.

No further explanation of this reference is given by Russell, but it is not too difficult to guess his meaning. He thought that he could interpret his ex-pupil's ideas so as to yield not only a solution to a number of problems in logic, but also a motive for changing the whole direction of his own philosophical researches. As he in fact says in a relatively late work of his (Russell, 1959), Wittgenstein's influence broadened his philosophical interests and led him to problems of meaning and truth, no longer purely with regard to logical symbolism, but in the realm of natural language and of human life in general. Moreover he came to think that the analysis of the structure of a perfect symbolism was a useful tool for a rigorous investigation of the ontological structure of the world. He gradually became convinced that the world had to consist of atomic facts, logically independent of one another, and of the elements that went to make up those facts, a point of view that seemed to many to have clear analogies with classical empiricism.

Thus Wittgenstein's name too, like that of his teacher, became associated with the traditions of British empiricism. This conception became more widely shared as the years passed and found confirmation particularly in historical reconstructions of the birth and development of logical atomism (cf., e.g., Urmson, 1956; Griffin, 1964). The general view was that the new logical tools supplied by Russell and Wittgenstein provided a theoretical framework within which research could proceed with clarity and rigour just where classical empiricism had had to confess itself defeated (cf. Urmson, op.cit., pp. 94–98).

Russell's attitude, of course, changed considerably over the next few years, as references to Wittgenstein in his later writings show (cf., e.g., Russell, 1928, 1936, 1959). His introductory note to the 1918–19 lectures, however, in which he describes his ex-pupil as the inspiration of logical atomism, was taken quite literally by a number of thinkers who continued along that line of thought in the 1920s and 1930s. For them it was natural to extend Russell's reference, which was intended to be to Wittgenstein's thought before the war, also to *Tractatus* once it was published. Thus a number of logical atomists treated the book as an authoritative and inspirational work that contained a valid nucleus of theory, even if in other respects it stood in need of more or less substantial changes.

A work in this tradition is A. J. T. D. Wisdom's *Logical constructions* (1931-3), which contains references to *Tractatus* that are of particular historical and theoretical value. Wisdom points out how difficult it is to apply Wittgenstein's picture theory to even the simplest propositions of ordinary language ('This is red' and the like): much has to be done to adapt them before they can satisfy some of the fundamental requirements of the theoretical model given in *Tractatus* (isomorphism, for instance, and that there should be the same number of elements in the proposition and in the 'fact', etc.). Though this point is not perfectly clear, one has the impression that Wittgenstein's 'pictures' are here being understood in a restricted sense, so as to fit in to an empiricist interpretation of his thought, which Russell in 1918-19 had been the first to give. In any case Wisdom's contribution did serve to reinforce a line of interpretation then much in the ascendancy.

The attempt to find in Wittgenstein's book a theory not valid for a 'logically perfect language' only (as Russell had suggested in his 'Introduction' to *Tractatus*) but directly applicable to historical languages is foreshadowed in the review by Ramsey that we have already discussed: 'there are, indeed, passages in which Mr. Wittgenstein is explicitly concerned with a logically perfect language . . . but in general he seems to maintain that his doctrines apply to ordinary languages in spite of appearances to the contrary' (Ramsey, 1923, p. 465). For most purposes Ramsey too was considered a logical atomist but in his contribution to the understanding of *Tractatus* he seemed content, as we have seen, to remain inside the sphere of logical problems and the foundations of mathematics. Indeed Ramsey's main contribution to logical atomism, *Facts and propositions* (1927), is also the work in which he breaks away for the first time from Wittgenstein's influence and starts out on a line of his own, to which he gives the name 'pragmatism'. It is worthy of note that he considers this theoretical innovation necessary 'in order to fill a gap in [Wittgenstein's] system'. Also largely philosophical in content are Ramsey's notes from the years 1928–29, which were included in the posthumous volume already referred to (Ramsey, 1931), but their provisional character and a certain obscurity in expression make it difficult to assess their precise relation to *Tractatus* though references to that work are not rare in them.

WITTGENSTEIN
AND NEOPOSITIVISM

So far we have been able to characterize the first steps that criticism and interpretation took in the years immediately following the publication of *Tractatus*. At that stage its practitioners emphasized the logical aspects of the work and preserved a relative neutrality on philosophical matters. Next were produced writings in which it was precisely philosophical starting-points and interests that prevailed. We saw, in particular, how Russell's attempt to insert Wittgenstein's thought into the framework of logical atomism led to a tendency to view *Tractatus* always from the standpoint of a more or less radical empiricism.

The latter style of interpretation became more and more marked during the 1930s and the works we have most recently mentioned may almost be considered as transitional, harbingers of a new phase of criticism. The onset of this new phase was directly connected with the formation of the Vienna Circle in the late 1920s, while, during the 1930s and 1940s, the ambages of the new style of interpretation followed those of logical positivism itself.

Wittgenstein's relations with the Circle were a matter of speculation at least until the beginning of the 1960s. Only those who had been directly involved were in a position to say what contact Wittgenstein had with Waismann, Schlick, Carnap, and other representatives of the Circle in the years from 1927 to 1929. To be sure, there were many references to Wittgenstein in the writings of these authors, but, as we shall see, these were sometimes too general in form and sometimes too obscure to be of much help in attaining a proper understanding of their relations with him. If anything they only increased the confusion.

Wissenschaftliche Weltauffassung, Der Wiener Kreis, which was considered to be the manifesto of the movement appeared in 1929 (q.v.). In it *Tractatus* is regarded as a source of inspiration of fundamental importance for the new movement. Along with the work of Russell and Einstein it was said to represent just that scientific conception of the world which the Circle existed to propagate. A tribute of this nature could not remain without effect, and indeed, for some years after it, commentators and historians took it for granted that *Tractatus* was indissolubly linked with the programmatic points set out in the manifesto. This was the origin of the opinion that the activity of clarification that Wittgenstein assigned to philosophy consisted, essentially, in showing how the meaning of statements proper, i.e., the statements of empirical science 'can be determined by logical analysis . . . through reduction to the simplest statements about the empirically given'. Statements for which this cannot be done say nothing, at best they 'express a certain mood and spirit' (ibid. p. 17). Wittgenstein from the start gave voice to rather negative judgements on the programme of the Circle and the spirit that animated it (cf., e.g., the letter to Waismann quoted in the introduction to *Wittgenstein und der Wiener Kreis*, p. 18). But they were uttered in private and reached no wide public, nor perhaps were taken seriously by those they did reach. After Wittgenstein's return to Cambridge in 1929, Schlick and Waismann were the only channel of communication with the Circle that he kept open, meeting them frequently for philosophical conversation during his vacation visits to Vienna. These two writers were at pains to acknowledge Wittgenstein's inspiration for their writings during this period: the theses defended are attributed to him or represented as derived from the conversations just mentioned (cf. Schlick, Waismann, 1930; Schlick, 1931, 1932; McGill, Waismann, 1936). Moreover, in the early 1930s, Waismann circulated notes in which not only were the main theses of *Tractatus* presented in palatable form but the latest developments in Wittgenstein's thought were incorporated (cf. Waismann, 1966).

A particularly striking instance of their attitude is given by the opening article of the new (or re-born) periodical 'Erkenntnis', *Die Wende der Philosophie* (E. T.: *The turning-point in philosophy*), a work of Schlick's (1930) and avowedly programmatic. The methods for the 'really final change in philosophy' now in progress 'proceed from logic. Their beginnings were obscurely perceived by Leibniz; in recent decades important stretches have been opened up by Gottlob Frege and Bertrand Russell: but the decisive turning-point was first reached by Wittgenstein in his *Tractatus*.' These new methods illuminate for us 'the nature of expression or presentation, that is, of any possible "language" in the most general sense of the term', and this in turn alone makes possible a rigorous distinction between what can be expressed or formulated without sacrifice of sense and, on the other hand, concatenations of terms to which no sense attaches. It is quite in conformity with this way of seeing matters that philosophy is no longer expected to be a body of knowledge but is recognized as 'that activity whereby the meaning of statements is established or discovered'.

The remarks by Schlick will immediately strike a chord with any reader of *Tractatus*, and will even seem to paraphrase some well-known paragraphs in that work. Similar echoes abound in other articles from early numbers of 'Erkenntnis' by authors such as Carnap, Waismann, Frank (all 1930), and Hahn (1931, see also Anon, 1930). Many took all this as proof beyond doubt of close ties that existed between Wittgenstein's thought and the programme of the Circle. In reality, however, there is a very problematic aspect to these references: it is far from clear how much in them really goes back to *Tractatus* and how much is owed to later developments in Wittgenstein's thought, developments known to these authors either from personal contact or by indirect means. We shall see that this uncertainty led critics to combine two phases that ought to have been kept distinct. So soon after the event, almost in the presence of the man, readers were not then capable even of considering such a possibility: one part of the truth (or at any rate of the new philosophy) could not differ from another. To be sure, Schlick and Waismann often mentioned in their writings new works on which Wittgenstein was engaged, but his day-to-day activity was not conducted in Austria and its difference from *Tractatus* not visible. Their mediation did indeed introduce some of his new ideas into the Circle, but imperceptibly since they themselves were not aware of the essential novelty of those ideas.

Wittgenstein's own attitude toward this form of mediation was complex and even inconsistent. He alternated between mistrustful reticence and a frank interest in the wider diffusion of his ideas. This uncertainty of attitude, together with other factors already indicated, lies at the root of many misunderstandings and much impreciseness of interpretation which in these years went to swell the inheritance of the first decade of our author's reception. Thus *Tractatus* was often understood in the light of solutions that Wittgenstein temporarily adopted in the early 1930s and that Schlick or Waismann perhaps gave currency to in their writings. The book was thought to anticipate the idea that the principle of verification was the test for the significance or sense of statements. It is a theme that recurs constantly in Waismann's unpublished papers from that period, and yet they were intended to assist a reader of *Tractatus*. The same question arises in a 1936 article by Schlick which has had considerable influence. In it Schlick traces back to his conversations with Wittgenstein the conviction that 'the meaning of a word or combination of words is determined by a set of rules which regulate their use'. He then proceeds to extend the scope of this principle somewhat unjustifiably, saying, 'Stating the meaning of a sentence amounts to stating . . . the way in which it can be verified.' A further important consequence of this point of view is that 'there is no way of understanding any meaning without ultimate reference to ostensive definitions', which, for the author, is an acknowledgement of the part that experience must play in explaining the functioning of language and solving the problem of meaning.

The frequency and the placing of the references to Wittgenstein in this article make it impossible to tell how much is meant to be attributed to him and how much is an independent account of Schlick's own views. We must remember that there were lively debates within the Circle in these years and widely divergent views held precisely on the topic of this article. All that is certain is that it is very hard to reconcile the views ascribed to Wittgenstein in such passages with the views that he was contemporaneously developing in his own manuscripts and in the typescripts that he had made for him, if, that is, any rigour of interpretation is to be observed. Even greater problems arise when the views attributed are placed alongside those of *Tractatus*. It looks as if these authors allowed their own theoretical preoccupations to take precedence over historical and exegetical accuracy, and perhaps Wittgenstein himself was more intent on the new points he had to make than on correcting the historical record. For all of this there may be some justification, but it has undoubtedly given rise to considerable misunderstanding with consequences that were not merely historiographical.

Apart from the verification principle there is another, though connected formula that was used as a key to the interpretation of Wittgenstein. It too was foreshadowed in some prior literature, but suited particularly well the theoretical framework of the Vienna Circle; and it too for many years dominated and perhaps distorted the reception of his thought.

We refer to the notion that the theses and the methods of *Tractatus* show that there was in Wittgenstein a fundamental aversion for metaphysics, a notion to which the writings of the first neopositivists gave very wide circulation. A fairly precise sense was given here to 'metaphysics': not arbitrary speculation on transcendent entities was meant but, more generally, any attempt to talk about what, in *Tractatus* terms, could only be 'shown' – such things as the pictorial relation between language and reality, the nature of the elements of a fully analysed proposition, the structure of the world as reflected in the structure of language, etc. In the first phase of neopositivism it was thought that such problems would disappear once a 'clear and meaningful' form of expression (i.e., one corresponding to logical syntax) had been found (cf. Schlick, 1930, p. 11). What we must here particularly note is the frequency with which the authors in question emphasize just those parts of *Tractatus* that seem to agree with their own philosophical convictions, ignoring other parts that have an opposite tendency. In particular, the closing sections of the book were regarded as suspect and some thought a fundamental revision of its theoretical framework might be necessary in order to avoid its mystical conclusions and its implications for ethics. Such a revision, it was thought, could be conducted on thoroughly Wittgensteinian lines, taking as its starting-point his own hostility to any question for which no meaningful answer could be expected, the very core of his doctrine as of theirs.

This approach is particularly evident in the writings of Carnap around the year 1930. Two works will serve to indicate this: *Der logische Aufbau der Welt* and *Scheinprobleme in der Philosophie* (for both see 1928), both extremely influential. References to *Tractatus* are few and generic in character: it is cited in connexion with the use of logic in philosophical research, the determination of the limits of scientific knowledge, the nature of ethical judgements, etc. (*Aufbau*, §§. 180, 183). But if we look beyond such courtesy references, we shall see that both works constantly have *Tractatus* in mind, as Carnap indeed allows in his introduction to the second edition of *Aufbau* (1961). This holds not only of general themes but of specific questions (as may be seen from Joergensen, 1951). The general supposition at the time was that in his two 1928 publications Carnap was developing and making explicit ideas that had been strikingly formulated in *Tractatus* but which Wittgenstein, largely for external reasons, had not carried through to their strict logical conclusion.

This is particularly evident in Carnap's remarks about the nature and scope of philosophy itself. These can be found not only in *Scheinprobleme*, already cited, but in *Überwindung der Metaphysik durch logische Analyse der Sprache* (1931). There the distinction between expressions that are possessed of sense and those that are not is found to reside in the fact that the former are reducible, directly or mediately, to primary propositions of a certain type (the *Protokollsätze*), which refer directly to 'the given'. Carnap here leaves the precise nature of the protocols undefined, because of a lack of agreement over them in the philosophical world, but goes so far as to say that a succession of words has sense only if it has a definite and ascertainable relation of deducibility with a set of protocols. This is an obvious attempt to adapt the *Tractatus* distinction between sense and nonsense, between science and metaphysics, to the Vienna Circle conception of a verifiability criterion based on the immediately given. 'Metaphysical words', which are denied meaning by such a criterion, have no theoretical value. They occur either in statements about the relation between language and the world (something that, as Wittgenstein said, can only be shown, not talked about) or else they are the expression of our feelings about life.

In papers of this kind Carnap, perhaps more than other neopositivists, remains true to the spirit of *Tractatus*, in that he recognizes that what falls outside the limits of sense may be of considerable importance. At the same time he insists that metaphysics is in the last analysis an unsatisfactory instrument of achieving its own aims, as well as being deceptive in the impression it gives of actually having a content. It now needs to be superseded by some more suitable mode of self-expression.

In his autobiographical notes written in 1963 Carnap lays some stress on differences between himself and Wittgenstein, especially as regards metaphysics and religion, that arose as early as 1927. His references at the time do not suggest a fundamental divergence of attitude and were certainly taken as an indication of how to understand Wittgenstein's thought, for Carnap was an influential figure both within and beyond the confines of the Circle.

In the mid-1930s, however, there is a sensible change in Carnap's attitude towards philosophy and towards Wittgenstein's philosophy in particular. Later he was to describe this as a liberalization: the principles he took as guide-lines during his first years of work within the Vienna Circle now seemed to him too restrictive. The revision to which this change of mind led had a curious effect as far as *Tractatus* was concerned. Having been taken as the Holy Writ of the first phase of neopositivism, it now had the flavour of archaism and intransigency, and was submitted to frequent criticism by those who had been (on a certain understanding of it) its adherents.

This is perhaps most easily seen, among Carnap's writings, in *Logische Syntax der Sprache* (1934) and in *Philosophy and logical syntax* (1935). In the former, Carnap reopens the crucial question of what can be expressed in meaningful language. Here he at once controverts Wittgenstein's thesis that the form of a proposition can only be shown, not meaningfully talked about. Carnap says that not only is such talk possible, by means of 'logical syntax', but is even possible within the very language whose formation and transformation rules are governed by that syntax. Thus Carnap holds that he has escaped the fundamental impasse of *Tractatus*, which consisted in the senselessness of the very statements in which its own logical theory is formulated (Carnap, 1935, ch. I, §. 7). In this way the word 'philosophy' begins to lose its rather negative connotations and can designate the activity of 'logic of science', which is presented in an entirely positive light. This change of direction in Carnap's thought is yet more clearly evident in *Testability and meaning* (1936). There the verifiability requirement (as a condition of the meaningfulness of sentences) is explicitly traced back to *Tractatus*, followed by the first publications of the Circle. As a criterion it is regarded as simplistic: it fails to take account of the complexity of the control and confirmation procedures employed in the experimental sciences. In those sciences, it is said, theoretical concepts are introduced on the basis of postulates and rules of coordination: their logical and methodological role does not permit of their being subjected to complete analysis or verification. The verificationist thesis is here attributed, it is interesting to see, to *Tractatus*, but also to Schlick and Waismann, the 'more conservative wing of the Circle' as Carnap puts it (ibid., §. 23). A similar judgement is found in later writings of Carnap (1936, 1942, 1947, and *Empiricism, semantics and ontology*, 1950) and we shall see that it soon became an accepted canon of interpretation.

In the second half of the 1930s Wittgenstein's fame began to spread beyond the restricted academic circles that had so far bounded it. This was principally due to the wider diffusion of neopositivism in these years, in the United States, in England, and in the Scandinavian countries, as many of its main representatives left Germany or Austria. News also spread that Wittgenstein in his Cambridge lectures was in the process of subjecting his views to a radical revision. Taken together these two circumstances served to confirm for most readers Carnap's view that *Tractatus* belonged to an outmoded and particularly intransigent phase of neopositivism. Among the many who took such a judgement for granted in the 1930s were Feigl and Blumberg (1931), Neurath (1931, 1935), and Reichenbach (1936, 1938).

Another, but less direct, contribution to this view was that of A.J.Ayer. In the opening passage of his 1936 preface to *Language, truth and logic*, the work that did more than any other to make known in the British Isles the new continental ways of thinking, he proclaims that his own views 'derive from the doctrines of Bertrand Russell and Wittgenstein, which are themselves the logical outcome of the empiricism of Berkeley and David Hume'. It must be said, of course, that some of Ayer's pronouncements later in the book are more guarded: many of the more radical positions of early neopositivism are held at arm's length: for example, the version of the verifiability principle adopted is a very liberal one (cf. also Ayer, 1933). Ayer is intransigent only in his insistence on the vacuousness of metaphysical statements and in his related determination to lay the foundations for a more rigorous philosophy, a 'scientific philosophy', to use the title he adopted in 1936 at the International Congress in Paris.

Ayer's passionate professions of adherence to the theses of *Tractatus* only served to confirm the impression that the work had been anticipated by Russell and in any case belonged to the tradition of British Empiricism. In this, and in his use of it in the course of attacks on metaphysics (1934 again), Ayer was applying *Tractatus* to ends to which its author, we now know, felt no great attachment.

A vigorous opponent of neopositivism in the early 1930s was K. R. Popper. In a letter of 1932 to the periodical 'Erkenntnis' he criticizes the attempt to found a theory of meaning on the principle of verifiability. Problems of meaning, in general, he regards as pseudo-problems, and he traces the rot back to *Tractatus*, finding there the principle that every proposition must be a truth-function of observation statements. But this would exclude the most characteristic part of science, the laws themselves, which cannot be deduced from observation statements. Popper, of course, has his own falsifiability criterion, which is not designed to solve the 'problem of meaning' but to draw a line between statements that are properly scientific and those that belong to metaphysics, religion, or pseudo-science (cf. also Popper, 1935).

Other critics who refer to *Tractatus* as a theoretical model with some valid elements but in general in need of fundamental revision are important figures such as G. Bergmann (1950, 1953), S. Stebbing (1932), J. R. Weinberg (1935). All, for varying reasons, will not accept that meaningful propositions must be completely analysable and ultimately consist of names for simple entities. The same themes appear in the retrospective section of many expositions of neopositivism: see J. R. Weinberg (again: 1936), E. Nagel (1936), R. von Mises (1939), J. A. Passmore (1942), I. M. Bochenski (1947), P. Frank (1949), F. Kaufmann (1950), F. Barone (1953), J. O. Urmson (1956). Weinberg, for example, the first historian of the movement, thinks that Wittgenstein is forced to admit the existence of simple objects in order to guarantee the exclusively empirical content of elementary propositions. This restrictive starting-point cried out for the liberating influence of physicalism, which brought an entirely new direction into philosophical research.

THE TWO WITTGENSTEINS

From the 1930s until Wittgenstein's death there was little change in critical judgement as regarded *Tractatus*. Echoes began to be heard, however, of his Cambridge lectures (1930–47), which aroused interest by reason of the unconventional nature both of their manner and setting and of the doctrines advanced in them. One oddity was the restriction to a small number of hearers and this naturally contributed to considerable confusion and misunderstanding among those who were not present. The most authoritative reports were Wittgenstein's own dictations, later published as *Blue and brown books*, but there were also accounts of his lectures composed by pupils, some now also published, but at the time circulated in typescript with a slight air of conspiracy. Not that sensationalism or intrusiveness were the motives of those who wrote or set them in circulation: these motives being much rather a recognition of the profound originality of Wittgenstein's thought and a sincere conviction that it should not be hidden from the intellectual community. Certainly this was the case with Waismann. His often revised summary of Wittgenstein's philosophy, *Logik, Sprache, Philosophie* (1965), was not published until both men were dead, for internal and external reasons, both partly attributable to Wittgenstein's distrust of the whole project.

Other references to Wittgenstein's new philosophy were made in the late 1930s by outsiders interested in the development of analytic philosophy at Cambridge and Oxford, who rightly saw that Wittgenstein's was a decisive influence (for these cf. Nagel,

1936; Black, 1939, 1950; Findlay, 1953), or by pupils who recognized their intellectual debt but were none the less bent on an independent development of the ideas derived from him (cf., e.g., Anscombe, 1957; Geach, 1957; Malcolm, 1959).

A. J. T. D. Wisdom is a particularly good example of this last group. He was one of the small number present at Wittgenstein's lectures during 1934–37 (cf. Wisdom, 1952) and in what he wrote (winning considerable acclaim) down to 1950 there are clear echoes of those lectures, both in theme and analytic method (cf. Wisdom, 1936, 1938, 1940, 1944, 1949). Above all the stress is on 'dissolving' problems belonging to the heritage of British philosophy: mind–body dualism, knowledge of other minds, identification of one's own mental states, etc.

All these varied references to Wittgenstein's new ideas had a decisive impact on his public image. A new trend in criticism declared itself, and indeed became prevalent. Whereas *Tractatus* had been interpreted on positivist lines, it was assumed that Wittgenstein had now completely turned his back upon such theories. Many of the obituaries by leading English-language philosophers that appeared just after his death lay particular stress on the notion of a complete break between the two supposed phases in his thought (cf. Russell, Ryle, 1951; Wisdom, 1952).

Inevitably the posthumous publication of *Philosophical investigations*, with its many critical references to the earlier work, was taken as a clear confirmation that the author had decisively rejected his former theoretical position. Also, Wittgenstein's stress on the need in philosophy to see how ordinary language functions (as opposed to knowledge of the idealized models studied by logicians) seemed to bring him near to the type of analytic philosophy developed in England after the war under the influence of such authors as G. E. Moore, G. Ryle, and J. L. Austin (cf. White, 1958; Russell, 1959).

This tendency to see Wittgenstein in terms of contemporary English philosophy (as Ayer and Russell had in the past, in quite other philosophical contexts) can be found particularly clearly in some of the articles in *The revolution in philosophy* (cf. Paul, Pears, 1956), a work professedly addressed to the general public.

The 'revolution' meant was the decisive turning-point introduced into the philosophy of the day by the new analytic approach. It was natural to attribute an important role here to the ideas of Wittgenstein, then becoming known through the publication of his literary remains. They had guided and inspired, just as *Tractatus* had done for a previous generation. But 'revolution' was also understood in its destructive and iconoclastic sense: traditional philosophy had to be attacked, and Wittgenstein's role was seen as a 'therapeutic' one, curing the 'mental cramps' of the metaphysician by undoing the conceptual knots that produced them (cf., e.g., Strawson, 1954; Urmson, 1956; Passmore, 1957; Quinton, Warnock, 1958; Ayer, 1959; Hartnack, 1960; Pitcher, 1964).

Those there were, indeed, who pointed out how Wittgenstein had attributed great power of illumination precisely to the conceptual knots he sought to untie, but most, and the best-regarded, of his interpreters in the 1950s and 1960s stressed the surgical nature of his therapy. This in turn led to a sharp reaction from other authors who found such a conception of analysis excessively limiting and wanted philosophy to assume a more constructive and less partisan role. Thus some suggested (cf. Strawson, 1954) that therapeutic analysis of problems occasioned by particular uses of language might be expanded to take the form of general and systematic research into the logic of language. Others thought that the appeal to current usage in language betrayed a conservative attitude which favoured widespread and established forms of expression and tended to overlook undeniable changes in our language and ways of thinking (cf. Pole, 1958). Yet others stressed the need for philosophy to free itself from the tyranny of correct use of language and to reassume its dynamic role of showing us new ways of looking at things, ways which would transform the whole intellectual scene (cf. Waismann, 1956).

Criticisms of this nature did not prevent the development throughout the 1960s and 1970s of an immense literature on Wittgenstein, in the English language for the most part, which concentrated on what were taken to be the central themes of his mature thought. Attention was paid above all to the philosophy of mind, as it came to be called: Wittgenstein's own term would have been 'philosophical psychology'. Typical problems here were the possibility of a private language, the rules (or absence of rules) for the use of expressions relating to inner states, the temptations of solipsism, etc. (cf. the indexes at the end of the present volume). These debates were among the most characteristic and most fertile preoccupations of analytical philosophy in the years in question. The authors concerned generally recognize the novelty and the historic importance of Wittgenstein's achievements in this area. He had called in question problems and solutions that formed the very core of the Anglo-Saxon philosophical tradition: under his influence many of the classical forms of associationist psychology, of empiricism, of phenomenalism, and of metaphysical dualism now faced radical and destructive criticism.

The historical importance lent to Wittgenstein by judgements of this kind chimed in very well with the anti-empiricist fervour observable in many Western countries in the decades immediately after the Second World War. This gave yet more colour to the idea of a 'later Wittgenstein' distinct from his earlier self, for *Tractatus* was everywhere taken to be wedded to the theses of the first neopositivists. Only recently, as we shall see, has a more balanced account of his philosophical evolution been attempted.

This apart, there is another striking aspect of criticism that appeared in the decades in question: authors were agreed in finding the origin of their own views in Wittgenstein, but substantially in disagreement, in many cases, as to what he actually meant, and that even in the case of the most basic and distinctive of his views. Disparities of understanding of this kind can be seen in the proceedings of many symposia held in the 1950s and 1960s, which none the less became accepted points of reference for future discussion. It must be asked whether such divergent judgements can possibly have issued from uniform or philologically admissible methods of interpretation. It seems that for a number of reasons, some already indicated, the time was not yet ripe for historical or exegetical rigour. Only in the 1970s, as we shall see, did conditions begin to emerge which permitted a fresh examination, historically more detached and philologically better prepared, of questions previously left undecided or even unattacked.

More Recent
Developments

We have had several occasions already to mention the changes that have taken place in the criticism and interpretation of Wittgenstein since 1970. These have been so numerous that we must here content ourselves with an indication of the main lines of the changes.

Many too have been the factors favouring change and making favourite earlier interpretations seem obsolete. Most important is the radical change in the philosophical climate precisely where Wittgenstein was most enthusiastically received. In the 1960s neopositivism was no longer the rage, but even inside its successor, analytic philosophy, with which Wittgenstein's later work was associated, important shifts of emphasis were taking place. It became evident that terms like 'analysis' and 'philosophy of language' had gathered under their banner authors of very diverse temperament and interests. At best such terms seemed to characterize a multiplicity of tendencies between which it was hard to discern the common features. If then the variety of analytic philosophy was read back into Wittgenstein, one of its inspirers, much room was left for uncertainty and imprecision in the understanding of his thought too.

A second factor was the regular publication, from the mid-1950s on, of a fair number of collections from his literary remains. This had a number of important consequences. First, the preparatory works that led to *Tractatus* became known to a large circle of readers. In this way the complexity and the difficulty of the genesis of that work came to be recognized.

Aspects previously neglected were brought into prominence and accepted interpretations were rendered problematic. A similar reversal of fortune took place as regarded Wittgenstein's later work. There too the works that came to light, though varied enough in subject and approach, were in no case easy to accommodate within the existing picture of 'the later Wittgenstein'.

At the same time, with the great increase in publication and also in translation into various languages, there came to be many more contributors to the whole discussion. Previously debate had been conducted almost exclusively in English: now there was a considerable body of writing in other languages. German (and Austrian) discussion had been practically non-existent before the late 1950s (we are not here considering the pre-War neopositivist phase): now in the 1970s it became more and more professional and introduced entirely new thematic directions, which we shall have to take into account. Further, from some ten years after the War, Italian writers made their presence felt: they had at their disposal one of the first (1954) translations of *Tractatus* into a language other than English, a bold enterprise and, in some ways, a pioneering one even in non-linguistic respects. French and Spanish recognition was slower to come (perhaps partly because of misunderstandings generated by the earlier interpretative literature) but come it did. Nor should we overlook the recent interest in our author among thinkers not directly stemming from our Western culture. Inevitably in such a diversity of interpreters there has been a great divergence also in points of view and forms of sensibility and this has led to the discovery of previously undetected aspects of Wittgenstein's thought.

Of all problems perhaps that of the relation between *Tractatus* and the later writings stood in greatest need of re-examination. Many thought that the new material that had come to light rendered untenable the old thesis of a clear opposition between the two chronologically distinct phases of Wittgenstein's thought: some organic connexion between them had to be found.

Two distinct tendencies emerged in this regard. Some authors (cf., e.g., Fann, 1969; Bogen, Hacker, 1972; Kenny, 1973; Hottois, 1976), on the basis of the works by then published, began to trace a coherent evolution and progress in the thought of our author. In particular they believed that a bridge could be built between the two major works using the writings of the period 1929–33 and the testimony contained in notes by Moore and Waismann. This material, they thought, gave evidence of an intermediate phase, during which Wittgenstein, returning to philosophy after a long absence, revised many of his original theses and, step by step, developed a new philosophy. Similarly the pre-*Tractatus* writings were thought to testify to a slow development leading Wittgenstein away from logic and from the influence of Frege and Russell to a position of substantial independence and marked theoretical originality. Whatever may be thought about the correctness of these conclusions, there is no doubt that this line of argument did draw attention to the writings of the intermediate period, which would otherwise have seemed to be of marginal interest. In general, however, looking at the intellectual biography of Wittgenstein as a whole, this school of thought had one essential feature in common with the school it sought to replace: it too recognized a substantial difference in methods employed and in theoretical results achieved between the initial and the final phases of Wittgenstein's development.

Other authors, especially after 1970, had recourse to a more radical solution. They tried to heal the breach between 'the two Wittgensteins' by stressing no longer the differences, but rather some of the common features and the analogies between the two. Thus, for example, they found in *Tractatus* anticipations of theses which previous criticism had ascribed solely to the mature Wittgenstein. Conversely they considered at least some of the theses of the so-called 'later Wittgenstein' to be nothing but fuller and more explicit formulations of intuitions already present in the early writings. Behind a small number of differences, much exaggerated, in their view, by previous critics, these authors held that it was possible to explain the whole of Wittgenstein's tortuous path on the assumption of a substantial unity of interests and of theoretical solutions (cf., e.g., *Studies* (ed. Winch), Toulmin, 1969; Pears, 1970; Engel, 1971; Janik and Toulmin, 1973).

Such tendencies in recent criticism may lead to divergent general conclusions, but they have in common a background which may now be regarded as now more or less established. They have been able to draw upon a large corpus of scholarly investigation devoted to individual works of Wittgenstein or to individual themes in his work. This gave more recent critics a solid and articulated argumentative base that would have been unthinkable for their predecessors.

This occurred in the first place with *Tractatus*, for which we have a number of works, beginning in the late 1950s, by Anscombe (1959), Stenius (1960), Black (1964), and the collection of articles edited by Copi and Beard (1966). These served as points of reference for later discussion. A general characteristic of writings from this time on is that as they liberated themselves from the shackles of too unreserved a commitment to Wittgenstein's solutions, so they gained in exegetical competence and even finesse. Many themes in *Tractatus* were now first submitted to a radical discussion: the logical aspects of the book, the theory of objects and the ontology generally, its theses on ethics and religion, its attitude towards philosophy. Historical aspects too were now touched on: the sources of the work were investigated, including the relations of Wittgenstein to Frege, Russell, and other contemporaries. All this led to the discovery of forgotten aspects of the work and to the forgetting of a number of interpretations that had enjoyed a wide diffusion.

In the case of *Philosophical investigations* too, criticism and discussion were put on a new path. Old answers to questions were revised and neglected aspects illuminated. Here, as well as monographs, we have a number of weighty volumes intended as a basis for further research, the concordance to the work by Kaal and McKinnon (1975), for example, and two large commentaries appearing within a few years of each other, from Hallett (1977) and from Baker and Hacker (1980 and in progress).

The new, more philological approach was not confined to the two major works. As other selections from the literary remains were published they found their own experts and provided material for discussion, sometimes of a highly specialized character. This certainly holds of *Remarks on the foundations of mathematics*. At first the interpretation of this publication was heavily influenced by three articles that appeared at the end of the 1950s, those by Kreisel (1958), Dummett (1959), and Bernays (1959). All three, for somewhat different reasons and in somewhat different tones of voice, concurred in the judgement that Wittgenstein's contribution to the philosophy of mathematics was confined to a few marginal aspects of that subject.

Still, in this field too, criticism was to undergo profound changes, partly in the light of further selections from Wittgenstein's writings later published. *Philosophical remarks* (1965), *Philosophical grammar* (1969), and the notes made from Wittgenstein's 1939 lectures contain many remarks on the foundations of mathematics. Some of the grounds for the more severe criticisms of Wittgenstein's treatment turned out to be based on passages ill-understood or on too narrow a conception of what problems Wittgenstein was attacking. Among the themes that have occupied this more recent literature, we may mention in particular the attempt to define the especial form of constructivism that was Wittgenstein's and the discussion of its relation to other twentieth-century schools in the philosophy of mathematics.

While the publications from Wittgenstein's literary remains drawn from his middle period served to bridge the gap, created by earlier critics, between *Tractatus* and *Philosophical investigations*, the publications drawn from Wittgenstein's writings in the years immediately before his death have tended to complicate the picture of his intellectual development. Particular attention has been devoted to *On certainty* (cf., e.g., *Essays* (ed. Hintikka) 1976; Hudson, 1977; Morawetz, 1978) and here commentators have seen a pronounced change in Wittgenstein's attitude towards constructive and systematic ways of doing philosophy. Certainly there seems to be a loss of interest in the 'therapeutic' aim of removing 'mental cramps', which alone was allowed to philosophy by Wittgenstein's 'analytic' interpreters. Similarly the more recent publication, *Remarks on the philosophy of psychology*, drawn from writings from the years 1946–9, provided an occasion to re-open the discussion on a number of problems in the philosophy of mind, previously debated when the picture of 'the two Wittgensteins' prevailed.

In the general change of perspective occasioned by these later publications a number of topics came into the centre of attention which had previously seemed of marginal importance because of the scantiness of references to them in the writings first published. The question of the basis of religious faith, in particular, the object of brief comment towards the close of *Tractatus*, attracted new interest after the publication (1966) of notes on lectures and conversations dedicated to this theme among others – still more so when it became known that there were many references to religion in unpublished writings from nearly every period in Wittgenstein's life. At first discussion was on purely 'Wittgensteinian' questions, but rapidly spread to the more general issues of fideism, of the possibility and limits of a rational foundation for religion, the nature of religious language, etc. (see the thematic index to the present volume).

A similar widening of interest occurred in the case of aesthetic questions. At first discussion was confined to the notes on the 1938 lectures but soon passed on to more general attempts to collect and harmonize ideas of Wittgenstein's drawn from more and more scattered parts of the corpus, and embracing in an organic vision many aspects of the theory of language: all this in the hope of throwing more light on the nature and logic of aesthetic evaluation. It is significant that this widening of the scope of discussion went hand in hand with an increasing tendency for references to Wittgenstein to occur in writings of a specialized kind dealing, for example, with literary criticism, the aesthetics of music, the analysis of the language of visual art, etc.

Connected with aesthetics by a celebrated equation, which in Wittgenstein's case goes back to *Tractatus*, is, of course, ethics, and this too has increasingly become a preoccupation of his interpreters. Here too discussion was originally purely exegetic and concerned with the short lecture of 1930 and the handful of remarks on the topic in *Tractatus*, but has since passed on to more and more ambitious reconstructions, sometimes seeing ethics as a central element in the whole theoretical edifice of Wittgenstein's thought. There is an ethical motivation, many authors have thought, in the way in which Wittgenstein attacks problems of the will and of intention at many different periods in his life: the approach is here clearly of Central European inspiration, derived from Kant and still more Schopenhauer, and has very little to do with English analytical philosophy. Here too, therefore, a multi-textual method of analysis has worked in favour of the thesis of substantial unity and coherence in Wittgenstein's thinking and against the thesis of 'the two Wittgensteins'.

We ought to add also that the tendency to seek for links between Wittgenstein and continental thought and culture has not been confined to limited areas of his interests but has been extended to his personality and his formation generally. A number of factors have contributed to this; above all a healthy historiographical drive to transcend the partisan and specialist context in which Wittgenstein first became known.

Naturally the widening of the nature of the interest taken in Wittgenstein has owed much to a flood of publications of a biographical nature. Friends and pupils have revealed hitherto unsuspected facets of his personality. His background too has been studied – the circumstances of his family, the culture of late-Hapsburg and early post-War Vienna in all its aspects: political, literary, artistic, and broadly cultural, as well as philosophical.

We must note especially the effect of the entry upon the scene of German or Austrian commentators, a phenomenon already noted. These have been apt to see Wittgenstein against the background of the other authors they were familiar with: Schopenhauer and even the later Heidegger will serve as instances. Some find place for him in the context of modern developments in Kantian scholarship. Historiographical principles of this nature have of course aroused fierce opposition in certain quarters, but even the controversy so generated has been useful to the study of our author, enriching and variegating it and attracting the attention of a larger learned public.

Obviously all of this is far from constituting a simplification of the panorama of Wittgenstein studies that we are attempting to give. Indeed it now becomes almost impossible to give a unitary picture of the literature. As specialist studies from diverse points of view have multiplied, the figure of our author has come to seem more and more enigmatic and shadowy, and the picture of his relation to his times has become more complex. The reader may well feel a certain disorientation: yet really it is the complexity of our own cultural scene that we are seeing mirrored in Wittgenstein. Lovers of nuance and chiaroscuro, we are fated to find them in him.

In a certain way, however, he is already beginning to escape us and to pass into philosophical history, so that these are perhaps the last years in which a unified Wittgenstein bibliography will be possible. There will always be specialist philological works paying close attention to the evidence, but, as with Plato, Descartes, or Kant, he will increasingly be cited by writers for whom he is merely the inspirer, merely a starting-point taken for granted, a peg, almost, on which to hang their own reflections, someone to teach from rather than to learn from. Hence the profusion of books or articles with the title Wittgenstein and X, where X is a writer or topic that the author is determined to relate Wittgenstein to. Such contributions are, of course, not always negligible. To take one of the best of them: Kripke's *Wittgenstein on rules and private language* (1982) has given rise to a great deal of discussion that has enlivened the philosophical scene. But on what topic? The book's author says that it 'should be thought of as expounding neither "Wittgenstein's" argument nor "Kripke's": rather Wittgenstein's argument as it struck Kripke, as it presented a problem for him'. Sure enough, the reader soon finds himself grappling with the problems of scepticism and a number of paradoxes of induction originally proposed by Nelson Goodman. *Habent sua fata libelli* – this is an ingenious application of some of the texts, but a number of reviewers have maintained that it would be hard to find anything further removed from the actual concerns or attitudes of Wittgenstein. Obviously if each can find his own dogmas in Wittgenstein, a type hierarchy of bibliographies will be required to deal with the multiplicity of possible Wittgensteins, but for the editors of the present volume his name is still, though perhaps barely, a rigid designator.

PART II
LISTS AND INDEXES

PUBLICATIONS OF WRITINGS BY WITTGENSTEIN[1]

Works are listed under their German and English titles when both exist in approximate order of composition and under the abbreviation used for the work in the present volume if any. Bibliographical indications are given for English and German versions only.

Review of C. Coffey, *The science of logic,* in 'Cambridge Review', 34, 1913, p. 351; reprinted in E. Homberger and others (eds.), *The Cambridge mind,* London, Cape, 1970.

N.L.
Notes on logic (September 1913), ed. by H. T. Costello, in 'Journal of Philosophy', 54, 1957, pp. 230-44. Reprinted in *Notebooks 1914-16.* (B. Russell's arrangement in I ed., original form in II ed.)

N.M.
Notes dictated to Moore in Norway (April 1914), in *Notebooks 1914-16,* pp. 107-18.

---

[1] The abbreviations above the majority of entries are used throughout the present volume. Most works originally published in German and English are now available in the two languages separately, sometimes only so. Most works have also been translated into the French, Italian, Spanish, and the majority of the other European languages, also into Japanese and in some cases into Chinese and Hebrew.

N.B.
Notebooks 1914-16, ed. by G. E. M. Anscombe and G. H. von
Wright; German text with facing English translation by G. E. M.
Anscombe, Oxford, Blackwell; New York, Barnes & Noble, 1961;
II ed., corrected and with the addition of an index, Oxford,
Blackwell; Chicago, Ill., University of Chicago Press, 1979.

P.T.
Prototractatus, ed. by B. F. McGuinness, T. Nyberg, G. H. von
Wright; German text with facing English translation by D. F.
Pears and B. F. McGuinness, with an introduction by G. H. von
Wright, London, Routledge & Kegan Paul; Ithaca, N.Y., Cornell
University Press, 1971.

Logisch-philosophische Abhandlung, 'Annalen der
Naturphilosophie', 14, 1921, pp. 185-262 (see following entry).

Tract.
Tractatus logico-philosophicus, German text with facing English
translation by C. K. Ogden and F. P. Ramsey, London, Kegan
Paul; New York, Harcourt & Brace, 1922; II ed. with corrections,
Routledge & Kegan Paul, 1933. New ed. with English translation
by D. F. Pears and B. F. McGuinness, London, Routledge & Kegan
Paul; New York, Humanities Press, 1961 (II ed., 1971).

W.V.
Wörterbuch für Volksschulen, Vienna, facsimile reproduction
Hölder-Pichler-Tempsky 1926; with an introduction by
A. Hübner, same publisher, 1977.

R.L.F.
Some remarks on logical form, PAS(SV), 9, 1929, pp. 162-71.
Reprinted in Copi and Beard (eds.), 1966.

C.V.
Vermischte Bemerkungen. Culture and value, ed. by G. H. von
Wright, Oxford, Blackwell; Frankfurt, Suhrkamp, 1977; with a
facing English translation by P. Winch and some additions,
Oxford, Blackwell, 1980; Chicago, Ill., University of Chicago Press.

L.E.
A lecture on ethics, PR, 74, 1965, pp. 3-12.

P.R.
Philosophische Bemerkungen. Philosophical remarks, ed. by
R. Rhees, Oxford, Blackwell; New York, Barnes & Noble;
Frankfurt, Suhrkamp, 1964. English translation by R. Hargreaves
and R. White, Oxford, Blackwell; New York, Barnes and Noble,
1975.

P.G.
Philosophische Grammatik. Philosophical grammar, ed. by
R. Rhees, Oxford, Blackwell; Frankfurt, Suhrkamp, 1969. English
translation by A. J. P. Kenny, Oxford, Blackwell; New York,
Barnes & Noble, 1974.

R.F.
*Bemerkungen über Frazers 'The golden bough'. Remarks on
Frazer's 'The golden bough'* ed. by R. Rhees, 'Synthese', 17,
1967, pp. 233-53. English translation by A. C. Miles, Atlantic
Highlands, N.J., Humanities Press, 1979. Revised ed., Retford,
Brynmill, 1979. Also in Luckhardt (ed.), 1979.

Letter to the editor, M, 42, 1933, pp. 415-16.

B.B.B. (or separately *Bl.B., Br.B.*)
The blue and brown books, (1933-35), ed. and with a preface
by R. Rhees, Oxford, Blackwell; New York, Harper & Row, 1958.

N.L.P.E.
Notes for lectures on 'private experience' and 'sense data', ed.
by R. Rhees, PR, 77, 1968, pp. 275-320 (introductory note by
R. Rhees, pp. 271-5). Repr. in Morick (ed.), 1967, and in Jones
(ed.), 1971.

E.P.B.
Eine philosophische Betrachtung, ed. R. Rhees, in *Schriften* 5,
Frankfurt, Suhrkamp, 1970, pp. 117-237.

Ursache und Wirkung: intuitives Erfassen. Cause and effect: intuitive awareness (various notes for and from W.'s lectures), ed. by R. Rhees, with an English translation by P. Winch, in 'Philosophia', 6, 1976, pp. 392–445.

R.F.M.
Bemerkungen über die Grundlagen der Mathematik. Remarks on the foundations of mathematics, ed. by G. H. von Wright, R. Rhees and G. E. M. Anscombe, facing English translation by G. E. M. Anscombe, Oxford, Blackwell; New York, Macmillan, 1956; II ed. (revised with considerable additions), Oxford, Blackwell; Cambridge, Mass., MIT Press, 1978.

P.I.
Philosophische Untersuchungen. Philosophical investigations, ed. by G. E. M. Anscombe and R. Rhees, with facing English translation by G. E. M. Anscombe, Oxford, Blackwell; New York, Macmillan, 1953. II ed. 1953, III ed. 1973.

R.P.P.
Bemerkungen über die Philosophie der Psychologie. Remarks on the philosophy of psychology. Vol. I, ed. by G. E. M. Anscombe and G. H. von Wright, facing English translation by G. E. M. Anscombe, Oxford, Blackwell; Chicago, Ill., University of Chicago Press, 1980.

R.P.P. II
Bemerkungen über die Philosophie der Psychologie. Remarks on the philosophy of psychology. Vol. II ed. by G. H. von Wright and H. Nyman, in German, with a facing English translation by C. G. Luckhardt and M. A. E. Aue, Oxford, Blackwell; Chicago, Ill., University of Chicago Press, 1980.

Z.
Zettel ed. by G. E. M. Anscombe and G. H. von Wright; with facing English translation by G. E. M. Anscombe, Oxford, Blackwell; Berkeley, Cal., University of California Press, 1967.

L.W.P.P.
Letzte Schriften über die Philosophie der Psychologie. Last Writings on the Philosophy of Psychology. (Vol. I: *Preliminary studies for Part II of the 'Philosophical Investigations'*, ed. by G. H. von Wright and H. Nyman with a facing English translation by C. G. Luckhardt and M. A. E. Aue, Oxford, Blackwell; Chicago, Ill., University of Chicago Press, 1982.

O.C.
Über Gewissheit. On certainty, ed. by G. E. M. Anscombe and G. H. von Wright, with facing English translation by D. Paul and G. E. M. Anscombe, Oxford, Blackwell; New York, Harper & Row, 1969.

R.C.
Bemerkungen über die Farben. Remarks on colour, ed. by G. E. M. Anscombe, with facing English translation by L. L. McAlister and M. Schättle, Oxford, Blackwell; Berkeley, Cal., University of California Press, 1977.

Schriften (German only), vols 1–7, Frankfurt, Suhrkamp: vol. 1 (1960): *Tract., N.B., P.I.*; vol. 2 (1964): *P.B.*; vol. 3 (1967): *W.V.C.*; vol. 4 (1969): *P.G.*; vol. 5 (1970): *Bl.B., E.P.B., Z.*; vol. 6 (1973): *R.F.M.*; vol. 7 (1978): *L.F.M.*; vol. 8 (1982): *R.P.P., R.P.P. II.*

Werkausgabe, vols. 1–8, Frankfurt, Suhrkamp, 1984 (German only, texts revised by J. Schulte) Vol. 1: *Tract., N.B., P.I.;* vol. 2: *P.R.*; vol. 3: *W.V.C.*, vol. 4: *P.G.*; vol. 5: *Bl.B., E.P.B., Br.B.*; vol. 6: *R.F.M.*; vol. 7: *L.F.M., L.W.*; vol. 8: *R.C., O.C., Z., C.V.*

Notes of Lectures and Conversations

W.V.C.
Wittgenstein und der Wiener Kreis. Wittgenstein and the Vienna Circle (conversations recorded by F. Waismann, 1929–31, with his *Thesen* as an appendix), in German, ed. with an introduction by B. F. McGuinness, Oxford, Blackwell; Frankfurt, Suhrkamp,

1967. English translation by B. F. McGuinness and J. Schulte: Oxford, Blackwell, 1979.

Notes on talks with Wittgenstein (notes by Waismann concerning ethics, 1929–30), with an English translation by M. Black, PR, 74, 1965, pp. 12–16 (included in *W.V.C.*).

W.'s lectures in 1930–33 (notes by G. E. Moore, see Moore, 1954).

W.'s lectures. Cambridge 1930–32 (based on notes taken by T. King and D. Lee), ed. by D. Lee, Oxford, Blackwell; Totowa, N.J., Rowman & Littlefield, 1980.

W.'s lectures. Cambridge 1932–35 (based on notes taken by A. Ambrose and M. Macdonald), ed. by A. Ambrose, Oxford, Blackwell; Totowa, N.J., Rowman & Littlefield, 1979.

L.C. (or separately *L.A.*, *C.F.*, *L.R.B.*)
Lectures and conversations on aesthetics, psychology and religious belief, Oxford, Blackwell, 1966; Berkeley, Cal., University of California Press.

L.F.M.
W.'s lectures on the foundations of mathematics – Cambridge 1939 (based on notes by R. G. Bosanquet, N. Malcolm, R. Rhees and Y. Smythies), ed. by C. Diamond, Hassocks, Harvester; Ithaca, N.Y., Cornell University Press, 1976.

Letters

Briefe, ed. by B. F. McGuinness and G. H. von Wright. Correspondence with B. Russell. G. E. Moore, J. M. Keynes, F. P. Ramsey, W. Eccles, P. Engelmann and L. von Ficker (in German, with original version of W.'s own letters, when English, in an appendix; German translations by J. Schulte), Frankfurt, Suhrkamp, 1980.

Letters to Russell, Keynes and Moore, ed. with an introduction by G. H. von Wright, German letters translated by B. F. McGuinness, Oxford, Blackwell; Ithaca, N.Y., Cornell University Press, 1974.

Eccles W., *Some letters of Wittgenstein, 1912-1939*, 'Hermathena' (Dublin), 97, 1963, pp. 57-65.

Briefe an L. von Ficker, ed. by G. H. von Wright, in collaboration with W. Methlagl, Salzburg, Müller, 1969. English translation by B. Gillette in *Wittgenstein: sources and perspectives*, 1979.

Engelmann P., *Letters from Wittgenstein, with a memoir*, ed. with a postword by B. F. McGuinness, letters in German with facing English translation by Lux Furtmüller, Oxford, Blackwell, 1967; New York, Horizon Press, 1968; German only version: *L.W. Briefe und Begegnungen*, Vienna and Munich, Oldenburg, 1970.

Letters to C. K. Ogden, ed. with an introduction by G. H. von Wright, with an appendix containing letters by F. P. Ramsey, 1923-24, Oxford, Blackwell, 1973.

ABBREVIATIONS OF TITLES
OF PERIODICALS

The following are the periodicals most frequently cited arranged in the order of the abbreviations used for them. Other periodicals' titles are given in full at the point of citation. Articles are listed under the year of the volume in which they appear or, when the volume straddles two years, under the earlier of the two.

A	Analysis
Ap	Aporia
Au	Auslegung
AA	Aut Aut
AF	Archivio di Filosofia
AGP	Archiv für Geschichte der Philosophie
AH	Analecta Husserliana
AIKP	Akten des XIV. Internationalen Kongresses für Philosophie
AJP	Australasian Journal of Philosophy
ANTW	Algemeen Nederlands Tijdschrift voor Wijsbegeerte
AP	Archives de Philosophie
AfP	Archiv für Philosophie
APF	Acta Philosophica Fennica
APQ	American Philosophical Quarterly
AS	L'Age de la Science
AZP	Allgemeine Zeitschrift für Philosophie
B	Behaviorism
Bi	Bijdragen

BBSMS	Bollettino Bibliografico per le Scienze Morali e Sociali
BJA	British Journal of Aesthetics
BJPS	British Journal of the Philosophy of Science
BSFP	Bulletin de la Société Française de Philosophie
BSPS	Boston Studies in the Philosophy of Science
C	Conceptus
Ca	Canocchiale
Cr	Crítica (Mexico)
Cri	Critique (Paris)
CA	Cahiers pour l'Analyse
CJP	Canadian Journal of Philosophy
CPR	Canadian Philosophical Review
D	Dialogue
Di	Dialectica
D(PST)	Dialogue (Phi Sigma Tau)
DR	Downside Review
DZP	Deutsche Zeitschrift für Philosophie
E	Erkenntnis
Ep	Epistemologia
Et	Ethics
EB	Eastern Buddhist
EP	Études Philosophiques
F	Filosofia
FL	Foundations of Language
FS	Filosofia della Scienza
FZPT	Freiburger Zeitschrift für Philosophie und Theologie
G	Gregorianum
GCFI	Giornale Critico della Filosofia Italiana
GM	Giornale di Metafisica
GPS	Grazer Philosophische Studien
GRP	Graduate Review of Philosophy

HJ	Heythrop Journal
HPL	History and Philosophy of Logic
HPQ	History of Philosophy Quarterly
HS	Human Studies
HW	Human World
I	Inquiry
Int	Intersezione. Rivista di Storia della Idee
IJP	Independent Journal of Philosophy
IndJP	Indian Journal of Philosophy
IJPR	International Journal for Philosophy of Religion
ILR	International Logic Review
IPQ	International Philosophical Quarterly
IndPQ	Indian Philosophical Quarterly
IS	Idealistic Studies
ISP	International Studies in Philosophy
ITQ	Irish Theological Quarterly
JAAC	Journal of Aesthetics and Art Criticism
JBSP	Journal of the British Society for Phenomenology
JCA	Journal of Critical Analysis
JCP	Journal of Chinese Philosophy
JHBS	Journal of the History of the Behavioral Sciences
JHP	Journal of the History of Philosophy
JICPR	Journal of Indian Council of Philosophical Research
JP	Journal of Philosophy
JPE	Journal of Philosophy of Education
JPL	Journal of Philosophy of Logic
JR	Journal of Religion
JSL	Journal of Symbolic Logic
JT	Journal of Thought
JTSB	Journal for the Theory of Social Behaviour
JVI	Journal of Value Inquiry
Ki	Kinesis
KS	Kant-Studien
LA	Logique et Analyse
LTP	Laval Théologique et Philosophique

M	Mind
Ma	Manuscrito
Me	Methodos
Mer	Merkur
Mo	Monist
Mp	Metaphilosophy
ML	Mind and Language
MS	Modern Schoolman
MSc	Methodology and Science
MW	Man and World
MWSP	Midwest Studies in Philosophy
N	Noûs
NDJFL	Notre Dame Journal of Formal Logic
NRT	Nouvelle Revue Théologique
NS	New Scholasticism
NZSTR	Neue Zeitschrift für Systematische Theologie und Religionsphilosophie
P	Philosophy
Pa	Paradigmi
Ph	Philosophia (Israel)
Phi	Philosophie (Paris)
Phy	Physis
Pr	Personalist
PACPA	Proceedings of the American Catholic Philosophical Association
PAS	Proceedings of the Aristotelian Society
PAS(SV)	Proceedings of the Aristotelian Society (Supplementary Volume)
PB	Philosophical Books
PC	Philosophy in Context
PE	Philosophic Exchange
PEW	Philosophy East and West
PF	Philosophical Forum
PhänF	Phänomenologische Forschungen
PH	Philosophy and History
PI	Philosophical Inquiry
PInv	Philosophical Investigations

PJ	Philosophisches Jahrbuch
PL	Philosophy and Literature
PLA	Philosophischer Literaturanzeiger
PM	Philosophia Mathematica
PP	Philosophical Papers
PPQ	Pacific Philosophical Quarterly
PPR	Philosophy and Phenomenological Research
PQ	Philosophical Quarterly
PR	Philosophical Review
PRd	Philosophische Rundschau
PRh	Philosophy and Rhetoric
PRA	Philosophy Research Archives
PS	Philosophical Studies
PS(I)	Philosophical Studies (Ireland)
PSc	Philosophy of Science
PSC	Philosophy and Social Criticism
PSS	Philosophy of the Social Sciences
PT	Philosophy Today
PTo	Philosophical Topics
R	Ratio
Ru	Russell
RBPH	Revue Belge de Philologie et d'Histoire
RCSF	Rivista Critica di Storia della Filosofia
RE	Rivista di Estetica
RF	Rivista di Filosofia
RaF	Rassegna di Filosofia
RevF(CR)	Revista de Filosofia de la Universidad de Costa Rica
RevF(Mex)	Revista de Filosofia (Mexico)
RevF(Sp)	Revista de Filosofia (Spain)
RFN	Rivista di Filosofia Neoscolastica
RIP	Revue Internationale de Philosophie
RLF	Revista Latinoamericana de Filosofia
RM	Review of Metaphysics
RMM	Revue de Métaphysique et de Morale
RNP	Revue Néo-Scholastique de Philosophie
RP	Research in Phenomenology
RPF	Revista Portuguesa de Filosofia

RPFE	Revue Philosophique de la France et de l'Étranger
RPL	Revue Philosophique de Louvain
RePL	Recherches sur la Philosophie et le Langage
RS	Religious Studies
RSF	Rassegna di Scienze Filosofiche
RStF	Rivista di Storia della Filosofia
RSPT	Revue des Sciences Philosophiques et Théologiques
RSR	Raccolta di Studi e Richerche
RTL	Revue Théologique de Louvain
RTP	Revue de Théologie et de Philosophie
RUB	Revue de l'Université de Bruxelles
RUS	Rice University Studies
S	Sophia (Australia)
Sy	Synthese
SAJP	South African Journal of Philosophy
SG	Studium Generale
SHPS	Studies in History and Philosophy of Science
SIF	Studi Internazionali di Filosofia
SJ	Schopenhauer Jahrbuch
SJP	Southern Journal of Philosophy
SJT	Scottish Journal of Theology
SL	Studia Logica
SP	Studia Philosophica
SR	Studies in Religion
SocR	Sociological Review
SST	Studies in Soviet Thought
SWJP	Southwestern Journal of Philosophy
SWPS	Southwest Philosophical Studies
T	Theoria
Ta	Tablet
Te	Telos
Teo	Teorema
Teor	Teoria
Th	Thomist
To	Topoi

TD	Theory and Decision
TF	Tijdschrift voor Filosofie
TLS	Times Literary Supplement
TP	Theologie und Philosophie
TeaP	Teaching Philosophy
TS	Theological Studies
TT	Theology Today
V	Verifiche
WJP	Wiener Jahrbuch für Philosophie
WW	Wissenschaft und Weltbild
WZPPP	Wiener Zeitschrift für Philosophie, Psychologie, Pädagogik
ZDP	Zeitschrift für Didaktik der Philosophie
ZKT	Zeitschrift für Katholische Theologie
ZPF	Zeitschrift für Philosophische Forschung

WRITINGS ON WITTGENSTEIN, 1914-1987

1914

1. Russell B., *Our knowledge of the external world,* Chicago, Ill., and London, Open Court Publishing Company, 1914; 2nd ed.: London, Allen & Unwin, 1926.
In the preface R. acknowledges that in the field of pure logic he has benefited from important results, not yet published, reached by his friend W.

1918

2. Russell B., *The philosophy of logical atomism*, Mo, 28, 1918, pp. 495-527; 29, 1919, pp. 32-63, 190-222, 345-380.
Reprinted in B. Russell, *Logic and knowledge*, see 1956; in *The collected papers of B. Russell*, vol. 8, London/Boston/Sydney, Allen & Unwin, 1986.
In an introductory note to these articles, which appeared before the publication of *Tract.*, R. says that they largely consist of an account of ideas learnt from his friend and former pupil W. *Inter alia* R. notes that W. prevailed upon him to accept the thesis that propositions are not names for facts (p. 187 of the 1956 edition).

1922

3. Anon, *Spinoza inverted*, TLS, 21 December 1922, p. 854.
Reprinted as *L. Wittgenstein 1922*, in TLS, 28 August 1953.

A favourable review of *Tract.* in Ogden's E.T. The work is found to be clear and lucid, while its conclusions have a mystical exaltedness which recalls Spinoza, even though W.'s methods are quite the reverse of Spinoza's. *Principia mathematica* and the works of Frege are indicated as the sources of *Tract.*

4. **Russell, B.**, Introduction to *Tractatus logico-philosophicus*, London, Routledge & Kegan Paul, 1922, pp. 7–23. Reprinted in the new ed. with trsl. by D. F. Pears and B. F. McGuinness, London, Routledge & Kegan Paul, 1961, pp. IX-XXII.
R. identifies the following as, in his view, the principal themes of the work: the principles of a perfect logical symbolism; the structural parallel between facts and propositions; the method of constructing truth-functions; the principle of the identity of indiscernibles; the nature of philosophical propositions; solipsism; intensional statements; the mystical. Of W.'s theses R. chiefly criticizes: the theory of numbers; the mystical conclusions drawn; the account of generality. The problem about symbolism raised by W. is, according to R., of a logical nature: it concerns the relation which the statement as a fact must have with another fact in order to be capable of being a symbol of it. Hence it raises the question of the conditions that must be satisfied by a logically perfect language. As for the mystical conclusions reached in the work, R. maintains that they can be avoided by the introduction of a hierarchy of languages, which could be effected without prejudice to the major part of W.'s theory.

1923

5. **Anon**, Pr, 4, pp. 207–8.
A rather unfavourable review of *Tract.* which is said to be exceptionally obscure and of little philosophical value.

6. **McTaggart J. E.**, *Propositions applicable to themselves*, M, 32, pp. 462–4.
McT. examines the thesis which he attributes to *Tract.* according to which 'a proposition cannot say anything about itself'. He shows the ambiguity of this statement and discusses possible interpretations of it.

7. **Ogden C. K.** and **Richards I. A.**, *The meaning of meaning*, London, Kegan Paul; New York, Harcourt Brace, 1923.

In an appendix (*On grammar*, pp. 395-399) the theory of *Tract.* is criticized inasmuch as it postulates a correspondence between the structure of propositional signs and the structure of facts. Such a theory can be valid only for elementary languages, and is unsuited to the complexity of historical or scientific languages.

8. **Ramsey F. P.**, *Critical notice of the Tractatus,* M, 32, pp. 465-78. Reprinted in F. P. Ramsey, *The foundations of mathematics* (see 1931); in I. M. Copi and R. U. Beard (eds.), 1966; in Canfield (ed.), vol. I, 1986; in Shanker (ed.), vol. I, 1986.

Although R. attributes a central importance to some advances made in *Tract.*, he regrets a certain imprecision in its exposition, especially in connection with some theses of a more technical nature. He also finds Russell's introduction (see 1922) rather unsatisfactory, for example because of its interpretation of *Tract.* as referring exclusively to a logical perfect language. R. therefore undertakes to clarify W.'s point of view, especially in relation to the following themes: the concepts of picture and of form of representation (pp. 466-78); the meaning of propositions (pp. 468-72); the nature of logical constants (p. 472); tautology and contradiction, necessity and impossibility (p. 473); internal and external properties and the nature of pseudo-propositions (pp. 472-76); the function of philosophy (pp. 476-78); the concept of 'world' (p. 478).

9. **S.** *A logical mystic,* 'Nation and the Athenaeum', 32, pp. 657-8.

1924

10. **De Laguna T.**, PR, 33, pp. 103-9. Reprinted in Copi and Beard (eds.), 1966.

Review of *Tract.* (1922 edition). A negative and ironic presentation of the 'principal themes' of the work, followed by equally negative criticisms of its usefulness and importance. The only merit it is willing to concede to the book is that it arrives at a *reductio ad insanitatem* of the theory of logical atomism. The English translation is also criticized and found to be full of errors, flat, and often incoherent.

11. **Keyser C. J.**, *A short notice of W.'s Tractatus,* 'Bulletin of the American Mathematical Society', 30, pp. 179-81.

A general presentation of the structure and content of *Tract.* The central problem of the work is considered to be the determination of the essential nature of a logically perfect language.

12. Russell B., *Logical atomism*, in J. H. Muirhead (ed.), *Contemporary British philosophy*, London, Allen & Unwin, 1924, pp. 356-86. Reprinted in B. Russell, *Logic and knowledge*, see 1956.

In confronting some problems in connection with the logical theory of relations, Russell recognizes his indebtedness to his 'friend W.', though stating that he does not accept all the doctrines contained in *Tract.*

1925

13. Ramsey F. P., *Universals*, M, 34, pp. 401-417. Reprinted in F. P. Ramsey, *The foundations of mathematics*, see 1931.

R. compares and discusses certain theories in relation to the distinction between 'particulars' and 'universals', Russell's and W.'s among them. In developing his own solutions, he shows how the logical theory of *Tract.* helps to throw light on the 'grave state of confusion' which reigns among the philosophers in this connection.

14. Whitehead A. N. and **Russell B.**, *Principia mathematica*, London, Cambridge University Press, 2nd ed., 1925-27.

In the introduction to the second edition (pp. XIII-XLVI) Wh. and R. (actually R.) admit to having revised their own theory in a rather radical fashion in the light of what W. recommends, for philosophic reasons, in *Tract.*: propositional functions are always truth-functions and a function can occur in a proposition only through its values. Such a thesis, R. adds, implies that all functions of functions are extensional and therefore expressions such as 'A believes p' cannot be functions of 'p'. R. then enumerates radical consequences which these theses entail regarding some aspects of the logical system of *Principia mathematica*. In 'Appendix C' R. discusses and tries to resolve certain difficulties connected to the thesis of extensionality, with particular reference to expressions such as 'A believes p'.

1926

15. Ramsey F. P., *Mathematical logic*, 'Mathematical Gazette', 13, pp. 185-194. Reprinted in F. P. Ramsey, *The foundations of mathematics*, 1931.
In outlining the developments of mathematical logic after the publication of *Principia mathematica*, R. attributes great importance to the contribution made by *Tract.* in particular by way of its treatment of general and existential propositions and of logical propositions.

16. Ramsey F. P., *The foundations of mathematics*, 'Proceedings of the London Mathematical Society', 25, pp. 338-384. Reprinted in F. P. Ramsey, *The foundations of mathematics*, see 1931.
R. tries to show how, adopting W.'s work, one can avoid certain difficulties inherent in *Principia mathematica*, which forced some logicians to abandon Russell's approach to logical problems. The most serious of such problems is that of the axiom of reducibility, whose truth or falsehood is a question of fact, and cannot therefore be used in mathematics. *Inter alia*, R. points out that the alternative solution proposed in *Tract.*, according to which mathematics consists of equations, encounters insuperable obstacles and ends in a blind alley (see spec. §1).

1927

17. Chadwick J. A., *Logical constants*, M, 36, pp. 1-11.
Briefly mentions (pp. 7-8) the reduction, proposed in W.'s *Tract.*, of logical necessity to tautology, and the consequent distinction between tautology and logical possibility. See C. H. Langford's observations on this article (1927).

18. Chadwick J. A., *On propositions belonging to logic*, M, 36, pp. 347-53.
A reply to Langford's (1927) article, which does not, however, make direct reference to *Tract.*

19. Feys R., *Le raisonnement en termes de faits dans la logistique russellienne*, RNP, 29, 1927, pp. 393-421; 30, 1928, pp. 154-92, 257-74.
In outlining the new tendencies of logic above all in the light of the 2nd edition of *Principia mathematica* F. makes frequent

references to *Tract.* which seems to him to carry this new direction to extremes while also exercising a visible influence on that second edition. To this end F. briefly presents W.'s method (compare 1927, pp. 416-18) as an attempt to prove the totality of logical laws (principles of contradiction and the excluded third) on the basis of their immediate intuitive evidence (*ibid.*, pp. 259-261).

20. Langer S. K., *A logical study of verbs*, JP, 24, pp. 120-9.
L. proposes to clarify whether and, if so, to what extent the function of assertion in verbs is to be considered as essentially logical. She maintains that in this regard the error of treating logic as a study of propositional forms presents considerable difficulties for Russell's theory and leads W. to mysticism. See Willis Moore's (1938) criticism of this article.

21. Langford C. H., *On propositions belonging to logic,* M, 36, pp. 342-346.
Referring to a previous article by Chadwick (*Logical constants,* 1927) L. makes some objections in connection with the analysis of logical propositions by W. in *Tract.* Compare Chadwick's reply to this article (1927).

22. Ramsey F. P., *Facts and propositions*, PAS (SV), 7, pp. 153-170. Reprinted in F. P. Ramsey, *The foundations of mathematics*, 1931.
Symposium with G. E. Moore. In developing his own theory of propositions R. underlines his debt to W. from whom (he declares) he derived his own concept of logic. Nevertheless, he stresses the fact that some of his theses reveal a pragmatist tendency which he considers necessary to fill some theoretical gaps in W.'s system.

23. Russell B., *The analysis of matter*, London, Kegan Paul, 1927.
Some references to *Tract.* concerning the principles of inference as applied to observation statements (p. 16), the tautological nature of logic (a theory which R. on p. 171 states he shares with W.) and the isomorphism between the structure of propositions and that of facts (p. 239). With reference to the latter problem R. admits to being greatly influenced by W.'s point of view.

1928

24. Carnap R., *Der logische Aufbau der Welt*, Berlin, Weltkreis-Verlag, 1928; 2nd ed. 1961. E.T. *The logical*

structure of the world, London, Routledge & Kegan Paul, 1967.
In §43 C. states that he has adopted a viewpoint close to *Tract.* as regards the thesis of extensionality. At the end of the volume (§§180, 183) C. again refers to *Tract.* as a work extremely valuable both for its logical derivations and for its ethical teaching, though unfortunately almost completely ignored. In the preface of the 2nd edition (1961) which includes his article *Scheinprobleme in der Philosophie* (1928) C. emphasizes the influence of *Tract.* on his own thought and on the Vienna Circle in general.

1929

25. Carnap R., *Abriss der Logistik*, Vienna, Springer, 1929, pp. 114.
C. refers to *Tract.* when dealing with the system of truth functions (p. 6), the mathematical concept of identity (p. 15) and the theory of types (p. 22).

26. Neurath O., Carnap R., Hahn H., *Wissenschaftliche Weltauffassung: der Wiener Kreis*, Vienna, Wolf, 1929, pp. 64. E.T. 'The scientific conception of the world. The Vienna circle' in O. Neurath, *Empiricism and sociology*, ed. by M. Neurath and R. S. Cohen, Dordrecht/Boston/London, Reidel, 1973, pp. 299-318.
In what was commonly considered as the manifesto of the Vienna Circle, the importance of *Tract.* for the formation of this philosophical movement is stressed, along with its influence on the members of the Circle. Among contemporary philosophers along with W., Einstein and Russell are picked out for their affinity with the Circle's programme. These three are said to be the most effective proponents of the scientific conception of the world.

1930

27. Anon, E, 1, 1930-31, p. 334.
At the conclusion of this volume, which is dedicated to the proceedings of the Prague Congress of 1929 (see below, Frank and others), in a bibliography containing a list of authors closest

in their thinking to the approach favoured by the Congress, a synopsis of *Tract.* is included. A more accessible account of this 'difficult' book is promised in F. Waismann's soon to be published 'Logik, Sprache, Philosophie' (a book which actually appeared in English in 1965 (see below) and in German in 1976).

28. Carnap R., *Die alte und die neue Logik*, E, 1, 1930-31, pp. 12-26. E.T. in A. J. Ayer (ed.), *Logical positivism*, Glencoe, Ill., Free Press, 1959.

This article appeared in the first number of 'Erkenntnis' together with an article of Schlick's (see below). C. mentions W.'s name among those who made a major contribution to the birth of the new logic. *Tract.* is mentioned in the bibliography for having introduced the theory of logic as tautology. In a note at the end of the English translation C. talks about changes which have in the meantime come about in respect to the theses set out in the article. In particular the original principle of verification, which was first expounded by W., is said to have been replaced by a weaker requirement of confirmability.

29. Dubislav W., *Über den sogenannten Gegenstand der Mathematik*, E, 1, 1930-1, pp. 27-48.

Reviewing the main directions taken by the philosophy of mathematics, D. distinguishes between the two different attitudes within 'logistics' – the first upheld by Russell and the second 'newer' one proposed by W. in *Tract.* According to this latter theory, logic and mathematics would constitute a system of tautologies. (See pp. 41ff.)

30. Frank P. and others, *Bericht über die 1. Tagung für Erkenntnislehre der exakten Wissenschaften* E, 1, 1930-31, pp. 93-339.

Acts of the 1st Congress on the theme of epistemology of the exact sciences (Prague 1929). Many speakers refer to the influence that *Tract.* had in giving rise to the theoretic demands which inspired the Congress. This influence is said to consist mainly of: the understanding of the nature of logic and mathematics (H. Hahn, pp. 100-1, P. Frank, pp. 139-40, A. Fraenkel, p. 301); the concept of probability (F. Waismann, cf. 1930); supersession of the metaphysics of the past (P. Frank, pp. 146 ff., O. Neurath, p. 312). See also Anon, 1930.

31. Frank P., *Was bedeuten die gegenwärtigen physikalischen Theorien für die allgemeine Erkenntnislehre?*, E, 1, 1930-3 pp. 126-157. E.T. P. Frank, *Modern science and its philosophy*, Cambridge, Mass., Harvard University Press, 1949.

In evaluating the contribution made by contemporary physics to theory of knowledge in general F. refers to the work of B. Russell and his pupils, in particular W., and to their efforts in trying to supersede the Aristotelian tradition of logic generally defended by philosophers.

32. Kaufmann F., *Das Unendliche in der Mathematik und seine Ausschaltung*, Leipzig and Vienna, Franz Deuticke, 1930. E.T. in F. Kaufmann, *The infinite in mathematics. Logico-mathematical writings*, ed. by B. McGuinness, Dordrecht/Boston/London, Reidel, 1978.

Several references to the logical theory of *Tract.*, especially in regard to the nature of the propositions of logic and of mathematics (pp. 26, 38 ff), the concept of identity (p. 40), the theory of classes (p. 82), and the theory of types (p. 193).

33. Langer S. K., *The practice of philosophy*, New York, Henry Holt, 1930.

In Chapter V ('The logical basis of meaning', especially pp. 118ff) some extracts from *Tract.* are re-examined and the work is characterized as a study of the logical basis of the problem of meaning.

34. Schlick M., *Die Wende der Philosophie*, E, 1, 1930-31, pp. 4-11. Reprinted in M. Schlick, *Gesammelte Aufsätze,* Vienna, Gerold, 1938 (q.v.); E.T.: *The turning point in philosophy*, in A. J. Ayer (ed.), *Logical positivism*, Glencoe, Ill., Free Press, 1959; in M. Schlick, *Philosophical papers*, vol. II (1925-36), Dordrecht/Boston/London, Reidel, 1979.

In the opening article of the first number of Erkenntnis S. presents the theoretical point of view to be sustained by that periodical, declaring it a decisive turning point in the history of philosophy. He identifies the origins of the new methods of investigation in Leibniz, Frege and Russell. He adds, however, that it was W. in *Tract.* who first fully recognized their value and made an exceptional contribution to their development.

35. Waismann F., *Logische Analyse des Wahrscheinlichkeitsbegriffs*, E, 1, 1930-1, pp. 228-48. Reprinted in his *Philosophical papers*, see 1977.

Wa.'s aim is to reach an understanding of the problem of
probability as part of a branch of logic. In Wa.'s view, some
difficulties arising from this analysis can be overcome following
the indications emerging from the research of W., whose results
'are being collected in a large work'.

1931

36. Braithwaite R. B., Introduction to F. P. Ramsey, *The
foundations of mathematics and other logical essays*
(Ramsey, 1931).
In a biographical note, which introduces a posthumous collection
of Ramsey's writings, B. recalls how Ramsey, brought up in the logic
of *Principia mathematica*, was soon to discover the importance
of the work of W., which was also largely the basis of the writings
published by Ramsey in his lifetime. Thus B. notes how the essay
on *Tract.* contained in the book (Ramsey, 1923) was the first
important philosophical work by Ramsey. Ramsey himself, having
written the review before having discussions with W., admitted
later that he had in many places misunderstood *Tract.*

37. Carnap R., Review of the 2nd ed. of A. N. Whitehead and
B. Russell, *Principia mathematica* (see 1925), E, 2,
pp. 73-74.
C. shows how the thesis of extensionality, proposed in *Tract.* can
solve the difficulties connected with the axiom of reducibility and
how its acceptance constitutes a step forward compared with the
theory maintained by Russell before the second edition of
Principia.

38. Carnap R., *Die logizistische Grundlegung der Mathematik*,
E, 2, pp. 91-105. E.T. in *Philosophy of mathematics*, ed.
by P. Benacerraf and H. Putnam, Englewood Cliffs, N.J.,
Prentice-Hall, 1964, pp. 41-52.
Refers to W.'s criticism of Russell's axiom of reducibility.

39. Carnap R., *Überwindung der Metaphysik durch logische
Analyse der Sprache*, E, 2, pp. 219-241. E.T. in A. J. Ayer
(ed.), *Logical positivism*, New York, Free Press, 1959.
C. attributes the thesis that the meaning of a proposition depends
on its method of verification to W. (p. 224). More generally he
refers to *Tract.* as a source of the conception of logic and
epistemology upheld in the article.

40. Feigl H. and **Blumberg A. E.**, *Logical positivism. A new movement in European philosophy*, JP, 28, pp. 281-96.
W.'s contribution to logical positivism is identified as his investigation of the relationship between logic and empirical knowledge, following the direction already taken by Frege and Russell (esp. pp. 282-285).

41. Hahn H., Carnap R. and others, *Diskussion zur Grundlegung der Mathematik*, E, 2, pp. 135-151.
An extract from discussions on the origins of mathematics between Carnap, Heyting and von Neumann at a Congress in Königsberg in September 1930. The authors occasionally refer to the report Waismann presented at that Congress on the theme of *The nature of mathematics: W.'s viewpoint* but not published (as explained in the preface of the volume) since the text did not arrive in time for inclusion (Waismann, 1982). Hahn (pp. 138-141) states specifically that he shares W.'s polemics and those of the intuitionists against the position of absolute realism taken for example by Russell, who sees the world as constituted by individuals, properties, properties of such properties, etc., and regards the axioms of logic as assertions about this world.

42. Jørgensen J., *A treatise of formal logic*, Copenhagen, Levin & Munksgaard; London, Humphrey Milford, 1931, 3 vols.
In volumes I and III *passim* some theoretical and historical references to the logical theory of *Tract*.

43. Neurath O., *Physikalismus*, 'Scientia', 50, pp. 297-303. E.T. in O. Neurath, *Philosophical papers, 1913-1946*, Dordrecht/Boston/Lancaster, Reidel, 1983.
W.'s thought together with Russell's is placed in relationship to the origins of the Vienna Circle and the programme of unified science pursued by that school. In the supplement of this review (pp. 117-122) a French translation of the article.

44. Neurath O., *Soziologie im Physikalismus*, E, 2, pp. 393-431. E.T. *Sociology and Physicalism*, in A. J. Ayer (ed.), *Logical positivism*, Glencoe, Ill., Free Press, 1959; in O. Neurath, *Philosophical papers, 1913-1946*, Dordrecht/Boston/Lancaster, Reidel, 1983.
Some references to W. and his influence on the diffusion of a scientific vision of the world free from all metaphysics. In spite

of his statement which attributes to philosophy the function of clarification of thought, W. has nevertheless introduced in the final sections of *Tract.* a kind of divergent secondary metaphysical doctrine. Thus W. did not adhere very strictly to the programme of avoiding metaphysical expressions and demonstrating their nonsensicality.

45. Neurath O., *Physicalism: the philosophy of the Viennese Circle*, Mo, 41, pp. 618-623. Reprinted in O. Neurath, *Philosophical papers, 1913-1946*, Dordrecht/Boston/ Lancaster, Reidel, 1983.

The programme of the Vienna Circle, 'strongly influenced by Russell and W.', consists essentially in 'sweeping away the last vestiges of theology and metaphysics' and establishing a method which would tend toward the clarification of scientific procedures.

46. Petzäll A., *Logistischer Positivismus*, Göteborg, Wettergren und Kerbers, 1931.

An analysis of the principal themes tackled by the Vienna Circle, whose general aim is taken to be the development of W.'s ideas. P. tends to interpret *Tract.* in the light of Waismann's *Thesen* (see *W.V.C.*) whose publication he considered imminent.

47. Ramsey F. P., *The foundations of mathematics and other logical essays*, London, Routledge & Kegan Paul, 1931 (2nd fully revised ed., 1978).

R.'s principal writings, some previously unpublished, are collected in this volume. Most contain important references to *Tract.* or constitute an attempt at developing its theory. Among those already published, which we have already considered above: *The foundations of mathematics* (1926), *Mathematical logic* (1926), *Universals* (1925), *Facts and propositions* (1927). Among the unpublished essays, we may here note *Truth and probability* (1926) and the last two sections of the book, in which are published notes made in 1928 and 1929, concerning *inter alia* the nature of theories, causality, the relationship between probability and truth, the nature of philosophic enquiry. R.'s *Critical notice of the Tractatus* (1923) is printed as an appendix.

48. Russell B., Critical notice of *The foundations of mathematics*, by F. P. Ramsey (1931), M, 40, pp. 476-482.

Contains numerous references to W. especially in connection with the first essay in the collection *The foundations of mathematics*, (cf. Ramsey 1926). Discussing Ramsey's review of *Tract.* (1923) R. brings out the cultural differences between the two philosophers: W. more radical and willing to sacrifice great intellectual structures for logical impeccability, Ramsey more fixed in the empirical tradition and more disposed to pragmatic solutions (p. 482).

49. Ryle G., *Systematically misleading expressions*, PAS, 32, pp. 139-70. Reprinted in A. G. N. Flew (ed.), *Logic and language*, Oxford, Blackwell, 1953; in R. Rorty (ed.), *The linguistic turn*, Chicago, Ill., and London, University of Chicago Press, 1967; in G. Ryle, *Collected papers*, vol. II, London, Hutchinson, 1971.

The concluding part of the article criticizes the theory attributed to W. and to the school of logical grammarians according to which there is a pictorial correspondence of a non-conventional nature between the elements of a proposition and those of the fact which it describes.

50. Schlick M., *The future of philosophy*, in *Proceedings of the VII International Congress of Philosophy*, Oxford, Oxford University Press, 1931, pp. 112-116. Reprinted in M. Schlick, *Philosophical papers*, vol. II, Dordrecht/Boston/London, Reidel, 1979.

The text of S.'s contribution to the VII International Philosophical Congress (Oxford, 1930). S. refers to W. *à propos* the conception of philosophy as an activity consisting in the logical clarification of thought. S. follows this up with a short history of precedents for such a view.

51. Wisdom A. J. T. D., *Logical constructions*, M, 40, 1931, pp. 188-216, 460-75; 41, 1932, pp. 441-64; 42, 1933, pp. 43-66 and 186-202. Reprinted in his *Logical constructions*, New York, Random House, 1969. The first part is also reprinted in Copi and Beard (eds.), 1966 (q.v.).

Throughout this long essay, the concept of *sketching* frequently recurs. Wis. defines it (see Section IV, entitled 'W. and picturing', pp. 200-205) and places it in relationship to the 'very similar' concept of *picturing* in *Tract.*. Wis. holds (and also ascribes to W.) the view that the *sentences* of ordinary language do not represent facts, as do the propositions of a logical language. In the first part of the essay (pp. 188-216) Wis., without explicitly referring to *Tract.*, lays down the conditions required to enable sentences to picture facts.

1932

52. Bell J., *An epistle on the subject of the ethical and aesthetic beliefs of Herr Ludwig Wittgenstein*, in Sherard Vines (ed.), *Whips and scorpions; specimens of modern satiric verse, 1914-31*, London, Wishart, 1932, pp. 21-31. Reprinted in Copi and Beard (eds.), 1966.

A satire in verse. B. specifies that it is not intended as a personal attack but as a criticism of W.'s theses regarding ethics and aesthetics.

53. Ginsburg E. B., *On the logical positivism of the Viennese Circle*, JP, 29, pp. 121-129.

The most important characteristic of logical positivism is seen in the rehabilitation of the positivist repudiation of metaphysics by the adoption of the logicism of Russell and W. The article attempts to give, from an American point of view, certain criticisms of the basis of this enterprise.

54. Jørgensen J., *Über die Ziele und Probleme der Logistik*, E, 3, pp. 73-102.

J. accepts the thesis of *Tract.* according to which all propositions in logic are on the same level, all being tautologies. The only aim of proof is to render more easily comprehensible the tautological character of a proposition (see esp. pp. 84-6).

55. Popper K., *Ein Kriterium des empirischen Charakters theoretischer Systeme*, E, 3, pp. 426-7. Reprinted in E.T. as an appendix to K. Popper, *The logic of scientific discovery*, London, Hutchinson, 1959.

P.'s letter to the editor contains two critical references to W. The first refers to the *status* of natural laws, which Schick 'influenced by W.' considered to be 'rules of transformation'. The second observation is in connection with the 'problem of demarcation' between assertions which belong to empirical science and those which are metaphysical. P. rejects W.'s attempt to resolve this problem by recourse to the notion of meaning, and by considering metaphysical propositions as nonsensical. The 'pseudo-problems' created by this solution can be avoided, P. maintains, by adopting the 'criterion of falsification' as a principle of demarcation between science and metaphysics.

56. Schlick M., *The future of philosophy*, in *Publications in philosophy*, Stockton Cal., College of the Pacific, vol. I,

1932, pp. 45–62. Reprinted in M. Schlick, *Gesammelte Aufsätze* (see 1938); in M. Schlick, *Philosophical papers*, vol. II (1925–36), Dordrecht/Boston/London, Reidel, 1979; in H. Feigl and W. Sellars (eds.), *Readings in philosophical analysis*, New York, 1949; in R. Rorty (ed.), *Linguistic turn*, see 1967.

A completely revised and extended version of S.'s 1931 article (q.v.). The view of philosophy to which S. refers is that formulated in *Tract.* Philosophy consists not in a theory but in an activity aimed at the logical clarification of thought. S. proceeds to investigate the precedents for this conception in the history of philosophy.

57. Stebbing L. S., *The method of analysis*, PAS, 33, pp. 65–94.
In section 3 (pp. 74ff.) S. discusses the method of analysis followed in England by Moore, Russell, Broad and W.

1933

58. Ayer A. J., *Atomic propositions*, A, 1, pp. 2–6.
If an atomic proposition is one which is incorrigible, i.e. which records what is directly experienced and is thus beyond doubt, then atomic propositions cannot be identified with what W. in *Tract.* calls elementary propositions, since W. does not maintain that these cannot be false.

59. Black M., *The nature of mathematics*, London, Routledge & Kegan Paul, 1933, pp. XIV, 218.
B. examines (pp. 129–34) those propositions and theses of *Tract.* that more directly concern the foundations of mathematics, i.e. the distinction between the equations of arithmetic and ordinary propositions; the multiplicity of a proposition; the impossibility of deducing the principle of induction; logical operations and use of indices (in this regard differences from the solutions proposed in *Principia mathematica* are pointed out). W.'s theory, B. maintains, constitutes a complete rejection both explicit and implicit of the theses of logistic. Pure mathematics is conceived in *Tract.* as the syntax of every possible system of symbols.

60. Braithwaite R. B., *Philosophy*, in H. von Wright (ed.), *University studies* (Cambridge, 1933), London, Ivor Nicholson and Watson, 1933, pp. 1–32.

B. sets himself the task of providing an overview of the progress of philosophic studies at Cambridge after the First World War. W's thought is discussed (especially pp. 18–32), not only in the light of *Tract.*, but also of various theories he is said to have put about after his return to Cambridge, especially concerning grammatical rules, the nature of a proposition, the verification principle, solipsism, etc. This article evcked a strenuous disavowal on the part of W.: in a letter to the periodical 'Mind' (42, 1933, pp. 415–16) he refuses to acknowledge as his own the theses which B. attributes to him. Parts of B.'s affirmations, W. states, can be taken as inaccurate representations of W.'s opinions; others clearly contradict them. See below (1933) B.'s reply to W.'s letter.

61. Braithwaite R. B., Letter to the editor of M, 42, p. 416.
A reply to W.'s letter published in the same number of the periodical (see 1933, above). B. clarifies his intentions in writing the article criticized by W.

62. Braithwaite R. B., *Solipsism and the 'Common sense view of the world'*, A, 1, pp. 13–15.
Contrary to what L. S. Stebbing maintains in her writing on 'logical positivism' (see below, 1933) not every form of solipsism is contrary to a view of the world which conforms 'to common sense', according to the meaning given to that expression by G. E. Moore. For example, the form of 'solipsism' defended by W. does not deny that there are beside myself other human beings who have analogous sensations to my own. See below (1933) the comments on this article by M. Cornforth and L. S. Stebbing.

63. Cornforth M., *Is solipsism compatible with common sense?*, A, 1, pp. 21–26.
Contrary to what Braithwaite holds (1933) W.'s 'solipsism' actually consists in reducing every experience to 'my' personal experience, and in deducing this thesis from a general verification principle (see esp. pp. 24–25).

64. Stebbing L. S., *Concerning solipsism: reply to R. B. Braithwaite*, A, 1, pp. 26–28.
S. acknowledges the truth of Braithwaite's observations (1933), which tend to distinguish between a form of solipsism incompatible with 'common sense' and the 'methodological solipsism' held by W.

65. Stebbing L. S., *Logical positivism and analysis*, London, Humphrey Milford, 1933, pp. 37. Extract from 'The Proceedings of the British Academy', vol. 19, pp. 53–87.
A lecture delivered to the British Academy. S. proposes to compare W.'s method of analysis with that of Moore. As far as W. is concerned, she examines *Tract.* and his lectures at Cambridge, explaining them in the light of the writings of the main exponents of the Vienna Circle (Schlick, Carnap, Waismann, Neurath). These latter philosophers, in fact, according to her, dedicated themselves to developing the consequences of W.'s conception of philosophy (cf. pp. 11–14). A common theoretic element in these different authors is the adoption of a principle of verification which was first stated in *Tract.* The major difficulties affecting these theories occur where they diverge from Moore's conception of analysis, i.e. in W.'s 'intentional' and Carnap's 'methodological' solipsism.

1934

66. Ayer A. J., *Demonstration of the impossibility of metaphysics*, M, 43, pp. 335–345. Reprinted in P. Edwards and A. Pap (eds.), *A modern introduction to philosophy*, London, Allen & Unwin, 1957.
In a preface to this article A. acknowledges that the ideas contained in it 'are not original' but 'inspired by W.'s work' and by the writings of M. Schlick and R. Carnap. The article is addressed to those who have hitherto ignored or misunderstood W.'s work and that of the Vienna Circle.

67. Carnap R., *Logische Syntax der Sprache*, Vienna, Springer, 1934. E.T. *Logical syntax of language*, London, Kegan Paul; New York, Harcourt Brace, 1937.
Numerous references to *Tract.* are scattered throughout the book. In pp. 282–4 (1937 ed.), C. underlines his basic agreement with many theses held by W. and declares his own work in a certain sense a development and clarification of *Tract.* All the same, he stresses two reasons for disagreeement: 1) W.'s thesis according to which there cannot be propositions about the logical form of the propositions; 2) the thesis that the logic of science (i.e. philosophy) cannot be formulated. According to C. on the contrary, not only can syntax be formulated, but this can be done in the very language whose rules of formation and transformation are to be defined.

68. Carnap R., *On the character of philosophical problems*, PSc, 1, pp. 9-19. Reprinted in R. Rorty (ed.), *Linguistic turn*, see 1967.

C. notes W.'s special emphasis in *Tract.* on the thesis which identifies philosophy with the 'logic of science', the propositions of metaphysics being considered to be without any meaning. C. goes on to attempt to give a positive reply to this problem, as an alternative to the negative conclusions of *Tract.*

1935

69. Ambrose A., *Finitism in mathematics*, M, 44, pp. 186-203, 317-40.

In evaluating the 'finitist' position regarding some problems in the philosophy of mathematics, A. states that her own theses were influenced by some indications she received from W. during his lectures in 1932-35. In the course of the discussion various examples and theses attributed to W. are cited.

70. Britton K., *Language, public and private*, Mo, 45, pp. 1-59.

Frequent references to *Tract.* especially in relation to discussion of the principle of the excluded middle (cf. pp. 43ff.).

71. Carnap R., *Philosophy and logical syntax*, London, Kegan Paul, 1935.

At §7 of the first chapter entitled 'The rejection of metaphysics', C. criticizes the thesis defended in *Tract.* according to which every philosophical statement is considered to be without sense, even if illuminating. C. then undertakes to demonstrate the correct philosophical method, which enables one to avoid W.'s difficulty, who was obliged to regard even his own propositions as senseless.

72. Dürr K., *Die Bedeutung der Negation*, E, 5, pp. 205-227.

D. refers to the concept of negation and to the thesis of the independence of atomic proposition in *Tract.*

73. Geymonat L., *Nuovi indirizzi della filosofia austriaca*, RF, 26, pp. 250-65. Reprinted with the title *Le idee direttive del neoempirismo*, in L. Geymonat, *Studi per un nuovo razionalismo*, see 1945.

G. undertakes to expound some of the motives that inspired

neo-empiricism, translating them into a philosophic language more familiar to the Italian reader. *Tract.* (G. laments the scanty knowledge of it in Italy) is considered the origin of the new way of thinking, and the most systematic account of its general orientation.

74. **Hempel C. G.**, *The logical analysis of psychology*, 'Revue de Synthèse', 10, pp. 27–42. Reprinted in H. Feigl and W. Sellars (eds.), *Readings in philosophical analysis*, New York, Appleton-Century-Crofts, 1949, pp. 373–384.
A review of principal results of the new analysis of psychology developed by the members of the Vienna Circle, in part 'based on the work of W.'.

75. **Morris C. W.**, *Philosophy of science and science of philosophy*, PSc, 2, pp. 271–286. Reprinted in his *Logical positivism, pragmatism, and scientific empiricism*, Paris, Hermann, 1937, pp. 7–21.
In the second section, 'Philosophy as clarification of meaning', M. examines the analytical way of thought represented by a branch of the Vienna school especially by W., Schlick, and Waismann, where philosophy is not seen as an inquiry into *a priori* logical forms, but as a 'clarification of ideas'; this, M. adds, is a conception which has always existed in American pragmatism.

76. **Popper K. R.**, *Logik der Forschung*, Vienna, Springer, 1935. E.T. *The logic of scientific discovery*, London, Hutchinson, 1959; 2nd edition 1968.
The work contains a number of references to W., especially in relation to the problem of the demarcation line between science and metaphysics (cf. especially the 'Introduction', 1st part, §4). P. maintains that the criterion of significance upheld in *Tract.* would lead to scientific laws being considered as lacking in significance. Further criticisms of W. are contained in the notes and appendices added to the English edition.

77. **Russell B.**, *The limits of empiricism*, PAS, 36, pp. 131–50.
R. refers to *Tract.* in order to exemplify the thesis (which he considers to be characteristic of empiricism) according to which it is impossible to justify the inference of a fact from other facts (see especially pp. 138ff.). The main defect of this theory, he maintains, is that it eliminates all those inferences which have a practical use.

78. **Weinberg J. R.**, *Are there ultimate simples?*, PSc, 2, pp. 387–99. Reprinted in Copi and Beard (eds.), 1966.

The method of reasoning by which W. attempts to demonstrate the existence of simple elements constitutes a *petitio principii*. Even the attempt to deduce logically the simple elements of the *Tract.* starting from independent facts (*Sachverhalte*), though it avoids this vicious circle, proves to be inadequate and purely verbal. Therefore both the existence of ultimate simple elements and the thesis stating that all (non-metaphysical) propositions are characterized by a final reference of an empirical nature are shown to be impossible to prove.

1936

79. Ayer A. J., *Language, truth and logic*, London, Gollancz, 1936 (2nd ed., 1946).

In the preface to the 1936 edition A. maintains that the theories supported in his own book derive from the doctrine of B. Russell and of W., which in their turn are the logical consequence of the empiricism of Berkeley and Hume. Numerous references to *Tract.* are contained in the work, especially in relation to questions of logic and the nature of philosophy.

80. Ayer A. J., *The analytic movement in contemporary British philosophy*, in *Actes du congrès international de philosophie scientifique* (Paris, 1935), Paris, Hermann, 1936, pp. 53–59.

The rehabilitation of English empiricism in the twentieth century, effected by Russell and Moore, was carried further by *Tract.* and by the critical development of that work, by S. Stebbing, J. Wisdom, and W.'s pupils.

81. Britton K., *Communication. A philosophical study of language*, London, Kegan Paul, 1936.

The work contains numerous references to *Tract.*, especially in relation to the following themes: the analysis of the 'propositional sign' (chs. V–VI), the nature of 'necessary propositions' (ch. VII), laws and their application to nature (pp. 194–5).

82. Carnap R., *Testability and meaning*, PSc, 3, 1936, pp. 420–471; 4, 1937, pp. 1–40. Reprinted by 'Graduate Philosophy Club', New Haven, Conn., Yale University Press, 1950.

In an historical introduction C. maintains that the requirement

of 'verifiability' for meaningful statements was formulated for the
first time in *Tract.* and that this point of view was developed in the
first publications of the Vienna Circle. C. judges this formulation
to be simplistic and restrictive and observes that it is still upheld
by the Circle's most conservative wing (especially Schlick and
Waismann). See also section 23, concerning the testability of
general statements and W.'s treatment of physical laws as rules
for the formation of statements. W.'s solution is compared to
those of Russell, Schlick, and Ramsey, and is then criticized.

83. **Carnap R.**, *Wahrheit und Bewährung*, in *Actes du congrès
internazional de philosophie scientifique* (Paris, 1935), IV,
Paris, Hermann, 1936, pp. 18-23. E.T. in a revised form in
R. Carnap, *Truth and confirmation*, see 1949.

84. **McGill V. F.**, *An evaluation of logical positivism*, 'Science
and Society', 1, pp. 45-80.
McG. gives an historical evaluation of 'logical positivism' from
the point of view of 'dialectical materialism', attempting to single
out its empiricist roots in classical empiricism. Then he analyses
Tract., which in his opinion anticipates the themes and solutions
of logical positivism (see in particular pp. 56-62).

85. **Nagel E.**, *Impressions and appraisals of analytic
philosophy in Europe*, JP, 33, pp. 5-53; reprinted in
E. Nagel, *Logic without metaphysics*, Glencoe, Ill., Free
Press, 1956.
Since N. did not obtain permission to attend W.'s lessons, he gives
(see in particular pp. 10-39) a description of the 'therapeutic'
method of investigation followed by W., based on notes circulated
privately and on conversations with pupils. He maintains that W.'s
philosophical activity after *Tract.* tends towards a genuine
restoration of the point of view of the man in the street and
therefore proves to be partly close to Moore's defence of common
sense.

86. **Reichenbach H.**, *Logistic empiricism in Germany and the
present state of its problems*, JP, 33, pp. 141-160.
R. sets himself the task of summarizing the results obtained in the
last fifteen years by the 'analytic-scientific' method in philosophy.
In his opinion, the element which links the works of W., Carnap,
Schlick and other representatives of the Vienna Circle is the
acceptance of the principle according to which every genuine
proposition must have a verifiable meaning.

87. Schlick M., *Meaning and verification,* PR, 45, pp. 339-369. Reprinted in M. Schlick, *Gesammelte Aufsätze* (see 1938); in M. Schlick, *Philosophical papers*, vol. II (1925-36), Dordrecht/Boston/London, Reidel, 1979; in H. Feigl and W. Sellars (eds.), *Readings in philosophical analysis*, New York, Appleton-Century-Crofts, 1949.

S. attributes the observations concerning 'meaning' and 'use', set out in this article, together with the notion of 'grammatical rule', largely to the conversations held with W, explaining that they profoundly influenced his own point of view on these subjects. An analogous acknowledgement is made concerning the analysis of expressions relating to private experiences. Here too S. declares that he follows closely ideas expressed by W. (cf. especially part V).

88. Waismann F., *Einführung in das mathematische Denken*, Vienna, Springer, 1936 (2nd ed., 1947). E.T. *Introduction to mathematical thinking*, London, Hafner; New York, Ungar, 1951.

Waismann acknowledges that he has drawn a number of the theses set out in this book from an unpublished manuscript by W.

89. Waismann F., *Über den Begriff der Identität,* E, 6, pp. 54-64. E.T. in F. Waismann, *Philosophical papers*, see 1977.

In order to clarify the concept of identity, Wa. analyses the different uses of the word 'identical' (*derselbe*). He notes that many of the ideas developed in the article were stimulated by conversations held with W.

90. Weinberg J. R., *An examination of logical positivism*, London, Routledge & Kegan Paul, 1936.

An investigation of the origins of 'logical positivism' centred above all on the logical thought of Frege and Russell and on its development in the context of the Vienna Circle and of physicalism. In this historical reconstruction, a great importance is also attributed to *Tract.* (see especially, in the first part, the chapters 'W.'s theory of meaning', pp. 31-68, and 'Logic and mathematics', pp. 69-103). While logical positivism was initially deeply influenced by *Tract.*, later it arrived at the construction of a more independent philosophy. This change can be explained as an attempt to overcome a number of difficulties deeply ingrained in W.'s work, in particular: 1) the thesis according to which the relationship between meaning and reality cannot be expressed by language; 2) the thesis that all meaningful sentences must have an empirical reference; 3) W.'s solipsistic conclusions, which made an intersubjective science impossible.

91. Wisdom A. J. T. D., *Philosophical perplexity*, PAS, 37, pp. 71–88. Reprinted in A. J. T. D. Wisdom, *Philosophy and psycho-analysis*, Oxford, Blackwell, 1953.

Wis. acknowledges his debt to W., not only with regard to the way of tackling single philosophical problems, but also and above all because of W.'s method of doing philosophy. In the article he examines a number of examples analysed by W. in the course of his lectures.

93. Wohlstetter A., *The structure of the proposition and the fact*, PSc, 3, pp. 167–84.

In re-formulating in his own terms the thesis which states that a proposition represents a fact by virtue of a structure identical to it, Wo. criticizes (pp. 173–175) the notion of structure used by W. in *Tract*.

NOTE   Entry 92, a doublet, was dropped in the course of production.

1937

94. Ambrose A., *Finitism and the 'Limits of empiricism'*, M, 46, pp. 379–85. Reprinted in a modified form in her *Essays in analysis*, see 1966.

A reply to the criticisms made by B. Russell (in PAS, 36, 1935–36 under the title given) of a previous article by A. (1935) concerning the conditions of significance of a mathematical expression and a number of questions connected with the development of π. A. mentions briefly a number of theses on the philosophy of mathematics maintained by W. in his 1932–35 lectures which could be applied to these problems.

95. Lazerowitz M., *Tautologies and the matrix method*, M, 46, pp. 191–205.

W. extends the validity of the matrix method, put forward in *Principia mathematica*, to tautological or self-contradictory functions, and considers these last to be truth-functions also. However, this theory proves not to be adequate. The matrix method is in fact applicable to tautologies and to contradictions in a different sense from that in which it is applicable to other truth-functions.

1938

96. Black M., *Some problems connected with language*, PAS, 39, pp. 43–68. Reprinted under the title 'Wittgenstein's Tractatus', in M. Black, *Language and philosophy*, Ithaca, N.Y., Cornell University Press, 1944; in Copi and Beard (eds.), 1966; in Shanker (ed.), 1986, vol. I.
B. defends what he judges to be the 'central thesis' of *Tract.*, i.e. the conception of philosophy as a critique of language, and replies to the criticisms raised for example by F. P. Ramsey (1931) and R. Carnap (*Logische Syntax*, see 1934). He also rejects the interpretation, supported by B. Russell in the introduction to the English edition (see 1922), according to which W. meant to construct a logically perfect symbolism to be opposed to the confused and imperfect one represented by ordinary language.

97. Moore W., *Structure in sentence and in fact*, PSc, 5, pp. 81–8. Reprinted in Copi and Beard (eds.), 1966.
M. considers a number of different interpretations which can be given of the notion of a 'structure' which, according to W.'s theory, facts should share with the statements that picture them. According to M., neither the answer put forward by S. Langer (1927), nor those of Russell and Schlick, nor other possible interpretations, provide a satisfactory solution to this problem.

98. Reichenbach H., *Experience and prediction*, Chicago, University of Chicago Press, 1938.
A particularly radical version of the principle of verification is said to go back to W., and the theoretical difficulties which this entails are analysed (pp. 49, 74ff.).

99. Schlick M., *Gesammelte Aufsätze, 1926–36*, ed. by F. Waismann, Vienna, Gerold, 1938, pp. 398. An enlarged and revised ed., with E.T. in M. Schlick, *Philosophical papers*, vol. II, ed. by H. L. Mulder and B. F. B. van de Velde-Schlick, Dordrecht/Boston/London, Reidel, 1979, pp. 538.

A posthumous collection of Schlick's writings, some of which contain important references to W. See, in particular, those which have been considered above: *Die Wende der Philosophie* (1930), *The future of philosophy* (1932), *Meaning and verification* (1936). See also the references contained in the introduction to the work, by F. Waismann, concerning the influence of W. on Schlick (pp. VII–XXXI).

100. Waismann F., *The relevance of psychology to logic*, PAS (SV), 17, pp. 54–68. Reprinted in H. Feigl and W. Sellars (eds.), *Readings in philosophical analysis*, New York, Appleton-Century-Crofts, 1949, pp. 211–21; and in Canfield (ed.), 1986, vol. V.
Wa. acknowledges his debt to W., and maintains that he owes the latter not only a large part of the opinions expressed in this article, but also its whole method of tackling philosophical problems.

101. Wisdom A. J. T. D., *Metaphysics and verification*, M, 47, pp. 452–499. Reprinted in A. J. T. D. Wisdom, *Philosophy and psychoanalysis*, Oxford, Blackwell, 1953.
The aim of the article is to show how the 'verification principle' is the generalization of a broad class of metaphysical theories. Wis. acknowledges his debt to W., especially in relation to the method of investigation followed, and uses numerous examples discussed by W. in his lectures.

1939

102. Black M., *Relation between logical positivism and the Cambridge school of analysis*, E, 8, pp. 24–35.
In examining the analogies and differences between these two philosophical movements, B. writes a brief account of the theses supported by W. in his Cambridge lessons, and compares the viewpoint emerging from the latter with that of Moore and Russell.

103. Stebbing S., *Language and misleading questions,* E, 8, pp. 1–6.
In her inaugural address at the 'Fourth International Congress for the Unity of Science' (Cambridge, 1938), on 'Scientific language', S. recalls how W. contributed more than any other to directing philosophy towards a critique of language.

Nevertheless *Tract.* does not succeed in explaining in what way sounds (or shapes) can be used as symbols. In order to argue in favour of this criticism, S. examines the distinction between 'sign' (*Zeichen*) and 'symbol' (*Symbol*), and also the notion of 'sense' according to *Tract.*

104. Urban W. M., *Language and reality*, London, Allen & Unwin; New York, Macmillan, 1939.

In chapter VIII a number of references to *Tract.* in relation to the pictorial theory of language (cf. pp. 252ff.).

105. von Mises R., *Kleines Lehrbuch des Positivismus*, The Hague, van Stockum, 1939. E.T. *Positivism: a study in human understanding*, Cambridge, Mass., Harvard University Press, 1951.

v.M. singles out in several places in *Tract.* a decisive contribution to the 'positivist' outlook and stresses the historical importance of W.'s thesis concerning the tautological character of the propositions of logic and mathematics.

106. Waismann F., *Was ist logische Analyse?*, E, 9, pp. 265-289. E.T. in F. Waismann, *Philosophical papers*, see 1977.

The logical analysis of *Tract.* is based on the existence of elementary propositions. Substantially, these have three characteristics: 1) they are irreducible; 2) they are reciprocally logically independent; 3) they are not truth-functions of one another. It is impossible to find examples of elementary propositions in ordinary language. Even those which seem to draw near to this concept do not actually possess these three requisite characteristics. This led W. to search for a model of artificial language that can be constructed on the basis of genuine elementary propositions.

1940

107. Findlay J., *Some reactions to recent Cambridge philosophy*, AJP, 18, 1940, pp. 193-211; 19, 1941, pp. 1-13. Reprinted in his *Language, mind and value,* London, George Allen & Unwin, 1963, pp. 13-38.

An analysis of the philosophical trends at Cambridge in the years 1930-40. F. maintains that the influence exerted by W. in his lectures during this period led to a rediscovery of the value of ordinary language and to avoiding the metaphysical flights of traditional philosophy. W.'s influence furthermore brought about the abandonment of the theory according to which language is composed of words or combinations of words with the exclusive function of expressing thoughts or of naming objects.

108. Russell B., *An inquiry into meaning and truth*, London, George Allen & Unwin, 1940.

Numerous critical references to *Tract.* in relation to the following themes: the theory of types (p. 62); the notion of identity (pp. 102–3); the principles of logical atomism and intensional statements (pp. 168–9, 262, 266–73).

109. Wisdom A. J. T. D., *Other minds*, M, 49, 1940, pp. 369–402; 50, 1941, pp. 97–121, 209–242, 313–329; 51, 1942, pp. 1–17; 52, 1943, pp. 193–211, 289–313. Reprinted in A. J. T. D. Wisdom, *Other minds*, Oxford, Blackwell, 1952.

In a note at the beginning of the first article of the series, Wis. acknowledges his debt to W. This debt will be appreciated properly only by those who have heard W. lecture and is certainly not confined to the few places where Wis. happens to recall that a specific passage derives from W.

1942

110. Carnap R., *Introduction to semantics*, Cambridge, Mass., Harvard University Press, 1942.

A number of references to the logical and semantic theory of *Tract.* C. attributes to W. *inter alia* the thesis that the truth conditions of a statement constitute its meaning, and that understanding it consists in knowing these conditions (pp. 28–29).

111. Moore G. E., *An autobiography*, in P. Schilpp (ed.), *The philosophy of G. E. Moore*, New York, Tudor, 1942 (2nd ed., 1952), pp. 3–39. Reprinted in part in Fann (ed.), 1967.

M. devotes a number of pages (especially pp. 33–35) to the analysis of his relationship with W., starting from 1912, the year in which the latter began to attend M.'s lectures on psychology.

This relationship was interrupted between 1914 and 1929, the year in which W. returned to Cambridge and began his own teaching. M. states that he felt great admiration when he attended these lectures, and that he somehow experienced the influence of W., even if he was never capable of fully understanding the philosophical method that W. was coming to adopt.

1943

112. Feigl H., *Logical empiricism*, in D.D. Runes (ed.), *Twentieth century philosophy*, New York, Philosophical Library, 1943, pp. 373–416.
W. is regarded as one of the pre-eminent figures of logical empiricism, even though the analytical method followed by him is distinct from the more systematic and constructive one adopted by Carnap and the other representatives of the Vienna School.

113. Passmore J. A., *Logical positivism*, AJP, 21, 1943, pp. 65–92; 22, 1944, pp. 129–53, 26, 1948, pp. 1–19.
The third part in particular of this work contains a number of references to W. The 'picture theory', P. maintains, is at the root of the greatest contradiction in *Tract.*: W. is forced to speak about that which, if he is to conform with his theory, he cannot speak about. P. then traces a line of development and continuity between *Tract.* and the work of Carnap (pp. 17–19).

1944

114. Wisdom A. J. T. D., *Philosophy, anxiety and novelty*, M, 53, 1944, pp. 170–175. Reprinted in A. J. T. D. Wisdom, *Philosophy and psycho-analysis* (1953).
Some examples tending to show how reminders of and respect for linguistic uses lead to the disintegration of a number of characteristic philosophical problems.

1945

115. Carnap R., *Remarks on induction and truth*, PPR, 6, pp. 590–602. Reprinted in a revised form in R. Carnap, *Truth and confirmation*, see 1949.

116. Geymonat L., *Studi per un nuovo razionalismo*, Turin, Chiantore, 1945.

A collection of essays, some of which already published in the years 1935–1945. They contain frequent references to W., especially in connexion with his relationship to neopositivism and to modern developments in formal logic (for the latter theme, cf. especially pp.57–75). Of particular interest here are the articles on 'The leading ideas of neoempiricism' (cf. 1935) and on the logical syntax of Carnap (especially pp. 142–5).

117. Kneale W., *Truths of logic*, PAS, 46, pp. 206–34.

In considering (pp. 218ff.) a number of authors who have attempted to define the logical notion of proposition in terms of certain properties and relationships between statements, K. evaluates W.'s contribution to this topic in *Tract*.

1946

118. Chisholm R. M., *The contrary-to-fact conditional*, M, 55, pp. 289–307. Reprinted in H. Feigl and W. Sellars (eds.), *Readings in philosophical analysis*, New York, Appleton-Century-Crofts, 1949, pp. 482–497.

In section IV of the article, the theory supported by W., Ramsey and others, concerning universal and existential quantifications, is considered inadequate for the purpose of explaining the contrary-to-fact conditional.

119. Cornforth M. C., *Science versus idealism*, London, Lawrence & Wishart, 1946, pp. 267. (2nd ed. rev. and extended, 1954.)

A treatment of the main developments of modern empiricism, from the 17th century up till the present day considered from the standpoint of Marxism or dialectical materialism. *Inter alia* C. considers W.'s thought, drawing only on *Tract*. (cf. especially ch. IX: 'The philosophy of Wittgenstein', pp. 141–66). In general, C. judges this work to be an updated, only apparently more accurate, version of 'subjectivism', characteristic of empiricist philosophy in its opposition to the innovative function of science. The whole of the *Tract*. theory leads to 'mysticism' and to subjective idealism in its most extreme form: namely solipsism. In the 1954 edition these criticisms are integrated with those previously set out in the work 'In defence of philosophy against positivism and pragmatism' (1950, see entry) and are substantially extended to W.'s later work. For a critique of the theses supported by Cornforth, see R. Rhees, 1947.

120. Farrell B. A., *An appraisal of therapeutic positivism*, M, 55, pp. 25–48, 133–50.

An analysis of the method of resolving and tackling philosophical problems followed at Cambridge and an evaluation of the influence exerted by W.'s lectures. F. calls this method 'therapeutic positivism'. A number of writings published by 'W.'s disciples' (J. Wisdom, G. A. Paul, N. Malcolm) are also examined.

121. Orr S. S., *Some reflections on the Cambridge approach to philosophy*, AJP, 24, pp. 34–76, 130–167.

An analysis of the relationship between the representatives of the 'Cambridge school' and 'logical positivism'. The article, although it makes no direct reference to W., considers his work to be representative of the 'Cambridge school' (p. 141).

122. Waismann F., *The many-level-structure of language*, Sy, 5, pp. 211–219. Reprinted in ch. IV of the posthumous collection of Waismann's works, edited by R. Harré, *How I see philosophy*, London, Macmillan, 1968.

Wa. sets himself the task of determining a theoretic model which will respect the actual complexity of the structure of language, and in contrast with the 'extraordinarily simple' model set out in *Tract.* W. supported the existence of atomic propositions placed at one and the same level and constructed according to a simple, uniform plan, and believed that all other linguistic expressions were truth-functions of atomic propositions.

123. Wisdom J. O., *Causation and the foundations of science*, Paris, Hermann, 1946.

In the section entitled 'Induction as a pseudo-problem' (pp. 37–42) Wis. examines the thesis, which he attributes to W., Russell and other 'positivists', according to which the inductive process does not require justification, since scientific laws do not describe reality, but our way of tackling it.

1947

124. Bochenski J. M., *Europäische Philosophie der Gegenwart*, Bern, Francke, 1947. E.T. *Contemporary European philosophy*, Berkeley, Cal., University of California Press, 1956.
An account of the main currents and philosophical theories of the XXth century. B. examines *Tract.* in the chapter devoted to neopositivism (pp. 60-67). The main theses of that school, he maintains, were already stated in that work.

125. Carnap R., *Meaning and necessity: a study in semantics and modal logic*, Chicago, Ill., University of Chicago Press, 1947.
In §2 of the first chapter C. refers to W. with regard to the method to be adopted in the definition of L-concepts. He also attributes to W. the thesis that to know the meaning of a statement is to know in which of the possible cases it is true, and in which false.

126. Rhees R., *Critical notice of Cornforth's 'Science versus Idealism'*, M, 56, pp. 374-92. Reprinted in his *Without answers*, London, Routledge & Kegan Paul; New York, Schocken Books, 1969.
R. examines and criticizes Cornforth's (1946) analysis of different forms of 'subjectivism' and their attitude toward science. As far as W. is specifically concerned, R. denies that it is possible to single out a form of solipsism in *Tract.*, at least in the meaning usually attributed to this term, and also denies that W. defines the sense of a proposition in terms of the method to be adopted for its verification.

1948

127. Blanshard B., *The new subjectivism in ethics*, PPR, 9, 1948-9, pp. 504-511. Reprinted in P. Edwards and A. Pap (eds.), *A modern introduction to philosophy*, New York, Free Press, 1957, pp. 434-441.
B. attributes to W. and other representatives of 'logical positivism' a subjectivistic theory in ethics, according to which

the assertion 'this is good' does not express a judgement but a favourable sentiment. The aim of the article is to criticize this theory.

128. Dürr K., *Der logische Positivismus*, Bern, A. Francke, 1948.
A concise presentation of the main problems confronted in the sphere of 'logical positivism', with an essential bibliography divided according to topic. W. (pp. 13–14) is considered to be among the most representative authors of this trend.

129. Langer S. K., *Philosophy in a new key*, Cambridge, Mass., Harvard University Press, 1948.
The work contains a number of references to *Tract.* (cf. especially ch. IV: 'Discursive and presentational forms', pp. 79–102). L. draws from this the logical theory upon which she bases her own analysis of symbolism, an analysis principally focused on implications in the field of aesthetics and philosophy of art.

1949

130. Carnap R., *Truth and confirmation*, in H. Feigl and W. Sellars (eds.), *Readings in philosophical analysis*, New York, Appleton-Century-Crofts, 1949, pp. 119–27. Reprinted in W. P. Alston and G. Nakhnikian (eds.), *Readings in twentieth-century philosophy*, London, Collier-Macmillan, 1963.
A revised version of the articles *Wahrheit und Bewährung*, see 1936, and *Remarks on induction and truth*, see 1945. C. considers his own confirmability requirement, together with Reichenbach's first principle of the probabilistic theory of meaning as liberalized versions of the verifiability requirement previously enunciated by C. S. Peirce, W. and others.

131. Copi I. M., *Language, analysis and metaphysical inquiry*, PSc, 16, pp. 65–70. Reprinted in R. Rorty (ed.), *The linguistic turn*, Chicago, Ill., and London, University of Chicago Press, 1967.
C. maintains that the plan formed by Russell and W. to investigate the metaphysical structure of the world through an enquiry into the logical structure of an ideal language must be rejected because compromised by a vicious circle.

132. Ferrater Mora J., *Wittgenstein o la destrucción*, 'Realidad', 1949, pp. 129–40. Republished in Italian (AA, 9, 1952, pp. 245–52) and in German (*W., Schriften/Beiheft*, see 1960).

A brief analysis of W.'s personality and an evaluation of the influence it has exercised on contemporary culture. W.'s contribution to logic and to language analysis, F. claims, is only one aspect of his work. What is more important is that he reflects, more clearly than other contemporary authors, the sense of 'crisis of his time'. This is expressed in his tendency to consider thought as 'man's essential sin', and thus to suppress it and to take refuge in silence.

133. Frank P., *Historical background*. Introduction to his *Modern science and its philosophy*, Cambridge, Mass., Harvard University Press, 1949.

In presenting a collection of his own writings (see in particular 1930, above), F. makes a retrospective analysis aimed at placing his thought in its historical setting. On pp. 31–34 he examines both W.'s and Carnap's contribution to the search for a scientifically-based philosophy. He underlines the substantial uniformity of viewpoint, in the 1920s and 1930s, between W. and the exponents of the Vienna Circle.

134. Gasking D. A. T., *Anderson and the Tractatus. An essay in philosophical translation*, AJP, 27, pp. 1–26.

G. attempts to translate into the terminology of the 'Sydney empiricists' (Anderson and Passmore) what he considers to be the core of the doctrines of *Tract.*: the definition of the limits of what can and what cannot be said. According to *Tract.*, the things which cannot be spoken about, and which therefore go beyond the limits of language, are: the form of representation; internal formal properties and relations; the existence of natural laws; questions concerning existence and the aims of life and of the world.

135. von Wright G. H., *Form and content*, Cambridge, Cambridge University Press, 1949, pp. 35. Reprinted in G. H. von Wright, *Logical studies*, London, Routledge & Kegan Paul, 1957.

A substantial contribution to the clarification of the notion of logical truth was given by W. in *Tract.*, where this notion is explained through the notion of tautology, which is in turn based on the concept of a truth-function (especially pp. 13ff.). v.W. then discusses the limits to the applicability of this theory.

136. Wisdom A. J. T. D., *The concept of mind*, PAS, 50, pp. 189–204. Reprinted in A. J. T. D. Wisdom, *Other minds*, Oxford, Blackwell, 1952.

Criticizing a number of aspects of Ryle's book, *The concept of mind*, London, Hutchinson, 1949, and at the same time proposing a development of some of his theses, Wis. recalls how W.'s analysis has contributed to the destruction of old myths such as those concerning the soul and mental mechanisms. He proceeds to point to a number of differences between W.'s position and that of Ryle.

1950

137. Anscombe G. E. M., *The reality of the past,* in M. Black (ed.), *Philosophical analysis*, Ithaca, N.Y., Cornell University Press, 1950, pp. 36–56 (see Black, 1950). Reprinted in G. E. M. Anscombe, *Metaphysics and the philosophy of mind. Collected philosophical papers*, vol. II, Oxford, Blackwell, 1981; in Canfield (ed.), 1986, vol. VIII.

A. acknowledges her debt to W. particularly as regards theses concerning the use of memory in the verification of statements referring to the past. For a critique of the article see Butler, 1956.

138. Barnes W. H. F., *The philosophical predicament*, London, A. & C. Black, 1950.

In ch. V (§3, pp. 102–105) a number of theses taken from *Tract.* are briefly and rather critically examined, in particular the principle of verification, the distinction between analytical statements and those of common sense and science, and the status of metaphysics.

139. Bergmann G., *Logical positivism*, in V. Ferm, (ed.), *A history of philosophical systems*, New York, Philosophical Library, 1950, pp. 471–82. Reprinted in G. Bergmann, *The metaphysics of logical positivism*, Madison, Wis., University of Wisconsin Press, 1954.

The publication of *Tract.* marked the birth of neopositivism. All the characteristic traits of the movement can be recognized in that work: a) the acceptance of Hume's theses on causality and induction; b) the thesis of the tautological nature of logical and mathematical truths; c) the concept of philosophy as an analysis of ordinary language; d) the rejection of metaphysics. The second and fourth aspects reflect W.'s contribution most directly, and differentiate neopositivism from previous empiricist philosophies.

140. Black M. (ed.), *Philosophical analysis*, Ithaca, N.Y., Cornell University Press, 1950.
In the 'Introduction' to this collection of articles, the editor sets out to show the complexity and variety of solutions adopted in the sphere of 'philosophical analysis', through a brief comparison of the thought of Russell, Moore and W.

141. Carnap R., *Empiricism, semantics and ontology*, RIP, 4, pp. 20–40. Reprinted in L. Linsky (ed.), *Semantics and the philosophy of language*, Urbana, Ill., University of Illinois Press, 1956; in R. Rorty (ed.), *Linguistic turn*, 1967.
A number of references to W. C. recalls how the Vienna Circle, under the influence of W., adopted a non-cognitive thesis in relation to the problem of the reality of the external world and of universals, and considered that the linguistic expressions referring to these notions were lacking in sense.

142. Carnap R., *Logical foundations of probability*, Chicago, Ill., University of Chicago Press, 1950.
Some references to *Tract.* The theory of L–concepts (p. 83) is said to be a development of an idea already conceived by W. (*Tract.*, 4.463).

143. Cornforth M., *In defence of philosophy against positivism and pragmatism*, London, Lawrence & Wishart, 1950; New York, International Publishers, 1965.
The criticism formerly voiced in *Science versus idealism* (1946), according to which W. is trying to defend a form of subjective idealism which is contrary to the spirit of science, and ideologically conservative, is carried further, and also applied to W.'s post-*Tract.* work.

144. Kaufmann F., *Basic issues in logical positivism*, in M. Farber (ed.), *Philosophic thought in France and the United States*, Buffalo, N.Y., Buffalo University Press, 1950, pp. 565–88.

K. sets out to define the contributions made by *Tract.* to the formation of logical positivism, and in particular the influence it has exerted on Carnap's thought. He maintains that, although Carnap generally agreed with some tenets of W.'s work, it was not without reservations that he did so. Amongst these were the impossibility of establishing the truth of an 'atomic proposition'; the difficulty of explaining, on the basis of *Tract.*, how general propositions (e.g. the laws of physics) come to have meaning; and W.'s phenomenalism, believed by K. to be in line with British and continental empiricism (Russell and Mach in particular).

145. Kraft V., *Der Wiener Kreis, der Ursprung des Neopositivismus*, Vienna, Springer, 1950. E.T. *The Vienna Circle*, New York, Philosophical Library, 1953.

The work contains a number of brief allusions to the relationship between W. and the Vienna Circle. According to K., *Tract.* heralds a variant of logical positivism, but many aspects of it diverge from the characteristic traits of the school.

146. Russell B., *Logical positivism*, RIP, 4, pp. 3-19. Reprinted in B. Russell, *Logic and knowledge*, London, Allen & Unwin, 1956, pp. 367-382 (see entry).

In carrying out a critical analysis of the origins and subsequent developments of 'logical positivism', R. recalls how *Tract.*, with its emphasis on the problems of logical syntax, stimulated the formation of the Vienna Circle. This school nevertheless introduced and developed the theory of the different levels of language, in order to avoid the logical mysticism of *Tract.*

147. Ryle G., *Logic and Professor Anderson*, AJP, 28, pp. 137-53. Reprinted in G. Ryle, *Collected papers*, vol. II, London, Hutchinson, 1971.

Despite the differences which exist between Anderson's spatio-temporal situations and the atomic facts of Russell and W., there are also analogies between them. Yet W., in *Tract.*, establishes a dichotomy between significant and nonsensical, which reflects the dichotomy between science and philosophy, and the representatives of the Vienna Circle do likewise. Anderson, on the other hand, does not admit that there are substantial differences between these two disciplines (a point also made by Gasking, 1949).

148. Toulmin S. E., *An examination of the place of reason in ethics*, Cambridge, Cambridge University Press, 1950.

In ch. 6, devoted to 'Reason and its uses', T. considers and criticizes (paragraph 6) the correspondence theory of truth, and considers *Tract.* to be of 'great historical importance' because of the ethical conclusions it derives from that doctrine.

1951

149. Anon, *Obituary. Dr. L. Wittgenstein. Philosophy of language*, 'The Times', London, 2 May 1951.
A few days after his death, the most significant stages in the philosopher's life are viewed, and the influence exerted by his work is recalled. Allusion is made to the existence of notes dictated to his pupils and circulated privately, and to that of unfinished manuscripts.

150. Anscombe G. E. M., Rhees R., von Wright G. H., Letter to M, 60, p. 584.
The literary executors express their reservations regarding any project of publishing those of W.'s notes that had been circulated privately. They announce the imminent publication of a book which has been left in almost complete form.

151. Barone F., *Il solipsismo linguistico di L. W.*, F, 2, pp. 543-70. Reprinted in F. Barone, *Il neopositivismo logico*, 1953.
B. particularly highlights the influence exerted by *Tract.* on the 'setting-up of the neopositivistic trend' and reconstructs, from this viewpoint, the different aspects of the theory by means of which W. investigates the possibility of a logically perfect language, and grounds his 'logical realism'.

152. Cranston M., *L. Wittgenstein*, 'World Review', December 1951, pp. 21-24.
A brief biographical sketch and analysis of the contents of *Tract.* C. mentions the existence of some later notes by W. circulating in a private form in Cambridge. At the end of the article he maintains that W., at the end of his life, drew near to the Catholic faith. In a note which follows this G. E. M. Anscombe (1952) firmly denies some of C.'s assertions.

153. Gasking D. A. T. and **Jackson A. C.**, *Ludwig Wittgenstein*, AJP, 29, pp. 73-80. Reprinted in Fann (ed.), 1967.

A short memoir written by two pupils on the occasion of W.'s death. The philosopher's personality, the environment in which his lectures took place, the method of philosophical investigation he adhered to, and his attitude towards religion are recalled. Furthermore, the thesis that W. had considered the principle of verification as a theory of meaning is firmly denied (p. 79).

154. Hänsel L., *L. Wittgenstein (1889–1951)*, WW, 4, no. 8, pp. 274–7.

An introduction to W.'s personality, and a brief explanation of *Tract.*, on the occasion of the philosopher's death. H. was a friend of W.'s and a prisoner-of-war with him in 1918–19.

155. Jørgensen J., *The development of logical empiricism*, Chicago, Ill., University of Chicago Press, 1951. Reprinted in O. Neurath, R. Carnap, C. Morris (eds.), *Foundations of the unity of science*, vol. II, Chicago, Ill. and London, University of Chicago Press, 1970, pp. 847–936.

J.'s contribution to what should have been the introductory section of the *International Encyclopedia of Unified Science*. While relating the story of the development of logical empiricism, J. recalls the importance of *Tract.* for the formation and development of this school (1970 edition, see especially pp. 848–58 and 863–74). Although W. never belonged to the movement, his work contributed to the crystallization of the philosophical perspective which was characteristic of the Vienna Circle.

156. Kraft V., *Ludwig Wittgenstein*, 'Wiener Zeitschrift für Philosophie, Psychologie, Pädagogik', 3, no. 3, pp. 161–3.

An evaluation of W.'s intellectual personality and of his work, made shortly after his death.

157. Russell B., *Ludwig Wittgenstein*, M, 60, pp. 297–98. Reprinted in Fann (ed.), 1967.

A number of memoirs and impressions concerning R.'s first meetings with W.; the years that W. spent at Cambridge as a student of logic; the period during which *Tract.* was prepared; the subsequent developments in the philosopher's thought. Despite the fact that Russell hints at a lack of intellectual sympathy, which damaged his relationship with his former pupil in the last years, he nevertheless judges his acquaintance with W. as one of the most exciting intellectual adventures of his life. R.'s work is preceded by an obituary in which news of W.'s death is given.

158. Ryle G., *Ludwig Wittgenstein*, A, 12, pp. 1-9. Reprinted in: Fann (ed.), 1967; in Copi and Beard (eds.), 1966; in G. Ryle, *Collected papers*, vol. I, London, Hutchinson, 1971. Italian translation in RF, 1952, 43, pp. 816-93.

A succinct presentation of the philosopher's biography, written a short time after his death, and an evaluation of his work within the framework of contemporary philosophy. R. emphasizes that W. was more a figure in English cultural life than in that of the continent and stresses the divergence in theoretical framework and in temperament which always set him apart from the logical positivists. R. then briefly recalls the development which led W. to abandon the primitive picture theory of language of *Tract.*, in favour of a new investigative method, no longer restricted to scientific propositions, but extending to the logical structure of all areas of language (a development anticipated by Moore).

1952

159. Anscombe G. E. M., *Wittgenstein*, letter to 'World Review', January 1952, p. 3.

A. denies some of the statements about W. contained in Cranston's article (1951). Amongst other things, she maintains, on the basis of personal acquaintance, that although W. read the New Testament and was interested in religion, he did not possess any form of religious belief.

160. Kaufmann W., *Critique of religion and philosophy*, New York, Harper & Row, 1952.

Three sections of the second chapter 'Positivism and existentialism' are devoted to W. (pp. 52-9). The first gives second-hand information on the philosopher's life, on his religious beliefs, on the sources of his works, and general observations on his method of inquiry. In the third K. criticizes W.'s followers' tendency to regard themselves as a philosophical school, and their way of understanding the master's work.

161. Malcolm N., *Knowledge and belief*, M, 61, pp. 178-189. Reprinted in N. Malcolm, *Knowledge and certainty*, London, Prentice-Hall, 1963; in Canfield (ed.), 1986, vol. viii.

At the end of the article M. acknowledges that he has drawn the main ideas of the work from conversations with W., in particular the thesis according to which there sometimes exists a logical resemblance between *a priori* assertions and empirical ones.

162. Paci E., *Negatività e positività di W.*, AA, 9, pp. 252-6. Reprinted in E. Paci, *Tempo e relazione*, Turin, Taylor, 1954; 2nd ed., 1967.
A critical analysis of the distinction, drawn in *Tract.*, between empirical and logical propositions, of W.'s conception of the nature of philosophical problems and of his method of dealing with them. Italian versions of articles by M. Cranston (1951) and J. Ferrater Mora (1949) are also published in the same issue of the review.

163. Popper K., *The nature of philosophical problems and their roots in science*, BJPS, 3, 1952, pp. 124-56. Reprinted in K. Popper, *Conjectures and refutations*, London, Basic Books, 1962.
P. examines the doctrine, attributed to the later W., according to which all genuine problems are of a scientific nature, the supposed problems of philosophy are pseudo-problems and, consequently, philosophy cannot contain any theory. While criticizing this point of view, P. reaffirms his own thesis, according to which genuine philosophical problems are always rooted in large problems outside philosophy.

164. Storer T., *Linguistic isomorphisms*, PSc, 19, pp. 77-85.
In attempting to determine the conditions under which precise rules of formation and transformation for a formal language can be given, S. examines a number of aspects of the logical theory of *Tract.*, in particular the pictorial function of language and the isomorphism between language and experience.

165. Wasmuth E., *Das Schweigen L.W.s. Über das Mystische im 'Tractatus Logico-Philosophicus'*, 'Wort und Wahrheit', 7, pp. 815-22.
A summary of the last sections of *Tract.*, with particular reference to the problem of the nature of 'that which cannot be said'.

166. Wisdom A. J. T. D., *L. Wittgenstein, 1934-37*, M, 61, pp. 258-60. Reprinted in his *Paradox and discovery*, Oxford, Basil Blackwell, 1966; in Fann (ed.), 1967; in Canfield (ed.), 1986, vol. V.

The record of a number of conversations held with W., and of the lectures Wis. attended at Cambridge between 1934 and 1937. Wis. took no notes during that period, and is relying on memory when he reports the following themes as dealt with by W.: the analysis of the uses of 'to understand' and 'to know'; 'family resemblances'; the function attributed to philosophical investigation; the analysis of sensation language; the problem of other minds.

167. **Wisdom J. O.**, *Foundations of inference in natural science,* London, Methuen, 1952.

In ch. IX, W. is mentioned as one of the authors who defend a 'descriptive' or 'operational' explanation of the nature of scientific laws.

1953

168. **Abbagnano N.**, *L'ultimo W*, RF, 44, pp. 447-56. Reprinted in N. Abbagnano, *Possibilità e libertà*, Turin, Taylor, 1956.

A critical analysis of the 'latest developments' of W.'s thought after *Tract.* in the light of the publication of *P.I.* Even in this new work W. lacks a historical perspective on language and treats the institutional use of it as something unchangeable.

169. **Anscombe G. E. M.**, *Note on the English version of W.'s 'Philosophische Untersuchungen'*, M, 62, pp. 521-2.

A number of errors in translation noticed by the author or drawn to her attention after the English publication of *P.I.*

170. **Bachmann I.**, *Zu einem Kapitel der jüngsten Philosophiegeschichte*, 'Kultur und Politik', 8, pp. 540-5. Reprinted in *W. Schriften/Beiheft*, pp. 7-15 (1960).

A general presentation of W.'s thought and of his intellectual personality in the light of *Tract.* According to B., it is above all the importance attributed by W. to the 'inexpressible', rather than to the precise language of science, which separates *Tract.*'s viewpoint from that of the neopositivists.

171. **Barone F.**, *Il neopositivismo logico*, Turin, Edizioni di 'Filosofia', 1953, pp. 408.

Besides including, in chapter form, an article previously printed on W.'s 'linguistic solipsism' (see 1951 entry), this work contains numerous references to W.'s thought. The influence of *Tract.* is followed from the first formation of the Vienna School to most recent developments such as C. Morris's semiotics and A. Tarski's semantics.

172. Barone F., *W. inedito*, Turin, Edizioni di 'Filosofia', 1953, pp. 16.

A brief examination of W.'s later philosophy considered in its opposition to the logical positivistic trend of *Tract.*

173. Bergmann G., *Logical positivism, language and the reconstruction of metaphysics*, RCSF, 8, pp. 453–481. Reprinted in his *The metaphysics of logical positivism*, New York, Longmans, 1954; in R. Rorty (ed.), *Linguistic turn*, 1967.

The common source of 'logical positivism' is sought in the writings and teaching of G. E. Moore, Russell and W. Four serious defects are singled out in the theory of *Tract.*, and in B.'s opinion these have negatively influenced the whole 'movement': 1) the thesis that language cannot speak about itself; 2) the absolutization of the notion of analyticity; 3) the thesis that sentences such as 'nothing is green and red at the same time' are analytic; 4) an unconscious and uncritical metaphysics particularly as regards the ontological aspects of the picture theory of language.

174. Cameron J., *The glass of language*, Ta, 202, 4 July 1953, pp. 11–12.

A brief examination of *Tract.* C. particularly considers W.'s biography and way of life.

175. Daitz E., *The picture theory of meaning*, M, 62, pp. 184–201. Reprinted under the name E. O'Shaughnessy in Copi and Beard (eds.), 1966, and in A. Flew (ed.), *Essays in conceptual analysis*, London, Macmillan, 1964.

D. examines the theory of meaning in Russell, in *Tract.*, and in Wisdom (*Logical constructions*, 1931–33). She maintains that in the model of language elaborated in *Tract.*, all the characteristics of a picture theory are respected, except one-to-one correspondence between sign and designation, and uniformity of role between the elements of the sign. In ordinary language statements expressing relations, the number of elements present exceeds by one unit the number of elements of the fact represented. The picture theory turns out to be not applicable to ordinary language, since statements have meanings in a quite different way from maps, drawings, or pictures. See the replies to this article by Evans ('Mind', 1955) and Copi ('Mind', 1958).

176. **Ferrater Mora J.**, *W., a symbol of troubled times*, PPR, 14, pp. 89-96. Reprinted in Fann (ed.), 1967.

W.'s 'genius' has not only made important contributions to logic and to metaphysics, but has also become a symbol of our age. W. 'understood that thought is the major factor of disturbance in human life', and tended towards its 'suppression' through his 'therapeutic positivism'.

177. **Findlay J. N.**, *W.'s 'Philosophical investigations'*, RIP, 7, pp. 201-16. Reprinted in 'Philosophy', 1955, 30, pp. 173-9; and in his *Language, mind and value*, London, Allen & Unwin, 1963.

The article is taken from two lectures, held at the Royal Institute of Philosophy, in February 1953. The analysis is not directly concerned with the content of *P.I.*, which had not yet been published at the time, but it aims to be an advance presentation of that work. With this in mind, F. bases his work on the record of what he has 'seen and heard', especially in relation to 'W.'s last teaching'.

178. **Freundlich R.**, *Logik und Mystik*, ZPF, 7, pp. 554-70.

An analysis of *Tract.*, with particular attention to the concluding sections and W.'s theses relating to 'that which cannot be said'.

179. **Hamburg C.**, *Whereof one cannot speak*, JP, 50, pp. 662-64.

The passage contained in section 7 of *Tract.* 'Whereof one cannot speak, thereof one must be silent', is an expression of the positivist *credo*. H. shows that this formula is ambiguous, whether taken to be analytic or synthetic or prescriptive.

180. **McPherson T.**, *Positivism and religion*, PPR, 14, pp. 319-31. Reprinted with the title *Religion as the inexpressible*, in A. Flew and A. MacIntyre (eds.), *New essays in philosophical theology*, London, SCM Press, 1955, pp. 131-143.

McP. examines the thesis on the nature of religious beliefs taken up by the 'positivists', and in particular by R. Otto and by W. in *Tract.* In his opinion it is erroneous to attribute to these

authors a conception contrary to religion, and not to see the
contribution that their ideas can make to theological studies.

181. Preti G., *Realismo ontologico e sense comune*, RCSF, 8,
pp. 533-544. Reprinted in G. Preti, *Linguaggio comune
e linguaggi scientifici*, Rome and Milan, Fratelli Bocca,
1953.
One section of the essay is devoted to an evaluation of the ethico-
cultural significance of *Tract.* That work is considered to be the
expression of a radical form of metaphysical and ontological
realism, which naturally terminates in an equally radical
scepticism.

182. Toulmin S., *The philosophy of science*, London,
Hutchinson University Library, 1953, pp. 176.
References here and there to *Tract.* particularly to sections 6.3ff.

183. Waismann F., *Language strata*, in A. Flew (ed.), *Logic
and language*, 2nd series, Oxford, Blackwell, 1953,
pp. 11-31. Reprinted in the second part of ch. IV of *How
I see philosophy*, ed. by R. Harré, London, Macmillan, 1968.

Wa. aims to provide a new investigation of language, as an
alternative to the one sustained for example by W. in *Tract.*,
according to which language is composed of assertions which
can without exception be derived from atomic propositions by
means of a uniform procedure.

184. Wisdom A. J. T. D., *Philosophy and psycho-analysis*,
Oxford, Blackwell, 1953.
Many writings collected in this volume, previously published
between 1933 and 1948 in periodicals, were intended as an
attempt to apply W.'s 'therapeutic' method. Some of them
contain explicit references to W., in particular: 'Philosophical
perplexity' (1936-37); 'Metaphysics and verification' (1938);
'Philosophy, anxiety and novelty' (1944).

1954

185. Anon, *W.'s philosophical views*, 'Nature' (London), 173,
p. 806.
Attention is briefly called to G. E. Moore's article (1954-55)
relating to W.'s 1930-33 lectures, and to P. F. Strawson's review
of *P.I.* (1954).

186. Anscombe G. E. M., *Misinformation: what W. really said*, Ta, 17 April, p. 374.

In reply to a series of articles and letters published by the review (see for example the contributions made by Smiley, 1954, Gregory, 1954, Colombo, 1954), A. maintains that W.'s thought is in reality irreconcilable with the Catholic faith, not because of a presumed empiricism in *Tract.*, but because of its teaching in the field of ethics. See the replies by Daly, 1956, and by Colombo, 1954.

187. Anscombe G. E. M., Letter to Ta, 15 May, pp. 478-9.

A reply to Colombo's letter (1954). W. was not an empiricist, at least not when he wrote *Tract.* As far as the reconciliation of *Tract.* with Christian faith is concerned, A. concludes that this would be a much less difficult task than a Christian assimilation of Plato.

188. Ayer A. J., *Can there be a private language?*, PAS(SV), 28, pp. 63-76. *Symposium* with R. Rhees (see below). Reprinted in A. J. Ayer, *The concept of person*, London, Macmillan, 1963; in Pitcher (ed.), 1966; in Morick (ed.), 1967; in Shanker (ed.), 1986, vol. II; in Canfield (ed.), 1986, vol. IX.

A language is private when only one person can understand it. In *P.I.*, such a language is considered to be logically impossible. According to W. the attribution of meaning to a sign must be justifiable, and the correctness of its use must be able to be verified in a public and independent way. This thesis is based on presuppositions which turn out to be false. Contrary to what is maintained by W., for example, it is possible to allow for cases in which memory alone is used as a criterion of correctness in the use of signs, or in order to identify private sensations.

189. Britton K., *Recollections of L. W.*, 'Cambridge Journal', 7, pp. 709-715. German translation in 'Merkur', 117, 1957, pp. 1066-1072.

In the first part of the article, there are a number of records of W.'s 1931 lectures, of his philosophical discussions with Moore, of his daily habits and of his attitude towards philosophy. In the second part, there is a description of brief meetings and conversations with W. in the 1940s.

190. Colombo G. C. M., *Introduzione critica al 'Tractatus logico-philosophicus'*, Milan and Rome, Fratelli Bocca, 1954, pp. 13–131.
A critical study which precedes the Italian translation of *Tract.* (with the German text on the opposite pages), also by C. In the first four sections C. sets himself the task of identifying the sources of *Tract.* and of setting out its theoretical principles. He insists above all on W.'s attempt to found empiricism through a theory of the proposition which envisages the elimination of every reference to a metaphysical or psychological subject in intensional expressions, and also the reduction of metaphysics to nonsense.

191. Colombo G. C. M., Letter to Ta, 15 May, p. 478.
The ethical teaching of *Tract.* is incompatible with the Catholic faith. As far as the existence of God is concerned, two different conclusions can be drawn from *Tract.*: see the reply by Anscombe in the same review (1954).

192. Dummett M., *Lo sfondo logico del 'Tractatus'*, in an appendix to the Italian translation edited by G. C. M. Colombo, 1954, pp. 303–311.
A brief exposition of the more technical aspects of W.'s logical theory, with frequent references to Frege and Russell.

193. Feyerabend P., *Ludwig Wittgenstein*, 'Merkur', 8, 1954, pp. 1021–38. Reprinted in *W. Schriften/Beiheft*, see 1960.
The solutions reached and the method of analysis followed in *P.I.* constitute a critique of the general philosophical tendencies of the first period of neopositivism. This is particularly valid for W.'s analysis of psychological language and for his critique of realistic theories of meaning.

194. Feyerabend P., *W. und die Philosophie*, WW, 7, pp. 212–20, 283–92.
A critical reconstruction of W.'s later philosophy and therapeutic method, and an attempt to define his position within neopositivism. F. criticizes him for reducing philosophy to an 'activity' with a purely critical and negative function.

195. Ficker L., *Rilke und der unbekannte Freund*, 'Der Brenner', 18, pp. 234–48. Reprinted in L. Ficker, *Denkzettel und Danksagungen*, Munich, Kösel, 1967, pp. 199–221.
F., editor of the review 'Der Brenner', gives information about

W.'s benefaction, in 1914, to artists lacking in means, from which the writers R. M. Rilke and G. Trakl, amongst others, benefited. Ficker describes how he came to know W. in July 1914, and provides a brief summary of the history of his relationship with him, together with a number of literary judgements of the significance of W.'s work. The article contains a number of previously unpublished letters, three written by Rilke and one by W. (16/11/1914), of which the last, addressed to the editor of the review, is about the benefaction in question.

196. Gabriel L., *Logische Magie. Eine Nachwort zum Thema W.*, WW, 7, pp. 288–93.

197. Gregory T. S., *Mere words? W. and the care of language*, Ta, 10 April 1954, pp. 343–5 (cf. Anscombe, 1954).

198. Harris E. E., *Nature, mind and modern science*, London, Allen & Unwin, 1954.
Frequent critical references to W. and to philosophical tendencies which take their inspiration from his work. See particularly the sections: 'Are there eternal problems in philosophy?' (especially pp. 6–18) and 'Modern empiricism: the third phase' (especially pp. 322–8). In W.'s work, and in particular in his 'hostility' towards metaphysics, H. sees a radical expression of a more general empirical attitude which is widespread in this century.

199. Lieb I. C., *W.'s Investigations*, RM, 8, pp. 125–43.
A critical examination of *P.I.*, centred above all on the theory of meaning and the philosophical method, this last considered to be essentially negative and unsystematic. On the whole L. believes that the atomistic theory of *Tract.* is more rigorous. In *P.I.*, W. seems to neglect the affinities which exist between the various propositions, emphasizing their differences.

200. Lukács G., *Die Zerstörung der Vernunft*, Berlin, Aufbau-Verlag, 1954. English translations: The destruction of reason, London, Merlin Press, 1980; Atlantic Highlands, N.J., Humanities Press, 1981.
A number of references to W. are contained in a 'Postscript' devoted to the 'irrationalism of the post-war period'. W.'s and Carnap's 'neo-Machism', together with the further development of pragmatism in Dewey's work, are considered to be socially determined by the new irrationalistic tendency which prevails in bourgeois thought.

201. Macdonald M., Introduction to *Philosophy and analysis*, Oxford, Blackwell, 1954, pp. 1-14.

The work contains a selection, edited by Macdonald herself, of articles published in the review 'Analysis' between 1933 and 1953. In the introduction M. includes a brief history of the review, emphasizing on several occasions the influence exerted by W. on the group of philosophers who launched it.

202. MacIvor C., Letter to 'Ta', 203, p. 140.

In a literary argument with Smiley (1954), M. examines the possibility of a reconciliation between modern anti-metaphysical tendencies and the Catholic faith.

203. Malcolm N., *W. 's 'Philosophical investigations'*, PR, 63, pp. 530-59. Reprinted in his *Knowledge and certainty*, Englewood Cliffs, N.J., Prentice-Hall, 1963. Reprinted also in V. C. Chappell (ed.), *The philosophy of mind*, Englewood Cliffs, N.J., Prentice-Hall, 1963; in G. Pitcher (ed.), 1966; in K. T. Fann (ed.), 1967; H. Morick (ed.), 1967; in Canfield (ed.), 1986, vol. IV.

M. sets out to analyse the way in which W. tackles the problem of the relationship between language and inner experiences, and, in relation to this, to show the implicit unity of W.'s work. The topics particularly examined are: the notion of private language; the identification and recognition of sensations; public and private rules; knowledge of other minds; the distinction between 'criterion' and 'symptom'; the differences between statements relating to sensations made in the first and third persons; the notion of 'form of life'. In the last section of the article he criticizes Strawson's interpretation (1954), according to which W.'s solutions show his hostility towards what is private and what cannot be observed by means of the outer senses. To this M. replies that W. does not deny that there are linguistic usages in which inner states of consciousness are named and described, recognized and identified. Nevertheless these usages do not justify the idea of a private language.

204. Mardiros A. M., *Shapers of the modern outlook. L. W. Philosopher*, 'Canadian Forum', 33, pp. 223-5.

W.'s work and intellectual contribution are considered to be important not only because of their philosophical significance, but above all in that they suggest a new way of looking at reality.

205. Moore G. E., *W. 's lectures in 1930-33*, M, 63, 1954, pp. 1-15, 289-315; 64, 1955, pp. 1-27. Reprinted in G. E.

Moore, *Philosophical papers*, London, George Allen & Unwin, 1959; in R. Ammerman (ed.), *Classics in analytic philosophy*, New York, McGraw-Hill, 1965. Extracts are also reprinted in Fann (ed.), 1967, and in Morick (ed.), 1967. This collection of notes taken from W.'s lectures between 1930 and 1933 is preceded by a biographical note and a record of a number of episodes dating from the same years: W.'s admission to Trinity College; the presentation of the article 'Some remarks on logical form' to the Joint Session of the Mind Association and the Aristotelian Society (July 1929); the discussions held with Ramsey until the latter's death, and the contrasts between the two philosophers, etc. W.'s lectures, together with his 'discussion classes', began in January 1930, and Moore took part in them fairly regularly until 1933. Two corrections to these notes were later published by Moore, 1955.

206. Nagel E., *Symbolism and science*, in *Symbolism and values*, New York, Harper, 1954. Reprinted in E. Nagel, *Logic without metaphysics*, Glencoe, Ill., Free Press, 1956, pp. 103–141.
In one section of the article N. criticizes the theory, which he attributes to Russell and to *Tract.*, according to which statements and facts have an analogical structure (especially pp. 196–132, 1956 edition).

207. Paci E., *W. e la nevrosi della filosofia*, in E. Paci, *Tempo e relazione*, Turin, Taylor, 1954; 2nd ed., 1967.
The 'crisis' of philosophy is made apparent in its tendency towards self-destruction. Substituting philosophy as activity for speculative philosophy, W. reflects an unresolvable contradiction (hence 'neurosis') which Kierkegaard, Feuerbach and Marx had already expressed, but in other terms. See also 'Perfect language and everyday situation', in the same collection.

208. Peduzzi O., *W. in Inghilterra*, AA, 19, pp. 46–49.
The influence exerted by W. on English philosophy from the beginning of his teaching at Cambridge (1929) is examined.

209. Preti G., *Le tre fasi dell'empirismo*, RCSF, 9, pp. 38–51. Reprinted in G. Preti, *Saggi filosofici*, vol. I, Florence, La Nuova Italia, 1976.
In the section devoted to the phase of 'strict' empiricism, represented by the first Vienna Circle, the influence exerted by *Tract.* on this trend is evaluated.

210. Rhees R., *Can there be a private language?*, PAS (SV), 77-94. *Symposium* with A. J. Ayer (see above). Reprinted in Pitcher (ed.), 1966; in Shanker (ed.), 1986, vol. II; in Canfield (ed.), 1986, vol. IX; in C. Caton (ed.), *Philosophy and ordinary language,* Urbana, Ill., University of Illinois, 1964.

In order to tackle correctly the problem of private langauge, the nature of the rules which govern the uses of language in general must be established. These rules exist so far as agreement about what people say and what they do exists. Thus, the problem of private language is reduced to the problem of establishing in what way words have meaning. This they do only if they are part of a language which is actually used. It is possible to invent names which stand for particular sensations only so far as a language is already spoken. Basing himself on this thesis R. criticizes Ayer's (1954) interpretation of the notion of a private language.

211. Sellars W., *Some reflections on language games*, PSc, 21, pp. 204-28. Reprinted in Canfield (ed.), 1986, vol. VI.

An independent reflection, without direct reference to W., on the possibility of applying the notion of game to problems of language and meaning.

212. Smiley P. O., *Importance of W.*, Ta, 203, p. 116.

In a controversy with other writers, S. emphasizes the importance and influence of W.'s thought. He maintains that, whether W.'s views are shared or not, his anti-metaphysical theses cannot be ignored, especially by a Catholic thinker. See Trethowan's reply (1954).

213. Stenius E., *Linguistic structure and the structure of experience*, T, 20, pp. 153-72.

In the course of setting out a 'picture theory' of his own which takes into consideration the distinction between objects and qualities, S. refers to the theory of language adhered to in *Tract.*, and compares his own theses to it.

214. Strawson P. F., *A critical notice of W.'s 'Philosophical investigations'*, M, 63, pp. 70-100. Reprinted in his *Freedom and resentment, and other essays*, London, Methuen; New York, Barnes & Noble, 1974. Reprinted also in Pitcher (ed.), 1966; in Morick (ed.), 1967; in Jones (ed.),

1971; in Canfield (ed.), 1986, vol. IV. German translation in *Über L.W.*, 1968.

S. examines a number of themes and topics occurring in *P.I.*, often suggesting an original interpretation and criticizing some of W.'s conclusions." These critical notes are above all concerned with the problems connected with the rules of the use of psychological language, with the relationship between public language and private states of consciousness (especially pp. 81ff.), and with the 'therapeutic' method of analysis (pp. 74–83). In particular, according to S., the thesis of W.'s which states that memory can never constitute a valid criterion, and that words never have the function of naming sensations, is groundless (pp. 81–85). In general, in tackling the problem of the relationship between public and private, W. demonstrates his hostility towards what is not observed (seen, heard, smelt, touched), and, above all, towards the thesis that that which is not observed can in any sense be recognized, described or referred to. According to S., this prejudice is to be linked to the old verificationist horror for what cannot be observationally confirmed. See Malcolm's reply, 1954.

215. Trethowan I., *Importance of W.*, Ta, 203, p. 140.

A critical reply to Smiley (1954), concerning the originality of W.'s ideas and the meaning that his anti-metaphysical philosophy can have for Catholic philosophy.

216. von Wright G. H., *L.W., en biografisk skiss*, 'Ajatus', 18, 1954, pp. 4–23. E.T. *L.W., a biographical sketch*, PR, 64, 1955, pp. 527–45. Reprinted in a modified form in N. Malcolm, *Memoir*, 1958; in *W. Schriften/Beiheft*, 1960; in Fann (ed.), 1967; in von Wright, 1982.

A succinct biography of the philosopher, accompanied by a short description of his personality and a general evaluation of the influence of his work on contemporary philosophy. v.W. singles out a radical change in W.'s thought, around 1933: after a transitional period (1929–1933), W. came to repudiate some of the fundamental ideas of *Tract.* While that work to a large extent betrayed the influence of Frege and Russell, W.'s new philosophy is completely beyond every philosophical tradition and is not influenced by literary sources. The original version of this biography, published in 'Ajatus', was variously modified in its different reprinted editions.

217. Wells R. S., *Meaning and use*, 'Words', 10, pp. 235–50.
We. evaluates the importance for linguistics and in particular
for semantics of the philosophical research promoted by Russell,
W. and those who have been influenced by their work.

1955

218. Aldrich V. C., *Images as things and things as imaged*,
M, 64, pp. 261–3.
A. discusses, in W.'s sense, the 'grammar' of descriptions of
sensory impressions. He makes a particular examination of the
types of justification and the criteria for correctness of such
linguistic uses.

219. Ambrose A., *W. on some questions in foundations of
mathematics*, JP, 52, pp. 197–213. Reprinted in A.
Ambrose, *Essays in analysis*, London, Allen & Unwin,
1966; in Fann (ed.), 1967; in Canfield (ed.), 1986, vol. XI;
in Shanker (ed.), 1986, vol. III.
The theses set out by W. in his 1934–35 and 1939 lectures show
how the propositions of mathematics provide criteria for the
use of propositions concerning factual data (empirical
propositions). The propositions of mathematics, being rules, are,
according to W., suggested by experience, but are not
generalizations of the data of experience. In this respect A. rejects
(pp. 206–14) the interpretation suggested by Moore ('W.'s
lectures', 1954) according to which W. would consider
arithmetical expressions to be at the same time necessary and
neither true nor false.

220. Bergmann G., *Intentionality,* in *Semantica*, 'Archivio di
Filosofia', 1955, pp. 177–216. Reprinted in G. Bergmann,
Meaning and existence, Madison, Wis., University of
Wisconsin, 1960.
The thesis, attributed to W., according to which what B. calls
'awarenesses' (units of consciousness) do not exist, is criticized.
The thesis is said to be shared by both *Tract.* and *P.I.*, and is
closely linked to W.'s other thesis, according to which language
cannot speak of itself.

221. Britton K., *Portrait of a philosopher*, 'The Listener', 53,
pp. 1071–2. Reprinted in Fann (ed.), 1967.

Records of the lectures held by W. in his room at Trinity College,
during 1931-32, which B. attended. W.'s physical appearance
is described, together with the method he followed in his
teaching and discussions, his lack of interest in the academic life,
his philosophical reading, his relationships with Moore and
Russell. Anecdotes and accounts of first-hand experiences. B.
also records the brief meetings he had with W. in 1945-46.

222. Chiodi P., *Essere e linguaggio in Heidegger e nel 'Tractatus' di W.*, RF, 46, pp. 170-91.

C. aims on the one hand to clarify the developments of
Heidegger's thought on the theme of language, from 'Being and
time' up to his most recent writings, and on the other to establish
a comparison with *Tract.* principally as regards logic, ontology,
philosophical method, and mysticism.

223. Evans E., *Tractatus 3.1432*, M, 64, pp. 259-60. Reprinted in Copi and Beard (eds.), 1966.

Against Daitz (1953) E. maintains that, according to *Tract.*
3.1432, there are four elements present both in the propositional
sign 'aRb' and in the fact aRb: 'a' (a), 'b' (b), 'R' (R), and the order
in which these constituents are placed. See the objections to this
interpretation in Copi, 1958, together with the reply by Evans,
1959.

224. Feibleman J. K., *Reflections after W.'s 'Philosophical Investigations'*, S, 23, 1955, pp. 322-8. Reprinted in J. K. Feibleman, *Inside the great mirror*, see 1958.

225. Feyerabend P., *W.'s 'Philosophical Investigations'*, PR, 64, pp. 449-483. Reprinted in his *Problems of empiricism. Philosophical papers*, vol. II, Cambridge, Cambridge University Press, 1984. Reprinted also in G. Pitcher (ed.), 1966; in Fann (ed.), 1967; in Canfield (ed.), 1986, vol. IV.

F. examines and discusses what he considers to be the central
aspect of W.'s work: the criticism of essentialism already upheld
in *Tract.* In the concluding sections he examines and criticizes
W.'s conception of the nature of philosophy and philosophical
method.

226. Mays W., *Note on W.'s Manchester period*, M, 64, pp. 247-8.

M. communicates the fact that a number of documents relating
to W.'s period of study in Manchester (1908-1911) have come

into his possession. These concern: 1) the records of a friend (W. Eccles) concerning W.'s research activity in the field of aeronautical engineering; 2) technical drawings relating to this research activity; 3) photographs and correspondence including letters exchanged between W. and Eccles, which contain 'interesting' philosophical observations. Copies of the documents are deposited in the University Library at Manchester.

227. Moore G. E., *Two corrections*, M, 64, p. 264.
Two corrections referring to the third article on W.'s lectures (see Moore, 1954).

228. Rougier L., *Traité de la connaissance*, Paris, Gauthier-Villars, 1955.
References to W. are contained in the following sections: ch. VI 'Le caractère tautologique des règles logiques'; 'La nouvelle théorie de la connaissance'. The discovery of the tautological character of logical rules, considered to be true by virtue of their form alone, is particularly attributed to *Tract.* (cf. pp. 120–125).

229. Russell B., *Philosophers and idiots*, 'The Listener', 10 February 1955, pp. 248–49. Reprinted in B. Russell, *Portraits from memory*, London, Allen & Unwin; New York, Simon & Shuster, 1956, pp. 23–29.
R. gives a number of particulars of his first meeting with W. at Cambridge. He then records, in anecdotal form, a number of episodes from W.'s life during and after W.'s imprisonment in Italy, the publication of *Tract.*, and R.'s philosophical disagreement with W. after his return to Cambridge.

230. Schiavone M., *Il pensiero filosofico di L. W. alla luce del 'Tractatus logico-philosophicus'*, RFN, 47, pp. 225–252.
An attempt to place *Tract.* in the story of the 'neopositivistic movement'.

231. White M., *The age of analysis*, New York, New American Library, 1955.
In a review of contemporary philosophers with the most diverse tendencies (from Husserl to Carnap, from Croce to Dewey), White devotes a chapter to W.'s later thought ('The uses of language: Ludwig Wittgenstein', pp. 225–236). W.'s main interest is identified as the therapy of metaphysical problems.

1956

232. Bochenski J. M., *Formale Logik*, Freiburg and Munich, Karl Alber, 1956. E.T. *History of formal logic*, University of Notre Dame Press, 1961.

In the section devoted to propositional logic (part V, §42) the theory of matrices, as set out by Peirce and by W. in *Tract.*, is examined.

233. Butler R. J., *A W.ian on 'The reality of the past'*, PQ, 6, pp. 11-12.

Referring to a preceding work by G. E. M. Anscombe (1950), B. criticizes W.'s followers who, in his opinion, have introduced a research method without having any opinion to sustain. He makes a particular examination of the problem of whether memory can constitute a criterion for deciding about the truth or falsity of sentences which refer to the past.

234. Campanale D., *Studi su W.*, Bari, Adriatica Editrice, 1956, pp. 269. 2nd ed., revised and brought up to date, 1970.

The work includes a number of articles previously published in 'Rassegna di scienze filosofiche' (1955-56). W.'s thought is reconstructed through the analysis of some sections of *Tract.* and of *P.I.* An implicit 'metaphysical' assumption is detected, which C. set himself the task of reconstructing.

235. Daly C. B., *Logical positivism, metaphysics and ethics: L.W.*, ITQ, 23, pp. 111-50.

D. examines, from a Catholic point of view, the problem of the mysticism, metaphysics and ethics in *Tract.* and in W.'s subsequent works, and mentions anticipations by Hume, Kant, and Russell.

236. Daly C. B., *Miss Anscombe and 'misinformation'*, ITQ, 23, pp. 147-50.

Response to an article by Anscombe, 1954, which purported to correct empirical interpretations of *Tract.*

237. Daly C. B., *W.'s 'objects'*, ITQ, 23, pp. 413-14.

In this brief note D. quotes some parts of a letter in which Anscombe criticizes D.'s interpretation (see above) of the objects of *Tract.* For his part, D. reaffirms the validity of his theses.

238. Ewing A. C., *The necessity of metaphysics*, in H. D. Lewis (ed.), *Contemporary British philosophy*, London, George Allen & Unwin, 1956, pp. 143-164.

At the beginning of the 1930s (cf. especially pp. 150ff.) the predominant influence of W. at Cambridge was reflected in the widespread acceptance of the principle of verification and in a hostile attitude towards metaphysics shared by the majority of philosophers.

239. Heath P. L., *W. investigated*, PQ, 6, pp. 66–71.

A critical examination of *P.I.* H. accuses W., *inter alia*, of defending a faulty theory of 'meaning'; of hesitating between a 'democratic' and a 'totalitarian' conception of language (p. 69); of dealing with the problem of private language in an inadequate and naive way; of maintaining a kind of 'linguistic phenomenalism' which has met with a surprising and undeserved success (p.71).

240. Hintikka K. J. J., *Identity, variables, and impredicative definitions*, JSL, 21, pp. 225–245.

A number of references to *Tract.* H. criticizes the interpretation of variables in that work.

241. McGuinness B. F., *Pictures and forms in W.'s Tractatus*, in E. Castelli (ed.), *Filosofia e Simbolismo*, Rome, Bocca, 1956, pp. 207–28. Reprinted in Copi and Beard (eds.), 1966.

The greatest difficulties encountered in the theory of *Tract.* are concerned with the distinction between structure and form (of a fact or of a representation), and the notion of relation. In fact W. seems not to notice that the existence of diverse forms of relation (corresponding to the logical forms of objects) implies different types of variables. Certain inconsistencies which can be found in *Tract.* concerning this subject derive from the fact that W. was sometimes referring to logical, and at others to spatial pictures. In order to interpret *Tract.* coherently, it must be acknowledged that there is a difference of logical type between the objects themselves.

242. Paul G. A., *Wittgenstein*, in G. Ryle and others, *The revolution in philosophy*, London, Macmillan, 1956, pp. 88–96. Reprinted in Fann (ed.), 1967.

P. gives a brief sketch of W.'s lines of research since 1929, basing himself on *P.I.* and concentrating on W.'s relation to the thought of Moore. According to P., W. follows Moore in his defence of common sense and ordinary language and in his sympathy for metaphysical philosophers. W. did not, however, share Moore's estimate of the primacy of consciousness and private experience.

243. Pears D. F., *Logical atomism: Russell and W.*, in G. Ryle and others, *The revolution in philosophy*, London, Macmillan, 1956, pp. 41–55.

The contribution made by Russell and, to a different extent, by W. and Moore, are considered in their common reaction (also shared by Bradley) to the psychological empiricism of Hume. Despite the authors' different aims, the solutions upheld by Russell and by W. still have a metaphysical nature and, unlike Moore, do not take the real function of language into account. Particularly, the theory of *Tract.* does nothing but recycle, in new terms, the metaphysical theory of individual subtances.

244. Russell B., *Logic and knowledge. Essays 1901–1950*, ed. by R. C. Marsh, London, Allen & Unwin, 1956, pp. 382.

In this collection are reprinted a number of writings about W. which have previously been considered in the present volume: 'The philosophy of logical atomism' (1918–1919), 'Logical atomism' (1924), 'Logical positivism' (1950). These articles are prefaced by introductions, written by the editor of the volume, in which the influence exerted by W. on Russell, especially between 1912 and 1919, is highlighted, as are the later developments which led Russell gradually to abandon W.'s ideas.

245. Shalom A., *Y a-t-il du nouveau dans la philosophie anglaise?* EP, 11, 1956, pp. 653–64; 12, 1957, pp. 47–63.

A summary of the philosophical situation in England, and an examination of the influence exerted by Moore's analaysis of everyday language and by W.'s 'therapeutic' philosophy (see above all the second part of the article).

246. Shwayder D. S., ' = ', M, 65, pp. 16–37.

W., in *Tract.*, following one of Frege's theses, considered assertions of identity to be statements about language, i.e. statements which affirm the possibility of substituting two symbols linked by the sign ' = ' (pp. 17ff.). This solution, however, (according to S.) turns out to be unsatisfactory.

247. Urmson J. O., *Philosophical analysis*, London, Oxford University Press, 1956.

U. aims at an examination of the origins and developments of 'analytical philosophy'. He looks at *Tract.* above all in its relationship to atomism and to logical positivism. In the field of atomism, W., who took up a most radical position on this point, held that the artificial language of truth-functions constitutes the skeleton of the language of ordinary discourse and shows the logical structure of the world (see in particular ch. V, 'Facts and pictures of facts', pp. 54-93). The contrast which emerged between the metaphysical approach of *Tract.* and the demand for a radical empiricism, which was shared by most of the exponents of logical positivism, is the explanation of the fact that the neopositivists later partially abandoned some of W.'s theories, and atomism in general (see the second part of the book).

248. Waismann F., *How I see philosophy*, in H. D. Lewis (ed.), *Contemporary British philosophy*, 3rd series, London, Allen & Unwin, 1956, pp. 447-490. Reprinted in A. J. Ayer (ed.), *Logical positivism*, Glencoe, Ill., Free Press, 1959; in the posthumous collection of Waismann's writings, edited by R. Harré, *How I see philosophy*, London, Macmillan, 1968.
In defining the nature and objectives of philosophical research, Wa. makes frequent references, sometimes only implicit, to W. Philosophy, Wa. maintains, does not only have the function of clarifying and solving badly-formulated problems, re-establishing a correct use of language. What is characteristic of philosophy is that it contributes to the affirmation of a new way of seeing, thus transforming the whole intellectual scene. The importance of W., like that of every other great philosopher, lies in this visionary capacity for renewal.

249. Wisan R. H., *A note on silence,* JP, 53, pp. 448-50.
A brief analysis of the meaning of W.'s dictum: 'Whereof one cannot speak, thereof one must be silent' (*Tract.*, prop. 7), controverting theses upheld by Hamburg (1953).

1957

250. Anscombe G. E. M., *Intention*, Oxford, Basil Blackwell, 1957.
The work contains numerous references to *P.I.*, and to theses maintained by W. concerning the rules for the use of various expressions of intention.

251. Anscombe G. E. M., Rhees R., von Wright G. H., *A note on Costello's version of the 'Notes on logic'*, JP, 54, p. 484.

The literary executors, assignees of W.'s manuscripts, believe that, for various reasons, the version of notes published by Costello (1957) is not to be relied on. Furthermore, they announce the imminent publication of W.ian manuscripts written before *Tract.* (See, however, McGuinness, 1972.)

252. Bergmann G., *The revolt against logical atomism*, PQ, 7, 1957, pp. 323–339; 8, 1958, pp. 1–13. Reprinted in G. Bergmann, *Meaning and existence*, Madison, Wis., University of Wisconsin Press, 1960.
B. examines the development of analytical philosophy between the two wars and pays particular attention to the reaction of Oxford philosophy against Russell and the theory of *Tract.* (pp. 334–39). Criticism of Urmson's historical interpretation (1956).

253. Broad C. D., *The local historical background of contemporary Cambridge philosophy*, in C. A. Mace (ed.), *British philosophy in the mid-century*, London, George Allen & Unwin, 1957, pp. 13–61.
W.'s contribution is analysed, together with those made by Whitehead and Russell, in a paragraph devoted to 'logico-mathematical' philosophy.

254. Costello H. T., *W.'s notes on logic*, JP, 54, pp. 230–45.
In an introductory note (pp. 230-1), C. explains how he received from Russell a number of W.'s manuscripts, dated September 1913, when the English philosopher made a trip to Harvard (1914). W.'s literary executors express reservations about the reliability of the notes published by Costello; cf. Anscombe and others, 1956. Later the executors accepted and published the Costello version, only to withdraw it still later in the light of considerations urged in McGuinness, 1972.

255. Duthie G. D., *Critical study of Remarks on the foundation of mathematics'*, PQ, 7, pp. 368–73.
The following topics are given particular emphasis: the conventional nature of logical inference; proofs and calculations; the theory of natural numbers and its relation with intuitionism; W.'s implicit rejection of Russell's theory of numbers; paradoxes and mathematical contradictions.

256. Fleming N., *Recognizing and seeing as*, PR, 66, pp. 161–79.
References to the discussion of the Jastrow figures in *P.I.* (pp. 174ff.).

257. Geach P. T., PR, 66, pp. 556-9.

A critical review of Colombo's Italian translation of *Tract.* (1954) in which G. claims to find a number of inaccuracies. Also Colombo's historical introduction is criticized for presenting a physicalistic interpretation and for treating mysticism as a superfluous appendix to *Tract.*

258. Geach P. T., *Mental acts: their content and their objects*, London, Routledge & Kegan Paul, 1957.

In the ch. 'W.'s alleged rejection of mental acts' (pp. 2-4) G. considers W.'s treatment of language referring to private events, and defends him from critics who accuse him of behaviourism.

259. Hampshire S., *Metaphysical systems*, in D. F. Pears (ed.), *The nature of metaphysics*, London, Macmillan, 1957, pp. 23-38.

W.'s thought is placed within the tradition of 'systematic philosophy' which dates back to Aristotle, and which takes a decisive turn with Kant. This tradition, maintains H., aims to determine both the necessary structure and the limits of human knowledge.

260. Hawkins D. J. B., *W. and the cult of language*, 'Aquinas paper', No. 27, London, Blackfriars Publications, 1957, pp. 14. Reprinted in D. J. B. Hawkins, *Crucial problems of modern philosophy*, Notre Dame, Ind., University of Notre Dame Press, 1962, pp. 66-79.

Tract., it is claimed, can be considered as an attempt to eliminate the Cartesian 'cogito' and its implications, making the subject coincide with its language (*Tract.*, 5.542). In *P.I.*, basing himself on a 'pragmatic conception of language', W. reaches, by other means, the same conclusions as in *Tract.* Thus all his work is reduced to an (unsuccessful) attempt to contest philosophy's speculative possibilities.

261. Hervey H., *The private language problem*, PQ, 7, pp. 63-79. Reprinted in Jones (ed.), 1971.

W.'s objections to an idea of a 'private language' are inadequate, according to H., particularly as regards the identification of sensations, the relation between them and observable behaviour and the grammar of expressions associated with them. H. develops these criticisms with reference to the articles by Ayer (1954), Rhees (1954) and Strawson (1954). See Hardin's observations (1959).

262. Linsky L., *W. on language and some problems of philosophy*, JP, 54, pp. 285-93. Reprinted in Fann (ed.), 1967, and in Canfield (ed.), 1986, vol. IX.

An attempt to interpret the paragraphs of *P.I.* in which the problem of 'private language' is tackled. According to L., by this term W. means a language which no one else, except the speaker, could understand, i.e. a language which does not have at its disposal criteria to decide on the correctness of the use to which it is put. At the end of the article there is a brief analysis of the concepts of 'symptom' and 'criterion' in *P.I.*

263. Melden A. I., *My kinaesthetic sensations advise me . . .*, A, 18, pp. 43-8.

M. examines the theses, contained in *P.I.* and in *Bl.B.*, on the role which kinaesthetic sensations play in the awareness we have of a movement or of our body's position. These theses, he states, constitute a significant part of the criticism made by W. of the previous theory of *Tract.*

264. Paci E., *La filosofia contemporanea*, Milan, Garzanti, 1957.

In the chapter 'Logical empiricism and the phenomenology of perception', there is a critical summary of W.'s work, carried out from a phenomenological point of view (especially pp. 247ff.).

265. Passmore J., *A hundred years of philosophy*, London, Duckworth, 1957, pp. 523. 2nd ed. revised and extended, 1966.

P. reviews the most significant works and trends to emerge in the last hundred years, especially in England, in the fields of epistemology, logic and metaphysics. At several points in the exposition he gives particular emphasis to the figure and work of W., devoting two chapters specifically to him: 'Some Cambridge philosophers and W.'s *Tractatus*' (XV, pp. 345-368) and 'W. and ordinary language philosophy' (XVIII, pp. 425-458). In the 2nd edition of the work (1966) a brief analysis of *R.F.M.* is included in ch. XVIII (pp. 441-444), the bibliography is brought up to date, and a final chapter is added (pp. 517-546) in which P. examines the developments in analytical philosophy after W.

266. Popper K. R., *Philosophy of science: a personal report*, in C. A. Mace (ed.), *British philosophy in the mid-century*,

London, George Allen & Unwin, 1957, pp. 155–191.
Reprinted in a revised form in K.R. Popper, *Conjectures
and refutations*, London, Basic Books, 1962.

While setting out the principal stages in his own thought from
1919 onwards, Popper (pp. 163–166) locates in *Tract.* a doctrine
according to which every genuine proposition must be a truth-
function of observation-statements. On the basis of this
interpretation P. attributes to W. a theory of meaning based on
a radical criterion of verifiability shared by most of the
representatives of the Vienna School. This criterion, claims P.,
excludes from science all that is most characteristic of it, for
example scientific laws, which cannot be deduced from
observation-statements.

267. Ryle G., *The work of an influential but little-known
philosopher of science: L.W.*, 'Scientific American', 197,
pp. 251–259. Reprinted in G. Ryle, *Collected papers*, vol.
I, London, Hutchinson, 1971. Reprinted in Shanker (ed.),
1986, vol. III.

A presentation of W.'s work and intellectual personality. The
importance which his philosophy holds for contemporary
scientific thought is emphasized.

268. Ryle G., *The theory of meaning*, in C. A. Mace (ed.), *British
philosophy in the mid-century*, London, George Allen &
Unwin, 1957, pp. 239–264.

A brief historical retrospective of the modern theories of
meaning. W., it is claimed, was among the authors who had the
greatest influence concerning this topic. He first, as early as
Tract., abandoned the purely denotative perspective of meaning,
and then developed, in a more complete way, in his later
writings, a theory which associates the meaning of a linguistic
expression with the rules governing its use (see especially
pp. 254ff, and 262–264).

269. Smart H. R., *Language-games*, PQ, 7, pp. 224–35.

A critical analysis of the concepts of 'language game' and 'family
resemblance', in the specific meaning with which they occur in
P.I.

270. Wilson C., *Religion and the rebel*, Boston, Mass.,
Houghton Mifflin; London, Gollancz, 1957.

In the chapter 'Wittgenstein and Whitehead', pp. 290–322,
literary reflections on W.'s personality and on his first work.

1958

271. Aldrich V. C., *Pictorial meaning, picture-thinking, and W.'s theory of aspects*, M, 67, pp. 70–79. Reprinted in Canfield (ed.), 1986, vol. XIII.

The aim of the article is to apply to problems of aesthetics the notion of seeing an aspect set out in *P.I.* According to A., what W., despite a certain ambiguity, is trying to show is that it is never a picture or image *per se* that exhausts the sense or meaning of an expression but rather the context of the use of the expression.

272. Ambrose A., *Proof and theorem proved*, JP, 55, pp. 901–2 (extract).

See Ambrose, 1959. Cf. also the observations made by J. W. Swanson, 1959, concerning this article.

273. Anderson A. R., *Mathematics and the 'language game'*, RM, 11, pp. 446–58. Reprinted in P. Benacerraf and H. Putnam (eds.), 1965, and in Canfield (ed.), 1986, vol. XI.

The general theoretical approach of *R.F.M.* turns out to be substantially similar to that of *P.I.* For W., neither the foundations of natural languages, nor those of mathematics can be sought in formal logical systems. In general, A. believes that the importance which has been attributed to W.'s philosophy of mathematics is exaggerated, and concludes that many of the aspects of his controversy with the formalists – in particular with Hilbert and Church – are superseded by later developments in the discussion of the foundations of mathematics.

274. Copi I. M., *Objects, properties and relations in the 'Tractatus'*, M, 67, pp. 145–65. Reprinted in Copi and Beard (eds.), 1966; in Canfield (ed.), 1986, vol. I.

A number of key passages and problems from *Tract.* are re-examined and re-interpreted from a different viewpoint from that adopted, for example, by Daitz, 1953, and Evans, 1955. The aim of *Tract.* was to determine a symbolic artificial language which conformed 'to the rules of logical grammar'; not to extend the picture theory and the theory of multiplicity (4.04) to ordinary language. The objects of *Tract.* are neither relationships nor properties, but 'pure particulars'. They do not have material properties, but only internal properties or forms, the form of an object being a possibility, and therefore a logical property. See Anscombe's reply, 1959, to this article.

275. Copi I. M., *Tractatus 5.542*, A, 18, pp. 102-4. Reprinted in Copi and Beard (eds.), 1966.

An interpretation of the analysis, proposed in *Tract.*, of sentences like 'A thinks (believes, says) p'.

276. Delius H., *Was sich überhaupt sagen lässt, lässt sich klar sagen. Gedanken zu einer Formulierung L.W.s*, AfF, 8, pp. 211-54.

The maxim of W.'s quoted in the title and taken from the preface to *Tract.* provides D. with the idea for reflections of his own on the nature of language and thought.

277. Feibleman J. K., *Inside the great mirror: a critical examination of the philosophy of Russell, W. and their followers*, The Hague, Martinus Nijhoff, 1958, pp. 228.

F. suggests a 'realistic' interpretation of the work of W. and of Russell, which, he specifies, is different from the various 'nominalistic' interpretations adopted by the American and European 'logical positivists', and by the 'English analysts'. In the second part of the work in particular, he analyses and comments upon several sections of *Tract.* (pp. 57-113) which he considers as a development of Russell's logical atomism, and as an attempt to overcome the difficulties implied in this. *Reviews*: Agassi J., BJPS, 1960-1, 11, pp. 83-4; Deledalle G., EP, 1959, 14, p. 78; Egidi R., CGFI, 1959, 38, pp. 418-22; Leroy A. R., RPFE, 1962, 87, pp. 448-50; Madden E.H., PPR, 1959-60, 20, pp. 561-2; Schiavone M., GM, 1960, 15, pp. 89-90; Wallraff C. F., Pr, 1960, 41, pp. 73-5.

278. Heller E., *L.W.: Unphilosophische Betrachtungen*, 'Merkur', 13, no. 142, pp. 1101-20. Reprinted in *W. Schriften/Beiheft*, 1960. E.T. in 'Encounter', 1959, 13, no. 3, pp. 40-8, and in Fann (ed.), 1967.

H. attempts to define the work and intellectual personality of W. within the framework of Western thought (Kant, Nietzsche) and of contemporary Austrian culture (Musil, Kafka and others).

279. Hintikka J., *On W.'s solipsism*, M, 67, pp. 88-91. Reprinted in Copi and Beard (eds.), 1966, and in Canfield (ed.), 1986, vol. III.

What is meant by solipsism in *Tract.* (5.62) is far from the meaning usually attributed to this word, i.e. the subject's inability to go beyond the limits of his own personal experience. On the contrary, 'solipsism' means for W. the elimination of the private, the recognition that the limits of a subject's thought and language are the limits of language in general.

280. **Khatchadourian H.**, *Common names and family resemblances*, PPR, 18, pp. 341-58. Reprinted in Pitcher, 1966.
K. examines the notion of 'family resemblances' (*Familienähnlichkeiten*) introduced in *P.I.* Contrary to what W. seems to maintain, he observes, at least in the case of some 'common names', the objects which they name have one or more features in common, even if this does not occur in relation to a determinate or relatively determinate characteristic.

281. **Klibansky R.** (ed.), *Philosophy in the mid-century*, 4 vols., Florence, La Nuova Italia, 1958-59.
The work of several authors, this is a review of the problems which were at the heart of the philosophical debate between 1949 and 1955, and of the main trends to emerge in that period. Here a list of the main contributions concerning W.'s thought is given: *Vol. I*: H. Putnam (see entry); M. Black (on induction and probability, especially pp. 155-160). *Vol. II*: C. A. Mace and R. S. Peters (on the philosophy of mind, cf. section 1); D. Pears (see entry); A. Quinton (see entry); G. J. Warnock (see entry). *Vol. III*: R.S. Hartman (on ethics, especially pp. 9-15); M. Weitz (on aesthetics, especially pp. 79-80).

282. **Kreisel G.**, *W.'s 'Remarks'*, BJPS, 9, pp. 135-58. Reprinted in Canfield (ed.), 1986, vol. XI.
The most significant contributions made to the philosophy of mathematics by W. concern certain problems relative to the foundations of elementary calculus and certain aspects of the 'theory of proof' which are often neglected by the mathematical logic. K. has little time for the solutions proposed by W. to questions within the philosophy of mathematics proper, in particular: the use of the criterion of *consistency*; the relationship between 'proof' and 'theorem'; Gödel's theorem; the nature of paradoxes. The article closes with reminiscences of the frequent discussions K. had with W. in the years 1942-51, and a list of corrections to the English translation by G. E. M. Anscombe.

283. **Malcolm N.**, *L. W.: a memoir*, London, New York, Oxford University Press, 1958, pp. 100. 2nd revised and enlarged

ed., 1984. Translations in French, Italian, German, Spanish and other languages.
The book is composed of two parts. In the first (pp. 1–22) is a reprint of an updated version of W.'s biography written by G. H. von Wright (see 1954). In the second part (pp. 22–100) Malcolm, who was W.'s student, describes his relationship with the philosopher from 1938 (the year in which he met W. for the first time in Cambridge) to 1951. These years cover three sojourns of Malcolm's in Cambridge and W.'s trip to the United States. For the remaining periods excerpts of a correspondence between W. and Malcolm are published. Brief summaries of lectures during 1938–40 and 1946–7 (pp. 47–50). Worth mentioning are notes that Malcolm made of certain conversations between him and W. in Ithaca, regarding the problem of 'knowledge' (pp. 87–92). In the 2nd ed. a new ch., 'W.'s letters to Malcolm' (1940–51), is added. *Reviews*: Bobbio N., RF, 1959, 50, pp. 233–4; Britton K., P, 1959, 34, pp. 277–8; Diamond C., CPR, 1985, 5, pp. 377–9; Jackson A. C., M, 1960, 69, pp. 269–70; Rollins C. D., JP, 1959, 56, pp. 280–3; Shalom A., EP, 1959, 14, p. 548, Vlastos G., PR, 1960, 6, pp. 105–8.

284. Malcolm N., *Knowledge of other minds*, JP, 55, pp. 969–78. Reprinted in V. C. Chappell (ed.), *The philosophy of mind*, Englewood Cliffs, N.J., Prentice-Hall, 1962; in N. Malcolm, *Knowledge and certainty*, Englewood Cliffs, N.J., Prentice-Hall, 1963; in Pitcher (ed.), 1966; in Canfield (ed.), 1986, vol. VIII.
The most important indication that *P.I.* supplies on the theme of the knowledge of other minds resides in the thesis that psychological expressions in the first person are not the result of an identification, recognition or observation of our own conscious state. Such a thesis, though demanding further study and a more rigorous formulation, has made a positive contribution to a radically new view of the 'other minds' problem as compared with the classical theories (J. S. Mill) which based themselves on analogical and inductive types of argument.

285. Nielsen H. A., *W. on language*, PS (I), 8, pp. 115–21.
A rather critical presentation of what N. considers to be the 'principal ideas' expounded in *P.I.* He examines, above all, the problem of language and of meaning and the philosophic method followed by W.

286. Palmer H., *The other logical constant*, M, 68, pp. 50-9.
A criticism of the analysis, proposed in *Tract*. 5.542, of sentences
like 'A believes (thinks) p', and an attempt to develop an
alternative.

287. Pap A., *Semantics and necessary truth*, New Haven,
Conn., Yale University Press, 1958.
In the paragraph entitled 'The concept of tautology'
(pp. 143-149) the author evaluates the contribution made by
Tract. toward the notion of logical truth.

288. Pears D., *Epistemology*, in R. Klibansky (ed.), 1958, vol.
II, pp. 109-116 (see above).
In *P.I.* there are to be found various examples of the application
of linguistic analysis to problems of epistemology. Among these,
particular historic importance attaches to the discussion of the
notion of private language, which is above all a criticism of a
basic tenet of empiricism.

289. Pole D., *The later philosophy of W.*, London, Athlone
Press, 1958, pp. 129.
In the first three chapters ('The linguistic approach to
philosophy', 'Logic and normative language' and 'Inner
experience') the author sums up the principal themes tackled
by W. in *P.I.* and in *R.F.M.* In Chapter IV ('Difficulties in W.'s
philosophy') P. criticizes some of the aspects of W.'s theory. This
theory, P. maintains, does not seem to contemplate the
·possibility that new systems of rules and new uses might be
introduced into the language which would contrast with those
adopted in common practice. In the last chapter P. examines
J. Wisdom's work and singles out some analogies and differences
between it and W.'s philosophy. *Reviews*: Bharati A., ZPF, 1962,
16, pp. 158-60; Britton K., P, 1960, 35, pp. 279-81; Jäger
H. W., PLA, 1960, 13, pp. 28-30; Nuchelmans G., FL, 1965, 1,
pp. 232-3; Ruytinx J., RIP, 1960, 14, pp. 106-7; Shalom A., EP,
1959, 14, p. 237; Strawson P. F., PQ, 1960, 10, pp. 371-2;
Teichman J., M, 1960, 69, p. 107.

290. Putnam H., *Elementary logic and foundations of set
theory*, in R. Klibansky (ed.), *Philosophy in the mid-
century*, 1958, vol. I, pp. 56-61 (see above).
In a review of the developments in the post-war study
of logic P. considers and evaluates *inter alia* the contribution
made by W. to inquiry into the foundations of mathematics.

W.'s position in this regard is considered in some of its aspects close to that of the intuitionists.

291. Quinton A., *Linguistic analysis*, in R. Klibansky (ed.), *Philosophy in the mid-century*, 1958, vol. II, pp. 146-202 (see above).

Q. traces the actual beginning of modern analytical philosophy (pp. 156-158) to *Tract.* and stresses the influence which it has had on logical positivism. Then, coming to the post-war period, he considers the impact that W.'s thought has had on the philosophy of language and on different methods of dealing with philosophical problems.

292. Shalom A., *W., le langage et la philosophie*, EP, 13, pp. 486-94.

The essential themes of W.'s 'ordinary language' methodology are considered in the light of some sections of *P.I.* and *Bl.B.*

293. Strawson P. F., *Persons*, in H. Feigl, M. Scriven, G. Maxwell (eds.), *Minnesota studies in the philosophy of science*, vol. II, Minneapolis, Minn., University of Minnesota Press, 1958. Reprinted in H. Morick (ed.), 1967; in Canfield (ed.) 1986, vol. XII.

Starting from some citations of *Tract.* (5.631-5.641) S. proposes to throw light on the philosophical notion of 'subject'. In the course of his discussion he also refers to W.'s theory of the subject in his 1930-32 lectures (Moore, 1954), defining it as an example of 'no-ownership doctrine of the self'. The article was reprinted in a revised form in Chapter III of Strawson's work, *Individuals*, London, Methuen, 1959.

294. Warnock G. J., *English philosophy since 1900*, Oxford, Oxford University Press, 1958. 2nd ed. revised and enlarged, 1969, pp. 126.

A large part of the book is dedicated to W.'s thought, particularly to the shift between *Tract.* and the later work. This radical change in his conception of language, Wa. maintains, had induced W. to distance himself progressively from the primitive 'logical atomism' which he shared with Russell, and whose presuppositions he had developed in a particularly uncompromising manner.

295. Warnock G. J., *The philosophy of W.*, in R. Klibansky (ed.), *Philosophy in the mid-century*, 1958, vol. II, pp. 203-207 (see above).

A brief analysis of relationships between *Tract.* and the maturer thought of W. and the influence this has had on contemporary English philosophy. In his posthumously published writings, Wa. maintains, W. arrives at an almost total repudiation of the philosophic positions which he held in his first work.

296. Weiler G., *On Fritz Mauthner's critique of language*, M, 67, pp. 80–87.

We. briefly examines the work of Mauthner, and in particular his 'criticism of language', stressing some analogies with W.'s thought.

297. White A., *G. E. Moore. A critical exposition*, Oxford, Basil Blackwell, 1958.

Wh. distinguishes three different methods of analysis in Moore (which he calls respectively inspection, division and distinction) and considers the analogies and the differences with the philosophy of Russell and W. (see esp. pp. 199–219). Both in *Tract.* and in Russell's logical atomism there are present, he maintains, ontological and metaphysical premises which are by contrast lacking in Moore: the analysis of language should have permitted one to draw conclusions about the ontological nature and the structure of the world. After 1929, however, (pp. 225–36) the method of research adopted by W. came considerably closer to that of Moore, especially in its aim of defending the uses of ordinary language against the confusions introduced by metaphysical speculation.

298. Wienpahl P. D., *Zen and the work of W.*, 'Chicago Review', 12, pp. 67–72.

Both in *Tract.* and in his later works, W. expressed detachment and scepticism regarding the powers of logic and of the intellect. These and other characteristics render his thought similar to that of important representatives of the Zen philosophy.

299. Winch P., *The idea of social science*, London, Routledge & Kegan Paul; New York, Humanities Press, 1958, pp. 143.

Winch examines the relationships between social sciences and philosophy on the one hand, and social sciences and natural sciences on the other. In Chapter I (§8, 'Rules: W.'s analysis', pp. 24–33) shows how in particular W.'s analysis of the concept of rule threw light on 'the nature of human society and social relationships between men'. In the following section ('Some misunderstandings of W.', pp. 33–9) Win. defends W. from criticisms made by Strawson, 1954 and by Ayer, 1954, in connection with the problem of private language.

1959

300. Agassi J., *W. the elusive*, TLS, 22 May, p. 305.
A. criticizes a previous article in the same journal (see Anon, 1959) for not having considered the interpretation of *Tract.* given by Russell (1922) and by Schlick. See below Anscombe's (1959) and Anon's (1959) answers.

301. Albritton R., *On W.'s use of the term 'criterion'*, JP, 56, pp. 845–857. Reprinted in Pitcher (ed.), 1966; in Shanker (ed.), 1986, vol. II; in Canfield (ed.), 1986, vol. VII.
An analysis of different meanings attributed by W. to the concepts of 'criterion' and 'symptom' in different parts of *P.I.*, *Bl.B.* and *Br.B.* See criticisms of this article by Scriven, 1959.

302. Allaire E. B., *Tractatus 6.3751*, A, 19, pp. 100–105. Reprinted in Copi and Beard (eds.), 1966; in Shanker (ed.), 1986, vol. I; in Canfield (ed.), 1986, vol. I.
According to the theory of *Tract.* (6.3751), the statement 'this is red and this is green' is contradictory when the demonstrative pronoun refers to one and the same patch of colour. In order to avoid errors of interpretation (Bergmann, 1957, and Urmson, 1956) 'red' and 'green' are to be understood, in *Tract.*, not as simples, but as definables.

303. Ambrose A., *Proof and the theorem proved*, M, 68, pp. 435–45. Reprinted in A. Ambrose, *Essays in analysis*, London, Allen & Unwin, 1966; in Canfield (ed.) 1986, vol. XI.
As W. was partly aware, the relationship outlined in *R.F.M.* between 'the proof of a proposition "p" ', 'the sense of a statement "p" ', and 'understanding "p" ' faces numerous theoretical difficulties, whose solution often appears rather difficult. See comments by Castañeda (1961).

304. Anon, *The passionate philosopher*, TLS, 1 May, pp. 249–250.
A review of three works on W.'s output published by N. Malcolm, 1958, G. E. M. Anscombe, 1959, D. Pole, 1958, respectively. See Agassi's criticism of this article, 1959.

305. Anon, TLS, 22 May, p. 305.

In reply to Agassi's interposition (1959), the reviewer records that W. expressed his own 'strong disapproval' of Russell's introduction to *Tract.* (1922), and did not accept Schlick's interpretation.

306. Anscombe G. E. M., *An introduction to W.'s 'Tractatus'*, London, Hutchinson, 1959. 2nd revised ed., 1963. Italian translation: Rome, Ubaldini, 1966. Spanish translation: Buenos Aires, Ateneo, 1978.

A reconstruction of the logical foundations of *Tract.* theory, placed in relationship to the work of Frege and Russell. The influence of the former, A. maintains (cf. above all the 'Introduction'), has not been sufficiently emphasized by the commentators. On the other hand, Russell's 'theory of descriptions', together with other aspects of his logical analysis, also influenced W.'s cultural development to a large extent. Nevertheless, the empiricist approach which characterized Russell's thought was somewhat alien to W. Another author with whom W. has much affinity, especially in his ethical theory and as regards mysticism, is Schopenhauer (cf. ch. XIII). A. develops this historical interpretation in relation to various topics, mostly logical, sufficiently indicated by the chapter titles, which follow: 'Elementary propositions'; 'Theory of descriptions'; 'Negation'; 'Consequences of the picture theory'; 'Sign and symbol'; 'W., Frege and Ramsey'; 'Operations'; 'Formal concepts and formal series'; 'The general form of proposition'; 'Generality'; 'Knowledge and certainty'; 'Mysticism and solipsism'. *Reviews*: Carney J. D., PSc, 1960, 27, p. 408; Cassirer E., BJPS, 1963–64, 14, pp. 359–66; Gill J. H., PPR, 1966, 27, pp. 137–8; Jarvis J. and Sommers F., P, 1961, 36, pp. 374–7; Plochman G.K., MS, 1959-60, 37, pp. 242–5; Rhees R., PQ, 1960, 10, pp. 21–31; Shalom A., EP, 1961, 16, p.239.

307. Anscombe G. E. M., *Mr. Copi on objects, properties and relations in the Tractatus*, M, 68, p. 404. Reprinted in Copi and Beard (eds.), 1966.

A brief reply to Copi's article (1958, M). According to A., the thesis which states that, in *Tract.*, the fact aRb contains exactly two elements is not justified.

308. Anscombe G. E. M., *Letter*, TLS, 29 May, p. 321.

The reply to a letter of Agassi's (1959). A. declares, amongst other things, that she is 'perplexed' about the thesis that W. shares Schlick's general philosophical opinions or his interpretation of *Tract.*

309. Ayer A. J. (ed.), *Logical positivism*, Glencoe, Ill., Free Press, 1959, pp. 455.

A collection of writings by different authors prefaced by an 'Introduction' by A. (pp. 3-20) in which a brief retrospective analysis is made of the neopositivist movement, with numerous references to W.'s work.

310. Ayer A. J., *Phenomenology and linguistic analysis. (Symposium)*, PAS (SV), 33, pp. 111-124.

Replying to C. Taylor's article (same title), in the same issue of the review, A. emphasizes the differences and analogies which exist between the phenomenological and analytical trends. In this regard A. also examines briefly a number of theses characteristic of W.'s more mature thought.

311. Bernays P., *Betrachtungen zu L. W.s 'Bemerkungen über die Grundlagen der Mathematik'*, R, 2, pp. 1-22. Reprinted and translated into English in P. Benacerraf and H. Putnam (eds.), 1964. Reprinted also in Shanker (ed.), 1986, vol. III; in Canfield (ed.), 1986, vol. XI.

Two problematical tendencies emerge from a reading of W.'s *R.F.M.* One leads W. to assume a Kantian position concerning mathematics (at least in the sense that mathematics creates the form of what are then called 'facts'); the other to maintain that the applicability of mathematics, and of arithmetic in particular, is based on empirical cognition. On the basis of these general observations B. criticizes W.'s theses concerning more specific questions: the nature of axioms in geometry; the difference between the propositions of mathematics and the principles of mechanics; the role of intuition in the development of mathematical concepts; impredicative definitions; the discussions of Dedekind; the function of formalization; the non-contradictory nature of formal systems; the reducibility of the theory of numbers to logic.

312. Charlesworth M. J., *Philosophy and linguistic analysis*, Pittsburgh, Penn., Duquesne University Press, 1959, pp. XIII, 256.

The most important works of English philosophy to emerge in this century are examined and critically analysed, from a point of view which C. himself defines as 'Thomist' and 'neoscholastic'. In the exposition, a particular emphasis is given to W.'s thought, and the relationship between his work and that of Frege, Moore, Russell and the 'philosophers of ordinary language' is considered (pp. 74-125).

313. Dummett M., *W.'s philosophy of mathematics*, PR, 68, pp. 324-48. Reprinted in Pitcher (ed.), 1966; Benacerraf and Putnam (eds.), 1964; Shanker (ed.), 1986, vol. III; Canfield (ed.), 1986, vol. XI; and in his *Truth and other enigmas*, London, Duckworth, 1978.

An analysis of *R.F.M.* from the point of view of the opposition between 'platonism' and 'constructivism' in the philosophy of mathematics. Of the two alternatives W. chooses a version of constructivism which is somewhat more radical than that supported by the intuitionists, and therefore adopts a conventionalistic solution concerning logical necessity which leads him to deny an objectively certain proof in mathematics and to face numerous other theoretical difficulties.

314. Evans E., *About 'aRb'*, M, 68, pp. 535-8. Reprinted in Copi and Beard (eds.), 1966.

A reply to a number of Copi's objections (1958, M) to a previous article by Evans (1955). Section 3.1432 of *Tract.* does not refer, as Copi maintains, to a perfect language, but to ordinary language. 'R' should be considered as a kind of name 'which refers to a particular type of object', i.e., to situations.

315 Garver N., *W. on private language*, PPR, 20, pp. 388-96. Reprinted in Klemke (ed), 1971.

W.'s *reductio ad absurdum* of the notion of private language does not connect with the problems raised by Ayer, 1954, and Rhees, 1954. Belief that a private language exists often rests on a philosophical acceptance of Cartesian dualism. §§256-270 of *P.I.* are also to be understood as a *reductio ad absurdum* of this dualism and of the philosophical theories connected with it.

316. Gellner E., *Words and things*, London, Gollancz, 1959.

In his critical, sometimes sarcastic and paradoxical exposition of Oxford analytical philosophy, G. often refers to W., who is considered to be the inspiration behind this trend.

317. Hadot P., *W. philosophe du langage*, 'Critique', 15, pp. 866-81 and 972-83.

An examination of *P.I.*, *R.F.M.* and *Bl.Br.B.* Despite the 'profound evolution' which has come into W.'s thought, H. finds the same inspiration and the same aim in these works that had, in his opinion, characterized *Tract.*: 'to bring a radical and definitive peace to metaphysical anxiety'.

318. Hadot P., *Réflexions sur les limites du langage: à propos du 'Tractatus logico-philosophicus' de W.*, RMM, 64, pp. 469–84. E.T. in 'Cross Currents', 1970, 20, pp. 39–54.
A critical examination of *Tract.*, with reference to the Italian translation edited by Colombo (1954). W.'s work is presented as one of the most serious attempts ever made to found a form of 'radical positivism' which nevertheless reserves an appropriate place for the inexpressible.

319. Hamlyn D. W., *Categories, formal concepts and metaphysics*, P, 34, pp. 111–24.
H. considers what W. calls 'formal concepts' in *Tract.* (cf. 4.126) and the relationships these have with grammatical analysis in W.'s later works, and therefore with the notions of 'use' and of 'language game'.

320. Hardin C. L., *W. on private languages*, JP, 56, pp. 517–528. Reprinted in Klemke (ed.), 1971.
W.'s thesis that memory facts cannot be verified without recourse to an independent authority (*P.I.* 265) is without foundation. H. also criticizes the articles by Hervey, 1957, Rhees, 1954, Ayer, 1954, from this viewpoint.

321. Horgby I., *The double awareness in Heidegger and W.*, I, 2, pp. 235–64. Reprinted in *Analytic philosophy and phenomenology*, ed. by H. A. Durfee, 1976.
In spite of many differences, W. and Heidegger have what H. calls 'double awareness' in common, i.e. the 'awareness of the fact that the world *is*' as distinct from or in addition to the 'awareness of how the world is'. For a critique of this article, cf. Weil 1960.

322. Kenny A., *Aquinas and W.*, DR, 77, pp. 217–35.
The critique (which was developed in *P.I.* and in *B.B.B.*) of essentialism, phenomenalism and logical atomism, the characteristic theses of neopositivism, is reminiscent, in certain regards, of the differences which separate St. Thomas from the theories on language and the awareness of Scotus, Ockham and the nominalists. Cf. Williams's criticism of this article, 1960.

323. Levi A. W., *Philosophy and the modern world*, Bloomington, Ind., Indiana University Press, 1959.
A review of the philosophical ideas and works which have had the greatest influence on modern culture. L. also examines the figures of Russell, Moore, W. and Carnap. See particularly ch. XI, 'G.E. Moore and L.W.' (pp.436-81).

324. Malcolm N., *Dreaming*, London, Routledge & Kegan Paul; New York, Humanities Press, 1959, pp. 128.
References to W.'s theses of the philosophy of mind and to his method of investigation are contained in particular in chs. XII and XIV.

325. Mills J. F., *A meeting with W.*, TLS, 12 June, p. 353.
A letter to the review which records a brief meeting, at Cambridge, between W. and 'a young American intellectual on holiday'.

326. Proctor G. L., *Scientific laws, scientific objects, and the Tractatus*, BJPS, 10, pp. 177–93. Reprinted in Copi and Beard (eds.), 1966.
Both scientific objects and scientific laws are logically constructed models and express indirectly the properties of the objects in the world. These models help us to organize and unify the propositions with which we describe our experiences. *Tract.* has inspired the development of this theory and can provide a number of important clues to clarify some of its aspects.

327. Rhees R., *W.'s builders*, PAS, 60, pp. 171–86. Reprinted in Fann (ed.), 1967; in Canfield (ed.), 1986, vol. VI.
What is to be understood by 'language'? The meaning which W. attributes to this term in his later writings is not clear. R. attempts to reply to this question particularly through an analysis of *P.I.* 3-5.

328. Russell B., *My philosophical development*, London, Allen & Unwin; New York, Simon & Schuster, 1959, pp. 279. Extracts reprinted in 'Encounter', January 1959, pp. 8–9.
This autobiographical work contains a chapter expressly devoted to the analysis of the relationship between R. and W. ('The impact of W.', pp. 110–127) besides numerous scattered references to W. in the remainder of the volume. R. attributes great importance to the influence exerted by W. on his thought, both in the years immediately preceding the First World War, through unpublished writings and conversations, and later, by *Tract.* In a chapter entitled 'Some replies to criticism', he

confirms his own scant regard for W.'s later work and that of those considered to be his disciples. W. (like Pascal and Tolstoy) is accused of having renounced his own genius from a misguided sense of humility and deference to 'common sense'.

329. Scriven M., *The logic of criteria*, JP, 56, pp. 857-68. Reprinted in Canfield (ed.), 1986, vol. VII.

Although S. adopts a different terminology to that used by W., he considers the results of his own analysis to be quite close to the theses supported in *P.I.*, which are the outcome of an interpretation suggested by Albritton (1959).

330. Stern J. P., *Lichtenberg: a doctrine of scattered occasions*, Bloomington, Ind., Indiana University Press, 1959.

In his study of G.C. Lichtenberg's personality and work, S. emphasizes (especially pp. 158-64) a large number of analogies which exist between his work and W.'s later writings. These comparisons, together with the enthusiasm with which W. speaks of L., lead S. to form a hypothesis on the influence exerted on W. by the latter.

331. Swanson J. W., *A footnote to Mrs. Lazerowitz on W.*, JP, 56, pp. 678-9.

S. sets out an instance, further to the one suggested by Mrs. Lazerowitz (= Ambrose, 1958), in which W.'s thesis, according to which it is the proof which gives meaning to a theorem, may be valid. S. adduces the intuitionistic theses of Heyting and Brouwer on this topic.

332. van Peursen C. A., *Edmund Husserl and L.W.*, PPR, 20, pp. 181-98. Reprinted in his *Phenomenology and reality*, Pittsburgh, Penn., Duquesne University Press, 1972, pp. 189-213. Reprinted also in Canfield (ed.), 1986, vol. XV.

Despite the fact that many differences exist between the works of Husserl and W., a number of analogies between them can also be found. Nevertheless, Husserl's philosophy, even in his last period, is structured with the subject as its centre, and thus approaches a form of idealism; W., on the other hand, places the object at the centre, thus reaching behaviouristic solutions.

333. Wellman C., *W. and the egocentric predicament*, M, 68, pp. 223-33.

We. examines and criticizes W.'s analysis of epistemological presuppositions which have theoretical egocentrism as their consequence ('I can know only my own experience', 'I understand only my own words').

334. Wisdom J. O., *Esotericism*, P, 34, pp. 338-54.
In the course of examining some of the themes of *R.F.M.*, Wis. attempts to locate the historical background to the work, and in particular its relationship with logical positivism.

1960

335. *Wittgenstein: Schriften/Beiheft, Arbeiten über W.*, Frankfurt, Suhrkamp, 1960, pp. 99.
A German collection of writings already published in various languages: I. Bachmann, 1953, M. Cranston, 1951, J. Ferrater Mora, 1949, P. Feyerabend, 1954, E. Heller, 1958, B. Russell, 1922, G. H. von Wright, 1954.

336. Bambrough J. R., *Universals and family resemblances*, PAS, 61, pp. 207-22. Reprinted in Pitcher (ed.), 1966; in Canfield (ed.), 1986, vol. V.
In his more mature work W. solved the problem of the nature of universals. In this connexion the notion of 'family resemblance' is a central one, and B. reconstructs its meaning by means of an examination of parallel steps drawn from *P.I.* and *B.B.B.* W.'s theses are then contrasted with the rival solutions of nominalism and realism.

337. Bergmann G., *Ineffability, ontology and method*, PR, 69, pp. 18-40. Reprinted in his *Logic and reality*, 1964, and in Klemke (ed.), 1971.
B. discusses two different arguments in favour of the thesis that 'the meaning of an expression is its use'; both are to be found in *P.I.* and in the 'philosophy of ordinary language'.

338. Carney J. D., *Private language: the logic of W.'s argument*, M, 69, pp. 560-5.
Controverting Wellman, 1959, C. re-examines and supports W.'s criticism of the thesis according to which all words derive their meaning from private experience.

339. Chastaing M., *W. et les problèmes de la connaissance d'autrui*, RPFE, 85, pp. 297-312.

340. Daly C. B., *New light on W.*, PS(I), 10, 1960, pp. 5-49; 11, 1961, pp. 28-62.

An extensive analysis of the recent writings by and on W., made from a Thomistic point of view, with particular attention (especially the 2nd part) paid to the ethical and religious implications.

341. Hartnack J., *W. og den Moderne Filosofi*, Copenhagen, Gyldendal, 1960. E.T. *W. and modern philosophy*, London, Methuen, 1965, pp. 124. A new English ed. with an 'Afterthought', Notre Dame, Ind., University of Notre Dame Press, 1986. Also translated into German, Italian, Spanish, and Japanese.

A brief comprehensive presentation of W.'s thought based on the opposition between *Tract.* (ch. II) and *P.I.* (ch. IV). While the former work (ch. III) is seen as standing apart from neopositivism, the influence which the therapeutic method of the second W. has on contemporary Anglo-Saxon philosophy is stressed. *Reviews:* A.G.C., RF, 1962, 53, pp. 357-8; Cassirer E., BJPS, 1964-5, 15, pp. 166-8; Copleston F. C., HJ, 1966, 7, pp. 321-5; Gill J. H., PPR, 1966, 27, pp. 137-8; Hennemann G., ZPF, 1966, 20, pp. 338-41; Narveson A., D, 1966, 5, pp. 101-2; Sluga H. D., PB, 1966, 7, p. 22; Stroll A., JHP, 1967, 5, pp. 190-3; Trinchero M., RF, 1964, 55, pp. 109-11; Wellman C., PR, 1967, 76, pp. 385-7.

342. Heller E., Drury M. O'C., Malcolm N., Rhees R., *L. W.: a symposium*, 'Listener', 63, pp. 163-5, 207-9. Reprinted in Fann (ed.), 1967, and in Canfield, 1986, vol. IV.

An informal and anecdotal presentation of the philosopher's personality and work. Heller researches into the sources in Austrian culture of W.'s formation and character. Drury (a doctor friend) testifies to the strictly metaphysical nature of his thought. Rhees dwells on the use of formalized languages in analysis, and on the significance of W.'s therapeutic method.

343. Kreisel G., *W.'s theory and practice of philosophy*, BJPS, 11, pp. 238-52. Reprinted in Canfield (ed.), 1986, vol. V.

A critical note concerning *B.B.B.*, whose main value is said to lie in its ability to deal with particular questions while avoiding useless abstract arguments. Its fundamental failings concern the problems of the foundations of mathematics, and there is also a frequent inability to grasp the wider nature of the philosophical problems discussed.

344. Lübbe H., *'Sprachspiele' und 'Geschichten'*, KS, 52, pp. 220-43.
A number of analogies between the more mature philosophy of W. and the most recent trends in phenomenology (especially W. Schapp).

345. Rhees R., *Miss Anscombe on the Tractatus*, PQ, 10, pp. 21-31. Reprinted in Canfield (ed.), 1986, vol. II.
Various criticisms of Anscombe's book (1959), including one of the fact that her interpretation of *Tract.* is presented in a predominantly logical key, rather than being centred on the problem of the limits between what can be said and what can merely be shown.

346. Shapere D., *Philosophy and the analysis of language*, I, 3, pp. 29-48. Reprinted in *Linguistic turn*, 1967.
S. singles out and criticizes two theses found in Russell, in *Tract.* and in the analytical philosophers (especially Ryle), which are concerned with the picture theory of language, according to which assertions register facts.

347. Stenius E., *W.'s Tractatus*, Oxford, Basil Blackwell; Ithaca, N.Y., Cornell University Press, 1960, pp. 241. German translation: Frankfurt, Suhrkamp, 1969.
The aim professed by the author is to give an interpretation of the semantic and metaphysical aspects of W.'s theory by means of a selective examination of the most significant steps in *Tract.*, starting from questions of an historical or genetic nature. The picture theory, which S. exemplifies with statements drawn from ordinary language, constitutes the central theme of this treatment. This theory revolves around the thesis, subsequently criticised by various authors, that in *Tract.* predicates are genuine components of reality on a level with objects (see particularly ch. V). In the final chapter, W.'s philosophical system is considered to be much closer to German metaphysics, and in particular to Kant, than to logical atomism 'of an Anglo-Saxon type'. The chapter headings are: 1) 'The structure of the Tractatus'; 2) 'The world as a fact'; 3) 'The concept of a Sachverhalt'; 4) 'Logical space'; 5) 'The concept of substance'; 6) 'The concept of a picture'; 7) 'The sentence as a picture'; 8) 'The descriptive concept of compound sentences'; 9) 'Descriptive content and mood'; 10) 'Internal structure of language and reality'; 11) 'W. as a Kantian philosopher'. *Reviews:*

Anon, TLS, 23 December 1961, p. 831; Bergmann G., T, 1963, 29, pp. 176-204; Copi I.M., PR, 1963, 72, pp. 382-90; Duthie G.D., PQ, 1962, 12, pp. 371-2; Garver N., PPR, 1962, 22, pp. 276-7; Jarvis J., JP, 1961, 58, pp. 584-96; Nerlich G.C., PB, 1960, 1, pp. 13-16; Nielsen H.A., PS, 1960, 10, pp. 265-6; Riverso E., RCSF, 1962, 15, pp. 255-6; Shwayder D.S., M, 1963, 72, pp. 275-88; Shalom A., EP, 1961, 16, pp.277-8; Stegmüller W., PRd, 1965-6, 13, pp. 116-38.

348. Weil G. M., *Esotericism and the double awareness*, I, 3, pp. 61-72.
This work develops and criticizes the comparison made by Horgby, 1959, between W. and Heidegger, and discusses the article by J. O. Wisdom, 1959.

349. Weiler G., *Is Humpty Dumpty vindicated?*, I, 3, pp. 278-81.
Taking part in a discussion with other authors previously contributing to the review, We. maintains that the well-known statement made by Humpty Dumpty in 'Alice' ('When I use a word, it means exactly what I have chosen it to mean – no more, no less') cannot seriously exemplify a possible theoretical attitude towards language. While developing this thesis, We. discusses a number of criticisms levelled at W.'s theory of language.

350. Williams C. J. F., *The marriage of Aquinas and W.*, DR, 78, pp. 203-12.
Contrary to the view of Kenny, 1959, the great theoretical differences between St. Thomas and W., in addition to the centuries which separate them, do not allow for a comparison between their works beyond a number of non-fundamental analogies.

351. Wolter A. B., *The unspeakable philosophy of the later W.*, PACPA, 34, pp. 168-93.

1961

352. Allaire E. B., *Types and formation rules: a note on 'Tractatus' 3.334*, A, 21, pp. 14-16.
A discussion of *Tract.* designed to show the futility and danger of using the notation of propositional functions.

353. Bennett J., *On being forced to a conclusion*, PAS(SV), 35, pp. 15-34.
A 'Symposium' with O. P. Wood (pp. 35-44). An analysis of the foundations of logical necessity and mathematical proof in their relationship with the theory of meaning. B. considers (especially pp. 17-20) the difficulties in the 'conventionalist' solution which are singled out by Dummett, 1959, in his analysis of W.

354. Bergmann G., *La gloria e la miseria di L. W.*, RF, 52, pp. 387-406. Published in English in G. Bergmann, *Logic and reality*, Madison, Wis., Wisconsin University Press, 1964; in Copi and Beard (eds.), 1966; in Klemke (ed.), 1971.
A critical analysis of W.'s thought focusing on the contrast between *Tract.* and *P.I.* The former represents a glorious failure, the latter is dictated by the desperation felt at that failure. At the end of the article, there is a comparison with Husserl (pp. 404-6).

355. Bernstein R. J., *W.'s three languages*, RM, 15, pp. 278-98. Reprinted in Copi and Beard (eds.), 1966.
The recent publications by and about W. lead to a belief that the previously-suggested interpretation of *Tract.* in a neo-positivistic and atomistic vein are unfounded, together with the thesis of the two W.s. The interest and historical influence exerted by these interpretations are all that remain. On the basis of these premises B. analyses the picture theory of the *Tract.*

356. Bouwsma O. K., *W. notes, 1949. The 'Blue Book'*, JP, 58, pp. 141-62. Reprinted in his *Philosophical essays*, Lincoln, Neb., University of Nebraska Press, 1965. Also reprinted in Fann (ed.), 1967, and in Canfield (ed.), 1986, vol. IV.

357. Castañeda H. N., *On mathematical proofs and meaning*, M, 70, pp. 385-90.
C. discusses a number of examples which do not agree with the constructivist interpretation suggested by Ambrose, 1959, with regard to mathematical proof in W.

358. Charlesworth M. T., *Linguistic analysis and language about God*, IPQ, 1, pp. 139-57.
In the course of analysing the 'serious deficiencies' shown by analytical philosophy in dealing with religious language, C. devotes a number of sections to W. (pp. 141-146), whom he considers to be among the fathers of this school of thought.

359. Chihara C. S., *W. and logical compulsion*, A, 21, pp. 136-40. Reprinted in Pitcher (ed.), 1966; in Canfield (ed.), 1986, vol. X.
Criticizing Nell, 1961, C. examines the nature of logical necessity in W.'s late work.

360. Cowan J. L., *W.'s philosophy of logic*, PR, 70, pp. 362-75. Reprinted in Fann (ed.), 1967.
A reply to the criticisms of W. made by Dummett, 1959, on the foundations of mathematics and logic.

361. Ferré F., *Colour incompatibility and language-games*, M, 70, pp. 90-94.
The observations made in *P.I.* regarding the incompatibility of different patches of colour permit a substantial clarification of the problem of the logical status of synthetic *a priori* propositions. See replies by Swiggart, 1963, and Arbini, 1963.

362. Hervey H., *The problem of the model language game in W.'s later philosophy*, P, 36, pp. 333-51.
An examination of the notion of language game in important passages drawn from *P.I.* and *Bl.B.* H. reveals diverse meanings of the term which are not always compatible, some of which seem to contrast with W.'s statement that his analysis does not have as its aim a reform of language, but only a description of it.

363. Jarvis J., *Professor Stenius on the Tractatus*, JP, 58, pp. 584-96. Reprinted in Copi and Beard (eds.), 1966; in Canfield (ed.), 1986, vol. I.
A critical examination of Stenius's book, 1960, centred on the picture theory. Stenius is criticized above all for extending the notion of object to properties and relations, and for applying the picture theory to logically composite statements. In conclusion, a discussion about the logical relationship between statements of colours ('x is red and blue').

364. Jünger F. G., *Satzsinn und Satzbedeutung. Gedanken zu den 'Schriften' von L.W.*, 'Merkur', 15, pp. 1009-23. Reprinted in his *Sprache und Denken*, Frankfurt, Klostermann, 1962.

365. Kempski J. von, *Über W.*, 'Neue Deutsche Hefte', 82, pp. 43-60.

366. Kempski J. von, *W. und die analytische Philosophie*,

'Merkur', 15, pp. 664–76. Reprinted in his *Brechungen,* Hamburg, Rowohlt, 1966.

367. Kraft W., *L. W. and Karl Kraus,* 'Die Neue Rundschau', 72, pp. 812–44. Reprinted in his *Rebellen des Geistes,* Stuttgart, Kohlhammer, 1968.

368. Marcuse H., *One-dimensional man,* Boston, Mass., Beacon Press, 1961.

In chapter 1, 'The triumph of positive thinking' (pp. 170–202) W.'s thought is included in M.'s criticism of analytical philosophy. W.'s 'therapeutic method' justifies the historically predominant forms of thought, and therefore subserves the 'ideological' function of conservation.

369. Maslow A., *A study in W.'s Tractatus,* Berkeley, Cal., University of California Press; Cambridge, Cambridge University Press, pp. 162.

As explained in the preface, this book was written in 1933, and is published in its original version. It largely reflects the viewpoint of logical positivism and has as historical and theoretical references Russell, Ramsey and Schlick. The exposition is divided into four parts: 'Objects, atomic facts and language'; 'Symbol and sign'; 'Truth functions of atomic propositions'; 'W.'s philosophy'. Overall *Tract.* is interpreted as a piece of research on formal aspects of consciousness and on 'symbolism in general', and is likened to a form of 'Kantian phenomenalism', in which language assumes the role of the transcendental in Kant. *Reviews:* McCall S., D, 1963, 2, pp. 114–15; Nerlich G. C., PB, 1962, 3, pp. 10–11; Rhees R., PR, 72, 1963, pp. 213–20; Ruytinx J., RPFE, 1955, 90, pp. 250–1.

370. Mays W., *W.'s Manchester period,* 'Guardian', 24 March 1961. Reprinted in Fann (ed.), 1967.

The reconstruction of a number of episodes from W.'s life at Manchester (1908–11) on the basis of the testimony of Eccles and others.

371. Mehta V., *A battle against the bewitchment of our intelligence,* 'New Yorker', 9 December 1961, pp. 59–159. Reprinted in his *The fly and the fly bottle: encounters with British intellectuals,* London, Weidenfeld & Nicolson, 1962.

Frequent references to W. and to his influence on contemporary analytical philosophy. A popular presentation.

372. Nell E., *The hardness of the logical 'must'*, A, 21, pp. 68–72. Reprinted in Canfield (ed.), 1986, vol. X.
N. criticizes the thesis, which he finds in *R.F.M.*, that it is possible to contravene the fundamental rules of logic. See the reply by Chihara, 1961.

373. Pole D., *W. et la philosophie*, AP, 24, pp. 450–67.
A general presentation of the main themes of W.'s mature thought, and of his 'revolutionary' philosophical method.

374. Rorty R., *Pragmatism, categories, and language*, PR, 70, pp. 197–223. Reprinted in Canfield (ed.), 1986, vol. XV.
Peirce and the later W. are likened to each other because of their rejection of positivism and their conception of the nature of language.

375. Taylor P. W., *W.'s conception of language*, in his *Normative discourse*, Englewood Cliffs, N.J., Prentice-Hall, 1961, pp. 263–79.
Chap. X of the book, divided into two sections, 'Language as a set of social practices' and 'Language as a set of instruments', examines W.'s ideas in order to clarify the concept of normative language.

376. Wein N., *Le monde du pensable et le langage*, RMM, 66, pp. 102–15.
W.'s critique of language is placed in the framework of a 'cosmological philosophy' (strictly post-Kantian and therefore of a critical trend). Its problem is that of the 'isomorphism between knowledge, language and reality'. In *Tract.* and in *P.I.* the philosophy of language reaches its self-destruction in different ways.

377. Wellman C., *Our criteria for third-person psychological sentences*, JP, 58, pp. 281–93.
In discussing Malcolm's thesis on knowing other people's minds, We. considers the notion of 'criterion' in *B.B.B.*

378. Wiplinger F., *L.W., Sprache und Welt in seinem Denken*, WW, 16, pp. 528–41.

379. Wisdom A. J. T. D., *A feature of W.'s technique*, PAS(SV), 35, pp. 1–14. Reprinted in J. Wisdom, *Paradox and discovery*, Oxford, Blackwell, 1966; in Fann (ed.), 1967; in Canfield (ed.), 1986, vol. V.

W.'s hostility towards generalization is discussed in relation to the problem of knowing other people's minds and to questions of method in philosophical analysis.

1962

380. Aldrich V. C., *Image-mongering and image-management*, PPR, 23, pp. 51-61.
Can it be imagined that a stone has consciousness? The question, posed by W. in *P.I.*, is tackled by means of an analysis of the diverse meanings which the question can assume.

381. Blanshard B., *Reason and analysis*, New York, Open Court; London, George Allen & Unwin, 1962, pp. 505.
Some sections devoted to W.: in the chapter 'Logical atomism' a demonstration, *inter alia*, of 'the incoherence of the picture theory', while in the chapter. 'The theory of meaning' solipsism is discussed and criticized.

382. Broad C. D., *W. and the Vienna Circle*, M, 71, p. 251.
A sardonic riposte to those who accuse B. of having identified W. with the Vienna Circle.

383. Cavell S., *The availability of W.'s later philosophy*, PR, 71, pp. 67-93. Reprinted in Pitcher (ed.), 1966; in Shanker (ed.), 1986, vol. II; in Canfield (ed.), 1986, vol. IV.
C. believes that Pole's exposition of W.'s thought, 1958, is superficial and false, and dismisses as unfounded the criticism that W. confines himself to defending to the last the current uses of ordinary language. In the final section there is an examination of W.'s literary style.

384. Gruender C. D., *W. on explanation and description*, JP, 59, pp. 523-30.
Both in *Tract.* and in *P.I.* philosophical 'explanations' are originally considered to be nonsense. The descriptive method, on the other hand, provides important results, for example in clarifying problems of the philosophy of the mind.

385. Hadot P., *Jeux de langage et philosophie*, RMM, 67, pp. 330-43.
A personal evaluation of W.'s thought particularly as regards the contrast between *Tract.* and *P.I.*

386. Hamlyn D. W., *The correspondence theory of truth*, PQ, 12, pp. 193-205.
Frequent references to the picture theory of language adhered to in *Tract.*

387. Harrison F. R., *W. and the doctrine of identical minimal meaning*, Me, 14, pp. 61-74.
The theory under discussion states that every general term has an essential meaning to which that term refers in each of its uses. H. opposes this theory to that of family resemblances adhered to by W.

388. King-Farlow J., *Postscript to Mr. Aune on a W.ian dogma*, PS, 13, pp. 62-4.
K.-F. discusses further examples, besides those given by Aune ('Phil. Studies', 12, pp. 53-8, 1961), where, contrary to what 'W.'s followers' maintain, it is sensible to state: 'He believes (knows) he is in pain.'

389. Kurtz P. W., *Letter to the editor*, JP, 59, pp. 78-9.
This letter concerns the authenticity of the version of 'Notes on logic' published under the editorship of H. T. Costello, 1957.

390. Llewelyn J. E., *On not speaking the same language*, AJP, 40, pp. 35-48, 127-45.
In the second part of the article (especially pp. 127-136) there is an evaluation of the theses on language in W.'s latest work in comparison with Collingwood's theory of absolute presuppositions.

391. Lübbe H., *W. ein Existentialist?*, PJ, 69, pp. 311-24.

392. Moore G. E., *Commonplace book*, London, George Allen & Unwin; New York, Macmillan, 1962, pp. 410.
The work contains numerous scattered references to W., especially in the sections: 'The same pain' (pp. 127-8), 'Saying that p' (pp. 180-1), 'Truth-possibilities' (*Tract.* 4.28-4.31) (pp. 282-3), 'W.'s sense of tautology' (in *Tract.*) (pp. 284-6).

393. Munson T. N., *W.'s phenomenology*, PPR, 23, pp. 37-50.
An investigation which tends to circumscribe what in W.'s thought comes close to the phenomenological method; M. pays particular attention to the problem of 'inner acts'. From this point of view he locates a substantial unity between the different phases of W.'s philosophy.

394. Plochmann G. K. and **Lawson J. B.**, *Terms in their*

propositional contexts in W.'s Tractatus: an index, Carbondale, Ill., Southern Illinois, Press, 1962, pp. 226.
An aid to finding occurrences of the principal terms in *Tract.* with summaries of the chief contexts in which they appear. Terms are given in an English translation which often varies from that usually employed. A list of equivalences to the original German terms is also provided. *Reviews:* Black, M., PR, 1963, 72, pp. 265–6; Fairbanks M.J., MS, 41, 1963–64, pp. 82–4.

395. Rest W., *Über W.s Wörterbuch für Volksschulen*, 'Rundschau', 16, pp. 680–86.

396. Richman R. J., *Something common*, JP, 59, pp. 821–30.
An analysis of the theory of meaning in *P.I.*, in its relationship to the notion of family resemblances. R. particularly dwells on the problem of whether elements falling under general terms which have a univocal meaning have common characteristics.

397. Rollins C. D. (ed.), *Knowledge and experience,* Pittsburgh, Penn., University of Pittsburgh Press, 1962, pp. 55–105.
The work contains two symposia about W. The first is composed of a presentation by N. Garver ('W. on criteria', pp. 55–71); the comments of C. Ginet, F. A. Siegler, P. Ziff; a reply by Garver. The second contains a presentation by H. N. Castañeda ('The private language argument', pp. 88–105); the comments of V.C. Chappell, J. F. Thomson; a reply by Castañeda. Castañeda's article has been reprinted in Klemke (ed.), 1971. The first of the two symposia has been reprinted in Canfield (ed.), 1986, vol. VII.

398. Schwyzer H. R. G., *W.'s picture-theory of language*, I, 5, pp. 46–64. Reprinted in Copi and Beard (eds.), 1966; Canfield (ed.) 1986, vol. I.
The theory of language in *Tract.* is not based on the isomorphism between statements and facts. Therefore the prevailing interpretation of the work given for example by Warnock, 1958, Anscombe, 1959, Stenius, 1960, turns out to be unfounded. Cf. the response by Stenius, 1963.

399. Sellars W., *Naming and saying*, PSc, 29, pp. 7–26. Reprinted in Copi and Beard (eds.), 1966; Klemke (ed.), 1971; Canfield (ed.), 1986, vol. I. Also reprinted in his *Science, perception and reality*, London, Routledge & Kegan Paul; New York, Humanities Press, 1963.
S. considers two alternative interpretations of the 'objects' of *Tract.*, according to which 1) they are always 'particular', 2) they

also include 'universals'. S. then shows that the first interpretation reflects W.'s thought more closely, and that it is theoretically correct.

400. Sellars W., *Truth and correspondence,* JP, 59, pp. 39–56.
An interpretation of the picture theory of language in *Tract.* (pp. 39ff.) is the starting-point for an investigation of the validity of the correspondence theory of truth.

401. Stigen A., *Interpretations of W.*, I, 5, pp. 167–75.
A critical analysis of Hartnack's book, 1960.

402. Suter R., *Augustine on time with some criticism from W.*, RIP, 16, pp. 378–94.
The theses of St. Augustine on time rest on an erroneous theory of meaning. The difficulties which these theses lead to can be avoided in the light of W.'s later writings.

403. Todd W., *Private languages,* PQ, 12, pp. 206–17.
Reprinted in Klemke (ed.), 1971.
Frequent references to individual passages of *P.I.*, in a comparison between different notions of 'private language'.

404. Trentman J., *A note on Tractatus 4.12 and logical form*, GRP, 4, pp. 29–33.

405. Wellman C., *W.'s conception of a criterion*, PR, 71, pp. 433–47. Reprinted in Morick (ed.), 1967.
An attempt to clarify the central notion of criterion, as an alternative to the interpretations suggested by Malcolm, 1954, and Albritton, 1959. In the final part, We. points out a number of limitations in W.'s thesis.

406. Wisdom J., *Mace, Moore and W.*, in *C. A. Mace, a symposium*, edited by Vida Carver, London, Methuen, and Harmondsworth, Middx., Penguin Books, 1962. Reprinted in J. Wisdom, *Paradox and discovery*, Oxford, Blackwell, 1966, pp. 148–66; in Fann (ed.), 1967.
A brief characterization of the personalities of the three philosophers, presented through anecdotes, remembrances and impressions.

1963

407. Allaire E. B., *The Tractatus: nominalistic or realistic,* in *Essays in ontology*, E. B. Allaire *et al.* (eds.), The Hague, Martinus Nijhoff, 1963, pp. 148-65. Reprinted in Copi and Beard (eds.), 1966.

A 'realistic' interpretation of *Tract.* in antithesis to the 'nominalistic' one proposed, amongst others, by Anscombe, 1959, and Copi, 1959; thus A. supports the thesis that properties and particulars are both constituents (of logically different types) of 'atomic facts'.

408. Arbini M., *Ferré on colour incompatibility*, M, 72, pp. 586-90. (See Ferré, 1961.)

409. Bergmann G., *Stenius on the Tractatus*, T, 29, pp. 176-204. Reprinted in his *Logic and reality*, Madison, Wis., Wisconsin University Press, 1964, pp. 242-271; in Klemke (ed.), 1971; Canfield (ed.), 1986, vol. I.

In the light of Stenius's interpretations (1960), a juxtaposition between B.'s own ontology and that of *Tract.* is presented.

410. Carnap R., *Intellectual autobiography*, in *The philosophy of R. Carnap*, edited by P. Schilpp, La Salle, Ill., Open Court, 1963, pp. 3-84. Extracts reprinted in Fann (ed.), 1967.

Frequent references to W., especially in the chapter devoted to the Vienna Circle (pp. 24-29). C. emphasizes the influence of *Tract.* on the members of the Circle and on his own formation. Further annotations on conversations held with W. and Schlick (summer 1927) and on the contrasts which emerged particularly on the themes of religion and metaphysics. Finally, an examination of the deep divergences which became manifest particularly in the years that followed.

411. Carney J. D., *Is W. impaled on Miss Hervey's dilemma?*, P, 38, pp. 167-190.

W. is not involved in a dilemma (see Hervey, 1961) concerning the necessity or otherwise of solving philosophical problems through an analysis of language. See Hervey's reply, 1963.

412. Cassirer E., *On logical structure,* PAS, 64, pp. 177-98.

C. makes a distinction between those statements of ordinary language for which *Tract.*'s picture theory can be valid (since the facts and the statements have the same logical structure) and those cases in which, on the contrary, this model turns out to be inapplicable.

413. Chihara C. S., *Mathematical discovery and concept formation*, PR, 72, pp. 17-34. Reprinted in Pitcher (ed.), 1966; in Shanker (ed.), 1986, vol. III; in Canfield (ed.), 1986, vol. XI.

In an attempt to shed light on the nature of the opposition between 'Platonism' and 'constructivism' in the philosophy of mathematics, C. examines W.'s theses (*R.F.M.*) as representatives of the latter trend. He maintains that W.'s doctrine not only contains many obscure aspects but also does not appear to be necessarily incompatible with certain forms of 'realism'.

414. Gardiner P., *Schopenhauer and W.*, in his *Schopenhauer*, Harmondsworth, Middx., Penguin Books, 1963, pp. 275-82.

415. Hallie P. P., *W.'s grammatical-empirical distinction*, JP, 60, pp. 565-78.

The distinction made in *P.I.* between grammatical statements and empirical ones is exaggerated and does not reflect the true function of certain linguistic expressions.

416. Harrison F. R., *Notes on W.'s use of 'das Mystische'*, SJP, 1, pp. 3-9. (See comments by Plochmann, 1964.)

417. Hervey H., *A reply to Dr. Carney's challenge*, P, 38, pp. 170-5.

Replying to Carney's criticisms, 1963, H. reaffirms her own thesis that there exists a conflict between W.'s concept of ordinary language and his idea of a philosophical therapy having as its object the uses of language itself.

418. Keyt D., *W.'s notion of an object*, PQ, 13, pp. 13-25. Reprinted in Copi and Beard (eds.), 1966.

Unlike Russell, W. accepts only one form of objects. In their role as substances, they are outside time and seem to be more similar to Plato's forms than to the concrete individuals of Aristotle. He concludes the article with a paragraph on solipsism.

419. Küng G., *Ontologie und logistische Analyse der Sprache*, Vienna, Springer, 1963. E.T. *Ontology and the logistic analysis of language*, Dordrecht, Reidel, 1967, pp. 210.

Two chapters of this 'inquiry into modern views on universals' are dedicated to *Tract.*: 'The relation of representation', pp. 51-59; 'L.W.', pp. 80-5 (on ideal language and predicate signs).

420. McCloskey A. J., *The philosophy of linguistic analysis and the problem of universals*, PPR, 24, pp. 329-38.
The problem of universals is an authentic metaphysical problem which cannot be resolved by means of a therapeutic method. Numerous critical references to the theory of family resemblances in *P.I.*

421. Rhees R., *The 'Tractatus': seeds of some misunderstandings*, PR, 72, pp. 213-20. Reprinted in Canfield (ed.), 1986, vol. II.
A critical anlysis of Maslow's book, 1961. R. sees in his interpretation of *Tract.* illicit inferences from theses that W. temporarily adopted at the beginning of the 1930s, and from a (later superseded) neopositivistic standpoint. There follows a detailed analysis on the incompatibility of colours. See Maslow's reply, 1964.

422. Shwayder D. S., *Critical notice of Stenius*, M, 72, pp. 275-89. Reprinted in abridged form in Copi and Beard (eds.), 1966; reprinted in Canfield (ed.), 1986, vol. I.
A critique of Stenius's book, 1960, examining both the method of analysis followed, and the interpretations suggested for single arguments, in particular for the picture theory (pp. 278ff.).

423. Specht E. K., *Die sprachphilosophischen und ontologischen Grundlagen im Spätwerk L. W.s*, Cologne, Kölner Universitätsverlag, 1963, pp. 176. E.T. *The foundations of W.'s later philosophy*, Manchester, Manchester University Press, 1967, pp. 209; New York, Barnes & Noble, 1969.
The aim of the work is to single out the 'ontological foundations' present in the theory of language contained in W.'s late writings, in his relationship to some classical problems and authors of philosophical thought, in particular to Plato and Kant. Having defined, in the first two chapters, the atomistic model of language in *Tract.*, especially by means of a comparison with Aristotle, S. follows the genesis and development of the 'model' for the linguistic game in later writings of W. The ontological implications (see chs. 5-6) reside in the attempt to arrive at the 'constitution of objects' along a path which avoids both nominalism and realism, and which safeguards the element of spontaneity and creativity that is found in grammatical rules. These rules take on a function similar in some aspects to the

synthetic *a priori* judgements of Kant, and ensure the correlation between sign and object without involving forms of conventionalism. *Reviews:* Feyerabend P., PQ, 1966, 16, pp. 79-80; Hartnack J., PR, 1971, 80, pp. 391-3; Hilgenheger N., AGP, 1968, 50, pp. 308-15; Norman R., RPL, 1970, 68, pp. 401-5.

424. Stenius E., *W.'s picture theory of language*, I, 6, pp. 184-95. Reprinted in Copi and Beard (eds.), 1966.
A reply to Schwyzer's criticisms, see 1962.

425. Swiggart P., *The incompatibility of colours*, M, 72, pp. 133-6.
S. criticizes Ferré's thesis, 1961, that the statements showing the incompatibility of different patches of colour can be considered both necessary and contingent.

426. Tanburn N. P., *Private languages again*, M, 72, pp. 88-102.
An analysis of the different ways in which the statement that 'There can't be private languages' can be restated and understood. Frequent references to the examples given in *P.I.*

427. von Morstein P., *Erfahrung bei L.W.*, AfP, 12, pp. 133-51.
An analysis of the notion of *Erfahrung* (experience) in several of W.'s writings.

428. Walsh W. H., *Metaphysics*, London, Hutchinson; New York, Harcourt, Brace & World, 1963, pp. 206.
Some sections of chap. VIII, 'Contemporary anti-metaphysics', are devoted to a critical examination of the bearing on metaphyics of both *Tract.* and *P.I.*, including a comparison between W. and E. Burke.

1964

429. Bambrough J. R., *Principia metaphysica*, P, 39, pp. 97-109.
B. sets himself the task of 'extracting from the writings of W. and Wisdom a general theory concerning the nature of knowledge' which also includes 'metaphysical knowledge'. The article sets out the principles of this theory.

430. Beard R.W., *Tractatus 4.24,* SJP, 2, pp. 14-17.

431. Benacerraf P. and **Putnam H.** (eds.), *Philosophy of mathematics*, Englewood Cliffs, N.J., Prentice-Hall; Oxford, Blackwell, 1964.
One section of this anthology (pp. 421-528) is devoted to W. It includes a selection from *R.F.M.* (pp. 421-480), and the republished version of the articles of Anderson, 1958, Dummett, 1959, and Bernays, 1959. In the introduction (pp. 25-27) the editors briefly examine the difficulties encountered in defining W.'s theses concerning logical necessity, in terms of the current trends in the philosophy of mathematics.

432. Black M., *A companion to W.'s Tractatus*, Ithaca, N.Y., Cornell University Press, pp. XV, 451. Italian translation, Rome, Ubaldini, 1967.
This work constitutes the most extensive and detailed study of *Tract*. It aims both to provide an aid to the reading of the work, and to suggest a number of solutions, on the basis of a careful discussion of various alternative possible interpretations, to some of the more controversial questions, for example: the significance of *Sachverhalt*; the notions of object, relation and property, and their reciprocal relationships; the existence of negative facts; the possibility that objects may enter into something more than an 'atomic fact'; the verifiabilify of elementary propositions; problems connected with solipsism and ethics, etc. In order to develop this analysis, B. divides the work into 90 paragraphs, each devoted to one theme, and corresponding to a group of sections in *Tract*. Each paragraph is composed of an introduction in an historical and theoretical vein, followed by a detailed analysis of the passages under examination. The work contains two concordances: one between the German terms and Ogden and Ramsey's English translation; and another with W.'s preparatory writings and the commentaries of Anscombe, 1959, and Stenius, 1960, both frequently referred to in the text. *Reviews*: Bastable J. D., PS (I), 1968, 17, pp. 390-3; Bogen J., PR, 1969, 78, pp. 374-82; Copleston Fr. C., JH, 1965, 6, pp. 321-7; Griffin J., PB, 1965, 6, pp. 2-4; Hinst P., PRd, 1968, 15, pp. 149-50; Kenny A., M, 1966, 75, pp. 452-3; Küng G., NS, 1966, 40, pp. 403-6; Narveson A., PSc, 1967, 34, pp. 69-73; Shwayder D. S., FL, 1969, 5, pp. 289-96; Sternfeld R., PPR, 1965-6, 26, pp. 287-90; Trinchero M., RF, 1968, 59, pp. 351-4.

433. Bogen J., *Was W. a psychologist?*, I, 7, pp. 374-8.
Some passages from *Tract.* and a letter to Russell could imply
a psychological theory of language, i.e. a correlation between
words and mental entities. The interesting points and limits of
this interpretation are discussed. See criticisms by Hannay,
1964.

434. Cavell S., *Existentialism and analytic philosophy*,
'Daedalus', 93, pp. 946-74. Reprinted in Canfield (ed.),
1986, vol.XV.
In section III there is a comparison between W. and Kierkegaard.

435. Fairbanks M. J., *C.S. Peirce and logical atomism*, NS,
38, pp. 178-88.
Contains a comparison of Peirce with W.

436. Favrholdt D., *Tractatus 5.542*, M, 73, pp. 557-62.
An examination of intensional statements and of the notion of
subject in *Tract.*

437. Favrholdt D., *An interpretation and critique of W.'s
Tractatus*, Copenhagen, Munksgaard, 1964; New York,
Humanities Press, 1966, pp. 229.
According to F., the fundamental thesis of *Tract.* is the thesis
of extensionality (chapter I). This has the function of a postulate
from which the 'picture theory' (chapter II), even in its
'psychological' aspects (the relationship between 'propositions'
and 'thought' (ch. III)), the nature of formal concepts and logical
relationships (ch. IV) and the theses on 'solipsism and the
ineffable'(ch. V) are derived. In the final chapter, the strictly
philosophical character of *Tract.* is defined, and some critical
remarks are made on the investigative method adopted by W.
and on the validity of some of his fundamental theses. *Reviews*:
Brown S., PQ, 1966, 16, pp. 78-9; Bubner R., PRd, 1968, 15,
pp. 161-84; Copi I. M., 1971, 80, pp. 530-2; Griffin J., M, 1965,
74, pp. 440-1; Nuchelmans G., FL, 1966, 2, pp. 271-3;
Plochmann G. K., MS, 1968-9, 46, pp. 157-60; Stroll A., JHP,
1967, 5, pp. 190-3.

438. Gill J. H., *W. and religious language*, TT, 21, pp. 59-72.

439. Granger G.-G., *L'argumentation du 'Tractatus'. Systèmes
philosophiques et métastructures*, in *Etudes sur l'histoire
de la philosophie en hommage à M. Guéroult*, Paris,
Fischbacher, pp. 139-54.

440. Griffin J., *W.'s logical atomism*, London, New York, Oxford University Press, 1964, pp. 164.

A study and interpretation of *Tract.* particularly centred on the representative theory of language, on the nature of 'atomic propositions', of objects, and of states of affairs. On the whole, G. proposes a reading of *Tract.* in a realistic rather than an 'epistemological' sense. The simple (indefinable) elements of language correspond not to sense data, but to substances from the outside world, whose existence is rendered necessary for purely logical, *a priori* reasons, in their capacity as a condition for the existence of a language which can describe the world. For the same reason, elementary statements are always relational (according to the interpretation also given by Copi, 1958). The 'atomism' of *Tract.* therefore turns out to be quite different both from that of Russell, and from the inductivism of Carnap, and historically can be much better understood as a development of the models that Hertz had applied to the study of classical mechanics. *Reviews*: Black M., PQ, 1966, 16, pp. 374-6; Blanché R., RPFE, 1967, 157, pp. 420-1; Bubner R., PRd, 1968, 15, pp. 161-84; Bunting I.A., PS, 1967, 16, pp. 363-4; C.C., DH, 1963, n.7-8, p. 259; Hunter J., D, 1965, 3, pp. 461-2; Keyt D., PR, 1965, 74, pp. 229-39; Kutschera F. von, PRd, 1964-5, 12, pp. 291-5; Rankin K.W., AJP, 1964, 42, pp. 439-44; Sloman A., PB, 1964, 5, pp. 8-10; Trinchero M., RF, 1967, 58, pp. 487-91.

441. Hannay A., *Was W. a psychologist?*, I, 7, pp. 379-86.

A critique of the interpretation given by Bogen, 1964, relating to the nature of a *Gedanke* in *Tract.*

442. Keyt D., *W.'s picture theory of language*, PR, 73, pp. 493-511. Reprinted in Copi and Beard (eds.), 1966.

The picture theory of *Tract.* does not manage to resolve the 'paradox' which has always accompanied this kind of theory: i.e. the inability to explain how, in relational propositions, three signs appear, while in the facts that these propositions represent, only two elements can be found.

443. Levi A. W., *W. as dialectician*, JP, 61, pp. 127-39. Reprinted in Fann (ed.), 1967.

A certain unity needs to be re-established in the development of W.'s thought. This unity can be detected in his dialectical research into the clarification of language in an effort to overcome the crisis of communication characteristic of our time.

444. Levison A. B., *W. and logical necessity*, I, 7, pp. 367–73.
The conventionalist interpretation of W. suggested by Dummett,
1959, is without foundation. In reality, W. does not deny 'logical
rules', nor that the results of the application of these rules are
'logically necessary', but rather attempts to explain the nature
and limits of these concepts.

445. Levison A. B., *W. and logical laws*, PQ, 14, pp. 345–54.
Reprinted in a modified form in Fann (ed.), 1967, and in
Canfield (ed.), 1986, vol. X.
The conventionalist and normative interpretations which have
been given for *R.F.M.* (for example, Nell, 1961, Cowan, 1961,
Dummett, 1959) rest on a common conceptual confusion
between the 'rules of a game' (which can have an optional
character) and principles on the basis of which every possible
game is played (for example, the laws of inference). W. did not
mean to deny the rigorous necessity for these principles, but only
to understand their nature.

446. Maslow A., Letter to PR, 73, p. 290.
A reply to the criticisms of Rhees, 1963.

447. Munz P., *Popper and W.*, in *The critical approach to
science and philosophy*, ed. by M.A. Bunge, London, and
New York, Free Press, 1964, pp. 82–91.

448. Narveson A., *The ontology of the Tractatus*, D, 3,
pp. 273–83.

449. Paul R., *B's perplexity*, A, 25, pp. 176–8.
P.I. 41, which examines an elementary linguistic game, provides
a convincing critique of *Tract.*'s theory of proper names.

450. Pitcher G., *The philosophy of W.*, Englewood Cliffs, N.J.,
Prentice-Hall, 1964, pp. 340. German translation, Freiburg
and Munich, Alber, 1967.
As P. himself explains, the aim of the work is to provide an
introduction to W.'s thought through an examination of *Tract.*
(part I) and of *P.I.* (part II). Of the former an interpretation is
given in which the relationship with Russell's theory of
descriptions is highlighted, and which, in regard to the
ontological aspects of the picture theory, comes close to the
theses of Copi, 1958: objects are 'simple permanent particulars',
and do not include relations and properties; a *Sachverhalt* is a
possible state of things and is distinguished from a fact. The part

devoted to *P.I.* makes a particular examination of W.'s
subsequent rejection of 'logical atomism', the critique of
essentialism, and the extension of these theses to the analysis
of language relating to sensations. In a final chapter, devoted
to method, a number of analogies are found, from this point of
view, between the first and the second W., and a summary of
his philosophical itinerary is given. *Reviews:* Ambrose A., PPR,
1964-5, 25, pp. 423-5; Bennett J., P, 1966, 41, pp. 86-7; Griffin
J., M, 1965, 74, pp. 438-40; Hinst P., PRd 1968, 15, pp. 51-66;
Horstmann H., DZP, 1968, 16, pp. 1152-7; Hunter J. F. M.,
D, 1964-5, 3, pp. 463-4; Keyt D., PR, 1965, 74, pp. 229-39;
Moss J. M. B., PB, 1966, 6, pp. 20-3; Narveson A., PSc, 1967,
34, pp. 80-2; Nuchelmans G., FL, 1965, 20, pp. 552-3; Rhees
R., R, 1966, 8, pp. 180-93; Shoemaker S., JP, 1966, 63,
pp. 354-8; Stenius E., PQ, 1966, 16, pp. 373-4.

451. Plochmann G. K., *A note on Harrison's notes on 'Das Mystische'*, SJP, 2, pp. 130-2 (cf. Harrison, 1963).

452. Riverso E., *Il pensiero di L.W.*, Naples, Libreria Scientifica Editrice, 1964. 2nd ed. revised and enlarged, 1970, pp. 484.
The updating of the 2nd edition is above all concerned with the
examination of writings of W. published in the meantime, but,
as R. warns, it leaves substantially unchanged the interpretation
given in the 1st edition. The first part of this is based on the
examination of *Tract.* (whose difference from the neoempiricism
and atomism of Russell is brought out), and the second part on
W.'s 'new philosophy', of which *P.I.* and *R.F.M.* are examples.
The passage from the one phase to the other is shown above
all by the way that W. goes beyond the ontological conception
of *Tract.*, and by the 'dissolution of solipsism'. In examining
these themes, frequent references are made to Husserl and to
phenomenological issues. *Reviews*: Strawson P. F., M, 1966, 75,
p. 447; Frongia G., BBSMS, 1971, 13-16, pp. 223-5.

453. Robinson G., *Following and formalization*, M, 73, pp. 46-63.
An examination of the foundations of logical necessity, in the
light of the first part of *R.F.M.* R. aims to show that the
opposition between 'conventionalism' and 'realism' (especially
Russell and Carnap) often rests on imprecise and preconceived
distinctions. Thus Dummett's conventionalist interpretation (see
1959) turns out to be unfounded. In reality W., placing

the notion of 'form of life' at the base of the necessity of grammatical statements, adopts a solution of an Aristotelian type (pp. 50–57).

454. Shwayder D. S., *Gegenstände and other matters*, I, 7, pp. 387–413. Reprinted in Canfield (ed.), 1986, vol. II.
A long critical review of the 'realistic' interpretation of *Tract.* given by Griffin, 1964. S. dwells in particular on the nature of the picture theory, on the notions of 'object' (pp. 402–412) (which Griffin understands as a simple material particle not subject to change) and of *Gedanke.*

455. Thomson J. J., *Private languages,* APQ, 1, pp. 20–31. Reprinted in *The philosophy of mind*, ed. by S. Hampshire, New York, Harper & Row, 1966; in Jones (ed.), 1981; in Canfield (ed.), 1986, vol. IX.
The interpretation given by 'W.'s followers' (especially Malcolm, 1954) concerning private language is based on the acceptance of a principle of verification that W. would never have shared.

456. von Morstein P., *W.s Untersuchungen des Wortes 'Schmerz'*, AfP, 13, pp. 132–40.
On the problem of verifying, and on the grammar of statements relating to sensations of pain.

457. Weiler G., *The 'world' of actions and the 'world' of events*, RIP, 18, pp. 439–57.
W. (pp. 440–47), Kant and Husserl are united in a common search for the definition of a 'world' understood as a unity between its optional and factual components (between reasons and causes).

458. Wienpahl P. D., *W. and the naming relation*, I, 7, pp. 329–47.
It is impossible to find in ordinary language examples of the entities postulated in *Tract.* (nouns, elementary propositions, etc.). In *P.I.* W. re-examines the problem of naming in order to overcome these difficulties.

459. Winch P., *Understanding a primitive society*, APQ, 1, pp. 307–24. Reprinted in his *Ethics and action*, London, Routledge & Kegan Paul, 1972; and in Canfield (ed.), 1986, vol. XIII.

460. Wolgast E. H., *W. and criteria*, I, 7, pp. 348–66.

The notion of 'criterion' is seen in relation to the definition and expression of mental states, and to scepticism regarding the minds of others.

461. Zemach E., *W.'s philosophy of the mystical*, RM, 18, pp. 39–57. Reprinted in Copi and Beard (ed.), 1966, and in Canfield (ed.), 1986, vol. III.
The mystical conclusions which *Tract.* reaches are seen as part of the work as a unitary whole and cannot be the object of a separate study. From this point of view, Z. examines the notion of God, ethics and aesthetics in *Tract.*

462. Zemach E., *Material and logical space in W.'s Tractatus*, Me, 16, pp. 127–40.
Z.'s aim is to show that, in *Tract.*, there cannot be a monadic *Sachverhalt*, and that every *Tatsache* is the combination of more than one (existing) *Sachverhalt*. In arguing the first thesis, he criticizes Sellars, 1962; for the second he discusses Russell's interpretation, 1922.

1965

463. Aaron R. I., *W.'s theory of universals*, M, 74, pp. 249–51.
Objections to Bambrough's thesis, 1960, which states that W. solved the problem of universals by means of his theory of family resemblances.

464. Anscombe G. E. M., *Retractation*, A, 26, pp. 33–6. Reprinted in her *The collected philosophical papers*, vol. I, 1981.
Are the objects of *Tract.* individuals or do they also include universals (properties and relations)? While analysing the reasons which make an unequivocal answer to this question difficult, A. returns to a discussion of a number of aspects of her own interpretation (see Anscombe, 1959), making a particular examination of Ramsey's article, 'Universals', 1931. She considers that, in any event, the reply made by Stenius, 1960, concerning this topic is incorrect. Cf. Stenius's answer, 1966.

465. Apel K.-O., *Die Entfaltung der 'sprachanalytischen' Philosophie und das Problem der Geisteswissenschaften*, PJ, 72, pp. 239–89. Reprinted in his *Transformation der Philosophie*, see 1973.

The elements which bring analytical philosophy close to hermeneutics. References to W. (*Tract.* and later works).

466. Bunting I. A., *Some difficulties in Stenius' account of the independence of atomic states of affairs*, AJP, 43, pp. 368–75. (Cf. Stenius, 1960.)

467. Campbell K., *Family resemblance predicates*, APQ, 2, pp. 238–44. Reprinted in Canfield (ed.), 1986, vol. V.
A critical examination of the thesis that there can be proper predicates which are applied to objects that do not have elements in common. An attempt, amongst other things, to clarify what the expression: 'having something in common' can mean in logical terms.

468. Chihara C. S. and **Fodor J. A.**, *Operationalism and ordinary language: a critique of W.*, APQ, 2, pp. 281–95. Reprinted in Pitcher (ed.), 1966; in Morick (ed.), 1967; in Canfield (ed.), 1986, vol. VII.
In the first part of the article C. and F. show how W., in his later writings, supports a theory in which an 'operationalist' viewpoint with regard to meaning and rules of confirmation acts as a support to his study of psychological language. In this context W. adopts a weak form of 'logical behaviourism', particularly in his criticism of scepticism concerning the knowledge of other people's minds, and in his distinction between 'criteria' and 'symptoms'. In the second part of the article C. and F. criticize the 'operationalist' point of view, demonstrating its inadequacy, for example, in the analysis of dreams.

469. Cook J. W., *W. on privacy*, PR, 74, pp. 281–314. Reprinted in Pitcher (ed.), 1966; in Klemke (ed.), 1971; in Canfield (ed.) 1986, vol. IX.
An examination of the idea of 'private sensation' going against some of the current interpretations of W. (e.g. Castañeda in Rollins, 1962).

470. Cornforth M., *Marxism and linguistic philosophy*, London, Lawrence & Wishart; New York, International Publishers, 1965.
Many critical references, made from a Marxist viewpoint, to W. and to the philosophical trends associated with him. Cf. in

particular ch. VI (pp. 111–130) which contains a critique of *Tract.*, seen in a neopositivistic light, and the section 'Linguistic philosophy' (pp. 133–188), on the 'philosophical therapy' of W. and 'his school'.

471. Egidi R., *Due tesi di W. sui fondamenti della matematica*, GCFI, 44, pp. 527–38. Reprinted in Egidi, 1971.

The two theses under examination are concerned with the impossibility of defining the concept of number and of deriving mathematics from logic. The implicit and explicit criticisms of the theory of *Principia mathematica*, which are contained in *Tract.*, are analysed, as are the implications of the rejection of the Russellian doctrine of classes.

472. Gargani A. G., *Linguaggio e società in Moore e W.*, GCFI, 44, pp. 98–118.

Analogies and differences between Moore and the 'second W.'. In both W. and Moore there prevails a static and conservative conception of philosophical investigation. The truisms of common sense are introduced in Moore as 'autonomous and unmodifiable structures'; analogously, W.'s 'antimentalistic polemic' leads to a passive and uncritical acceptance of the current rules of language.

473. Heller E., *W. and Nietzsche*, in his *An artist's journey into the interior and other essays*, New York, Random House, 1965, pp. 201–226. Reprinted in Canfield (ed.), 1986, vol. XV.

474. Hintikka J., *Are logical truths analytic?* PR, 74, pp. 178–203.

Criticizing the thesis that logical truths are analytic, H. examines (pp. 181ff.) the *Tract.* solution, according to which these truths are tautologies. He then considers the applicability of this thesis to the theory of quantifications.

475. Kerr F., *Language as hermeneutic in later W.*, TF, 27, pp. 491–520.

See also criticisms by M. Gosselin, *ibid.*, 1966, 28, pp. 72–81, and reply by Kerr, ibid., pp. 84–89.

476. Keyt D., *A new interpretation of the Tractatus examined*, PR, 74, pp. 229–39.

A comparison and a critique of the interpretations of *Tract.* given

by Griffin, 1964, and Pitcher, 1964. K. dwells in particular on
the nature of objects and of elementary propositions.

477. Long T. A., *The problem of pain and contextual
implication*, PPR, 26, pp. 106-11.
A critique of the distinction made by Malcolm, 1954, between
criterion and symptom, in relation to the problem of knowing
the minds of others.

478. Mandelbaum M., *Family resemblances and generalization concerning the arts*, APQ, 2, pp. 219-28.
M. applies W.'s theory on family resemblances to the
examination of the notion of art.

479. Mood J. J., *Poetic languaging and primal thinking; a
study of Barfield, W., and Heidegger*, 'Encounter', 26,
pp. 417-33.

480. Naess A., *Moderne filosofer: Carnap, W., Heidegger,
Sartre*, Copenhagen and Stockholm, Almqvist & Wiksell,
1965. E.T. Chicago, Ill., University of Chicago Press;
London, Phoenix Books, 1968.
A brief presentation of the biography and work of the four
authors, taken as representative of twentieth-century
philosophy. The section devoted to W. (pp. 67-171, 1968
edition) is composed of a brief examination of *Tract.* and *P.I.*,
with a final chapter dealing with their influence on 'linguistic
philosophy'. In the final paragraph (pp. 167-171) there is a
comparison with Heidegger. *Review*: A. Manser, M, 1971, 80,
pp. 623-6.

481. Nelson, J. O., *The influence of the later W. on American
philosophy*, in F.H. Donnell Jr, (ed.), *Aspects of
contemporary American philosophy*, Würzburg, Vienna,
Physica Verlag, pp. 50-60.

482. Olscamp P. J., *W.'s refutation of skepticism*, PPR, 26,
pp. 239-47.
A critical examination of W.'s argumentation against scepticism
concerning the knowledge of other minds, in the light of the
distinction between 'criterion' and 'symptom'. Among others,
Malcolm's interpretation, 1954, is discussed.

483. Perkins M., *Two arguments against a private language*,

JP, 62, pp. 443-58. Reprinted in Morick (ed.), 1967.
An interpretation of W.'s private language argument, based on
P.I. 258-9 and a discussion of its scope and validity.

484. Pitcher G., *W., nonsense, and Lewis Carroll*,
'Massachusetts Review', 6, pp. 591-611. Reprinted in Fann
(ed.), 1967; in Shanker (ed.), 1986, vol. IV; in Canfield (ed.),
1986, vol. V.
A constant element in W.'s thought is his interest in the nature
of nonsense. P. looks at the deep affinity which links him, in
this respect, to L. Carroll.

485. Plochmann G. K., *Mathematics in W.'s Tractatus*, PM,
2, pp. 1-12.

486. Rhees R., *Some developments in W.'s view of ethics*, PR,
74, pp. 17-26. Reprinted in Canfield (ed.), 1986, vol. III.
In the light of W.'s lecture on ethics, published in the same issue
of the review (pp. 3-12), and of Waismann's notes (*ibid.*,
pp. 12-16, see works by W.), an examination of W.'s
developments in ethics as regards *Tract.* R. also refers to some
notes drawn from a conversation with W. (1942) on the conflict
between duties (pp. 22-25).

487. Richter V., *Logik in W.s Tractatus* and *Von Brouwers
Intuitionismus zu W.s Spätwerk*, in his *Untersuchungen
zur operativen Logik der Gegenwart*, Freiburg and Munich,
Alber, 1965, pp. 15-52.

488. Saran A. K., *A W.ian sociology?*, Et, 75, pp. 195-200.
W.'s writings could have important implications for a
philosophical sociology, but not in the sense indicated by Winch,
1958. Winch's thesis, indeed, is founded on an erroneous
understanding of the nature of philosophy in W., and of the
nature of scientific investigation.

489. Stegmüller W., *L.W. als Ontologe, Isomorphietheoretiker,
Transzendentalphilosoph und Konstruktivist*, PRd, 13,
pp. 116-52.
A critical examination of Stenius (1960) and *R.F.M.*, dealing in
particular with a number of comparisons between W. and Kant.

490. Stegmüller W., *L.W.*, in his *Hauptströmungen der
Gegenwartsphilosophie*, 3rd ed., Stuttgart, Kröner, 1965,
pp. 526-696. E.T. in his *Main currents in contemporary*

German, British and American philosophy, Bloomington, Indiana University Press; Dordrecht, Reidel, 1970, pp. 394-527.

491. Stern K., *Private language and scepticism*, JP, 60, pp. 745-59.

Contrary to what many interpreters of W. have maintained, his thesis about the impossibility of private language is in the tradition of Cartesian scepticism and confronts problems which have received an appropriate analysis in the sphere of American pragmatism, in particular from Peirce.

492. Stroud B., *W. and logical necessity*, PR, 74, pp. 504-18. Reprinted in Pitcher (ed.), 1966; in Klemke (ed.), 1971; in Shanker (ed.), 1986, vol. III; in Canfield (ed.), 1986, vol. X.

Controverting Dummett, 1959, S. suggests an interpretation of *R.F.M.* which places it halfway between Platonism and constructivism and salvages the objectivity of logical inference.

493. Waismann F., *The principles of linguistic philosophy*, edited by R. Harré, London, Macmillan; New York, St. Martin's Press, 1965. German original, *Logik, Sprache, Philosophie*, edited by G. P. Baker and B. McGuinness, Stuttgart, Reclam, 1976.

This work was originally written halfway through the 1930s, to spread W.'s ideas, though afterwards modified. It contains a chapter (pp. 304-322) in which the theory of the isomorphism between language and reality in *Tract.* and in Schlick is criticized. The original German was published subsequently and includes as an 'Appendix' a new chapter on 'Hypotheses' (see, for an English translation of this, Waismann, 1977) and a 'Nachwort' by the editors in which various aspects of the relation between Waismann and W. are analysed.

494. Winch P., *Can a good man be harmed?* PAS, 66, pp. 55-70. Reprinted in his *Ethics and action,* London, Routledge & Kegan Paul, 1972; in Canfield (ed.), 1986, vol. XIV.

What is the relationship linking the moral notion of good and that of punishment? In examining this question Winch (pp. 63ff.) attempts to explain the sense of W.'s expression 'I am absolutely safe' (*L.E.*). References to Kierkegaard.

1966

495. Ambrose A., *Essays in analysis*, London, George Allen & Unwin; New York, Humanities Press, 1966, pp. 262.
A number of articles by A. on W. are here republished. Cf. Ambrose, 1937, 1955, 1959, 1966.

496. Ambrose A., *W. on universals*, in W. E. Kennick and M. Lazerowitz (eds.), *Metaphysics: readings and reappraisals*, Englewood Cliffs, N.J., Prentice-Hall, pp. 80–91. Also printed in her *Essays in analysis*, see 1966; in Fann (ed.), 1967; in Canfield (ed.), 1986, vol. V.
A. makes an examination, partly in the light of the notes taken during the 1933–34 lectures, of W.'s critique of the problem of universals. A correct understanding of this aspect, she maintains, shows that many current interpretations of the nature of W.'s philosophical inquiry are unfounded.

497. Ambrose A. and **Lazerowitz M.**, *W.: philosophy, experiment and proof*, in *British philosophy in the mid-century*, edited by C. A. Mace, London, George Allen & Unwin, 1966. Partly reprinted in Fann (ed.), 1967; fully reprinted in Canfield (ed.), 1986, vol. V.
A presentation of W.'s mature work. 1st part: its relationship with contemporary English philosophy (Moore) and the problems of philosophy of the mind; 2nd part: the nature of logical necessity and of proof in mathematics. Reference is made to notes taken by Ambrose during the 1939 lectures, and to *Y.B.*

498. Apel K.-O., *W. und das Problem des hermeneutischen Verstehens*, 'Zeitschrift für Theologie und Kirche', 63, pp. 49–87. Reprinted in Apel, 1973.
W.'s development from the neopositivism of *Tract.* to a hermeneutics which brings him closer to the phenomenological method of Husserl and Heidegger.

499. Casey J., *W. and the philosophy of criticism*, in his *The language of criticism*, London, Methuen, 1966, pp. 1–34.
An analysis of the implications for aesthetics and ethics of W.'s conception of language, of his treatment of the 'seeing as' problem and of his philosophical method.

500. Copi I. M. and **Beard R. W.** (eds.), *Essays on W.'s*

Tractatus, New York, Macmillan; London, Routledge & Kegan Paul, pp. 414.

A collection of 30 articles dealing with various aspects of *Tract.* and ranging from 1923 (Ramsey) to 1964 (Keyt), which have had a notable influence on discussions about the work. *Reviews*: Bunting I. A., PS, 1968, 17, pp. 273–4; Copleston F. C., HJ, 1968, 9, pp. 344–6; Gale R. M., PPR, 1968, 29, pp. 146–7.

501. Cornman J. W., *Metaphysics, reference and language*, New Haven, Conn., Yale University Press, 1966, pp. 288.

See especially ch. 4, 'Linguistic references and external questions', sections on picture theory of meaning.

502. Diamond C., *Secondary sense*, PAS, 67, pp. 189–208. Reprinted in Canfield (ed.), 1986, vol. XIV.

What W. calls, in *L.C.*, the 'absolute sense' of ethical and religious terms presents a number of logical analogies with what he later called, in *B.B.B.* and in *P.I.*, the 'secondary sense' of words.

503. Donagan A., *W. on sensation*, in Pitcher (ed.), 1966, pp. 324–51. Reprinted in Canfield (ed.), 1986, vol. IX.

W.'s analysis of the language of sensations, in its double opposition to 'Cartesianism' and 'behaviourism'. Pitcher's interpretation (1964) is criticized.

504. Dufrenne M., *W. et Husserl*, in his *Jalons*, The Hague, Martinus Nijhoff, 1966, pp. 188–207.

505. Fairbanks M., *W. and James*, NS, 40, pp. 331–40.

506. Filiasi Carcano P., *Introduzione alla lettura del 'Tractatus' di W.*, Rome, De Santis, 1966, pp. 115.

507. Gargani A. G., *Linguaggio ed esperienza in L.W.*, Florence, Le Monnier, 1966, pp. XII, 504.

The aim of the work is to reconstruct the development of W.'s thought from *Tract.* to the 'second phase', represented by *P.I.* According to G., this development is distinguished by the passage from a 'logico-linguistic apparatus which supposes a closed system of meanings rigidly defined by experience' to a theory which assumes 'plans of linguistic articulation made available by the forms of life and systems of behaviour of humanity'. While the examination of the 'first phase' is centred upon the 'theory of language as representation' (chapter II, in which Frege's influence and that of the dynamic models of H. Hertz are highlighted), the 'second' W. is above all seen in relation to the semantic criticism of essentialism (a criticism which W. derived 'from intuitionism and from conventionalist mathematical constructivism', see ch. IV) and to the problem of a private language (chs. V–VI); his attitude to this last is seen as being in antithesis to the solipsism of *Tract.* and to neopositivistic phenomenalism. *Reviews*: A.M., RH, 1968, 22, p. 144; Ferriani M., RCSF, 1969, 24, pp. 101–4; Marietti A. K., EP, 1968, p. 459; Novielli V., F, 1968, 19, pp. 321–30; Rieser M., JHP, 1970, 8, pp. 108–11; Trinchero M., RF, 1968, 59, pp. 225–30.

508. Giacomini U., *Appunti sull'etica di W.*, AA, 92, pp. 72–81.

509. Gill J. H., *W.'s concept of truth*, IPQ, 6, pp. 71–80.
The notion of truth in *P.I.* and therefore the objectivity of knowledge rest on the fact that a linguistic game, in whose terms truth itself is defined, is correlated to a 'form of life' which does not have an arbitrary character.

510. Hackstaff L. H., *A note on W.'s truth-function-generating operation in Tractatus 6*, M, 75, pp. 255–6.
A critique of Anscombe's interpretation, 1959, of this aspect of *Tract.*

511. Hallie P. P., *W.'s exclusion of metaphysical nonsense*, PQ, 16, pp. 97–112.
Starting from section 500 of *P.I.*, a critical examination of the notion of nonsense and of W.'s 'therapy' for the illnesses of language.

512. Harris R., *The semantics of self-description*, A, 27, p. 144.
An analysis and interpretation of *Tract.* 3.332.

513. Hawkins B., *Note on a doctrine of Frege and W.*, M, 75, pp. 583–5.
The 'doctrine of Frege' examined concerns the general form of the proposition (*Tract.* 6). A critique of Anscombe's theses, 1959, on this theme.

514. Hester M. B., *Metaphor and aspect seeing*, JAAC, 25, pp. 205–12.
The theory of aspects in *P.I.* applied to the study of poetic metaphor.

515. Hester M. B., *W.'s analysis of 'I know I am in pain'*, SJP, 4, pp. 274–9.

516. Janik A. S., *Schopenhauer and the early W.*, PS (I), 15, pp. 76-95. Reprinted in Janik, 1985.
An examination of the influence of Schopenhauer on *Tract.* and *N.B.*, with the aim of bridging the gap between the logical W. and the mystical W.

517. Katz J. J., *Ordinary language philosophy*, in his *Philosophy of language*, New York, Harper & Row, 1966, pp. 68-93.
The later W., considered to be amongst the founders of the philosophy of language, is examined as an example of the inadequacy of philosophers in the study of language.

518. Kenny A., *Cartesian privacy*, in Pitcher, 1966, pp. 352-70. Reprinted in his *The anatomy of the soul*, Oxford, Blackwell, 1974, pp. 113-28; in Canfield (ed.), 1986, vol. IX.
The innovation introduced by Descartes into the philosophy of mind consists essentially in identifying what is mental with the private. W.'s criticism of Cartesian dualism consists in highlighting the public aspects linked to the use of language.

519. McGuinness B. F., *The mysticism of the Tractatus*, PR, 75, pp. 305-28. Reprinted in Canfield (ed.), 1986, vol. III.
An examination of the particular kind of mysticism found in the *Tract.*, of its genesis, of its analogies with and differences from Russell ('Mysticism and logic') and Schopenhauer, its relationship to logic, ethics, solipsism, and the experience of feeling absolutely safe.

520. Mundle C. W. K., *Private language and W.'s kind of behaviorism'*, PQ, 16, pp. 35-46. Reprinted in Jones (ed.), 1971.
Despite the fact that W. claims he does not defend philosophical theories, he nevertheless adopts a particular form of behaviourism which M., from an analytical viewpoint, rejects. Criticisms of Rhees, 1954.

521. O'Brien D., *The unity of W.'s thought*, IPQ, 6, pp. 45-70. Reprinted in Fann (ed.), 1967.
In a controversy with the kind of interpretation upheld for example by Urmson, 1956, O'B. inquires into the elements of unity between *Tract.* and the later writings. These are located in the conception of philosophy as an 'activity' rather than a source of metaphysical theories.

522. Osborne H., *W. on aesthetics*, BJA, 6, pp. 385-90.
A critical examination of *L.C.*

523. Pears D. F., *W. and Austin*, in *British analytical philosophy*, edited by B. Williams and A. Montefiore, London, Routledge & Kegan Paul, 1966, pp. 17-39. Reprinted in Canfield (ed.), 1986, vol. XV.
For both W. and Austin the analysis of language is a way through to the solution of philosophical problems. Nevertheless, unlike Austin, W. remains much more tied to the classical philosophical problems, and in particular to the continental tradition (Kant).

524. Pitcher G., (ed.), *The 'Philosophical investigations'*, New York, Doubleday, 1966; London, Macmillan, 1968, pp. 510.
A collection of writings, most of which have been previously published: A. M. Quinton, 1964 (extracts); P. F. Strawson, 1954; N. Malcolm, 1954; P. Feyerabend, 1955; S. Cavell, 1962; R. Bambrough, 1960; H. Khatchadourian, 1957-58; R. Albritton, 1959; A. J. Ayer and R. Rhees, 1954; J. W. Cook, 1965; A. Donagan, 1966, pp. 324-51 (here published for the first time); A. Kenny, 1966, pp. 352-70 (here published for the first time); N. Malcolm, extracts from *Knowledge and certainty*, 1963; C. S. Chihara and J. A. Fodor, 1965; M. Dummett, 1959; C. S. Chihara 1963 and 1960-1; B. Stroud, 1965.

525. Rankin K. W., *W. on meaning, understanding and intending*, APQ, 3, pp. 1-13.
A critical examination of the relationship between an understanding of the meaning of a linguistic expression and its use.

526. Rosenberg J. F., *New perspectives on the Tractatus*, D, 4, pp. 506-17.

527. Specht E. K., *W. und das Problem der Aporetik*, KS, 57, pp. 309-22.

528. Stegmüller W., *Eine modelltheoretische Präzisierung der W.schen Bildtheorie*, NDJFL, 7, pp. 181-95. E.T. in his *Collected papers*, vol. 1, Dordrecht and Boston, Mass., Reidel, 1977, pp. 137-53.

529. Stocker M. A. G., *Memory and the private language argument*, PQ, 16, pp. 47-53.

A critique of W.'s argument concerning private language in the interpretation of it given by Malcolm, 1954.

530. Tanner M., *W. and aesthetics*, 'Oxford Review', no. 3, pp. 14–24.

531. Thyssen J., *Sprachregelung und Sprachspiel*, ZPF, 20, pp. 3–22.
A critical note to *P.I.*

532. van de Vate D., *Other minds and the uses of language*, APQ, 3, pp. 250–4.
A critical examination of W.'s thesis which states that 'language does not have an essence', and of his argument concerning solipsism.

1967

533. *The linguistic turn: recent essays in philosophical method*, ed. by R. Rorty, Chicago, Ill., and London, University of Chicago Press, 1967, pp. 393.
Many of the 28 essays collected here refer to the analytical method in philosophy and W.'s contribution to it. See in particular the reprinted Schlick, 1933, Carnap, 1934, Copi, 1949, Bergmann, 1953, Carnap, 1950, Ryle, 1931, Wisdom, 1937, Shapere, 1960. In an introductory essay by R. Rorty, *Metaphilosophical difficulties of linguistic philosophy*, pp. 1–39, consideration is given to aspects of the relation between W. and such contemporaries as Husserl and Heidegger.

534. Allaire E. B., *Things, relations and identity*, PSc, vol. 34, pp. 260–72.

535. Antiseri D., *Dopo W. dove va la filosofia analitica*, Rome, Abete, 1967, pp. 485.
An examination of *Tract.*, of the intermediate writings and of *P.I.* is contained in the central sections of the volume (chapters 2–6).

536. Apel K.-O., *W. und Heidegger. Die Frage nach dem Sinn von Sein und der Sinnlosigkeitsverdacht gegen alle Metaphysik*, PJ, 75, pp. 56–94. Reprinted in O. Pöggler (ed.), *Heidegger. Perspektiven zur Deutung seines Werks*,

Cologne and Berlin, Kiepenheuer und Witsch, 1970,
pp. 258-96; in Apel's *Transformation der Philosophie*, see
1973.
The analogies and differences between the two philosophers are
brought out by means of a comparison between, on the one
hand, *Tract.* and Heidegger's fundamental ontology, and on the
other, *P.I.* and Heidegger's critical metaphysics.

537. Apel K.-O., *The origin of the ambivalence in W.'s
Tractatus*, in his *Analytic philosophy of language and the
'Geisteswissenschaften'* (Foundations of language,
Supplementary series, vol. 4), Dordrecht, Reidel, 1967,
pp. 4-13.

538. Barrett C., Paton M., Blocker H. (symposium), *W. and
problems of objectivity in aesthetics*, BJA, 7, pp. 158-74.
Ba., with reference to *L.C.*, dwells in particular on the distinction
between an aesthetic explanation and a psychological one, in
relation to W.'s search for objectivity in critical judgement. P.
examines the nature of rules in aesthetic judgement, and
particularly W.'s thesis which states that correctness is not the
key concept in aesthetics. Bl. considers the possibility of applying
the theory of aspects to the aesthetic judgement of painting.

539. Carse J. P., *W.'s lion and Christology*, TT, 24, pp. 148-59.

540. Coder D., *Family resemblances and paradigm cases*, D,
6, pp. 355-66.

541. Cristaldi M., *Nota sulla possibilità di un'ontologia del
linguaggio in W. e in Heidegger*, 'Teoresi', 22, pp. 47-86.

542. De Mauro T., *L.W.: his place in the development of
semantics*, Dordrecht, Reidel; New York, Humanities
Press, 1967, pp. 63.
Here a number of theses already set out in *Introduzione alla
semantica* (Bari, Laterza, 1965) are developed. According to De
M., *Tract.* carries to extreme and paradoxical conclusions the
theory of language as naming, whose origins go back to Aristotle,
and whose developments can be traced throughout the whole of
the history of semantics. *P.I.* (see especially De M.'s last chapter),
on the other hand, develops a radical and systematic critique
of this concept, and reflects, together with the contributions
made by Saussure and Martinet, the rise of a new form of
semantics. *Reviews*: Bastable J. D., PS(I), 29, p. 258; Geach P. T.,
BJPS, 20, pp. 277-9; Leyvraz J.-P., RTP, 1970, pp. 204-5.

543. Dilman I. and **Ishiguro H.** (symposium), *Imagination*, PAS(SV), 41, pp. 19–36, 37–56.

In an analysis of the notion of imagination, particularly in relation to artistic activity, D. considers (pp. 22–31) the theory of aspects in *P.I.* and *B.B.B.* I. replies.

544. Dorfles G., *Appunti per un'estetica W.iana*, RE, 12, pp. 134–50. Also published in *L'estetica del mito (da Vico a W.)*, Milan, Mursia, 1967.

545. Dwyer P. J., *Thomistic first principles and W.'s philosophy of language*, PS(I), 16, pp. 7–29.

546. Engel S. M., *W.'s 'foundations' and its reception*, APQ, 4, pp. 257–68. Reprinted in Shanker (ed.), 1986, vol. III.

547. Engelmann P., *Letters from W. with a memoir*, ed. by B. F. McGuinness, Oxford, Blackwell, 1967, pp. 150. German edition: Vienna and Munich, Oldenburg, 1970. Italian edition: Florence, La Nuova Italia, 1970.

The first part of the book (pp. 1–59) contains in German with an English translation *en face* the text of about 50 letters from W. to his friend and disciple E. falling into the period 1916–37 (see list of W.'s writings above). In the second part (pp. 60–136) E. analyses and interprets the personality of W. and gives an account of their relationship. The chapters are: 'W. in Olmütz'; 'Religious matters'; 'Literature, music and cinema'; 'Observations on the *Tract.*'; 'W.'s family'; 'Kraus, Loos and W.'; 'Wordless faith'. In a concluding 'Editor's appendix' (pp. 137–44) McGuinness gives further details of the period, of the family surroundings of W., of his relations with Ficker, Loos, and Schlick, and of the history of the publication of *Tract. Reviews*: see under 'Reviews of W.'s Own Writings'.

548. Fann K. T., *A W. bibliography: writings by and about him*, IPQ, 7, pp. 311–39.

The most extensive general bibliography published up to that date. Successive additions bringing it up to date are contained in Fann, 1969, and in *Actes du colloque*, etc., 1969.

549. Fann K. T. (ed.), *W., the man and his philosophy*, New York, Dell, 1967; Atlantic Highlands, N.J., Humanities, 1978; Hassocks, Sussex, Harvester, 1978.

A collection of 29 essays, republished here sometimes in modified or shortened forms, on various aspects of W.'s biography and thought. All of them have been already considered above. The only contribution which is partly original is the one by Mays, 1967.

550. Fodor J. A., *Meaning, convention and the Blue Book*, in J. J. McIntosh and S. C. Coval (eds.), *The business of reason*, London, Routledge & Kegan Paul, 1967, pp. 73-94. Reprinted in Canfield (ed.), 1986, vol. VI.

551. Gill J. H., *'W.'s 'Philosophical investigations'*, IPQ, 7, pp. 305-10.
An index, divided into chapters and paragraphs, of the themes confronted in *P.I.*

552. Gill J. H., *W. on the use of 'I'*, SJP, 5, pp. 26-35.

553. Granger G.-G., *Sur le concept du langage dans le Tractatus*, 'Word', 23, pp. 196-207.

554. Gustafson D. F., *On Pitcher's account of 'Investigations'*, §43, PPR, 28, pp. 252-8.

555. Gustafson D. F., *A note on a misreading of W.*, A, 28, pp. 143-4.
Donagan, 1966, is merely the latest of the interpreters to misread *P.I.* 246, attributing to W. what belongs to an imaginary (Cartesian) adversary of his.

556. Habermas J., *Zur Logik der Sozialwissenschaften*, PRd, Beiheft 5, pp. 195.
In the section entitled *'Der linguistische Ansatz'* (pp. 124-149), an examination of W.'s philosophy is given from the 'linguistic transcendentalism' of *Tract.* to the analytical method of W.'s later work. This second aspect is examined critically using the interpretation of it given by Winch, 1966.

557. Hallett G., *W.'s definition of meaning as use*, Bronx, N.Y., Fordham University Press, 1967, pp. 210.
After an initial chapter in which he examines the picture theory of *Tract.* and the distinction between *Bedeutung* and *Sinn*, H. follows, in the central sections of the work, W.'s search for a new theory of meaning related to the notion of use. H. maintains that although such a solution is already anticipated in a number of places in *Tract.* and the intermediate writings, it is nevertheless set out in its entirety in *P.I.* In a final chapter, an examination of the critical literature dealing with this argument

and with the various objections to W. is to be found. *Reviews*:
Binkley T., PPR, 1970-1, 31, pp. 429-32; Frank W.A., RM,
1972-3, 26, pp. 160-1; Gill J.H., 'Thought', 1968, 43,
pp. 632-3; Pitcher G., PR, 1969, 78, pp. 555-7; Röper P., HJ,
1968, 9, pp. 427-8; Zaslawsky D., RTP, 1969, 102, pp. 427-8.

558. Henze D. F. and **Saunders J. T.**, *The private-language problem: a philosophical dialogue*, New York, Random House, 1967, pp. 205.

An imaginary dialogue between a supporter of W. and a 'traditionalist' on the possibility of a (logically) private language, in the various senses which this term can assume. These senses are defined in an introduction where the historical importance of the problem is also analysed. *Review:* Holborow L.C., PQ, 1970, 20, pp. 185-6.

559. Hester M. B., *The meaning of poetic metaphor: an analysis in the light of W.'s claim that meaning is use*, The Hague, Mouton, 1967, pp. 229.

Having examined the theory of meaning in late W., H. attempts to apply a number of its elements to the analysis of metaphor. From this point of view, he maintains that W.'s insistence on the public nature of the rules of language compromises the understanding of all that is most characteristic of poetic language. *Review:* Wieck D.T., JAAC, 1969-70, 28, pp. 400-1.

560. High D. M., *Language, persons, and belief. Studies in W.'s 'Philosophical investigations' and religious uses of language*, New York, Oxford University Press, 1967, pp. 216.

H. applies suggestions derived from the examination of the theses on language in *P.I.*, in the first part of his work, to a personal analysis of 'the religious use of language'. In particular, H. dwells upon the uses of 'to believe' in the first and third persons (chapter V, 'Belief utterances'); upon the distinction between 'believe in' and 'believe that' (chapter VI); upon the problem of the justification of religious language and 'fideism' (chapter VII). In this analysis the most frequent references are to authors such as Barth, Tillich, Bultmann. *Reviews:* A.M., RM, 1968, 22, pp. 144-5; Dubois P., RPFE, 1974, 99, pp. 366-7; Dunbar S., RS, 1968-9, 4, pp. 294-7; Griffiths L., P, 1970, 45, pp. 257-8; Hallett G., TS, 1968, 29, pp. 150-2; Weissman D., PPR, 1969, 29, pp. 471-2.

561. Holborow L. C., *W.'s kind of behaviorism?*, PQ, 17, pp. 345-57. Reprinted in Jones (ed.), 1971.
A critique of the behaviourist interpretation of W.'s theses on private language (see Mundle, 1966).

562. Hunter J. F. M., *W.'s theory of linguistic self-sufficiency*, D, 6, pp. 367-78.

563. Johnstone H. W., *On W. on death*, Proceedings of the Seventh Inter-American Congress of Philosophy, Quebec, Les Presses de l'Université Laval, 1967, vol. II, pp. 66-71.

564. Jones J. R., *How do I know who I am?*, PAS(SV), 41, pp. 1-18.
In analysing some aspects of the *cogito* problem, J. examines the concept of the 'ego' in W., especially in connection with the solipsism of *Tract.* (pp. 6-11).

565. Kambartel, F., *Formales und inhaltliches Sprechen (Frege, Hilbert, W.)*, in Gadamer, H. G. (ed.), *Das Problem der Sprache*, Akten Deutscher Kongress für Philosophie, Heidelberg, 1966; Munich, Wilhelm Fink, 1967, pp. 293-312.

566. Knüfermann B., *Theorien W.s in der Bildsprache*, Munich, Willing, 1967, pp. 140.

567. Lenk H., *Zu W.s Theorie der Sprachspiele*, KS, 58, pp. 458-80.
In his theory of language W. does not, as he claims, follow a purely descriptive method, but has to introduce evaluative and normative elements.

568. Lewy C., *A note on the text of the Tractatus*, M, 76, pp. 417-23.
L. has come upon Ramsey's copy of *Tract.* containing corrections of Ogden and Ramsey's translation in W.'s hand. He gives a list of these corrections (some of which have been followed in the 1933 edition of *Tract.*) and advances an hypothesis as to their date.

569. Malcolm N., *The privacy of experience*, in A. Stroll (ed.), *Epistemology: new essays in the theory of knowledge*, New York, Harper & Row, 1967, pp. 129-58.

570. Malcolm N., in *The encyclopedia of philosophy*, ed. by

P. Edwards, vol. 8, London and New York, Macmillan, 1967, pp. 327-40. s.v. *Wittgenstein*.

571. Manser A. R., *Games and family resemblances*, P, 42, pp. 210-24.

Contrary to what Bambrough says, 1960, the concept of 'family resemblance' is not very important in the analysis of the traditional problem of the universals and has only a very limited philosophical interest.

572. Mays W., *Recollections of W.*, in Fann (ed.), 1967, pp. 79-88.

M. attended W.'s lectures in 1940. Memories of the ambience and of the philosopher's personality. In the second part of the article Mays, 1961, is republished.

573. Micheletti M., *Lo Schopenhauerismo di W.*, Bologna, Zanichelli, 1967; 2nd ed., Padua, La Garangola, 1973, pp. 190.

The influence of Schopenhauer in some themes of *Tract.* is described: the picture theory, solipsism, ethics and aesthetics. *Reviews*: Babolin A., RFN, 1973, 65, pp. 630-3; Guerrero Brezzi F., 'Aquinas', 1975, 18, pp. 293-5; L.L., RFN, 1968, 60, pp. 329-30; Pieretti A., 'Studia Patavina', 1969, 16, pp. 177-9; Rossi F., 'Sapienza', 1977, 30, pp. 114-16; Salmona B., GM, 1970, 25, pp. 142-4.

574. Morick H., (ed.), *W. and the problem of other minds*, New York, McGraw-Hill, 1967, pp. 231; Atlantic Highlands, N.J., Humanities Press, 1981.

A collection of reprints of the following writings: Strawson P. F., *Critical notice of W.'s Philosophical investigations,* pp. 3-44 (1954); Malcolm N., *W.'s Philosophical Investigations*, pp. 45-81 (1954); Ayer A. J., Can there be a private language?, pp. 82-96 (1954); Perkins M., Two arguments against a private language, pp. 97-118 (1965); Moore G. E., *From W.'s lectures in 1930-1933*, pp. 119-126 (1954, abstracts); Strawson P. F., *Persons*, pp. 127-153 (1958, abstracts); Wellman C., *W.'s conception of a criterion*, pp. 154-169 (1962); Chihara C. S., and Fodor J. A., *Operationalism and ordinary language: A critique of W.*, pp. 170-202 (1965); Geach P., *Could sensuous experience occur apart from an organism?*, pp. 205-210 (1957, abstracts); Geach P., *The fallacy of Cogito, ergo sum*, pp. 211-214 (ibid.); Malcolm N., *The concept of dreaming*, pp. 215-227 (1959, abstracts).

Reviews: Frongia G., GCFI, 1971, 50, pp. 516–17; Laycock H., D, 1969–70, 8, pp. 337–8; Röper P., HJ, 1969, 10, pp. 198–202; Trainor P., MS, 1983, 60, pp. 69–70.

575. Müller A., *Ontologie in W.'s Tractatus*, Bonn, Bouvier, 1967, pp. XIII, 250.
Although M. realizes that all the logico-linguistic analysis contained in *Tract.* has important consequences for its 'theory of being', he none the less devotes the central sections of his work to strictly ontological themes; the nature of a *Gegenstand* (halfway between Aristotelian substances and *materia prima*, pp. 61–69), the properties and states of non-relational things (pp. 71–102), the nature of a *Tatsache* and the relationship between *Sachverhalt* and *Gegenstand* (pp. 131–150). In conclusion, the final chapters are concerned with the notions of 'the logic of the world' and 'logical space', the nature of the 'metaphysical subject' and the problem of limits. *Review*: Heintel E., WJP, 1969, 2, pp. 366–9.

576. Nielsen K., *W.ian fideism*, P, 42, pp. 191–209. Reprinted in Nielsen, 1982, and in Canfield (ed.), 1986, vol. XIV.
The 'fideistic' position which appears in a number of 'W.ians' (for example Winch, Hughes, Malcolm, Geach and others) consists of identifying religion with a 'form of life' which, as such, is in order as it is, and cannot therefore be subjected to a philosophical critique. N. discusses and rejects this point of view. See Hudson's criticism, 1968.

577. Pole D., *Cook on W.'s account of privacy*, P, 42, pp. 277–9.
A critique of Cook's 1965 article.

578. Pompa L., *Family resemblance*, PQ, 17, pp. 63–9.
There are three possible interpretations of the notion of family resemblance in W., only one of which is of philosophical interest. A critique of this interpretation. See the reply made by Huby, 1968.

579. Rajan R. S., *Cassirer and W.*, IPQ, 7, pp. 591–610.
Beyond their most obvious differences, the two philosophers show strong analogies, for example in their common Kantian foundation, and in their common criticism of empiricism and realism. Analogies also exist between 'symbolic forms' and 'language games'.

580. Rankin K. W., *The role of imagination, rule-operations, and atmosphere in W.'s language-games*, I, 10, pp. 279-91.

R. analyses critically the role which, in W., emotive and dispositional states play in the understanding of language.

581. Ricoeur P., *Husserl and W. on Language*, in E. N. Lee and M. H. Mandelbaum (eds.), *Phenomenology and existentialism*, Baltimore, Md, Johns Hopkins University Press, 1967, pp. 207-17. Reprinted in H. A. Durfee (ed.), *Analytic philosophy and phenomenology*, 1976, and in Canfield (ed.), 1986, vol. XV.

582. Russell B., *Autobiography,* London, George Allen & Unwin; New York, Simon & Schuster, 3 vols, 1967-9.

Russell's autobiography contains numerous references to W. The most important are: Vol. 2: in the chapter 'Russia', a summary of his relationship with W. and a series of letters from W. and from Ogden concerning the publication of *Tract.* (1919-21); in chapter VII correspondence with Moore concerning Russell's report to Trinity College on W.'s research on the foundations of mathematics (1930). Vol. 3, chapter XVI: correspondence with A.J. Ayer concerning the inclusion of Russell's introduction to *Tract.* in the new translation by Pears and McGuinness, 1961.

583. Schmidt S. J., *Der Versuch, nicht 'über unsere Verhältnisse' zu denken (A. I. Wittenberg, L.W. und W. Schapp)'*, in E. Oldemeyer (ed.), *Die Philosophie und die Wissenschaften*, Meisenheim, Hain, 1967, pp. 124-44.

584. Schulz W., *W.: die Negation der Philosophie*, Stuttgart, Neske, 1967, pp. 113; 2nd ed., 1979. Spanish translation: Madrid, Del Toro, 1970.

S. finds both in the 'positivism' of *Tract.* and in the 'philosophy of language' contained in *P.I.* the tendency to deny itself through a 'negation of the reflecting subject', a tendency which is to a great extent typical of contemporary philosophy (including structuralism). *Reviews:* Bharati A., ZPF, 1970, 24, pp. 313-15; Boschheurne C. J., 'Streven', 1967-8, 21, p. 821; Bubner R., PRd, 1968, 15, pp. 161-84; Del Negro W. von, PLA, 1968, 21, pp. 330-4; König C., PH, 1968, 1, pp. 192-3.

585. Scott-Taggart M. J., *Private language and linguistic stipulation*, in J. J. McIntosh and S. C. Coval (eds.), *The* *business of reason*, London, Routledge & Kegan Paul, pp. 228–43.

586. Stenius E., *Miss Anscombe's retractation*, A, 27, pp. 86–96.
A reply to Anscombe's criticism, 1965, particularly in relation to the notion of *Gegenstand* in *Tract.*

587. Stenius E., *Mood and language game*, Sy, 17, pp. 254–74.
(Comments by D. Follesdal, ibid., pp. 275–80.) Reprinted in his *Critical Essays* (Acta Philosophica Fennica, vol. 25), Amsterdam, North-Holland, 1972.

588. Weissman D., *Ontology in the Tractatus*, PPR, 27, pp. 475–501.
The two translations of *Sachverhalt*, as 'possible state of things' and 'existing state of things', are not incompatible. In fact, although the central aspect of W.'s metaphysics is concerned with every possible world, nevertheless it also has implications for the ontology of our current world. We. also discusses the interpretation of this given by Black, 1964.

589. Wennerberg H., *The concept of family resemblances in W.'s later philosophy*, T, 33, pp. 107–32.
A critique of Bambrough's interpretation, 1960.

590. Wilson F., *The world and reality in the Tractatus*, SJP, 5, pp. 253–60.

1968

591. *Über L. Wittgenstein*, Frankfurt, Suhrkamp, pp. 172.
A German translation and collection of the essays by N. Malcolm, 1954, P. Strawson, 1954, N. Garver, 1959–60, S. Cavell, 1962.

592. Albrecht E., *Zur Kritik der Auffassungen L.W.s über das Verhältnis von Sprache, Logik und Erkenntnistheorie*, DZP, 16, pp. 813–29.

593. Borgis I., *Index zu L.W.s Tractatus logico-philosophicus*, Freiburg, Alber, 1968, pp. 112.
An index of more than 300 terms from *Tract.*, often with brief indications of the context.

594. Bubner R., *Die Einheit in W.'s Wandlungen*, PRd, 15, pp. 161–85.

An examination of recent publications by and about W. which tends to emphasize the substantial unity of his work.

595. Cohen M. F., *W.'s anti-essentialism*, AJP, 46, pp. 210-24.
With his unfounded criticism of generality and essentialism, W. has sacrificed all that is most important in philosophical inquiry.

596. Coleman F. J., *A critical examination of W.'s aesthetics*, APQ, 5, pp. 257-66. Reprinted in Canfield (ed.), 1986, vol. XIV.
An exegesis and an attempt at a critical development of the problems which W. has left open in *L.C.*

597. Cornman J. W., *Private languages and private entities*, AJP, 46, pp. 117-26.
An examination of the private language argument, which aims to show that in W. the first-person statements which refer to sensations are not always pure verbal expressions, but sometimes have a descriptive function (they are reports).

598. Daly C. B., *Polanyi and W.*, in T. A. Langford and W. H. Poteat (eds.), *Intellect and hope: essays in the thought of Michael Polanyi*, Durham, North Carolina, Duke University Press, 1968, pp. 136-68.

599. Dilman I., *Imagination*, A, 28, pp. 90-7.
Frequent references to *P.I.*

600. Erickson S. A., *Meaning and language*, MW, 1, pp. 563-86. Reprinted in *Analytic philosophy and phenomenology*, 1976.
A comparison between W. and Heidegger.

601. Fogelin R. J., *W. and intuitionism*, APQ, 5, pp. 267-74. Reprinted in Shanker (ed.), 1986, vol. III; in Canfield (ed.), 1986, vol. XI.
In *B.G.M.*, the 'intuitionist' elements of W.'s philosophy of mathematics are identified: his criticism of an uncircumscribed use of the law of the excluded middle; his constructivistic notion of 'proof'; his hostility towards the thesis that mathematics needs a foundation.

602. Funke G., *Einheitssprache, Sprachspiel und Sprachauslegung bei W.*, ZPF, 22, pp. 1-30, 216-47.

603. Gallagher M. P., *W.'s admiration for Kierkegaard*, 'Month', 39, pp. 43-9.

604. Goff R. A., *W.'s tools and Heidegger's implements*, MW, 1, pp. 447–62.

605. Granger G., *Le problème de l'espace logique dans le Tractatus de W.*, AS, pp. 181–95.
The notion of 'logical space' is analysed in its relationship to objects, and states of things, and as a general notion which is the source of *a priori* necessity.

606. Gustafson D. F., *A note on a misreading of W.*, A, 28, pp. 143–4.
A reply to Donagan, 1966, concerning the correct interpretation of *P.I.* 246.

607. Haller R., *L.W. und die österreichische Philosophie*, WW, 21, no. 2, pp. 77–87. Reprinted in Haller, 1979.

608. Harries K., *W. and Heidegger*, JVI, 2, pp. 281–91.
Analogies between the two authors in their use of language for the aims of philosophical inquiry.

609. Harries K., *Two conflicting interpretations of language in W.'s Investigations*, KS, 59, pp. 397–409.
In *P.I.*, two incompatible conceptions of language co-exist, one 'realistic' and the other 'transcendental'.

610. Hems J. M., *Husserl and/or W.*, IPQ, 8, pp. 547–78. Reprinted in *Analytic philosophy and phenomenology*, 1976.
Apart from a number of superficial similarities, emphasized by some commentators, the philosophy of these two authors remains substantially different.

611. Huby P. M., *Family resemblance*, PQ, 18, pp. 66–7.
A criticism of Pompa's interpretation, 1967. With his theses on family resemblances, W. does not intend to resolve a general philosophical problem, but merely to clarify the use of a class of terms which are of great philosophical importance. See Pompa's reply, 1968.

612. Hudson W. D., *On two points against W.ian fideism*, P, 43, pp. 269–73.
A critique of Nielsen's criticism, 1967, of W.'s 'fideism', in relation to religion.

613. Hudson, W. D., *L. W.: the bearing of his philosophy upon religious belief*, London, Lutterworth; Richmond, Va, John Knox, 1968, pp. 74.

This small volume, part of the series 'Makers of contemporary theology', is designed to introduce W. to theologically oriented readers. After a summary of W.'s earlier and later thought, the chapter 'Theology as grammar' discusses the implications of W.'s method of analysis for theological problems.

614. Hunter J. F. M., *'Forms of life' in W.'s 'Philosophical investigations'*, APQ, 5, pp. 233-43. Reprinted in Klemke (ed.), 1971; in Shanker (ed.), 1986, vol. II; in Canfield (ed.), 1986, vol. XIII.

An examination of four possible interpretations of the term 'form of life'. The first three are those normally accepted by the critics, but only the last one turns out to be justified.

615. Keyt D., *W., the Vienna Circle and precise concepts*, in AIKP, 2, pp. 237-246.

In Frege, in Schlick and in *Tract.* there recurs the common thesis that, in ordinary language, 'elementary propositions' are absolutely 'precise'.

616. Kultgen J. H., *Can there be a public language?*, SJP, 6, pp. 31-44.

617. Lazerowitz M., *W.: The nature of philosophy*, in his *Philosophy and illusion*, London, Allen & Unwin; New York, Humanities, 1968, pp. 53-70.

618. Levin D. M., *More aspects to the concept of aesthetic aspects*, JP, 65, pp. 483-9.

A critical examination of the thesis, attributed to W., that 'aesthetic qualities' are not qualities in a proper sense, but only 'aspects'.

619. Leyvraz J. P., *A propos des objets simples dans le Tractatus*, AIKP, 2, pp. 254-62.

620. Llewelyn J. E., *Family resemblance*, PQ, 18, pp. 344-6.

A number of criticisms of Pompa's article, 1967. W. does not apply the notion of 'resemblance' to all general terms, but only to some of them, those which are fundamental to philosophical analysis. See Pompa's reply, 1968.

621. Locke D., *The private language argument*, in his *Myself and others*, Oxford, Oxford University Press, 1968, pp. 72-109 (cf. Thornton, 1969).

622. Lyon A., *Family resemblance, vagueness and change of meaning*, T, 34, pp. 66-75.

L. enters into the debate between Wennerberg, 1967, and Bambrough, 1960, about the problem of universals in W. W.'s 'anti-essentialism' as applied to mental states.

623. Mace C. A., *On the directedness of aesthetic responses*, BJA, 8, pp. 155-60.
According to W., aesthetic response is directed towards an object. The historical sources of this thesis and the element of novelty in it.

624. Mandelbaum M., *Language and chess: De Saussure's analogy*, PR, 77, pp. 356-7.
Passages from Saussure, concerning the analogy between language and game, which suggest a comparison with W.

625. Morrison J. C., *Meaning and truth in W.'s Tractatus*, The Hague, Mouton, 1968, pp. 148.
The book aims to provide a concise introduction to and exposition of *Tract.* centred above all on the picture theory and the theory of truth. The first two chapters are devoted to ontological aspects (the nature of objects and of facts) and to a critique of the phenomenalistic and positivistic interpretations. In chapter V an analysis is made of the logical problem of negation. Finally, the mystical conclusions reached in *Tract.* are analysed, with a critical evaluation of W.'s philosophical method. *Reviews*: Couprie D. L., FL, 1970, 6, pp. 562-4; Stenius E., PR, 1970, 79, pp. 573-5.

626. Murphy J. P., *Another note on a misreading of W.*, A, 29, pp. 62-4.
A criticism of Donagan's interpretation of *P.I.* 246, 1968.

627. Norman J., *Russell and Tractatus 3.1432*, A, 29, pp. 190-2.
Russell, 1904, has anticipated some *Tract.* theses concerning the 'conceptual representation of a complex'.

628. Pompa L., *Family resemblance: a reply*, PQ, 18, pp. 347-53.
P. replies to the criticisms, made by Huby, 1968, and Llewelyn, 1968, of one of his previous articles, 1967.

629. Rosenberg J. F., *W.'s theory of language as picture*, APQ, 5, pp. 18-30. Reprinted in Canfield (ed.), 1986, vol. I.
The *Tract.*'s theory of language contains important elements which throw light on the correspondence theory of truth. This theory is critically developed.

630. **Rosenberg J. F.**, *Intentionality and self in the Tractatus*, N, 2, pp. 341-58. Reprinted in Canfield (ed.), 1986, vol. III.
A critical examination of the analysis of intensional statements ('A believes p').

631. **Rossi-Landi F.**, *Per un uso marxiano di W.*, 'Nuovi Argomenti', n. 1, pp. 187-230; included in his *Il linguaggio come lavoro e come mercato*, Milan, Bompiani, 1973. German translation: Munich, Hauser, 1972. E.T. in *Austrian philosophy*, 1981; in Canfield (ed.), 1986, vol. XV.

632. **Rotenstreich N.**, *The thrust against language; a critical comment on W.'s Ethics*, JVI, 2, pp. 125-36.

633. **Rovatti P. A.**, *La positività del paradosso in W.*, AA, 103, pp. 79-92.
An examination of the differences between the 'first' and 'second' W., with regard to his conception of philosophy, and the possibility of going beyond the limits defined in *Tract.*

634. **Schmidt S.**, *Sprache und Denken als sprachphiloso-phisches Problem von Locke bis W.*, The Hague, Nijhoff, 1968, pp. 202.
Central chapters on the philosophy of language of Locke, Herder, W. von Humboldt, and various 19th century authors. Chap. VI, 'L.W.s Prinzipienforschung', pp. 148-72, is a critical analysis of W.'s method of analysis, his treatment of the relation between thought and language, and his conception of the nature of philosophy. *Reviews*: Bodammer T., Prd, 1973, 20, pp. 111-18; Bumann W., PLA, 1971, 24, pp. 87-90; König G., PH, 1971, 4, pp. 43-5; Paterson R.W.K., PQ, 1970, 20, pp. 398-9.

635. **Simon M. A.**, Games, essences and family resemblances, AIKP, vol. 3, pp. 476-81.

636. **Spiegelberg H.**, *The puzzle of W.'s 'Phänomenologie'*, APQ, 5, pp. 244-56. Reprinted in a modified form in his *The context of the phenomenological movement*, The Hague, Nijhoff, 1981; in Canfield (ed.), 1986, vol. XV; in Shanker (ed.), 1986, vol. I.
In *P.R.*, the term 'Phänomenologie' appears for the first time, which could suggest that W. is, temporarily at least, drawing near to the phenomenological movement.

637. Suszko R., *Ontology in the Tractatus*, NDJFL, 9, pp. 7-33.

638. Teichman J., *Universals and common properties*, A, 29, pp. 162-65.
The different versions of the 'problem of universals', with reference to the notion of family resemblance in *P.I.* and *B.B.B.*

639. Walker J., *W.'s earlier ethics*, APQ, 5, pp. 219-32. Reprinted in Canfield (ed.), 1986, vol. III.
An examination of the ethics of *Tract.*, in the light of *L.E.* and of W.'s later philosophy. W. moves from the mystical rejection of metaphysics and a 'scientific model of intelligibility' to a conception in which philosophy is limited to a description of the role which ethical, aesthetic and religious statements play in observable human culture.

640. Winch P., *W.'s treatment of the will*, R, 10, pp. 38-53; reprinted in *Ethics and action,* London, Routledge & Kegan Paul, 1972; and in Canfield (ed.), 1986, vol. III.
Through the examination of the notion of will in *Tract.*, Winch also aims to throw light on various philosophical aspects of the later writings.

641. Wolniewicz B., *A difference between Russell's and W.'s logical atomism*, AIKP, 2, pp. 263-7.
Russell's 'logical atoms' are 'objects'; in the *Tract.*, on the other hand, the atoms are *Sachverhalte.*

1969

642. *Actes du colloque d'Aix-en-Provence*, RIP, 23, pp. 151-378. Reprinted in volume with title *W. et le problème d'une philosophie de la science*, Paris, Editions du C.N.R.S., 1970, pp. 225.
The individual articles are followed by a debate with brief interpositions by some of the participants in the congress. McGuinness B. F., *Philosophy of science in the Tractatus*, pp. 155-64 (reprinted in Canfield (ed.), 1986, vol. II); Specht E. K., *W. und das Problem des 'a priori'*, pp. 167-78; Pariente J. C., *Bergson et W.*, pp. 183-200; Imbert C., *L'héritage frégéen du Tractatus*, pp. 205-18; Granger G., *W. et la métalangue*, pp. 223-33; Clavelin M., *Élucidation philosophique et 'écriture conceptuelle' logique dans le Tractatus*, pp. 237-56; Wright G. H. von,

W.'s views on probability, pp. 259-79 (reprinted with some changes in von Wright, 1982); Black M., *Verificationism and W.'s reflections on mathematics*, pp. 284-94 (reprinted in Shanker (ed.), 1986, vol. III); Vuillemin J., *Remarques sur 4.442 du Tractatus*, pp. 299-313; Bouveresse J., *La notion de 'grammaire' chez le second W.*, pp. 319-35; Raggio A. R., *'Family resemblance predicates', modalités et réductionisme*, pp. 339-55; Fann K. T., *Supplement to the W. bibliography*, (cf. Fann, 1969), pp. 363-70.

643. *Studies in the philosophy of W.*, ed. by P. Winch, London, Routledge & Kegan Paul; New York, Humanities Press, 1969, pp. 210.

A collection of writings, none of which had previously been published: H. Ishiguro, *Use and reference of names*, pp. 20-50 (criticism of the thesis that there is a clear distinction between *Tract.* and *P.I.* concerning the problem of meaning. Reprinted in Canfield (ed.), 1986, vol. II); R. Rhees, *Ontology and identity in the Tractatus*, pp. 51-65 (in a debate with M. Black, 1964. Reprinted in Canfield (ed.), 1986, vol. II); D.S. Shwayder, *W. on mathematics*, pp. 66-116 (a combined examination of the *Tract.*, *P.B.* and *R.F.M.*, based on the thesis that W.'s philosophy of mathematics has a unitary and Kantian nature. Reprinted in Canfield (ed.), 1986, vol. XI); J. W. Cook, *Human beings*, pp. 117-151 (on the problem of other minds, W. rejects both 'Cartesianism' and 'behaviourism'. Reprinted in Canfield (ed.), 1986, vol. XII); L. R. Reinhardt, *W. and Strawson on other minds*, pp. 152-165; A. Manser, *Pain and private language*, pp. 166-183; F. Cioffi, *W.'s Freud*, pp. 184-210. (Reprinted in Canfield (ed.), 1986, vol. XV.) In the introduction to the work, P. Winch (*The unity of W.'s philosophy*, pp. 1-19) examines the development of W.'s philosophy and criticizes the thesis that there is an opposition between its two phases. *Reviews*: Blackburn S., BJPS, 1970, 21, pp. 385-6; Lyas C. A., P, 1970, 45, pp. 330-2; Mounce H. O., PB, 1970, 11, n. 1, pp. 27-9; Rose R., D, 9, pp. 268-71; Teichman J., PQ, 1970, 20, p.276.

644. Anscombe G. E. M., *On the form of W.'s writing,* in *Contemporary philosophy,* edited by R. Klibansky, vol. III, Florence, La Nuova Italia, 1969, pp. 373-8. Reprinted in Canfield (ed.), 1986, vol. V.

On W.'s expository style, and the relationship it has to his philosophical method.

645. Arrington R. L., *W. on contradiction*, SJP, 7, pp. 37-44. Reprinted in Shanker (ed.), 1986, vol. III.
With reference to *R.F.M.* and *P.I.*

646. Beard R. W., *On the independence of states of affairs*, AJP, 47, pp. 65-8.
Bunting's interpretation (1965), according to which in *Tract.* objects can be constituents of only one existing state of affairs, compromises W.'s fundamental thesis about the logical independence of states of affairs.

647. Becker O., *Heidegger und W.*, in *Heidegger: Perspektiven zur Deutung seines Werks*, edited by Otto Pöggeler, Cologne, Kiepenheuer und Witsch, 1969.

648. Bell R. H., *W. and descriptive theology*, RS, 5, pp. 1-18.

649. Bouveresse J., *Philosophie des mathématiques et thérapeutique d'une maladie philosophique: W. et la critique de l'apparence 'ontologique' dans les mathématiques*, CA, 10, pp. 174-208. Reprinted in Bouveresse, 1971.

650. Bywater W. G., *W.'s elementary propositions*, Pr, 50, pp. 360-70.
With a critique of Keyt's article, 1964.

651. Ehrlich L. H., *Mysticism or metaphysics? A juxtaposition of W., T. Aquinas, and Jaspers*, AIKP, 3, pp. 651-659.

652. Engel S. M., *Schopenhauer's impact on W.*, JHP, 7, pp. 285-302.
Schopenhauer's influence on W. is extended from *Tract.* to his later works. There are also strong analogies with S.'s little-known works on logic and language.

653. Engel S. M., *W. and Kant*, PPR, 30, pp. 483-513.
The debt owed by W. to K. is somewhat greater than that which emerges from current criticism. This thesis is argued by showing strong analogies in *Tract.* and *P.I.*, especially in relation to the problem of the nature of metaphysics.

654. Fann K. T., *W.'s conception of philosophy*, Berkeley, University of California Press; Oxford, Blackwell, 1969, pp. 178.
A concise, comprehensive exposition of the passage from an

early W. to a later W. through a period of 'transition' (pp. 41-53) during which, under the influence of Sraffa, Ramsey and Moore, W. gradually abandons the *Tract.*'s *a priori* method of analysis. In a final chapter ('Understanding W.') F. examines and discusses a number of widespread criticisms of W. (for example, Pole, 1958, Pitcher, 1964) concerning above all his method of analysis and his attitude towards philosophy. An extensive general bibliography concludes the work, bringing up to date the one previously published in 1967 (see entry). Further updatings in *Actes du colloque*, 1969. *Reviews*: Bambrough J. R., PB, 1970, 11, pp. 8-9; Lycan W. G., Mp, 1972, 3, pp. 301-9; Richards W. M., PPR, 1972-3, 33, pp. 134-5.

655. Giegel H. J., *Die Logik der seelischen Ereignisse. Zu Theorien von L. W. und W. Sellars*, Frankfurt, Suhrkamp, pp. 162.

656. Goff R., *Aphorism as Lebensform in W.'s 'Philosophical investigations'*, in *New essays in phenomenology. Studies in the philosophy of experience*, ed. with an introduction by James M. Edie, Chicago, Ill., Quadrangle Books, 1969, pp. 58-71.

657. Granger G. G., *L. Wittgenstein*, Paris, Seghers, 1969, pp. 185.
An anthological selection of W.'s works, prefaced by an historico-critical introduction. *Reviews*: Blanché R., 'Journal de psychologie normale et pathologique', 1970, 67, pp. 232-3; Gochet P., RIP, 1969, 23, pp. 371-8.

658. Hartnack, J., *Kant and W.*, KS, 60, pp. 131-4.
A number of analogies between the two philosophers, especially in their conception of the limitations and duties of philosophy.

659. Hintikka J., *Quantification and the picture theory of language*, Mo, 53, pp. 204-230. Reprinted in Hintikka, 1973.
H. suggests an extension of the *Tract.*'s picture theory, on the basis of the interpretation of it given by Stenius, 1960, which makes it compatible with the theory of quantification.

660. Hintikka J., *W. on private language: some sources of misunderstanding*, M, 78, pp. 423-5. Reprinted in Canfield (ed.), 1986, vol. IX.
Some errors of interpretation concerning language have their

origin in the English translation of *P.I.* 245 and 265, which is the source of misunderstandings.

661. Hochberg H., *Negation and generality*, N, 3, pp. 325–43. Reprinted in Klemke (ed.), 1971.
On the logical theory of *Tract.*, do facts corresponding to general statements and do true disjunctive statements exist?

662. Holmer P. L., *W. and theology*, in *New essays in religious language*, ed. by D. M. High, Oxford, Oxford University Press, 1969, pp. 25–35.

663. Hope V., *The picture theory of meaning in the 'Tractatus'*, P, 44, pp. 140–8.
The theory of meaning in *Tract.* as a development of the 'theory of judgement' of Moore and Russell.

664. Huby P. M., *Is 'Tractatus' 5.542 more obscure in English than it is in German?*, P, 44, p. 243.
On the translation of '"p" sagt p'.

665. Hudson W. D., *Some remarks on W.'s account of religious belief*, in *Talk of God*, ed. by G. N. A. Vesey, London, Macmillan, 1969, pp. 36–51.

666. Keyt D., *Letters from L.W.*, D, 8, pp. 128–31.

667. King-Farlow J. and **O'Reilly E. W.**, *Contructor reconstructus: a symposium on W.'s primitive languages*, PS(I), 18, pp. 100–10 and 110–18.
In the first of two contributions ('W.'s primitive languages'), the interpretation given by Rhees of primitive language, 1959, is examined and criticized, and a number of difficulties in W.'s theories are identified by K.-F. In the second, O'R. re-examines W.'s theses, especially in relation to his criticism of the nominalism of St. Augustine, and discusses K.-F.'s criticisms.

668. Klein P. D., *The private language argument and the sense-datum theory*, AJP, 47, pp. 325–343.
W.'s argumentation is based on an erroneous analysis of memory as a criterion for identification. Therefore the 'theory of sense data' is exempt from the criticism of it made by W.

669. Kolakowski L., *L.W.*, in his *The alienation of reason*, New York, Anchor Books, pp. 174–7.

670. Leinfellner E., *Zur nominalistischen Begründung von*

Linguistik und Sprachphilosophie: F. Mauthner und L. W.,
SG, 22, pp. 209-51.

671. Long P., *Are predicates and relational expressions
incomplete?*, PR, 78, pp. 90-8. Reprinted in Canfield (ed.),
1986, vol. II.
An analysis based on *Tract.* 3. 1432. Predicates and relations are
'incomplete' expressions and merely serve as 'indexes'.

672. Moore J. D., *Facts and figures*, AJP, 47, pp. 145-60.
A critical examination of Gasking and W. on the nature of the
propositions of arithmetic.

673. Morrison J. C., *Heidegger's criticism of W.'s conception
of truth*, MW, 2, pp. 551-73. Reprinted in *Analytic
philosophy and phenomenology*, 1976.

674. Muehlmann R., *Russell and W. on identity*, PQ, 19,
pp. 221-30.
In *Tract.* W. attempts to avoid the errors made in Russell's theory
of identity.

675. Murray D., *Disembodied brains*, PAS, 70, pp. 121-138.
A critical examination in the light of W.'s philosophy of mind
of the ('materialistic') thesis, which identifies mind and brain.

676. Nielsen K., *W.ian fideism again*, P, 44, pp. 63-5.
Replying to Hudson, 1968, N. reaffirms his own thesis that a
correct theory must allow for rational doubt concerning the
coherence of religious language.

677. Novielli V., *W. e la filosofia*, Bari, Adriatica, 1969, pp. 144.
A comprehensive study of W. from *Tract.* to *P.I.* In the latter
work, N. singles out the supersession of the static and solipsistic
conception of language, with results which leave W. in a position
not too far from the phenomenology of Husserl. *Reviews*: Becci
S. C., GCFI, 1970, 49, pp. 586-8; L.M.P., RM, 1970-1, 24,
pp. 751-2; Namer E., RPFE, 1970, 95, p. 256; S.R., RF, 1970,
61, pp. 102-4; Thiry L., D, 1971, 10, pp. 207-9.

678. Pears D., *The development of W.'s philosophy*, 'New York
Review of Books', 16 January 1969, pp. 21-30.
There is a relationship of substantial unity between *Tract.* and
the later works. The historical sources of W.'s philosophy. The
theses contained in this article are taken up and developed in
Pears, 1970.

679. Rosen S., *W. and ordinary language*, in his *Nihilism. A philosophical essay*, New Haven, Conn., and London, Yale University Press, pp. 1–27.
Attempts to find in *Tract.*, in *P.I.* and in authors influenced by W. elements (judged so by R.) of nihilism 'in the sense defined by Nietzsche and subsequently elaborated by Heidegger'.

680. Ruf H., *Wolniewicz on W. and Aristotle*, BSPS, 4, pp. 218–25 (cf. Wolniewicz, 1969).

681. Sellars R. W., *A few words on W.*, in his *Reflections on American philosophy from within*, Notre Dame, Ind. and London, University of Notre Dame Press, 1969, pp. 91–95.

682. Sheridan G., *The electroencephalogram argument against incorrigibility*, APQ, 6, pp. 62–70.
An examination of the validity of the recourse to an experimental check in the discussion of W.'s thesis concerning the incorrigibility of first-person expressions of sensations and feelings.

683. Shibles W., *W., language and philosophy*, Dubuque, Iowa, Brown, 1969, pp. 100; Whitewater, Wisc., Language Press, 1974. German translation, Bonn, Bouvier, 1973. Portuguese translation, São Paulo, Cultrix, 1974.
A collection of writings of different types, some of which contain only indirect references to W. The first two are essentially concerned with the literary nature of his style; in the third the problem of 'the limits' is discussed with some reference to Lewis Carroll's nonsense; the fourth and fifth are entitled 'Memory and remembering' and 'Intention'; the last is devoted to a comparison between W.'s 'philosophy of ordinary language' and Zen Buddhism (pp. 84–100). *Reviews*: Hegenberg L., 'Convivium', 1974, 13, pp. 470–2; Malherbe J.F., RPL, 1976, 74, p. 309; McKim V.R., NS, 1970, 44, p. 471; Pisani A., RSF, 1973, 26, pp. 443–5.

684. Simon M. A., *When is a resemblance a family resemblance?* M, 78, pp. 408–16.
Dissenting from some critics, S. defends W.'s thesis that things which do not have characteristics in common with each other can be grouped under the same general term.

685. Smart R. N., *W., death and the last judgement*, in his *Philosophers and religious truth*, 2nd revised ed., London, S.C.M. Press; New York, St. Martin's Press, 1969.

686. Steinvorth U., *W.s transzendentale Untersuchung der ostensiven Definition*, KS, 60, pp. 495–505.

A criticism of the prevailing interpretations which tend to identify the notion of use with that of rule in *P.I.*

687. Thomas G.B., *W. on sensations,* PS, 20, pp. 19–23.

A criticism of the interpretation given by Pitcher, 1964.

688. Thornton M. T., *Locke's criticism of W.*, PQ, 19, pp. 266–71.

The criticism of Don Locke, 1968, is based on an erroneous understanding of W.'s argumentation about private language.

689. Tillman F. A. and **S. M. Cahn** (eds.), *Philosophy of art and aesthetics: from Plato to W.*, New York and London, Harper & Row, 1969, pp. 791.

As well as a reprint of W.'s *L.E.* this volume contains an essay by S. Cavell, *Aesthetic problems of modern philosophy*, pp. 687–706, showing the use that can be made of W.'s later philosophy in the analysis of the problems of aesthetics.

690. Toulmin S. E., *L.W.*, 'Encounter', 32, January 1969, pp. 58–71.

A concise presentation of some fundamental features of W.'s personality and philosophy, with the aim of tracing their development and defining their sources historically. These are, in general, sought within the sphere of Central European culture and, from a philosophical point of view, in Kant and Schopenhauer. Thus the central role which reflection on ethics and religion plays in W.'s thought is emphasized, together with the strong unity and coherence which mark the different phases of his work.

691. Toulmin S. E., *From logical analysis to conceptual history*, in *Legacy of logical positivism*, edited by P. Achinstein and S. Baker, Baltimore, Md., Johns Hopkins Press, 1969, pp. 25–53.

Treats W.'s development from *Tract.* onwards particularly in connexion with the Vienna Circle.

692. van Peursen C. A., *L. Wittgenstein. An introduction to his philosophy*, London, Faber & Faber, 1969; New York, Dutton, 1970, pp. 120.

English translation and revision of a work previously published in Dutch, 1965. A rapid examination of W.'s personality and some of his themes, considered in their links with traditional continental philosophy (Leibniz, Kant, Schopenhauer, Meinong). *Reviews*: Blackburn S., BJPS, 1970, 21, pp. 385-6; Newell R.W., PQ, 1970, 20, pp. 275-6.

693. Watson R. A., *Sextus and W.*, SJP, 7, pp. 229-37.
Analogies with Sextus Empiricus in W.'s criticism of phenomenalism.

694. Wienpahl P., *W.'s notebooks*, 1914-1916, I, 12, pp. 287-316.
An examination of the picture theory of language.

695. Wolniewicz B., *A note on Black's 'Companion'*, M, 78, p. 141.
The term *Urbild* in *Tract.* cannot be translated *picture*, as Black does, 1964.

696. Wolniewicz B., *A parallelism between W. and Aristotelian ontologies*, BSPS, 4, pp. 208-17.
Cf. H. Ruf's comment, 1969.

697. Wright G. H. von, *The W. papers*, PR, 78, 483-503.
Published in a modified and enlarged version in von Wright, 1982; in Canfield (ed.), 1986, vol. IV; in Shanker (ed.), 1986, vol. v.
A complete catalogue of W.'s manuscripts and typewritten documents, collected in the library of Trinity College at Cambridge (Wren Library). It is accompanied by an historical note, by a description of the systems of classification adopted, by a number of comments on individual texts, and by a brief note on the directions followed by the literary executors in the posthumous publications.

698. Wuchterl K., *Struktur und Sprachspiel bei W.*, Frankfurt, Suhrkamp, 1969, pp. 220.
Examines W.'s thought concerning the foundations of logic and of mathematics in its development from *Tract.* to the second 'phase', in which W. approaches a 'constructivist' position.
Review: Hanak T., PLA, 1970, 23, pp. 341-4.

1970

699. Ambrose A., *Philosophy, language and illusion*, in C. Hanly and M. Lazerowitz (eds.), *Psychoanalysis and* *philosophy*, New York, International Universities Press, 1970, pp. 14–34.

Despite W.'s later rejection of Freudian theory, some of his most original views depend upon likenesses between psychoanalytic insight into the workings of the mind and his understanding of philosophy.

700. Amdur S. and **Horine S.**, *An index of philosophically relevant terms in W.'s Zettel*, IPQ, 10, pp. 310–21.

701. Binkley T., *On reading Investigations §43*, PPR, 31, pp. 429–32.

In *P.I.* 43, W. does not give a definition or theory of 'the meaning of a word' (see Pitcher, 1964, Hallett, 1967), but adopts a purely descriptive method.

702. Black M., *W.'s views about language*, in his *Margins of precision. Essays in logic and language*, Ithaca, N.Y., Cornell University Press, 1970, pp. 246–68.

Originally published in Hebrew in 1966. The mode of language presented in *P.I.*, although a vast improvement upon the 'picture theory' of *Tract.*, still has serious limitations, which encourage misinterpretations of some of W.'s important insights and reinforce the tendency to label him as a behaviourist and dogmatic conventionalist.

703. Coope C., Geach P., Potts T., White R., *A W. workbook*, Berkeley, Cal., University of California Press; Oxford, Basil Blackwell & Mott, 1970, pp. 51. German translation: Frankfurt, Suhrkamp, 1972.

A book conceived in order to facilitate undergraduate study of W. It is divided into eighteen sections devoted to the main themes (from the picture theory, to 'philosophical method'). Each of these is provided with: information on the most significant passages of W.'s works that are concerned with this theme; an indication of classical works and authors or relevant contemporaries; a list of questions designed to guide inquiry and to test the level of understanding reached. *Reviews*: Fletcher J. J., RM, 1972, 26, pp. 154–5; Wolter A. B., Th, 1971, 35, pp. 551–2.

704. Cristaldi M., *W.: l'ontologia inibita*, Bologna, Patron, 1970, pp. 394.

An examination of *Tract.*, suggesting that a 'fundamental ontology' having affinity with that of Heidegger should be the outcome of the book, but that this result is 'inhibited' by W.'s mystical refusal to speak of what transcends the limits of language.

705. Crittenden C., *W. on philosophical therapy and understanding*, IPQ, 10, pp. 20-43. Reprinted in Canfield (ed.), 1986, vol. V.
The method followed in *P.I.* is not purely therapeutic and negative in its attitude towards philosophy.

706. Dilman I., *W., philosophy and logic*, A, 31, pp. 33-42.
W. always believed that the study of mathematics and logic is fundamental to philosophy, even if he did not maintain that such a study should be carried out using the purely formal method followed by Russell. The fundamental differences between the two philosophers in this respect.

707. Doss S. R., *Copernicus revisited*, PPR, 31, pp. 193-211.
The theses on time in *P.I.* contain the elements of a 'Copernican revolution' similar to that brought about by Kant.

708. Erickson S. A., *Language and being: an analytic phenomenology*, New Haven, Connecticut, Yale University Press, 1970, pp. 165.
Addressing himself to philosophers of both phenomenological and analytical persuasion, E., in the third chapter, 'Phenomenology and language', tries to define what is the philosophical significance of language and compares Heidegger's views with those held by W., both in *Tract.* and in *P.I.*

709. Fahrenbach H., *Die logisch-hermeneutische Problemstellung in W.'s Tractatus*, in R. Bübner *et al.* (eds.), *Hermeneutik und Dialektik*, vol. 2, Tübingen, Mohr, 1970, pp. 25-54.

710. Ferguson A. T., *Quine, Carnap and W.: analyticity and logical compulsion*, D(PST), 12, pp. 1-15.

711. Gill J. H., *On 'I'*, M, 79, pp. 229-240.
An examination of the notion of subject in W. (*B.B.B.*, *P.I.*), in Ryle and in Strawson.

712. Ginet C., *W.'s argument that one cannot obey a rule privately*, N, 4, pp. 349-65. Reprinted in Canfield (ed.), 1986, vol. IX.
An analysis of *P.I.* 202.

713. Gross B. R., *L. W.: meaning and reference, sensations and mental acts*, in his *Analytic philosophy. An historical introduction*, New York, Pegasus, 1970, pp. 141-80.

714. Hallett G., *Did W. really define 'meaning'?*, HJ, 11, pp. 294-8.

A reply to Binkley, 1970.

715. Hallett G., *W. and the 'contrast theory of meaning'*, G, 51, pp. 679-710.

The thesis under examination (*Tract.* and later writings) is the one according to which a statement whose opposite is inconceivable is devoid of sense. Mathematics and philosophy.

716. Halloran S. M., *W.ian grammar*, Pr, 51, pp. 212-21.

The opposition between the 'anthropocentric' conception of grammar and the formalistic approach. The advantages and limitations of both approaches.

717. Hampshire S., *Wittgenstein,* in his *Modern writers and other essays*, New York, Knopf, 1970, pp. 130-7.

718. Hartshorne C., *A logic of ultimate contrasts: W. and Tillich. Reflections on metaphysics and language*, in his *Creative synthesis and philosophical method*, London, SCM Press, 1970, pp. 131-58.

719. Kielkopf C. F., *Strict finitism. An examination of W.'s 'Remarks on the foundations of mathematics'*, The Hague, Mouton, 1970. pp. 192.

After an opening chapter in which he defines the nature of the philosophical problems connected with mathematics, K. analyses and interprets (chs. II, III) some central sections of *R.F.M.*, in a strictly 'finitistic' vein (W. is shown to have given an explanation of the necessary truth of simple geometry and of the arithmetic of small numbers without the slightest hint of Platonism). K. then examines (ch. IV) W.'s criticism of other philosophical positions ('logicism' and 'Platonism' in particular), and gives a judgement of the value of the 'finitistic' solution, defending it from a number of possible objections (ch. V).

720. Leitner B., *W.'s architecture*, 'Artforum International', 8, pp. 59-61.

721. Lenk H., *War der späte W. ein Essentialist?*, MW, 3, pp. 16-25.

722. Leyvraz J. P., *W.-orientierter Vortrag zum Struktur-alismus*, SP, 30-1, pp. 167-95.

723. Malcolm N., *W. on the nature of mind*, APQ (Monograph series), 4, pp. 9-29. Reprinted in his *Thought and knowledge*, 1977; in Shanker (ed.), 1986, vol. II; in Canfield (ed.), 1986, vol. XII.
An examination of the role played by private experiences in the use of some verbs (to intend, to understand, to remember, etc.). W. does not deny the need for internal events, but criticizes some uses which have been made in philosophy of the notion of privacy.

724. Mayr F. K., *L. W. und das Problem einer philosophischen Anthropologie*, TF, 32, pp. 214-89.

725. Morick H., *Cartesian privilege and the strictly mental*, PPR, 31, pp. 546-51.
M. enters into the debate on private language in defence of a 'Cartesian' position.

726. Mulligan R. W., *The nature of person in W.*, NS, 44, pp. 565-73.
A comparison between W. and Strawson (1958) concerning the notion of person.

727. Mundle, C. W. K., *A critique of linguistic philosophy*, Oxford, Oxford University Press, 1970, pp. 192; 2nd rev. ed., London, Glover & Blair, 1979, pp. XI-282.
Part II of this 'deliberately provocative' book has the title 'L.W., the instigator of the revolution in philosophy', pp. 153-252, and is devoted to a criticism of W.'s philosophy and of contemporary trends influenced by his work. It includes chapters on a comparison between 'The roles of G. E. Moore and W.', on *Tract.*, on W.'s later accounts of language and of philosophy, on his method of analysis, and on 'W.'s legacy'. The 2nd edition contains some passages of self-criticism, some replies to critics and a section on 'The private language argument'. *Reviews*: Abelson R., Mp, 1976, 7, pp. 276-286; Graham K., BJPS, 1983, 34, pp. 84-8; Olin D., PR, 1973, 82, pp. 246-249; Shorter M., PQ, 1972, 22, pp. 172-174; Wencelius M., EP, 1972, pp. 283-285.

728. O'Shaughnessy R. J., *On having something in common*, M, 79, pp. 436-40.

In discussing whether W. has resolved the problem of universals (see Bambrough, 1960, and Manser, 1967), the examination of the characteristics which different objects must have in common in order to belong to one and the same class has been unduly restricted to a limited number of cases.

729. Pears D. F., *Wittgenstein*, New York, Viking Press, 1970, pp. 208; London, Fontana, 1971. Translations in French, German, Spanish, Portuguese, Dutch.

Although it is divided into two distinct parts, devoted to a first and second philosophy of W. respectively, the aim of this short work is to show, through a rapid exposition, the substantial unity which links themes and solutions that are apparently opposed to or far from each other. The central source of inspiration in the whole of W.'s work is located as a (Kantian) need to define the possibilities of reason, and to establish the limits of its speculative claims. In this perspective P. seeks the bonds which link W. to classical works in the history of philosophy. *Reviews*: Blanché R., RPFE, 1972, 97, p. 118; Burns S.A.M., D, 1972, 11, pp. 478-80; Hartz C., PL, 1987, 11, pp. 199-201; Levin M.E., 'Social Research', 1973, 40, pp. 192-207; Lycan W. G., Mp, 1973, 4, pp. 152-62; Rabossi E. A., RLF, 1975, 1, pp. 72-3; Robert J. D., RPL, 1973, 11, pp. 629-30; Serrano J. A., RevF(Mex), 1974, 7, pp. 404-6; Stroud B., JP, 1972, 69, pp. 16-26; Villanueva E., Cr, 1972, 6, pp. 131-38.

730. Phillips D. Z., *Religious beliefs and language games*, R, 12, pp. 26-46. Reprinted in his *Faith and philosophical enquiry*, London, Routledge & Kegan Paul, 1970; in Shanker (ed.), 1986, vol. IV; in Canfield (ed.), 1986, vol. XIV.

A discussion of the difficulties encountered in applying the theory of language games to religious language, in an attempt at a rational foundation of religious belief.

731. Poulain J., *Le mysticisme du Tractatus logico-philosophicus et la situation paradoxale des propositions religieuses*, in D. Dubarle *et al.* (eds.), *La recherche en philosophie et en théologie,* Paris, Éditions du CERF, pp. 75-155.

732. Radford C., *Characterizing-judgments and their causal counterparts*, A, 31, pp. 65-75. Reprinted in Canfield (ed.), 1986, vol. XIV.

Two possible interpretations concerning the relationship found by W. to exist between aesthetic judgement and its explanation in hypothetico-causal terms.

733. Raggio A. R., *Einige Betrachtungen zum Begriff des Spiels*, KS, 61, pp. 227-37.
The notion of rule in relation to the theory of linguistic games in W. and in Lorenzen.

734. Rhees R., *Discussions of W.*, London, Routledge & Kegan Paul; New York, Schocken Books, 1970, pp. 161.
The following, previously-published works by R. are here reprinted: 1954 (PASSV), 1959-60 (PAS), 1960 (PQ), 1963 (AR), 1965 (PR), 1966 (R), 1966 (PASSV), 1969. In the final article, *On continuity: W.'s ideas, 1938* (pp. 104-157), published here for the first time, R. sets out W.'s theses on continuity inside and outside mathematics. In the second part of the article, he uses notes taken on the occasion of conversations held with W. on this subject in 1938 (reprinted in Canfield (ed.), 1986, vol. XI). *Reviews*: Audi R., PF, 1971, 10, pp. 163-5; Bharati A., ZPF, 1973, 27, pp. 330-2; Burnheim J., AJP, 1971, 49, pp. 119-20; Dilman I., PB, 1970, 11, pp. 23-8; Manser A.R., M, 1973, 82, pp. 298-300; Unsigned, TLS, 8 Jan. 1970, no. 3541, p. 36; Wagner J. U., RM, 1971, 25, pp. 366-7; Wolf M., PS(I), 1973, 21, pp. 287-91.

735. Rorty R., *W., privileged access, and incommunicability*, APQ, 7, pp. 192-205. Reprinted in Shanker (ed.), 1986, vol. II; in Canfield (ed.), 1986, vol. IX.
A critical examination of the interpretation given by Pitcher, 1965, and by Cook, 1965: both have failed to grasp the meaning of the private language argument, and therefore attribute paradoxical theses to W.

736. Rosenberg J. F., *W.'s self-criticism, or 'Whatever happened to the picture theory?'*, N, 4, pp. 209-23.
The criticism contained in *P.I.* of *Tract.* picture theory is misleading ('A great philosopher can be his own worst interpreter').

737. Scalafani R. J., *'Art', W., and open-textured concepts*, JAAC, 29, pp. 333-41.

738. Smerud W. B., *Can there be a private language?*, The Hague and Paris, Mouton, 1970, pp. 120.

A critical examination of some arguments used by N. Malcolm,
J. D. Carney and N. Garver in support of the anti-private-language
thesis and as an explication of W.'s doctrine. The relevance of
this thesis to such philosophical topics as sense-datum theory,
phenomenalism, and the problem of other minds is also
discussed. *Reviews:* Cua A.S., RM, 1973-4, 27, pp. 412-13;
García S.A., Teo, 1973, 3, pp. 159-61.

739. Stegmüller W., *Aufsätze zu Kant und W.*, Darmstadt,
Wissenschaftliche Buchgesellschaft, 1970, pp. 76.
Review: Kleinschneider M., KS, 1972, 63, pp. 281-2.

740. Struhl P. R., *The language only I understand*, JCA, 2,
pp. 31-34.
On *Tract.* 5.62 and solipsism.

741. Weiler G., *Mauthner's critique of language*, Cambridge,
Cambridge University Press, 1970, pp. 346.
References to W. throughout: one chapter, *Critique of language,
W. and Mauthner*, pp. 298-306, discusses the possible
importance of Mauthner's influence on W.

742. Wolniewicz B., *Four notions of independence*, T, 36,
pp. 161-64.
Out of four possible notions of independence of propositions,
that contained in *Tract.* is the strongest and implies the others.
Demonstration of this theorem.

743. Zemach E. M., *The unity and indivisibility of the self*,
IPQ, 10, pp. 542-55.
An examination of W.'s theories on the ascription of sensations
and the nature of the subject.

1971

744. Belohradsky V., *Interpretazioni italiane di W.*, Milan,
Marzorati, pp. 326.
An examination of the Italian literature on W. divided into
chapters which deal with the main themes and interpretative
trends. Each work is summarized at generous length.

745. Bier J. P., *Quelques traces du 'mythe' et de la pensée de
L. W. dans la littérature allemande contemporaine*, RUB,
nos 2-3, pp. 212-28.

746. Bloom S. L., *A completeness theorem for 'theories of kind W.'*, SL, 27, pp. 43–56.
On Suszko's theses (NDJFL, 1968, 9, pp. 7–33) for a formalization of *Tract.*

747. Bouveresse J., *La parole malheureuse*, Paris, Editions de Minuit, 1971, pp. 475.
A collection of works, some of which are directly concerned with W.: 'Philosophie des mathématiques' (previously published, see 1969); 'Sur le finitisme de W.' (pp. 183–226); 'La compétence', etc. (previously published, see *Actes du colloque*, 1969). *Review*: Kenny A., AP, 1974, 37, pp. 343–5.

748. Carney J. D., *The private language argument*, SJP, 9, pp. 353–9.

749. Clegg J. S., *Symptoms*, A, 32, pp. 90–8.
W.'s distinction between symptom and criterion analysed in 'diagnostic terms' and defended.

750. Cornman J. W., *The private language argument*, in his *Materialism and sensations*, New Haven, Conn., and London, Yale University Press, 1971, pp. 85–96.

751. Durrant M., *The use of pictures in religious belief*, S, 10, pp. 16–21.
A criticism of Hudson, 1969. See also the reply by Hudson, 1973.

752. Egidi R., *Studi di logica e filosofia della scienza*, Rome, Bulzoni, 1971, pp. 245.
This contains two works concerning W.: 'Material for a study of W.'s philosophical grammar'; 'Two theses of W. on the foundations of mathematics' (cf. Egidi, 1965).

753. Engel S. M., *W.'s doctrine of the tyranny of language. An historical and critical examination of his 'Blue Book'*, Introduction by S. Toulmin, The Hague, Martinus Nijhoff, 1971, pp. 145.
Although this work is specifically devoted to the examination of *Bl.B.*, it aims to group together some essential features of W.'s whole work and intellectual personality. E. maintains that the theoretical tensions present in *Bl.B.* can in fact only be explained by taking into account the strong links which tie W. to the Kantian problems of the limits of reason and the nature of metaphysics (ch. III, pp. 43–73), to Schopenhauer (ch. IV, pp. 74–95), and to continental philosophy in general (Spinoza,

Kierkegaard, etc). Far from representing a break with or a rejection of traditional Western philosophy, the whole of W.'s work only acquires unity and coherence in relation to it (ch. VII). *Reviews*: Bertman M. A., PRh, 1975, 8, pp. 131–33; Collins J., MS, 1972–3, 50, pp. 383–4; De Pater W. A., TF, 1973, 35, pp. 653–5; Flew A., PB, 1973, 14, pp. 14–15; Klemke E.D., Ph, 1982–3, 12, pp. 435–9; Larive A., JHP, 1974, 12, pp. 132–3; Shiner R.A., D, 1973, 12, pp. 161–4; Sterling J.W., RM, 1971–2, 25, p. 750; Wolf M., PS(I), 1974, 22, pp. 274–9.

754. Finch H. L., *W.: the early philosophy. An exposition of the Tractatus*, New York, Humanities Press, 1971, pp. 291.
A somewhat personal examination of *Tract.*, centred above all on ontological themes, the picture theory and religious and ethical aspects. There are comparisons with Plato, Kant and Buddhist logic in appendices to the work. *Review:* Teske J.R., MS, 1971–2, 51, pp. 241–2.

755. Frongia G., *L.W.: etica, estetica, psicoanalisi e religione*, GCFI, 50, pp. 120–30.
Topics concerning ethics and aesthetics are central in W.'s thought, and as such shed light also on the general theory of *Tract.*

756. Garver N., *Pantheism and ontology in W.'s early work*, IS, 1, pp. 269–77.

757. Gebauer G., *Wortgebrauch, Sprachbedeutung. Beiträge zu einer Theorie der Bedeutung im Anschluss an die spätere Philosophie L.W.s.* Munich, Bayerischer Schulbuch-Verlag, 1971, pp. 116.

758. Gill J. H., *W. and the function of philosophy*, Mp, 2, pp. 137–49.
The conception of philosophy in *P.I.* is different from the 'positivistic' one, according to which philosophical problems are dissolved.

759. Goldberg B., *The linguistic expression of feeling*, APQ, 8, pp. 86–92. Reprinted in Canfield (ed.), 1986, vol. IX.
What does it mean to associate a sensation with a sign? A detailed analysis of the diary example (*P.I.* 258) and of the problem of private language.

760. Greenwood E. B., *Tolstoy, Wittgenstein, Schopenhauer: some connections*, 'Encounter', 36, pp. 60–72.

761. Gustafson D. F., *The natural expression of intention*, PF, 2, pp. 299-315.
A discussion of the interpretations given by Melden, 1957, and Anscombe, 1957, of intention in W.

762. Gustason W., *Miss Anscombe on the 'general propositional form'*, A, 32, pp. 195-6.
An examination and a critique of Anscombe's interpretation, 1954, ch. X.

763. Habermas J., *W.s Rückkehr (1965)*, in his *Philosophisch-politische Profile*, Frankfurt, Suhrkamp, 1971; 3rd enlarged ed., 1981, pp. 217-225. E.T. London, Heinemann, 1983.

764. Hacker P. M. S., *W.'s doctrines of the soul in the Tractatus*, KS, 62, pp. 162-71.

765. Hardwick C. S., *Language learning in W.'s later philosophy*, The Hague, Mouton, 1971, pp. 152.
A somewhat critical examination of the theories of the second W. on language (interpreted in a 'pragmatic' sense and compared with J. Dewey and G.H. Mead) and of its implications in the field of teaching and linguistic learning in children. In general, W.'s viewpoint is considered to be somewhat backward in the light of advances in linguistics and psychology. Furthermore, W.'s theory of language games would give a distorted and over-simplified picture of the complex functioning of language.

766. Hart W. D., *The whole sense of the Tractatus*, JP, 68, pp. 273-88. Reprinted in Canfield (ed.), 1986, vol. III.
An examination of the maxim contained in the preface of *Tract.*, which contains, according to W., the whole sense of the work: 'What can be said at all, can be said clearly'. See reply by Block, 1975.

767. Hunter J. F. M., *W. and knowing the meaning of a word*, D, 10, pp. 294-304.

768. Jones O. R. (ed.), *The private language argument*, London, Macmillan; New York, St. Martin's Press, 1971, pp. 284.
A collection of 16 essays on the problem of private language, one new (see Kenny, 1971), the others republished here, often with new titles or in a reduced version. W.'s *N.L.P.E.* is also reprinted, at the end of the volume, with R. Rhees's introduction (see 'Publications of writings by Wittgenstein').

769. Kaplan B., *Some considerations of influences on W.*, IS, 1, pp. 73-88.

770. Kenny A., *The verification principle and the private language*, in Jones (ed.), 1971. Reprinted in Canfield (ed.), 1986, vol. IX.

771. Klemke E. D. (ed.), *Essays on W.*, Urbana, Ill., University of Illinois Press, 1971, pp. 552.
A collection of 23 essays, about half previously published, divided into three sections: 'W.'s ontology'; 'Epistemology and philosophy of language'; 'Philosophy of logic and mathematics'. The contributions published here for the first time are: E. D. Klemke, *The ontology of W.'s Tractatus*, pp. 104-19; H. Hochberg, *Material properties in the Tractatus,* pp. 120-2; N. Garver, *W.'s pantheism. A new light on the ontology of the Tractatus,* pp. 123-37; H. G. Petrie, *Science and metaphysics. A W.ian interpretation*, pp. 138-71; M. S. Gram, *Privacy and language*, pp. 298-327; F. Zabeeh, *On language games and forms of life,* pp. 328-73; J. Hunter, *W. on meaning and use*, pp. 374-93 (reprinted in Canfield (ed.), 1986, vol. VI); A. Oldenquist, *W. on phenomenalism, skepticism and criteria*, pp. 394-422; D. W. Stampe, *Tractarian reflections on saying and showing*, pp. 423-45; H. Hochberg, *Facts, possibilities and essences in the Tractatus*, pp. 485-533; H. Hochberg, *Arithmetic and propositional form in W.'s Tractatus*, pp. 534-42 (reprinted in Canfield (ed.), 1986, vol. II).

772. Kuhns R., *Philosophy as a form of art*, in his *Literature and philosophy: Structures of experience*, London, Routledge & Kegan Paul, 1971, pp. 215-72.
'Symbolism' and 'imagism' share with W. a close attention to language. The close association between knowledge and aesthetic and ethical values.

773. Lang M., *W.'s 'Philosophische Grammatik'. Entstehung und Perspektiven der Strategie eines radikalen Aufklärers*, 's-Gravenhage, M. Nijhoff, 1971, pp. 160.
Reviews: G. Hottois, RBPH, 1976, 54, pp. 137-9; Parret H., TF, 1972, 34, pp. 594-5.

774. Lycan W. G., *Noninductive evidence: recent work on W.'s criteria*, APQ, 8, pp. 109-25. Reprinted in Canfield (ed.), 1986, vol. VII.

An examination of the literature on the notion of criterion in relation to the awareness of other minds. L. dwells in particular on the opposition between those who maintain and those who deny the thesis that this notion constitutes a middle course between inductive and deductive evidence. An extensive analytical bibliography on the subject.

775. Lycan W. G., *Gombrich, W., and the duck-rabbit*, JAAC, 30, pp. 229-37. Reprinted in Canfield (ed.), 1986, vol. XIV.
L. detects a substantial agreement between W.'s theory of aspects and Gombrich's theses set out in *Art and illusion*.

776. Magee B. (ed.), *Modern British philosophy*, London, Secker & Warburg; New York, St. Martin's Press, 1971, pp. 234.
A series of broadcast conversations with various philosophers. The interview with D. Pears, 'The two philosophies of W.', pp. 31-47, concerning the continuity between *Tract.* and the later writings, is particularly interesting here.

777. Malcolm N., *Problems of mind. Descartes to W.*, New York, Harper & Row, 1971; London, George Allen & Unwin, 1972, pp. 103. Italian translation, Milan, ISEDI, 1973.
An independent treatment of three aspects of the philosophy of mind (mind–body dualism; mind–brain monism; 'logical behaviourism') with frequent references to W., and with the aim of providing an introduction to his later writings. *Reviews*: Bertman M. A., MS, 1973-4, 51, pp. 249-50; Donnelly J., IPQ, 1973, 13, pp. 305-8; Largeault J., 'Revue de Synthèse', 1978, 99, pp. 372-8; Largeault J., RIP, 1978, 32, pp. 135-40; Larreta J., RLF, 1975, 1, pp. 175-6; Mayberry T. C., PF, 1975, 14, pp. 289-95; Torretti R., 'Dialogos', 1972, 23, pp. 238-9; Whiteley C.H., PQ, 1972, 22, p. 367.

778. Marconi D., *Il mito del linguaggio scientifico. Studio su W.*, Milan, Mursia, 1971, pp. 165.
M. aims to give a definition of W.'s work, from *Tract.* to his more mature works, in the framework of the 'rationalistic' tradition, in which 'neopositivism' also finds a place. Unlike the latter, W. none the less never treated scientific knowledge as absolute, nor did he give a value-free explanation of it. In fact, the theme of value (ethical, aesthetic and religious value) and of its transcendental nature is present throughout his work, and

confers homogeneity on works of different periods. *Reviews*:
Buzzetti D., RF, 1972, 63, pp. 87-9; Drago G., GM, 1974, 29,
pp. 106-8.

779. Mondadori F., *W. sui fondamenti della necessità logica*,
RCSF, 26, pp. 57-78.
A critique of the conventionalist interpretation of W.'s philosophy
of mathematics given by Dummett, 1959, Bennett, 1961, and
Pears, 1969. M. seeks rather an intermediate solution 'between
the concept of demonstration as choice and the concept of
demonstration as obligation'.

780. Nuchelmans G., *Tractatus 4.113*, M, 80, pp. 106-7.
The problems encountered in translating from German the
passage in *Tract.* which is concerned with philosophy and the
limits of natural science.

781. Piana G., *Husserl, Schlick e W., sulle cosiddette 'proposi-
zioni sintetiche a priori'*, AA, no. 122, pp. 19-41.

782. Place U. T., *Understanding the language of sensations*,
AJP, 49, pp. 158-66.
A critique of W.'s theses on private language as they appear in
Kenny's interpretation.

783. Riteris J. M., *Early W.'s 'fundamental mistake'*, JT, 6,
pp. 240-5.
On the nature of the objects in *Tract.* and in *N.B.*

784. Rohatyn D. A., *A note on Heidegger and W.*, PT, 15,
pp. 69-71.
The examination of a remark of Heidegger's about W., contained
in his last book *Heraklit*. A comparison of the two philosophers
and a bibliography.

785. Rudich N. and **Stassen M.**, *W.'s implied anthropology:
remarks on W.'s notes on Frazer*, 'History and Theory',
10, pp. 84-9.

786. Thompson J. L., *About criteria*, R, 13, pp. 30-43.
Reprinted in Canfield (ed.), 1986, vol. VII.
A discussion of the criticisms made by Chihara and Fodor, 1965,
and by Putnam, 1962, of the distinction between criterion and
symptom in W.

787. von Wright G. H., *The origin of W.'s Tractatus*,

published as an introduction to the *Prototractatus* (see 'Publications of writings by Wittgenstein').
A history of the events which led to the publication of *Tract.* Revised and expanded versions of this essay have been published in *W., Sources and perspectives*, 1979; in von Wright, 1982; in Canfield (ed.), 1986, vol. I.

788. Wuchterl K., *W. und die Idee einer operativen Phänomenologie*, ZPF, 25, pp. 6-24.
The search for phenomenological elements in the different phases of W.'s thought. Analogies with Husserl's notion of *Lebenswelt*.

1972

789. *L.W.: philosophy and language*, edited by A. Ambrose and M. Lazerowitz, London, George Allen & Unwin; New York, Humanities Press, 1972, pp. 326.
Articles by: Ambrose A., *L.W.: a portrait*, pp. 13-25; Wisdom J., *W. on private language*, pp. 26-36; Cook J. W., *Solipsism and language*, pp. 37-72; Hanly C., *W. on psychoanalysis*, pp. 73-94; Redpath T., *W. and ethics*, pp. 95-119 (reprinted in Canfield (ed.), 1986, vol. XIV); Pitcher G., *About the same*, pp. 120-39; Kennick W. E., *Philosophy as grammar and the reality of universals*, pp. 140-85; Ebersole F., *Saying and meaning*, pp. 186-211 (reprinted in Canfield (ed.), 1986, vol. VI); Fujimoto T., *The notion of Erklärung*, pp. 222-32; Lazerowitz M., *Necessity and language*, pp. 233-70 (reprinted in Lazerowitz and Ambrose, 1985); Goodstein R.L., *W.'s philosophy of mathematics*, pp. 271-86 (reprinted in Canfield (ed.), 1986, vol. XI); Ambrose A., *Mathematical generality*, pp. 287-318. *Reviews*: Butterworth R., HJ, 1974, 15, pp. 81-4; Lyas L., PB, 1972, 13, no. 3, pp. 1-3; Proudfoot M., PQ, 1973, 23, pp. 263-5; Radford C., M, 1975, 84, pp. 295-7.

790. *Sobre el Tractatus logico-philosophicus*, Valencia, Universidad de Valencia, 1972, pp. 166.
A special number of 'Teorema', 1972, containing the following contributions: Pears D., *The ontology of the Tractatus*, pp. 49-58; Wolniewicz B., *The notion of fact as a modal operator*, pp. 59-66; Lorenz K., *Zur Deutung der Abbildtheorie*

in W.'s Tractatus, pp. 67-90; Favrholdt D., *The relation between thought and language in W.'s Tractatus*, pp. 91-100; Blasco J. L., *El lenguaje ordinario en el Tractatus*, pp. 101-12; Spisani F., *Il concetto di identità in W.*, pp. 113-15; García Suarez A., *¿Es el lenguaje del Tractatus un lenguaje privado?*, pp. 117-30; Hartnack J., *The metaphysical subject*, pp. 131-8; Garrido M., *La lógica del mundo*, pp. 139-52; Vera F., *Bibliografía*, pp. 153-66.

791. Bertman M. A., *Non-extensional propositions in W.*, ILR, 3, pp. 73-7.

792. Bogen J., *W.'s philosophy of language. Some aspects of its development*, London, Routledge & Kegan Paul; New York, Humanities Press, 1972, pp. 244.

An examination of the 'gradual development' of W.'s thought which has as its central theme the problem of the truth and falsity of non-necessary statements. After an exposition of the picture theory and of the ontology of *Tract.* (ch. I), B. dwells at length, in part using unpublished material, on the theoretical reasons which led W., from the beginning of the 1930s, to revise some aspects of *Tract.* and to formulate a new truth theory (calculus theory) according to which 'to assert something is to use signs as projections according to strict rules' (chs. II and III). The third phase is represented by the subsequent revision of the calculus theory (ch. III). *Reviews*: Frank W., RM, 1974, 27, p. 604; Hallett G., JH, 1973, 14, pp. 445-7; Llewelyn J. E., I, 1973, 16, pp. 431-9; Lyas C., PB, 1973, 14, n. 1, pp. 3-5; Merrill G. H., MS, 1974-5, 52, pp. 207-11; Shiner R. A., D, 1973, 12, pp. 683-99; Sievert D., PR, 1975, 84, pp. 117-22; Stock G., M, 1974, 83, pp. 300-3; Wolf M., PS(I), 21, pp. 285-7.

793. Bouwsma O. K., *A difference between Ryle and W.*, RUS, 58, n. 3, pp. 77-87. Reprinted in Bouwsma, 1982.

From a 'Symposium on G. Ryle', with a reply by Ryle (ibid., pp. 107-10).

794. Brady P., *Period style terms and concepts. The W. perspective*, JCA, 4, n. 2, pp. 62-70.

795. Canfield J. V., *A model Tractatus language*, PF, 4, pp. 199-217. Reprinted in Canfield (ed.), 1986, vol. I.

An interpretation of the picture theory, in contrast to the one suggested by Anscombe (1959) and Copi ('Mind', 1958).

796. Dauer F. W., *Empirical realists and W.ians*, JP, 69, pp. 128-147.
On the notion of criterion.

797. Dazzi N. and **Simone R.**, *Philosophische Untersuchungen* §§1-3, RF, 63, pp. 59-74.
An analytical examination of the first three sections of *P.I.*, interspersed with comments of an historico-critical nature. In particular, W.'s criticism of the conception of language as naming is considered, with reference to the development of semantic theories, from Aristotle to Saussure.

798. Downing F. G., *Games, families, the public and religion*, P, 47, pp. 38-54.
Nielsen's 'fideistic' interpretation, 1972, of W. and his followers is not justified, and furthermore, it fails to grasp the nature of religious belief.

799. Ebersole F. B., *Reconsidering some passages in W.*, CJP, 2, pp. 1-28. Reprinted in Canfield (ed.), 1986, vol. V.
The passages under examination, taken from *P.I.* and *B.B.B.*, are concerned with family resemblances and the problem of generality.

800. Fay T. A., *W.'s critique of metaphysics in the Tractatus*, PS(I), 20, pp. 51-61.
The paradox of *Tract.*, which, in the final sections, refutes itself.

801. Findlay J. N., *My encounters with W.*, PF, 4, pp. 167-185. Reprinted in *Studies in the philosophy of J. N. Findlay*, 1985.
Encounters and philosophical interviews held with W. during the period 1930-39.

802. Frommke P., *Die Grammatik der Hypothese. Zur Wissenschaftstheorie des mittleren W.*, ZPF, 26, pp. 426-38.

803. Genova J. A., *W. and Caligari*, PF, 4, pp. 186-98.
W.'s development and aesthetic sensitivity in relation to Vienna at the beginning of the century. The aesthetic implications of *Tract.*

804. Hacker P. M. S., *Insight and illusion. W. on philosophy and the metaphysics of experience*, Oxford, Clarendon Press, 1972, pp. XVI, 324. German translation: Frankfurt,

Suhrkamp, 1978. A radically revised edition: Oxford, Clarendon Press, 1986, pp. 341 (see 1986).

A comprehensive examination of W.'s evolution from *Tract.* to his more mature 'phase' (distinguished by a 'radical constructivism'), paying particular attention to the metaphysical elements behind the three essential constituents of experience: the self, other minds and objects. After an examination of *Tract.* (chs. II–III) and intermediate period (ch. IV), H. considers the 'new phase', which marks a radical turning-point as far as the theses of *Tract.* are concerned, and hinges on the discovery of the notion of criterion as non-inductive evidence. This notion, together with the related one of 'grammar', have a decisive function in the analysis and dissolution of that classical philosophical problem (the 'metaphysical illusion') represented by solipsism and by the notion of private language (chs. VII–VIII). The historical significance of this critique is illustrated with a large number of references to Locke (pp. 224–31), to Russell, and to neopositivism, while W.'s own theses are explained with frequent references to Kant. In the final chapters there is a critical examination of W.'s 'non-cognitivist' theses concerning psychological statements in the first person. *Reviews*: Ameriks K., NS, 1975, 49, pp. 94–118; Burns S. A., D, 1974, 13, pp. 384–8; Druet P. P., RPL, 1973, 71, pp. 628–9; Hallett G., G, 1973, 54, pp. 590–1; Hunter J. F. M., IPQ, 1973, 13, pp. 295–8; Hunter J. F. M., CJP, 1974, 4, pp. 201–11; Llewelyn J. E., I, 1973, 16, pp. 439–45; Lyon A., M, 1975, 84, pp. 293–5; Mounce H. O., PB, 1973, 14, n. 1, pp. 18–21; Richman R. J., PR, 1975, 84, pp. 113–17; Wolf M., PS(I), 22, pp. 277–9.

805. Hacker P. M. S., *Frege and the private language argument*, IS, 2, pp. 265–287.

The critique of Frege's philosophy is implicitly one of W.'s objectives in his examination of private language. A comparison beteen the two authors.

806. Harris C. E. Jr., *The problem of induction in the later W.*, SWJP, 3, pp. 135–46.

Five different argumentations by W. (all of which H. considers to be inadequate) which aim to give a philosophical foundation to induction.

807. Harward D. W., *W. and the character of mathematical* *propositions*, ILR, 3, pp. 246-51. Reprinted in Shanker (ed.), 1986, vol. III.

808. High D. M., *Belief, falsification, and W.*, IJPR, 3, pp. 240-50.
The difficulties faced in applying the principle of falsifiability to religious language.

809. Hoche H.-U., *Phänomenologie und Sprachanalyse. Bemerkungen zu W., Ryle und Husserl*, in *Aufgaben und Wege des Philosophieunterrichts*, F. Borden (ed.), Frankfurt, Hirschgraben, 1972, pp. 68.

810. Katz J. J., *Two contrasts with W.*, in his *Linguistic philosophy*, New York, Harper & Row, 1971; London, George Allen & Unwin, 1972, pp. 5-17.
A critical comparison between the 'early' and the 'later' W.'s theory of language, in an attempt to show that the manner in which language appears to us in speech and writing is very far from reflecting its true nature.

811. Kellenberger J., *The language-game view of religion and religious certainty*, CJP, 2, pp. 255-75.

812. Leblanc H., *W. and the truth-functionality thesis*, APQ, 9, pp. 271-4.
The relationship between the branching theory of Russell's types, the axiom of reducibility and *Tract*.

813. Leyvraz J. P., *B. Russell et l'impact de W.*, RIP, 26, n. 102, pp. 461-82.
The developments in Russell's thought which took place under W.'s influence.

814. Leyvraz J. P., *La notion d'attente chez Wittgenstein*, SP, 32, pp. 141-61.

815. Lübbe H., *Bewusstsein in Geschichten. Studien zur Phänomenologie der Subjektivität: Mach, Husserl, Schapp, W.*, Freiburg, Verlag Rombach, 1972, pp. 174.
Reviews: Gralhoff R., 'Archiv für Rechts- und Sozialphilosophie', 1974, 60, pp. 296-9; Nyíri J. C., PLA, 1974, 27, pp. 13-15; Pfafferott G., AGP, 1975, 57, pp. 114-18.

816. MacCormac E. R., *W.'s imagination*, SJP, 10, pp. 453-61.
The use of metaphor and the inventive nature of W.'s method of analysis, which aims to explore the limits of language.

817. McCormick P., Schaper E., Heaton J. M., *Symposium on saying and showing in Heidegger and W.*, JBSP, 3, pp. 27-35, 36-41, 42-5.
The differences (cf. in particular the first contribution) and analogies between the two philosophers, concerning the nature of metaphysics.

818. McGuinness B., *B. Russell and L.W.'s 'Notes on logic'*, RIP, 26, n. 102, pp. 440-60.
An examination of the genesis of *N.L.* and a comparison of the different manuscript versions of the work.

819. Marconi D., *W.: contesto e fondamento*, F, 23, pp. 255-74.
An examination of *P.G.*, and *O.C.*, paying particular attention to W.'s method of analysis and to his conception of philosophy. References to Heidegger.

820. Moran J., *Wittgenstein and Russia*, 'New Left Review', no. 73, pp. 85-96.

821. Mouloud N., *La logique et les 'jeux du langage'. Quelques suggestions de W. pour une philosophie des signes*, in Mouloud N. (ed.), *Les signes et leur interprétation*, Paris, Éditions Universitaires, 1972, pp. 31-50.

822. Nielsen K., *The coherence of W.ian fideism,* S, 11, no. 3, pp. 4-12.
A defence of W. against critics who find incoherencies in his 'fideistic' solution on the theme of religion (see also Downing, 1972).

823. Novielli V., *La problematica del significato nell'ultimo W.*, F, 23, pp. 389-410.

824. Nyíri J. K., *Das unglückliche Leben des L.W.,* ZPF, 26, pp. 585-608.

825. Pears D. F., *W.'s treatment of solipsism in the Tract.*, Cr, 6, pp. 57-80. Reprinted in Pears, 1975; in Canfield (ed.), 1986, vol. III; in S.G. Shanker (ed.), 1986, vol. I.

826. Pettit P., *W. and the case for structuralism*, JBSP, 3, pp. 46-57. Reprinted in Shanker (ed.), 1986, vol. IV.
A careful examination of the relationship between W., Lévi-Strauss and Saussure with regard to the theme of language.

827. Pitkin, H. F., *W. and justice. On the significance of L.W. for social and political thought*, Berkeley, Cal., University of California Press, 1972, pp. 360. Spanish translation: Madrid, Centro de Estudios Constitucionales, 1984.
P., who describes herself as an amateur philosopher, aims to provide an introduction for those studying politics to some topics treated by the later W., and to some theses of the 'philosophy of ordinary language', on the assumption that this 'revolutionary way of conceiving of language' can provide such students with a deeper understanding of the foundations of their own discipline. *Reviews:* Beehler R., CJP, 1976, 6, pp. 755-71; Erler E. J., 'Western Political Quarterly', 1973, 26, pp. 788-9; Flatham R. E., 'Journal of Politics', 1973, 35, pp. 747-53; Helm P., 'Political Studies', 1973, 21, pp. 530-1; Price J. T., MW, 1974, 7, pp. 78-87; Reinhardt L. R., M, 1976, 85, pp. 151-4; Richards W. M., 'Social Praxis', 1973, 1, pp. 319-23; Thomas D. A. L., PQ, 1974, 24, pp. 76-7; Whelan J. Jr., PR, 1974, 83, pp. 540-4.

828. Prange K., *Können, Üben, Wissen. Zur Problematik des Lernens in der Sprachphilosophie L.W.s*, 'Pädagogische Rundschau', 26, pp. 707-734.

829. Premo B. I., *The early W. and hermeneutics*, PT, 16, pp. 43-65.
On the possible relationship between *Tract.* and the phenomenology of K. O. Apel.

830. Radford C., *Pain and pain behaviour*, P, 47, pp. 189-205.
An examination of the relationship between pain sensations and behaviour in W., with a critique of Chihara and Fodor, 1965.

831. Ross G. A., *W. on persons*, NS, 46, pp. 368-71.
A critique of Mulligan, see 1970, and an examination of the debate between Strawson (1958) and Ayer (*The concept of a person*, London, 1963).

832. Schwartz E., *Remarques sur 'l'espace des choses' de W. et ses origines frégéennes*, Di, 26, pp. 185-226.

833. Sherry P., *Truth and the 'religious language game'*, P, 47, pp. 18-37.
S. criticizes the way in which Phillips ('Faith and philosophical enquiry', 1970) and others have tried to apply the theories on language of the later W. to the philosophy of religion.

834. Sherry P., *Is religion a 'form of life'?*, APQ, 9, pp. 159-67.
Contrary to what authors such as Malcolm, 1954, maintain, W.
never identified religion with a 'form of life', and never took
up a relativistic position.

835. Shirley E. S., *The illusion of a private language,* SWJP,
3, pp. 55-64.

836. Solomon R. C., *W. and Cartesian privacy*, PT, 16,
pp. 163-79.
A critical examination of W.'s theses on private language, which
are opposed to Husserl's 'Cartesianism'.

837. Steinvorth U., *L.W.: Sprache und Denken*, in Speck J.
(ed.), *Grundprobleme der grossen Philosophen.
Philosophie der Gegenwart*, Göttingen, Vandenhoeck &
Ruprecht, 1972, pp. 98-150.

838. Thorp J. W., *Whether the theory of family resemblances
solves the problem of universals*, M, 81, pp. 567-570.
Bambrough's theses, 1960, are based on an erroneous
understanding both of W.'s theory and of the traditional problem
of universals.

839. Tilghman B. R., *W., games, and art*, JAAC, 31, pp. 517-24.

840. Todd D. D., *A note on 'criteria'*, JCA, 3, no. 4,
pp. 198-207.
A critique of the interpretation of the notion of 'criterion' given
by Albritton, 1959, and by Malcolm, 1954, and its application
to the problem of other minds.

841. van Buren P. M., *The edges of language: an essay in the
logic of a religion*, London and New York, Macmillan,
1972, pp. 178.
Many references to W., and a discussion of the implications that
P.I. can have for Christian theology.

842. van Peursen C., *Phenomenology and analytical
philosophy*, Pittsburgh, Penn., Duquesne University Press,
pp. 190.
Large parts of this volume are devoted to an analysis of some
of W.'s later work, considered from the point of view of its
relation to phenomenological tendencies: see, in particular, chap.
9, 'From logical positivism to analytical philosophy: the uses of
language', and chap. 10, 'Linguistic analysis of the forms of life'.

843. **von Wright G. H.**, *W. on certainty*, in *Problems in the theory of knowledge*, edited by G. H. von Wright, The Hague, M. Nijhoff, 1972, pp. 47–60. Reprinted in von Wright, 1982.
Followed by a comment from B. F. McGuinness (pp. 61–5).

844. **Weissman D.**, *Platonism in the Tractatus*, IS, 2, pp. 51–80.

845. **Wertz S. K.**, *On W. and James*, NS, 46, pp. 446–8.
James's influence on W.'s mature works: objective analogies examined.

846. **Winkler E. R.**, *Scepticism and private language*, Mind, 81, pp. 1–17.

847. **Zemach E. M.**, *The reference of 'I'*, PS, 23, pp. 68–75. Reprinted in Canfield (ed.), 1986, vol. XII.
An interpretation of the analysis of first-person statements in *P.I.*

1973

848. **'Logos'**, n. 2, pp. 219–331.
A special issue of the review for the fiftieth anniversary of the publication of *Tract.* Twenty short contributions on various subjects.

849. **Aldrich V.**, *Something really unheard of*, PPR, 44, pp. 528–38.
A critical examination of *O.C.* 531. The general nature of W.'s claim leaves room for misunderstandings. A series of examples is discussed.

850. **Apel K.-O.**, *Transformation der Philosophie*, 2 vols, Frankfurt, Suhrkamp, 1973.
A collection of essays, previously published, centred on the relationship between hermeneutics and analytical philosophy, with frequent references to W.'s work (cf. 1965, 1966, 1967). A selection of these essays is translated into English in Apel, 1980.

851. **Bartley W. W.**, *Wittgenstein*, New York, Lippincott, 1973, pp. 192; London, Quartet Books, 1974, pp. 145; rev. ed., London, Cresset Library; La Salle, Ill., Open Court, 1985, pp. 218.

A reconstruction of W.'s biography and personality, in particular in the years following the First World War. A particular emphasis is placed on the existential and psychological crisis which occurred during that crucial period, and on W.'s activities as a teacher in small Austrian villages. Part of B.'s aim is to throw light, by means of this reconstruction, on the meaning of *Tract.* and of the later writings. *Reviews:* Unsigned, TLS, 17 August 1973, pp. 953-54; Bouveresse J., Cri, 1975, 31, pp. 796-804; De Angelis W., PPR, 1974-5, 35, pp. 289-90; Frank W., RM, 1974-5, 27, pp. 601-2; Goodstein R. L., P, 1974, 48, pp. 403-4; Hottois G., RIP, 1980, 33, pp. 293-5; Haller R., C, 1977, 11, pp. 422-4; Jarvie I. C., BJPS, 1974, 25, pp. 195-8; Price J. T., MW, 1974, 7, pp. 423-32; Soto C. H., 'Dialogos', 1978, 11, pp. 163-5.

852. Bearsley P. J., *Aquinas and W. on the grounds of certainty*, MS, 51, pp. 301-34.

853. Bensch R., *L.W. Die apriorischen und mathematischen Sätze in seinem Spätwerk*, Bonn, Bouvier, 1973, pp. 164.
After a short, comprehensive examination (section 3) of the problem of *a priori* statements in *Tract.* and in the later writings, B. dwells in particular on *R.F.M.* (section 4), and then (section 5) looks, within the framework of W.'s thought, for a reply to the Kantian question of how synthetic *a priori* statements are possible. According to B., W. in his more mature works tries (without success) to reconcile the ontological solution given in *Tract.* with the extreme 'conventionalism' of *R.F.M. Reviews:* Pittioni V., C, 1973, 7, pp. 96-9; Hallett G., G, 1973, 54, pp. 789-90.

854. Binkley T., *W.'s language*, The Hague, Martinus Nijhoff, 1973, pp. 227.
B.'s main intention is to analyse the expository style adopted by W. in *P.I.*, and to show that it is carefully adapted to W.'s therapeutic conception of philosophy and to the nature of the problems under examination. *Reviews:* Lichtigfeld A., TF, 1975, 37, pp. 147-9; Malherbe J. F., RPL, 1976, 74, pp. 309-10; Goff R., MW, 1975, 8, pp. 227-32; Soto C. H., 'Dialogos', 1975, 11, pp. 163-5; Todd D. D., PRh, 1975, 8, pp. 187-9.

855. Bloor D., *W. and Mannheim on the sociology of mathematics*, SHPS, 4, pp. 173-91. Reprinted in Shanker (ed.), 1986, vol. III.

856. Bouveresse J., *W., la rime et la raison. Science, éthique et esthétique*, Paris, Editions de Minuit, 1973, pp. 239. Italian translation: Bari, Laterza, 1982.
A collection of essays. Controverting, sometimes polemically, the interpretative trends which have emerged in Anglo-Saxon literature, B. dwells on the relationship between rationality and the need to transcend the limits of reason. The titles are: 'Mysticisme et logique' (pp. 21-72, concerning *Tract.*), 'La voie et le moyen' (pp. 72-116, republished in a modified form, see 1972); 'La volonté, le destin et la grâce' (pp. 117-152, devoted, like the preceding essay, to themes of ethics and religion); 'La voix universelle et le discours critique' (pp. 153-204, on aesthetics in W.), 'Les causes, les raisons et les mythes' (pp. 205-234, the relationship with psychoanalysis, with references to Frazer). *Reviews:* Kenny A. J. P., AP, 1974, 37, pp. 343-347; Penco C., 'Proteus', 1973, 4, pp. 206-210.

857. Bouveresse J., *W. et la philosophie*, BSFP, 67, pp. 85-122.
The text of a lecture. B. insists on the unitary aspect of W.'s thought, and on the strictly philosophical, rather than logical or linguistic, nature of his philosophy. A debate follows (pp. 122-137), with a critical note by M.M. Matschinski on Bouveresse's presentation, and a brief reply by the latter.

858. Chihara C., *Operationalism and ordinary language revisited*, PS, 24, pp. 137-57. Reprinted in Canfield (ed.), 1986, vol. III.
C. replies to Cook's criticisms (see *Studies in the philosophy of W.*, 1969) of one of C.'s previous articles (1965), and reaffirms his own interpretation, which attributes a form of logical behaviourism to W.

859. Cohen S. M., *Family resemblance in the thirteenth century*, P, 48, pp. 391-4.
There are clear precedents of W.'s theory on family resemblances, particularly in St. Thomas. This claim is followed by criticisms of Bambrough's and Thorp's theses, 1960 and 1972 respectively.

860. Daniels C. B. and **Davison J.**, *Ontology and method in W.'s Tractatus*, N, 7, pp. 233-47.
There are two radically distinct kinds of ontological entity in *Tract.*: 'objects' and 'facts'. Material properties and general terms, on the other hand, are analysable.

861. Dietrich R. A., *Sprache und Wirklichkeit in W.s Tractatus*, Tübingen, Niemeyer, 1973, pp. 215.

862. Dilman I., *Induction and deduction. A study in W.*, New York, Harper & Row; Oxford, Blackwell, 1973, pp. 225. The work is mainly concerned with philosophical scepticism about the possibility of giving a rational justification of the principles of inductive (with particular reference to Hume and Russell) and deductive reasoning. In the first part, D. considers W.'s reply to scepticism concerning inductive inference. In the second part he examines the theory of 'formal inference' in *Tract.* (ch. 8) and the theses on logical necessity in the later writings. *Reviews*: Bogen J., D, 1974, 13, pp. 198–201; Lyas C., PB, 1974, 15, n. 1, pp. 1–3; Mackenzie P.T., CJP, 1975, 5, pp. 309–21; Wilkerson T.E., M, 1975, 84, pp. 297–9.

863. Engel S. M., *W., existentialism and the history of philosophy*, in *Deutung und Bedeutung*, ed. by B. Schuldermann *et al.*, The Hague and Paris, Mouton, 1973, pp. 228–47.

864. Erde E. L., *Philosophy and psycholinguistics* (Janua Linguarum, Series Minor, 160), The Hague and Paris, Mouton, 1973, pp. 235. In Part 3, especially in the chapter 'In defense of W.', pp. 164–202, E. develops parallels between the later W.'s theses on language, innate ideas, and behaviourism and those of Chomsky, claiming a real compatibility and also defending W. against critics such as Fodor, Katz and Chihara, who interpret him as a behaviourist.

865. Fay T. A., *Early Heidegger and W. on world*, PS(I), 21, pp. 161–171.

866. Gargani A. G., *Introduzione a W.*, Bari, Laterza, 1973, pp. 195.

867. Ginet C., *An incoherence in the Tractatus*, CJP, 3, pp. 143–51. Reprinted in Canfield (ed.), 1986, vol. I. The fact that W. abandoned the thesis concerning the independence of elementary propositions in 1929 should not necessarily be taken to mean a repudiation of the whole theory of *Tract.*

868. Griffin N., *W., universals and family resemblances*, CJP, 3, pp. 635–51. Reprinted in Canfield (ed.), 1986, vol. V.

The theory of family resemblances does not constitute an alternative solution to the problem of universals (contrary to what Bambrough, 1960, maintains) in that it does not provide clear criteria for the application of general terms.

869. Hallett G., *Is there a picture theory of language in the Tractatus?*, HJ, 14, pp. 314–21. Reprinted in Shanker (ed.), 1986, vol. I.
An interpretation of *Tract.* (4.001) which aims to extend the picture theory of assertions ('statements') to commands and questions.

870. Headlee M. B., *W.'s philosophy: old and new*, D, 15, pp. 39–44.
Despite the profound differences between *Tract.* and *P.I.*, some of W.'s aims remain unchanged.

871. Hintikka J., *Logic, language-games and information. Kantian themes in the philosophy of logic*, Oxford, Clarendon Press, 1973, pp. 291.
A collection of essays on general philosophical topics, frequently referring to W. and developing in an independent manner notions derived from him. Contains a reprint of Hintikka, 1969.

872. Hodges M., *W. on universals*, PS, 24, pp. 22–30.
The ambiguity of the 'family resemblances' theory, as it affects the opposition between nominalism and realism.

873. Hudson H., *W. and Zen Buddhism*, PEW, 23, pp. 471–81.
In spite of some objective analogies, there are substantial differences between the two trends.

874. Hudson W. D., *'Using a picture' and religious belief*, S, 12, pp. 11–17.
A reply to the criticisms made by Durrant, 1971.

875. Hunter J. F. M., *Essays after W.*, London, George Allen & Unwin; Toronto, University of Toronto Press, 1973, pp. 202.
A collection of essays. While some have a mainly exegetic purpose, others aim rather at a theoretical development of W.ian subjects. Amongst the former, the following are particularly worthy of mention: *Telling* (pp. 91–114); *The concept of pain* (pp. 115–146); *Logical compulsion* (pp. 171–202). *Reviews*: Bambrough R., CJP, 1977, 7, pp. 869–76; Burns S., D, 1975, 14,

pp. 341-53; Cooke V. M., IPQ, 1975, 15, pp. 122-4; Dilman I.,
M, 1976, 85, pp. 460-2; Edwards J. C., PR, 1978, 87, pp. 76-99;
Hallett G. L., G, 1975, 56, pp. 181-2; Newell R. W., P, 1975,
50, pp. 368-70; Nielsen K., Mp, 1976, 7, pp. 241-64; Pletcher
G. K., MS, 1976, 53, pp. 71-5; Price J. T., FL, 1975, 13,
pp. 307-8; Stroud B., JP, 1976, 73, pp. 277-81.

876. **Janik A.** and **Toulmin S. E.**, *W.'s Vienna*, London,
Weidenfeld & Nicolson; New York, Simon & Schuster,
1973, pp. 314. Spanish translation, Madrid, Taurus, 1974.
Italian translation: Milan, Garzanti, 1975. Dutch translation:
Meppel, Boom, 1976. French translation: Paris, Presses
Universitaires de France, 1978. German translation: Munich
and Vienna, Hanser, 1984.

A reconstruction of Viennese culture in the decades before
the fall of the Hapsburg empire. With this as a background, J.
and T. aim to provide, in the second part of the work, a picture
of W.'s intellectual personality and philosophy which is in
many ways novel. Dealing with both *Tract.* (esp. ch. VI) and
the later writings, J. and T. emphasize the fundamental problems
treated and place them historically in the continental tradition
derived from Kant. Thus it turns out that all W.'s work is
clearly distinguished from both contemporary neopositivism
and Anglo-Saxon analytical philosophy (see ch. VIII). *Reviews*:
Bartley W. W., PSS, 1975, 5, pp. 88-91; Bouveresse M. J.,
Cri, 1975, 31, pp. 781-96; Boyer J. W., 'Journal of Modern
History', 1976, 47, pp. 703-11; Cunningham N., MW, 1976, 9,
pp. 313-19; De Ruyter R., 'Krisis', 1981, 5, pp. 103-7; Evan-
Granboucan G., RMM, 1978, 84, p. 258; Frank W., RM, 27,
pp. 612-13; Henderson C., Zeman V., JHP, 1976, 14,
pp. 118-21; Hoffman R. L., 'Dissent', 1975, 22, pp. 203-5;
Hottois G., RIP, 1980, 34, pp. 298-301; Largeault J., RPFE, 1979,
104, pp. 326-7; Linsky L., 'Modern History', 1975, 47,
pp. 699-703; Nyíri J. K., PLA, 1975, 28, pp. 95-9; Presas M. A.,
RLF, 1976, 2, pp. 85-7; Steiner G., 'The New Yorker', 23 July
1973, pp. 73-7.

877. **Kenny A. J. P.**, *Wittgenstein*, London, Allen Lane;
Cambridge, Mass., Harvard University Press, 1973, pp. 240.
German translation: Frankfurt, Suhrkamp, 1974. Spanish
translation: Madrid, Alianza, 1974. Flemish translation:
Utrecht and Antwerp, Het Spectrum, 1974. French

translation: Verviers, Marabout, 1975. Italian translation: Turin, Boringhieri, 1984.
The work considers the development of W.'s thought through the examination of themes held to be central. The part concerning *Tract.*, whose historical background is said to be located in the work of Frege and Russell (chs. 2–3), is centred above all on the picture theory (ch. 4) and on its metaphysical and ontological implications (ch. 5). The central part of the book traces W.'s gradual detachment from 'logical atomism', through the works of the intermediate period. The examination of the later works is limited to the problems of the philosophy of mind (ch. 10) and to the discussion on scepticism, paying particular attention to *O.C.* (ch. 11). In a concluding chapter K. re-affirms the thesis of the continuity in the development of W.'s thought which is due not only to the gradual (non-traumatic) modification of his theories on language and philosophy, but also to the persistence of some of the main themes and solutions. *Reviews*: Ameriks K., NS, 1975, 49, pp. 94–118; Brown S., P, 1975, 50, pp. 248–9; Burns S. A. M., D, 1974, 13, pp. 196–8; Byrne P., RS, 1975, 11, pp. 489–90; Ellis A., M, 1978, 87, pp. 270–75; Graham G., IPQ, 1975, 15, pp. 369–72; Manser A., M, 1975, 84, pp. 619–21; Meggle G., E, 1975, 9, pp. 145–52; Palmer A., PB, 1974, 15, n. 1, pp. 6–8; Stroud B., PR, 1975, 84, pp. 576–80.

878. Klein J. T., *W.'s analysis of the use of 'I' in the 'Philosophical investigations'*, MS, 51, pp. 47–53.

879. Kluge E. H. W., *Objects as universals: a re-appraisal of the Tractatus*, D, 12, pp. 64–77.

880. Koenne W., *Die Beziehung W.s zu Frege im Tractat*, WW, 26, pp. 135–45.

881. Leavis F. R., *Memories of W.*, HW, 10, pp. 66–79. Reprinted in *L.W.: personal recollections*, 1981.

882. Leitner B., *The architecture of L.W.*, London, Studio International Publications, 1973, pp. 127.
The work is essentially composed of a photographic documentation, external and internal, of the house built by W. together with P. Engelmann in 1927–9, with reproductions of documents and plans (pp. 34–124). This is preceded by a brief historical introduction and extracts from 'Family recollections', notes written by W.'s sister Hermine, at the beginning of the

1940s, concerning episodes from W.'s life, especially during the period of the planning of the house (reprinted in *L. W.: personal recollections*, 1981). Texts in English and German. *Reviews*: Aldrich V., SWJP, 1975, 6, pp. 168-9; Eichner H., D, 1974, 13, pp. 388-9; Frank W., RM, 1974, 27, p. 801.

883. Lucier P., *Le statut du langage religieux dans la philosophie de L. W.*, SR, 3, no. 1, pp. 14-28.

884. Machan T. R., *W. and meta-ethics*, JT, 8, pp. 252-9.

885. Mackenzie N., *Basic sentences and objectivity: a private language argument*, D, 12, pp. 217-32. Reprinted in Canfield (ed.), 1986, vol. IX.
An analysis and defence of W.'s private language argument based on an interpretation of *P.I.* 243-317.

886. Moran J., *Towards the world and wisdom of W.'s Tractatus*, The Hague and Paris, Mouton, 1973, pp. 126.
An attempt to determine a systematic relationship between the 'technical' and logical parts of *Tract.* and those parts which deal with the problems of the limits of language, the subject, the will, ethics, death, God, etc. Hence a refusal to interpret W. one-sidedly, in theoretical and cognitive terms: it must not be overlooked that for W. philosophy should improve our thinking about the important questions of everyday life. *Reviews*: Bramann J. K., RM, 1975-6, 29, pp. 350-1; Goldstein L., PQ, 1975, 25, pp. 84-5; Stine G. C., PR, 1975, 84, pp. 570-5.

887. Mounce H. O., *Understanding a primitive society*, P, 48, pp. 347-62.
The application of the notion of 'language game' in anthropological analysis. Criticism of Winch, 1964.

888. Nammour J., *Resemblances and universals*, M, 82, pp. 516-24.
Does W.'s notion of 'family resemblances' apply only to complex words like 'chair' and 'game' or to all general words? An examination and criticism of Bambrough's interpretation, 1960.

889. Nielsen K., *The challenge of W. An examination of his picture of religious belief*, SR, 3, pp. 29-46. Reprinted in Nielsen, 1982.

890. Pascal F., *W.: a personal memoir*, 'Encounter', 41, pp. 23-39. Reprinted in *W.: sources and perspectives*, 1979, and in *L.W.: personal recollections*, 1981.

891. Piana G., *Interpretazione del Tractatus di W.*, Milan, Il Saggiatore, 1973, pp. 172.

An examination, in particular, of the 'theory of symbolism' and of the philosophy of logic and mathematics of *Tract.* following a 'formalistic' interpretation'. In one chapter, 'On the ideology of *Tract.*', the theses on the subject, on ethics and on mysticism are dealt with.

892. Poulain J., *La possibilité des propositions ontologiques dans le Tractatus*, EP, no. 4, pp. 529-52.

893. Poulain J., *Logique et religion. L'atomisme logique de L.W. et la possibilité des propositions religieuses*, The Hague and Paris, Mouton, 1973, pp. 228.

The French text is followed by an English version, modified and abridged, entitled 'Logic and religion', in which P. dwells in a more analytical manner on some aspects of his exposition. *Review*: Reix A., RPFE, 1977, 102, pp. 99-100.

894. Price J. T., *Language and being in W.'s P.I.*, The Hague and Paris, 1973, Mouton, pp. 122.

A critical discussion of some themes (language, philosophy of mind, philosophical method) in the later work of W. *Review*: Baldwin H.W., RM, 1975, 29, pp. 144-5.

895. Rappaport S., *Aune's W. on the empiricist thesis*, PS, 24, pp. 258-63.

W.'s critique of private language fails to show that the empiricist thesis placing the foundation of empirical knowledge in immediate experiences is unfounded. Critical references to B. Aune's *Knowledge, mind and nature*, New York, 1967.

896. Saunders J. T., *Persons, criteria and scepticism*, Mp, 4, pp. 95-113.

A discussion of the 'W.ian-Strawsonian notion of criteria', in its connection with the problem of knowledge of other minds.

897. Schlagel R. H., *Contra W.*, PPR, 34, pp. 539-50.

The claim that philosophical problems can be solved through the analysis of ordinary language is based on an erroneous understanding of the nature of philosophy.

898. Schwyzer H., *Thought and reality: the metaphysics of*

Kant and W., PQ, 23, pp. 193-206. Reprinted in Canfield (ed.), 1986, vol. XV; in Shanker (ed.), 1986, vol. II.
The unity of W.'s thought is placed in relation to the Kantian nature of the solution given to the problem of the relationship between reality and thought.

899. Shibles W., *L'originalité de W.*, RIP, 27, pp. 526-34.
The most original feature of *P.I.* is identified as its analytical method and its conception of philosophy. Contrasts and analogies with the thought of W.M. Urban.

900. Shirley E. S., *Castañeda on the private-language argument. A refutation of a refutation*, SWJP, 4, no. 1, pp. 133-8 (see Castañeda, 1962).

901. Studhalter K., *Ethik, Religion und Lebensform bei L.W.*, Innsbruck, Universität Innsbruck, 1973, pp. 78.
Review: Walgrave J. H., TF, 38, pp. 169-70.

902. Teichman J., *W. on 'can'*, A, 34, pp. 113-17. Reprinted in Canfield (ed.), 1986, vol. XIII.
The examination of a series of 'language games', drawn from *Br.B.*, designed to shed light on the relationship between functional ability and physical structures (brain, nervous system, etc.).

903. von Wright G.H., Introduction to *Letters to C.K. Odgen* (see 'Publications of writings by Wittgenstein'), pp. 1-13.
An examination of the events leading to the publication and first English translation of *Tract*.

904. Walker J., *W.'s early theory of the will: an analysis*, IS, 3, pp. 179-205.
An interpretation in a Kantian sense of ethics in W.

905. Wallace K., *Nietzsche's and W.'s perspectivism*, SWJP, 4, pp. 101-7.
Analogies between Nietzsche and the 'ontology' of the later W.

906. Weitz M., *W.'s aesthetics*, in *Language and aesthetics*, ed. by B. R. Tilghman, Lawrence, Kan., University Press of Kansas, 1973, pp. 7-19.

907. Wertz S. K., *On placing W. in history*, SJP, 11, pp. 337-50.
With reference to Toulmin's interpretation, 1969.

908. Wilkerson T. E., *Seeing-as*, M, 82, pp. 481–96.
Various criticisms of W.'s distinction in *P.I.* between 'seeing'
and 'seeing as'. It is maintained that this distinction is of no great
philosophical interest.

909. Wollheim R., *The art lesson*, in his *On art and the mind*,
London, Allen Lane; Cambridge, Mass., Harvard University
Press, 1973, pp. 130–45.
A lecture on teaching art, taking into account W.'s views on 'the
way we learn or are taught language'.

1974

910. *Understanding W.*, ed. by G. Vesey, London, Macmillan;
New York, St Martin's Press, 1974, pp. 285.
This important collection of essays, which appeared in vol. 7
of the series of Royal Institute of Philosophy Lectures (1972-73)
includes: A. Kenny, *The ghost of the Tractatus*, pp. 1–13 (an
evaluation of the references to *Tract.* in W.'s later works.
Reprinted in Kenny, 1984); R. M. White, *Can whether one
proposition makes sense depend on the truth of another* (*Tract.*
2.0211-2), pp. 14–29; R. Rhees, *Questions on logical inference*,
pp. 30–48; B. McGuinness, *The Grundgedanke of the Tractatus*,
pp. 49–61 (*Tract.* 4.0312: an historical and theoretical evaluation
of the thesis that logical constants do not represent anything);
G. Stock, *W. on Russell's theory of judgment*, pp. 62–75;
B. Williams, *W. and idealism*, pp. 76–95 (solipsism and the
nature of the subject in *Tract.* and in the later writings); A. P.
Griffiths, *W., Schopenhauer, and ethics*, pp. 96–116;
R. Bambrough, *How to read W.*, pp. 117–131 (an account of
W.'s expository style); J. Teichman, *W. on persons and human
beings*, pp. 133–148; G. Vesey, *Other minds*, pp. 149–161;
I. Dilman, *W. on the soul*, pp. 162–192; L. Holborow, *The
prejudice in favour of psychological parallelism*, pp. 193–207
(with reference to *Z.* 611); R. Squires, *Silent soliloquy*,
pp. 207–225; A.J. Ayer, *W. on Certainty*, pp. 226–245 (reprinted
in his *Freedom and morality*, Oxford, 1984); C. Coope, *W.'s
theory of knowledge*, pp. 246–267 (knowledge and certainty,
with particular reference to *O.C.*). The essays by I. Dilman,
B. McGuinness, R. Rhees, J. Teichman, R. M. White, B. Williams
have been included in Canfield (ed.), 1986; that by A. Kenny
in Shanker (ed.), 1986, vol. I. *Reviews*: Agassi J., E, 1978, 13,

pp. 305-326; Burke T. E., PB, 1975, 16, pp. 32-33; Block I., Ph, 1978, 7, pp. 717-733; Genova J. A., MW, 1978, 11, pp. 199-207; Janik A. S., 'Modern Austrian Literature', 1980, 13, p. 208; Lichtigfeld A., TF, 1975, 37, pp. 540-544; Manser A. R., P, 1975, 50, pp. 478-481; Newell R. W., PQ, 1975, 25, pp. 363-365; Palmer A., M, 1976, 85, pp. 619-621.

911. *Wisdom: twelve essays*, ed. by J. R. Bambrough, Oxford, Blackwell, 1974, pp. 300.

Many references to the relationship and the contrasts between Wisdom and W. See in particular: I. Dilman, *Paradoxes and discoveries*, pp. 78-106; J. R. Bambrough, *Literature and philosophy*, pp. 274-92.

912. Abrams M. H., *A note on W. and literary criticism*, 'Journal of English Literary History', 41, pp. 541-54. Reprinted in Shanker (ed.), 1986, vol. IV.

913. Baker G., *Criteria: a new foundation for semantics*, R, 16, pp. 156-189. Reprinted in Shanker (ed.), 1986, vol. II; in Canfield (ed.), 1986, vol. XII.

A defence of the originality and coherence of the notion of criterion in W., and of its uses for a 'constructivistic' semantic theory.

914. Bartley W. W., *Theory of language and philosophy of science as instruments of educational reform; W. and Popper as Austrian schoolteachers*, in *Methodological and historical essays in the natural and social sciences*, ed. by R. S. Cohen *et al.* ('Boston Studies in the Philosophy of Science', vol. 14), Dordrecht and Boston, Mass., Reidel, 1974, pp. 307-337.

915. Bickenbach J. E., *The status of the propositions in the Tractatus*, D, 13, pp. 763-72.

Examines *Tract.* 6.45 and the criteria for recognizing a proposition as devoid of sense.

916. Birnbacher D., *Die Logik der Kriterien. Analysen zur Spätphilosophie W.s*, Hamburg, Meiner, 1974, pp. 155.

In an analysis of different works written by W. after 1930, B. singles out two prevailing meanings of the notion of 'criterion': semantic criteria and criteria of evidence. This distinction is then used in a critical examination of the problem of private language in W. *Reviews*: Reitzig G. H., PLA, 1976, 29, pp. 299-301;

Heidelberger M., GPS, 1977, 4, pp. 172-84; Zimmermann R., PRd, 1979, 26, pp. 208-13.

917. Black C., *'Philosophical investigations'. Remark 43 revisited*, M, 83, pp. 596-8.
On the relationship between meaning and use. W. avoids solutions which do not take into account the great variety of linguistic cases.

918. Bogen J., *W. and skepticism*, PR, 83, pp. 364-73.
Reprinted in Canfield (ed.), 1986, vol. VIII; in Shanker (ed.), 1986, vol. II.
The relationship between O.C. and some classical forms of scepticism, in particular 'verificationism' and 'Cartesianism'.

919. Brown C. H., *W.ian linguistics*, The Hague, Mouton, 1974, pp. 135. Italian translation: Rome, Armando, 1978.

920. Broyles J. E., *An observation on W.'s use of fantasy*, Mp, 5, pp. 291-7.
The role played by imagination in W.'s philosophical method.

921. Canfield J. V., *Anthropological science fiction and logical necessity*, CJP, 4, pp. 467-79.
An examination of the notion of necessity in mathematical inference, and a critique of Stroud's interpretation, 1965.

922. Canfield J. V., *Criteria and rules of language*, PR, 83, pp. 70-87.
An examination of the notion of criterion and a defence of Albritton's interpretation, 1959.

923. Cherry C., *Professor Schwyzer's entitlement question*, PQ, 24, pp. 261-4. (cf. Schwyzer, 1973).

924. Clegg J. S., *W. on verification and private language*, CJP (Suppl.), 1, pp. 205-13. Reprinted in King-Farlow J. and Shiner R.A. (eds.), *New essays on the philosophy of mind*, Edmonton, University of Alberta, 1976.

925. Cohen M., *Truth-tables and truth*, A, 35, pp. 1-7.
A comment on the thesis from *Tract.* (6.111) that the terms 'true' and 'false' do not express properties.

926. Cohen M., *Tractatus 5.542*, M, 83, pp. 442-4.
The analysis of intensional statements.

927. Cohen T., *Chihara on Cook on other minds*, PS, 26, pp. 299–300.
Cf. Chihara, 1973. See also Chihara's reply, 1976.

928. Cooke V. M., *W.'s use of the private language discussion*, IPQ, 4, pp. 25–49.
The outcome of an examination of *P.I.*, 242–270 is that W. did not so much intend to show the impossibility of private language, but rather to point out the source of two erroneous philosophical theories: those of behaviourism and dualism.

929. Dumitriu A., *W.'s solution of the paradoxes and the conception of the scholastic logician Petrus de Allyaco* [Pierre d'Ailly], JHP, 12, pp. 227–37. Reprinted in Shanker (ed.), 1986, vol. III.

930. Fann K., *W. and bourgeois philosophy*, 'Radical Philosophy', no. 8, pp. 24–7.

931. Fogelin R. J., *Negative elementary propositions*, PS, 25, pp. 189–97. Reprinted in Shanker (ed.), 1986, vol. I.
The possibility of negative elementary propositions in *Tract.*, although it is in contrast to prevailing interpretations, and although it was denied by W. himself, appears to be more in keeping with the doctrine of *Tract.* itself.

932. Frongia G., *L.W.-Recenti studi e tendenze della critica*, BBSMS, nos. 25–26, pp. 17–63.

933. Gill J. H., *On reaching bedrock*, Mp, 5, pp. 277–290.
Hume, Kant and W. *(O.C.)* on the foundations of knowledge and on the most suitable philosophical method for an understanding of their nature.

934. Gill J. H., *Saying and showing. Radical themes in W.'s 'On certainty'*, RS, 10, pp. 279–90.
The limits of what can be said and their relevance to the grounds of certainty.

935. Gudmunsen C., *On the Mahāyāna and W.*, JRR, 4, no. 2, pp. 96–103.
A comparison between W.'s philosophy and some of the theses of Zen Buddhism.

936. Gustafson D. F., *Expressions of intentions*, M, 83, pp. 321–40. Reprinted in his *Intention and agency*,

Dordrecht and Boston, Mass., Reidel, 1986, pp. 69–83; in Canfield (ed.), 1986, vol. XIII.
Frequent references to W.'s analysis of the notion of intention.

937. **Gustason W.**, *Tractatus, 2.0201-2.0212*, CJP, 4, pp. 515–27.
The analysis of the 'propositions of ordinary discourse' in elementary propositions. The relation of this to Russell's theory of descriptions.

938. **Haller R.**, *Sprachkritik und Philosophie: W. und Mauthner*, in Doppler A. (ed.), *Sprachthematik in der österreichischen Literatur des 20. Jahrhunderts*, Vienna, Hirt, 1974, pp. 41–56.

939. **Hollinger R.**, *Natural kinds, family resemblances, and conceptual change*, Pr, 55, pp. 323–33.

940. **Hollinger R.**, *The role of aspect seeing in W.'s later thought*, 'Cultural Hermeneutics', 2, pp. 229–41.

941. **Hopkins J.**, *W. and physicalism*, PAS, 75, pp. 121–46.
W.'s criticism of the 'Cartesian' conception of sensations as identifiable objects.

942. **Hudson W. D.**, *A philosophical approach to religion*, London, Macmillan, 1974, pp. 200.
Contains a chapter 'The logical structure of religious belief' on the value of W.'s ideas for understanding religious belief.

943. **Hülser K.**, *Die Unterscheidung 'sagen-zeigen', das Logische und die 'Wahrheit' in W.s Tractatus*, KS, 65, pp. 457–75.

944. **James D.**, *Le problème de l'erreur dans les 'Investigations philosophiques' de L.W.*, SP, 34, pp. 25–56.

945. **Levin M. E.**, *When is it five o'clock on the sun?*, SJP, 12, pp. 65–70.
The origin of philosophical problems and their solutions in W., with particular reference to the problem of the knowledge of other minds.

946. **Lütterfelds W.**, *Die Dialektik 'sinnvoller Sprache' in W.s Tractatus*, ZPF, 28, pp. 562–84.

947. **Marks C. E.**, *Can one recognize kinds of private objects?*, CJP (Suppl.), 1 (2nd part), pp. 216–28. Reprinted in Canfield (ed.), 1986, vol. IX.

948. Marks C. E., *Ginet on W.'s argument against private rules*, PS, 15, pp. 261-71 (cf. Ginet, 1970). Reprinted in Canfield (ed.), 1986, vol. IX.

949. Morawetz Th. H., *W. and synthetic a priori judgments*, P, 40, pp. 429-34.
Far-reaching analogies between Kant and *O.C.* as regards the nature of *a priori* synthetic judgements and of metaphysics.

950. Murray M., *A note on W. and Heidegger*, PR, 83, pp. 501-3. Reprinted in *Heidegger and modern philosophy,* edited by M. Murray, New Haven, Conn., and London, Yale University Press, 1978, pp. 80-3.
Combating a widespread lack of understanding among 'analytical philosophers' of the interest of this comparison, M. points to analogies between W. and Heidegger, with reference to a brief passage in Waismann's notes on W.'s conversations *(W.W.K.)*.

951. Musciagli D., *Logica e ontologia in W. Proposta d'analisi su struttura e conoscenza nel Tractatus*, Lecce, Milella, 1974, pp. 197.

952. Paskow A., *A phenomenological view of the beetle in the box*, NS, 48, pp. 277-304.
P. examines W.'s theses on private language from a 'phenomenological' viewpoint.

953. Price J. T., *Dream recollection and W.'s language*, D, 13, pp. 35-41.

954. Schwyzer H., *Essence without universals*, CJP, 4, pp. 69-78. Reprinted in Canfield (ed.), 1986, vol. V.
Criticisms of Bambrough, 1960.

955. Sefler G. F., *Language and the world. A methodological-structural synthesis within the writings of M. Heidegger and L.W.*, Atlantic Highlands, N.J., Humanities Press, 1974, pp. 228.
Reviews: Balowitz V. H., SIF, 1975, 7, pp. 218-19; Harries K., PR, 1976, 85, pp. 422-6; J.D.C., RM, 1975, 28, pp. 764-5; Moulines C. U., Cr, 1981, 13, pp. 120-3; Tollinchi E., 'Dialogos', 1977, 11, pp. 316-17.

956. Shibles W., *Wittgenstein*, in his *Death: an interdisciplinary*

analysis, Whitewater, Wis., Language Press, 1974, pp. 69-80.
Comments on passages about death drawn from *Tract.* and *L.C.*

957. Shibles W., *W.'s language-game, theory of sensations and emotions*, in his *Emotion: the method of philosophical therapy*, Whitewater, Wis., Language Press, 1974, pp. 145-56.

958. Shiner R. A., *W. on the beautiful, the good and the tremendous*, BJA, 14, pp. 258-71. Reprinted in Canfield (ed.), 1986, vol. XIV.
A critique of some of the later W.'s theses on aesthetics *(L.C.)* which, according to S., still retain traces of the *Tract.* view.

959. Shiner R. A., *W. and Heraclitus: two river-images*, P, 40, pp. 191-7.
The two philosophers' recourse to the metaphorical image of the river *(O.C.)*.

960. Solomon R. C., *On Cartesian privacy*, SJP, 12, pp. 527-36.
In controversy with Kenny, 1966, S. maintains that W.'s private language argument does not affect the foundation of 'Cartesianism', especially in its 'phenomenological' form. Kenny's reply follows (pp. 537-8).

961. Solomon R. C., *Husserl's private language*, SWJP, 5, pp. 203-28.
The rejection of 'subjectivism' in W., and a comparison with Husserl.

962. Stetter C., *Sprachkritik und Transformationsgrammatik. Zur Bedeutung der Philosophie W.s für die sprachwissenschaftliche Theoriebildung*, Düsseldorf, Schwann, 1974, pp. 168.

963. Strawson P. F., *Freedom and resentment and other essays*, London, Methuen; New York, Barnes & Noble, pp. 214.
Apart from a reprint of S.'s review of *P.I.* (see no. 1954), this volume contains *Imagination and perception*, pp. 45-65, which develops a comparative historical analysis of the concept of 'imagination' in Kant's *Critique of Pure Reason* and similar topics in W.'s later work.

1975

964. *Forms of representation*, ed. by B. Freed, A. Marras, P. Maynard, Amsterdam, North Holland, 1975, pp. 245. Proceedings of the 1973 Philosophy Colloquium at the University of Western Ontario. The contributions concerned with W. are: D.S. Shwayder, *W.'s 'picture theory' and Aristotle*, pp. 161–88 (reprinted in Canfield (ed.), 1986, vol. I); H. Ishiguro, *Representation: an investigation based on a passage in the Tractatus*, pp. 189–202; D. F. Pears, *Representation in W.'s Tractatus*, pp. 203–220; D. W. Stampe, *Show and tell*, pp. 221–45.

965. *Sprachanalyse und Soziologie. Die sozialwissenschaftliche Relevanz von W.s Sprachphilosophie*, ed. by R. Wiggershaus, Frankfurt, Suhrkamp, 1975, pp. 350.
W.'s text *Remarks on Frazer* is followed by a collection of contributions, of a quite varied nature and on various subjects, which aims to evaluate the relevance of the 'philosophy of language' of the second W. for a 'social science' with a critical tendency. All the contributions are contained in previously published works, except the last one, by J. Habermas, *Sprachspiel, Intention und Bedeutung. Zu Motiven bei Sellars und W.* (pp. 319–340). The other authors are: P. Winch, A. MacIntyre, M. Roche, A.V. Cicourel, H. Berger, J.R. Searle. A bibliography on the subject follows.

966. Amendolagine F. and **Cacciari M.**, *Oikos, da Loos a W.*, Rome, Officina Edizioni, 1975, pp. 117.
A book essentially composed of two essays: C.'s *Loos-Wien*, pp. 13–60 (with a section on 'L'oikos di W.'. Also contained in Cacciari, 1986), A.'s *La casa di W.*, pp. 63–105. The middle pages of the book give a photographic documentation of the house planned by W. and of other Austrian works of architecture from the first thirty years of the century.

967. Ameriks K., *Recent work on W. and the philosophy of mind*, NS, 49, pp. 94–118.
A critical examination of W.'s literature on this subject, from 1972 onwards.

968. Block I., *Hart on the 'Tractatus'*, ILR, 6, pp. 145–57. Reprinted in Canfield (ed.), 1986, vol. III.
A critique of Hart, 1971.

969. Block I., *'Showing' in the Tractatus: The root of W.'s and Russell's basic incompatibility*, Ru, no. 17, pp. 4-22. Reprinted in Shanker (ed.), 1986, vol. I.

970. Bouveresse J., *Les derniers jours de l'humanité*, Cri, 31, pp. 753-805.
An examination of W.'s biography and personality, particularly his cultural links with Vienna before the First World War.

971. Bramann J. K., *Kafka and W. on religious language*, S, 14, n. 3, pp. 1-9. French translation in 'Diogène', 1975, no. 90, pp. 31-42.

972. Brand G., *Die grundlegenden Texte von L.W.*, Frankfurt, Suhrkamp, 1975, pp. 217. E.T. *The central texts of L.W.*, Oxford, Blackwell; New York, Basic Books, 1979. Spanish translation: Madrid, Alianza, 1981.
An anthology of passages from W. arranged according to subject such as: certainty, the world, the subject, temporality, language, understanding, complex and thing, language game, rules, exactness and vagueness, grammar and logic, the will, religion, ethics, philosophy. *Reviews:* Ales Bello A., 'Filosofia e Societa', 1976, 4, pp. 101-3; Bayertz K., 'Argument', 1976, 18, pp. 840-3; Cobb-Stevens R., RM, 1980-1, 34, pp. 598-9; Coyne M. U., IPQ, 1981, 21, pp. 226-7; König I., AZP, 1978, 3, pp. 77-9; Iglesias M. T., PS(I), 1981, 28, pp. 351-2; Smith P., Th, 1982, 46, pp. 161-3; Teskee R. J., MS, 1982, 60, p. 49; Vossenkuhl W., ZPF, 1977, 31, pp. 467-70; Zimmermann R., PRd, 1979, 26, pp. 198-201.

973. Burch R. W., *Why elementary propositions cannot be negative*, PS, 27, pp. 433-5.
A critique of Fogelin, 1974.

974. Burke T. E., *W.'s conservatism*, 'Radical Philosophy', no. 10, pp. 27-8.

975. Canfield J. V., *Anthropological science fiction and logical necessity*, CJP, 4, pp. 467-79. Reprinted in Canfield (ed.), 1986, vol. X.
A reply to Stroud, 1966, on 'W.'s anthropological view of language'.

976. Canfield J. V., *W. and Zen*, P, 50, pp. 383-408. Reprinted in Canfield (ed.), 1986, vol. XV; in Shanker (ed.), 1986, vol. IV.

Analogies between the 'mystical basis' of the later W.'s theory
of language, and the Zen practice of acting 'with an empty mind'.
See Gudmunsen's criticisms, 1977.

977. Carney J. D., *Defining art*, BJA, 15, pp. 191–206.
The opposition between the model of 'work of art' in Mill and
in W. An attempt to go beyond this alternative.

978. Cherry C., *Games and language*, M, 84, pp. 528–47.
The recourse to the notion of 'game' in the exposition of the
theory of family resemblances is logically unnecessary and has
a purely illustrative value.

979. Clark R. W., *The life of B. Russell*, London, Jonathan Cape
and Weidenfeld & Nicolson; New York, Knopf, 1975,
pp. 766.
Drawing on correspondence and autobiographical writings of
Russell, C. makes numerous references to the personal relations
between R. and W., bringing out the fascination exercised by
the latter from the start: see especially ch. 7, 'Enter W.',
pp. 166–98.

980. Davant J. B., *W. on Russell's theory of types*, NDJFL, 16,
pp. 102–8.

981. D'Hert I., *W.'s relevance for theology*, Frankfurt, Lang,
pp. 238.
W.'s theses on religion are discussed from a Catholic viewpoint,
in a comparison with St. Thomas and Heidegger, and within the
sphere of a general treatment of concepts and problems of a
theological nature. *Reviews:* Reix A., RPL, 1977, 75, pp. 709–12;
Sherry P. J., PB, 1977, 18, pp. 32–34; Wuchterl K., PLA, 1977,
30, pp. 358–62.

982. Dilman I., *Matter and mind: two essays in epistemology*,
London, Macmillan, 1975, pp. 225.
Two essays, with numerous references to W.: *Moore's 'Proof
of an external world'*, pp. 3–112 (compares the different
approaches of Moore and W. to scepticism); *Solipsism and our
knowledge of other minds*, pp. 115–219 (draws on *Tract.* and
also on later writings of W.).

983. Epstein M. F., *The common ground of Merleau-Ponty's
and W.'s philosophy of man*, JHP, 13, pp. 221–34.
Reprinted in Canfield (ed.), 1986, vol. XV.

984. Finch H. Le Roy, *W.'s last word: ordinary certainty*, IPQ, 15, pp. 383-95.
The novel elements introduced by the publication of *O.C.* should affect the evaluation of W.'s philosophical method.

985. Gellner E., *A W.ian philosophy of (or against) the social sciences*, PSS, 5, pp. 173-99. Reprinted in Shanker (ed.), 1986, vol. IV.
Comments on A. R. Louch's book, *Explanation and human action*, (Oxford, Blackwell, 1966). See Louch's reply, 1977.

986. Gill J. H., *Tacit knowing and religious belief*, IJPR, 6, pp. 73-88.
Wisdom, W. *(O.C.)* and Polanyi on the basis of religious belief.

987. Goodman R. B., *Style, dialectic, and the aim of philosophy in W. and the taoists*, JCP, 3, pp. 145-57.

988. Grabner-Haider A., *W. und 'das Mystische'. Folgerungen für die Theologie*, ZKT, 97, pp. 282-96.

989. Hacker P. M. S., *W. on ostensive definition*, I, 18, pp. 267-87.
In his mature works W. is criticizing nine fundamental errors involved in normal notions of ostensive definition, or, in many cases, in *Tract.* itself.

990. Hacker P. M. S., *Laying the ghost of the Tractatus*, RM, 29, pp. 96-116. Reprinted in Shanker (ed.), 1986, vol. I.
An examination of passages from *P.I.* and *P.G.* in which W. rejects *Tract.*'s ontological theory of objects. Critique of the thesis (Kenny, 1974) according to which W. gives an unreliable version of *Tract.* in his later works.

991. Hacker P. M. S., *Frege and W. on elucidations*, M, 84, pp. 601-9.
The thesis in *Tract.* (3.263) according to which primitive logical signs (Russell's 'indefinables') can be explained by means of *Erläuterungen*. W.'s criticism of Russell's theses. Analogies with and differences from Frege.

992. Hacking I., *L. W.'s articulation*, in his *Why does language matter to philosophy?*, Cambridge, Cambridge University Press, 1975, pp. 82-92. German translation: Königstein, Hain, 1984.

993. Hazard P. A., *A problem with W.'s 'family resemblance'*, LTP, 31, pp. 265-91.

994. Heller E., *Revival of L.W.: the philosopher rediscovered at home*, 'Austria Today', no. 3, pp. 48-52.

995. Hudson W. D., *W. and religious belief*, New York, St. Martin's Press; London, Macmillan, 1975, pp. 206.
The work aims to analyse W.'s theoretical attitude towards religion in the 'three stages' of its development. After a comprehensive presentation of the more general theses of the earlier and the later W., H. dwells more particularly on the ethico-religious implications of *Tract.* (pp. 78-112), on W.'s relationship to neopositivistic 'verificationism' as regards metaphysics and religion in the 'intermediate' period (ch. IV); finally (ch. V), H. analyses the problem of the nature of and justification for religious belief, in relation to the notions of form of life and language game, in the light of *P.I.* and *L.R.B.* in particular. In this analysis H. develops themes already tackled more briefly in a previous work, 1968. *Reviews:* Brown S., M, 1978, 87, pp. 293-5; Butterworth R., HJ, 1976, 17, pp. 453-5; Coburn R. C., PR, 1978, 87, pp. 126-32; Diamond M. L., RS, 1979, 15, pp. 107-18; Rowe W. L., SIF, 1978, 10, pp. 247-8; Sell A. P. F., PS(I), 25, pp. 380-2; Sherry P., PB, 1977, 18, no. 1, pp. 32-4; Tomasini A., Cr, 1981, 13, pp. 113-19.

996. Ihde D., *W.'s phenomenological reduction*, in *Phenomenological perspectives, historical and systematic, in honor of H. Spiegelberg*, ed. by P. H. Bossert, The Hague, Nijhoff, 1975, pp. 47-60.

997. Kaal H. and **McKinnon A.**, *Concordance to W.'s Philosophische Untersuchungen*, Leiden, E. J. Brill, 1975, pp. XII, 596.
The work provides a computer-based concordance of a list of (it is hoped) all 'philosophically relevant' German terms, in *P.I.* The context of each occurrence is indicated in a lemma of a line's length. *Reviews:* Black M., 'Computers and the Humanities', 1975, 10, pp. 301-2; Dubois P., 'Erasmus', 1976, 10, pp. 833-4; George R. A., D, 1978, 16, pp. 545-6; Klemke E. D., Ph, 1976, 6, pp. 505-6; Schwyzer H. R. G., JHP, 1978, 16, pp. 365-7.

998. Kemmerling A., *Regel und Geltung im Lichte der Analyse W.'s 'Rechtstheorie'*, 16, pp. 104-31.

999. Klemke E. D., *W.'s lecture on ethics*, JVI, 9, pp. 118-27.

1000. Lagache A., *W.: la logique d'un dieu*, Paris, Éditions du Cerf, 1975, pp. 148.
Review: Gilbert P., NRT, 1976, 108, p. 262.

1001. Lemoine R. E., *The anagogic theory of W.'s Tractatus*, The Hague and Paris, Mouton, 1975, pp. 215.
Review: Reix A., RPL, 1977, 75, pp. 709-12.

1002. Levin M. E., *Kripke's argument against the identity thesis*, JP, 72, pp. 149-67.
In the second part of the article an interpretation and analysis of W.'s private-language argument in *P.I.*

1003. Leyvraz J. P., *Le problème moral chez W.*, RTP, no. 4, pp. 280-90.

1004. Ludwig J., *Zero-remarks and the numbering system of the 'Tractatus'*, JCA, 6, n. 1, pp. 21-9.

1005. Marks C. E., *Verificationism, scepticism, and the private language argument*, PS, 28, pp. 151-171. Reprinted in Canfield (ed.), 1986, vol. IX.
An interpretation of W.'s theses on private language, based on the analysis of ostensive definition and of the notion of rule: an alternative to the interpretation put forward by Kenny, 1973.

1006. Marsh J. L., *The triumph of ambiguity: Merleau-Ponty and W.*, PT, 19, pp. 243-55.

1007. Martland T. R., *On 'The limits of my language mean the limits of my world'*, RM, 29, pp. 19-26.
Tract. 5.6, and its implications for artistic language.

1008. Moutafakis N. J., *Of family resemblances and aesthetic discourse*, PF, 7, pp. 71-89.

1009. Noonan H. W., *Tractatus 2.0211-2.0212*, A, 36, pp. 147-9.
The existence of objects as substances. *Tract.*'s relationship to the theory of the proposition in Frege.

1010. Osheroff S. S., *W.: psychological disputes and common moves*, PPR, 36, pp. 339-63.
An examination of W.'s theses on psychoanalytic language (*L.C.*), in relation to the theories of language games.

1011. Packard D. J., *A note on W. and cyclical comparatives*, A, 36, pp. 37–40.
An attempt to extend Bambrough's interpretation, 1960, of family resemblances from the examination of properties to that of relationships.

1012. Pears D., *Some questions in the philosophy of mind*, London, Duckworth; New York, Barnes & Noble, 1975, pp. 296.
A collection of articles, some theoretical, others historical, many containing references to W. The last, *W.'s treatment of solipsism in the Tract.*, pp. 272–92, is an attempt to detach W.'s transcendental solipsism from the solipsism of his middle period and to connect it with both Russell's and Schopenhauer's theories of the ego.

1013. Radford C., *Religious belief and contradiction*, P, 50, pp. 437–44.
Can a non-believer reason against a believer? A critique of the theses contained in *L.C.*

1014. Rembert A., *W. on learning the names of inner states*, PR, 84, pp. 236–48.
R. criticizes the interpretation given by Malcolm, 1954, concerning the relationship between internal states and names, and the role played in this by behaviour.

1015. Robinson I., *Linguistics and philosophy: Chomsky's failure with W.*, in his *The new grammarian's funeral: a critique of Noam Chomsky's linguistics*, Cambridge, Cambridge University Press, 1975, pp. 145–55.

1016. Rotella O., *Santo Tomás y W.*, RevF, 8, pp. 301–17.

1017. Sbisà M., *Che cosa ha veramente detto W.*, Rome, Ubaldini, 1975, pp. 144.

1018. Shirley E. S., *Hintikka on 'Investigations' 265*, SWJP, 7, pp. 67–73.
A critique of Hintikka's article on 'private language', see 1969.

1019. Smith P., *Solitary speakers*, M, 84, pp. 590–4.
S. controverts the interpretation given by Manser (in *Studies in the philosophy of W.*, 1969) on the notion of private language in W.

1020. Sprengard K. A., *Neue Möglichkeiten der Ethik: Kant, W.,*

Sartre, in *Bewusst Sein*, ed. by A. J. Bucher *et al.* Bonn, Bouvier, Grundmann, 1975, pp. 290–308.

1021. Steiner M., *Mathematical knowledge*, Ithaca, N.Y., Cornell University Press, 1975, pp. 164.
Many references to W. and to his criticism of logicist philosophy in *R.F.M.*, especially in the chapters 'Logic and mathematical knowledge' and 'Logicism reconsidered'.

1022. Sutherland S. R., *On the idea of a form of life*, RS, 11, pp. 293–306.

1023. White D. A., *The labyrinth of language: Joyce and W.*, 'James Joyce Quarterly', 12, pp. 294–304. Reprinted in Canfield (ed.), 1986, vol. XV.

1024. Zemach E. M., *'Sachverhalte', 'Tatsachen' and properties*, R, 17, pp. 49–51.
A demonstration of the logical complexity of a *Tatsache* in *Tract.* See also the 'Postscript', ibid., pp. 258-9.

1025. Zimmermann J., *W.'s sprachphilosophische Hermeneutik*, Frankfurt, Klostermann, pp. 318.
Z. develops a general interpretation of W. which aims to bring his thought back within the sphere of a linguistico-philosophical 'hermeneutics', and which is therefore distinct from the interpretation which sees W. as a philosopher of ordinary language. In this connexion Z. singles out a substantial continuity between *Tract.* (1st part, pp. 1–86) and the later works (2nd part, 'Die Hermeneutik der Sprachspiele', pp. 87–268). In both cases, aesthetic understanding becomes a paradigm of 'hermeneutic reflection' about language. The place of this in W.'s development is made clear by references to Kant, Schopenhauer, Kierkegaard, Valéry, Heidegger, Gadamer. *Reviews:* Keller A., TP, 1976, 51, pp. 398–401; Leinfellner E., PH, 1977, 10, pp. 172-5; Zimmermann R., PRd, 1979, 26, pp. 201-5.

1976

1026. *Analytic philosophy and phenomenology*, ed. by H. A. Durfee, The Hague, Nijhoff, 1976, pp. 277.

Practically half the book is devoted to the contrast between
W. and Husserl and Heidegger. The following articles are
republished: J.M. Hems, *Husserl and/or W.*, pp. 55-86 (see
1968); P. Ricoeur, *Husserl and W. on language*, pp. 87-95 (see
1969); I. Horgby, *The double awareness in Heidegger and W.*,
pp. 96-124 (see 1959); J. Morrison, *Heidegger's criticism of
W.'s conception of truth*, pp. 125-46 (see 1969); S. A. Erickson,
Meaning and language, pp. 147-69 (see 1968).

1027. *Essays on W. in honour of G. H. von Wright*, ed. by
J. Hintikka, (APF 28, 2-3) Amsterdam, North-Holland,
1976, pp. 516.

Includes the following articles: K. E. Tranøy, *W. in Cambridge
1949-51. Some personal recollections*, pp. 11-21; M. O'C.
Drury, *Some notes on conversations with W.*, pp. 22-40
(reprinted in *L.W.: Personal recollections*, 1981); A. Kenny,
From the big typescript to the 'Philosophical grammar',
pp. 41-53 (reprinted in Kenny, 1984); P. Geach, *Saying
and showing in Frege and W.*, pp. 54-70; E. Stenius, *The
sentence as a function of its constituents in Frege and in the
Tractatus*, pp. 71-84; R. M. Gale, *Could logical space be
empty?*, pp. 85-104; J. Hintikka, *Language-games*, pp. 105-25;
L. Hertzberg, *On the factual dependence of the language-
game*, pp. 126-53; C. Ginet, *W.'s claim that there could
not be just one occasion of obeying a rule*, pp. 154-65;
G. Kreisel, *Der unheilvolle Einbruch der Logik in die
Mathematik*, pp. 166-87; G. E. M. Anscombe, *The question
of linguistic idealism*, pp. 188-215; N. Malcolm, *Moore
and W. on the sense of 'I know'*, pp. 216-40; J. Hartnack,
Me and my body, pp. 241-9; D. Sachs, *W. on emotion*,
pp. 250-85; F. Stoutland, *The causation of behavior*,
pp. 286-325; R. Martin, *The problem of the 'Tie' in von
Wright's schema of practical inference: a W.ian solution*,
pp. 326-63; R. Tuomela, *Psychological concepts and
functionalism*, pp. 364-93; C. Wellman, *The meaning of
good*, pp. 394-416; F. Cioffi, *Aesthetic explanation and
aesthetic perplexity*, pp. 417-49; R. Rhees, *W. on language
and ritual*, pp. 450-84 (reprinted in *W. and his times*,
B. McGuinness (ed.), see *W.s geistige Erscheinung*, 1979);
N. Rotenstreich, *Between persuasion and deeds*, pp. 485-502;
J. C. Nyíri, *W.'s new traditionalism*, pp. 503-12. The
essays by G. E. M. Anscombe, F. Cioffi, P. Geach, C. Ginet,
L. Hertzberg, J. Hintikka, N. Malcolm, D. Sachs have been
reprinted in Canfield (ed.), 1986.

1028. *Thought and reality: central themes in W.'s philosophy*, Milton Keynes, Open University Press, 1976.

A series of texts for advanced courses of the Open University, UK, each of which is devoted to a particular theme or aspect of W.'s thought. A. Kassman, *Cartesian scepticism*, pp. 83; S. K. Zaw, *J. Locke: the foundations of empiricism*, pp. 82; S. Brown, *Realism and logical analysis*, pp. 62; G. H. R. Parkinson, *Saying and showing: an introduction to W.'s 'Tractatus'*, pp. 89; S. Brown, *Verification and meaning*, pp. 85; S. Brown, *Language and reality: 'Philosophical investigations' 1-137*, pp. 63; G. Vesey, *Meaning and understanding: Locke and W.*, pp. 79; O. Hanfling, *Language and the privacy of experience*, pp. 89; O. Hanfling, *The grammar of feelings*, pp. 67; O. Hanfling, *Solipsism and the self*, pp. 66; D. Collinson, *The will*, pp. 67; C. Wilde, *Certainty*, pp. 89; S. Guttenplan, *Meaning and truth*, pp. 30.

1029. Adler L., *L.W.: eine existenzielle Deutung*, Basel and Munich, S. Karger, 1976, pp. 110.
Reviews: Köchler H., PH, 1979, 12, pp. 3-4; Hügli A., SP, 1979, 38, pp. 237-48.

1030. Aldrich V., *Linguistic mysticism*, Mo, 59, pp. 470-92. Reprinted in Canfield (ed.), 1986, vol. XIV.
Part II of the article is on W.'s distinction between saying and showing, both in *Tract.* and later works.

1031. Almond P. C., *Winch and W.*, RS, 12, pp. 473-82.

1032. Altieri C., *W. Consciousness and language: a challenge to Derridean literary theory*, 'Modern Language Notes', 91, no. 6, pp. 1397-1423.

1033. Bertman M. A., *Criterion and defining criterion*, PS(I), 24, pp. 118-30. Reprinted in ILR, 1977, 8, pp. 170-81.

1034. Bouveresse J., *Le mythe de l'intériorité. Expérience, signification et langage privé chez W.*, Paris, Les Éditions de Minuit, 1976, pp. 702.
After an analysis (ch. I) of solipsism in *Tract.*, B. sketches W.'s later theory on language (ch. II: 'Le signe, le sens, et le système') and then comes to a discussion of private language (ch. III: 'Le problème de l'égocentricité de l'expérience'; ch. IV: 'L'idiolecte commun'). In the last chapter ('Des choses que l'on ne peut révoquer en doute'), these themes are taken up again with frequent references to Descartes, to the *cogito* (pp. 569-92)

and to the problem of the relationship between believing and knowing *(O.C.)*. *Reviews:* Brykman G., RPFE, 1977, 102, pp. 95-9; Brykman G., 'Pensée', 1978, 200, pp. 133-5; Dubarle D., RSPT, 1977, 61, pp. 644-7; Michaud Y., EP, 1979, 2, pp. 242-4; Mouchard C., 'Quinzaine littéraire', 1976, 44, pp. 19-20.

1035. Bruening W. H., *W.'s view of death*, PS(I), 25, pp. 48-68.

1036. Burke T. E., *Theological originality*, RS, 12, pp. 1-20.
A defence of Whitehead's theses on religion, as opposed to those of W.

1037. Burr, R. L., *W.'s later language-philosophy and some issues in philosophy of mysticism*, IJPR, 7, pp. 261-87.

1038. Cacciari M., *Krisis. Saggio sulla crisi del pensiero negativo da Nietzsche a W.*, Milan, Feltrinelli, 1976, pp. 189.

1039. Canfield J. V., *Tractatus objects*, Ph, 6, pp. 81-99.
Reprinted in Canfield (ed.), 1986, vol. II.

1040. Cherry C., *Explanation and explanation by hypothesis*, Sy, 33, pp. 315-39.
The problem of explanation in psychoanalysis, with reference to Cioffi's interpretation of W. on Freud (see *Studies in the philosophy of W.*, 1969).

1041. Chihara C. S., *Cohen's defence of Cook*, PS, 29, pp. 353-5 (see Cohen, 1974).

1042. Clammer J., *W.ianism and the social sciences*, Soc.R, 24, pp. 775-91.

1043. Cook M., *W.'s appeal to particular cases*, MS, 54, pp. 56-66.
W.'s appeal to examples rather than to definitions, with special reference to *Bl.B.*

1044. Copi I. M., *Frege and W.'s Tractatus*, Ph, 6, pp. 447-61.
Reprinted in Shanker (ed.), 1986, vol. I.

1045. Cox C. H. and **Cox J. W.**, *The mystical experience. With an emphasis on W. and Zen*, RS, 12, pp. 483-91.

1046. Dambska I., *Les idées kantiennes dans la philosophie des mathématiques de W.*, 'Organon', 11-13, pp. 249-60.

1047. Dayton E. B., *Tractatus 5.54-5.5422*, CJP, 6, pp. 275-85.
The analysis of non-extensional statements ('A believes that p') is a direct consequence of the picture theory and of the theory of judgement. Criticisms of the interpretations put forward by Anscombe, 1959, Pitcher, 1964, and Black, 1964, on this subject.

1048. Elgin C. Z., *Analysis and the picture theory in the Tractatus*, PRA, 2, pp. 568-80.

1049. Fogelin R. J., *Wittgenstein*, London and Boston, Mass., Routledge & Kegan Paul, 1976, pp. 223; 2nd ed., 1987, pp. 255.
An expository presentation of *Tract.* and of W.'s later work (above all, *P.I.* and *R.F.M.*), paying particular attention to the problems of the philosophy of mind. The second edition differs from the original in a number of ways. In the first part the major changes concern the discussion on *Tract.;* in the second part, the private language argument and the discussion of following a rule. A closing chapter, examining the place of W.'s later philosophy in the history of philosophy, is added. *Reviews:* Bogen J., TeaP, 1981, 4, pp. 67-9; Candlish S., AJP, 1978, 56, pp. 81-6; De Angelis W. J., PInv, 3, no. 3, pp. 80-3; Janik A., JHP, 1980, 18, pp. 108-10; Largeault J., AP, 1978, 41, pp. 684-7; Mounce H. O., PQ, 1977, 27, pp. 366-70; Rolston H. L., PR, 1978, 87, pp. 296-9; Winch P., M, 1978, 87, pp. 443-5; Wolf M., PS(I), 26, pp. 271-2.

1050. Forgie J. W., *W. on naming and ostensive definition*, ISP, 8, pp. 13-26. Reprinted in Canfield (ed.), 1986, vol. VIII.

1051. French P. A., *W.'s limits of the word*, MWSP, 1, pp. 114-124. Reprinted in Shanker (ed.), 1986, vol. I.

1052. Grandy R. E., *The private language argument*, M, 85, pp. 246-50.
A critical examination of the interpretations put forward by Kenny, 1973, and Thomson, 1964.

1053. Grene M., *Life, death, and language. Some thoughts on W. and Derrida*, 'Partisan Review', 43, pp. 265-79. Reprinted in Canfield (ed.), 1986, vol. XV.

1054. Grennan W., *W. on religious utterances*, S, 15, pp. 13-18.

1055. Griffiths A. P., *W. and the four-fold root of the principle of sufficient reason*, PAS(SV), 50, pp. 1–20. Reprinted in Canfield (ed.), 1986, vol. III.
Schopenhauer is the source of the theory of necessity in *Tract.* and *N.B.*, and is the key to an understanding of central passages in both.

1056. Hanfling O., *Hume and W.*, in *Impressions of empiricism*, edited by G. Vesey, London, Macmillan, 1976, pp. 47–65.
If the more obvious differences are left out of consideration, the two philosophers have many more elements in common than criticism generally allows. For example, in both of them a 'therapeutic' method of investigation predominates.

1057. Harward D. W., *W.'s saying and showing themes*, Bonn, Bouvier Verlag H. Grundmann, 1976, pp. 71.
H. claims that the central theme of W.'s philosophy is the saying/showing distinction. He analyses its origin in the pre-Tractatus materials, its development in *Tract.* and in the later writings, including *R.F.M., P.G., B.B.B., O.C.* He argues that the saying–showing distinction is not ancillary to the picture theory of language, but can be defended on independent grounds.

1058. Hodges M., *Nominalism and the private language argument*, SJP, 14, pp. 283–91.

1059. Hottois G., *Aspects du rapprochement par O. Apel de la philosophie de M. Heidegger et de la philosophie de L.W.*, RIP, 30, pp. 450–485.
Validity and limits in the comparison between the 'first Heidegger' and the second W. (see Apel, 1973).

1060. Hottois G., *La philosophie du langage de L.W.*, Brussels, Éditions de l'Université de Bruxelles, 1976, pp. 220; preface by J. Bouveresse.
A 'genetic' presentation of the development of W.'s thought, addressed to a French-speaking public. This development is divided into three 'phases', paying particular attention to the 'intermediate period' (pp. 57–112). In the examination of the 'second W.', a certain amount of space is devoted to the use of metaphor and to aesthetics. *Reviews:* Hallett G., G, 1977, 58, pp. 207–8; Parret H., TF, 1980, 42, pp. 160–4; Reix A.,

RPL, 1977, 75, pp. 712-3; Stock G., M, 1978, 87, pp. 291-3; Zimmermann R., PRd, 1979, 26, pp. 205-8.

1061. Hunter J. F. M., *W. on describing and making connections*, PQ, 26, pp. 243-50.
In the use of certain expressions we make a connection rather than describe it. An examination of the passages in *P.I.* in which this thesis recurs.

1062. Hunter J. F. M., *Why animals don't talk*, D, 15, pp. 290-5.
Interpretation of, and comments on, *P.I.* 25.

1063. Jones P., *Strains in Hume and W.*, in *Hume: a re-evaluation*, ed. by D. W. Livingstone and J. T. King, New York, Fordham University Press, 1976, pp. 191-209.

1064. Keightley A., *W., grammar and God*, London, Epworth, 1976, pp. 176.
As mentioned in the preface, this work aims essentially to be an introduction to the way in which W. tackles the problem of religious belief in *Tract.* and in the later works (especially chs. 1-2). K. then discusses some developments of W.'s ideas, in particular the work of D. Z. Phillips (chs. 3-4), and applies the results of this analysis to themes of a more typically theological nature (chs. 5-6). Bibliography on the subject.
Review: Bell R.H., RS, 1978, 14, pp. 547-8.

1065. Klenk V. H., *W.'s philosophy of mathematics*, The Hague, Nijhoff, 1976, pp. 128.
The examination is restricted above all to *R.F.M.* In the first part K. reviews the theoretical positions criticized by W. (Platonism, intuitionism, formalism, conventionalism), then (second part) he analyses W.'s attempt to develop a viewpoint which takes account of the 'constructive' and creative nature of mathematics ('behavioural theory'). Finally he examines, and largely rejects as unfounded, the criticisms which have most frequently been made of W.'s philosophy of mathematics.
Reviews: Klemke E.D., Ph, 1983, 13, pp. 153-64; Stroud B., ISP, 1979, 11, pp. 235-6; Tomasini A., Cr, 1981, 13, pp. 110-14; Tragesser R., N, 1980, 14, pp. 130-3.

1066. Kutschera F. von, *W.'s philosophy of language in the P.I.*, in his *Philosophy of language*, Dordrecht, Reidel, 1976, pp. 304 (translation from German: *Sprachphilosophie*, Munich, Fink, 1971).

1067. Lewis P. B., *W. on seeing and interpreting*, in *Impressions of empiricism*, edited by G. Vesey (Royal Institute of Philosophy Lectures, 9), London, Macmillan; New York, St. Martin's Press, 1976, pp. 93-108.
An examination of passages from *P.I. II,* xi concerned with change of aspect.

1068. Ludwig J., *'Substance' and 'simple objects' in Tractatus 2.02ff.*, PS, 29, pp. 307-18. Reprinted in Canfield (ed.), 1986, vol. II.
Tract. 2.01ff. contains important clues for a correct interpretation of the relationship between 'substance' and 'simple object'.

1069. Marcuschi L. A., *Die Methode des Beispiels. Untersuchung über die methodische Funktion des Beispiels in der Philosophie, insbesondere bei L.W.*, Erlangen, Verlag Palm & Enke, 1976, pp. 236.
Review: Wallner F., PLA, 1980, 33, p. 272.

1070. Mijuskovic B. L., *The simplicity argument in W. and Russell*, Cr, 8, pp. 85-99.

1071. Phillips D. Z., *Religion without explanation*, Oxford, Blackwell, 1976, pp. 198.
Many references to W., especially in ch. X ('Does God exist?'), where P. explores the treatment that the sceptical doubts receive in *O.C.* in connection with the analysis of the fundamental beliefs of religion.

1072. Raffman, R. L., *L.W.'s concept of family resemblances and contemporary music*, 'Music and Man', 2, pp. 117-23. Reprinted in Shanker (ed.), 1986, vol. IV.

1073. Richardson J. T. E., *The grammar of justification. An interpretation of W.'s philosophy of language*, New York, St. Martin's Press; London, Chatto & Windus, 1976, pp. 147.
R. begins with the assumption that the influence of Brouwer, 1928, was decisive in the formation of W.'s later thought. In each of his central notions ('Meaning and use', ch. III; 'Family resemblance', ch. IV; 'The theory of criteria', ch. V) W. develops a 'constructivist' point of view, according to which the meaning of a statement is explained in terms of the

conditions which are are considered appropriate for its use. *Reviews:* Burke T.E., PB, 1977, 18, pp. 42-3; Parret H., TF, 1980, 42, pp. 163-4; Stock G., M, 1978, 87, pp. 291-3; Weston M., PQ, 1977, 27, pp. 180-2.

1074. Rosenberg J. F., *The concept of linguistic correctness*, PS, 30, pp. 171-84.
P.I. embodies a thesis concerning the correctness of a descriptive application of language which is not only of great philosophical importance but also arguably right.

1075. Seligman D. B., *W. on seeing aspects and experiencing meanings*, PPR, 37, pp. 205-17.
An examination of *P.I.* II, xi.

1076. Senchuk D. M., *Private objects. A study of W.'s method*, Mp, 7, pp. 217-40.

1077. Shibles W., *Comments on 'W.'s limits of the world'*, MWSP, 1, pp. 132-4. (See French, 1976.)

1078. Thorlby A., *Anti-mimesis: Kafka and W.*, in F. Kuna (ed.), *On Kafka: semi-centenary perspectives*, London, Elek Books; New York, Barnes & Noble, 1976, pp. 59-82.

1079. Tilghman B. R., *Seeing and meaning*, SJP, 14, pp. 523-33. A critical examination of *P.I.* II, xi, and of the theory of aspects.

1080. Tugendhat E., *Vorlesungen zur Einführung in die sprachanalytische Philosophie,* Frankfurt, Suhrkamp, 1976, pp. 534. E.T. *Traditional and analytical philosophy. Lectures on the philosophy of language,* Cambridge, Cambridge University Press, 1982, pp. XII, 438.
Designed to analyse the philosophy of linguistic analysis and to build a bridge between it and continental approaches to philosophy, whether traditional or Heideggerian. Frequent references to W. especially in the central chapters dedicated to the themes of the meaning and use of expressions.

1081. Vesey G., *Locke and W. on language and reality*, in *Contemporary British philosophy (4th series)*, edited by H. D. Lewis, London, George Allen & Unwin, 1976, pp. 253-73.
In what sense and to what extent is W.'s critique of private language indirectly aimed at a theory of sense data like that upheld by Locke?

1082. **Warnock M.**, *The nature of the mental image. Phenomenology, Sartre and W.*, in her *Imagination*, Berkeley and Los Angeles, Cal., University of California Press, 1976, pp. 131–95.

1083. **Wuchterl K.**, *Die Hermeneutik und der operative Aufbau der Philosophie, dargestellt an der Philosophie W.s*, ZPF, 30, pp. 350–68.

1977

1084. **'Nuova Corrente'**, nos. 72–3, pp. 229.
A special issue devoted to W. It contains the following contributions (titles translated from the Italian): Rella F., *For W.*, pp. 3–15; De Monticelli R., *Frege, Husserl, W. Notes on the problem of foundation*, pp. 16–45; Franck G., *The foundation of knowledge and the foundations of operating (Moore and W.)*, pp. 46–58; Cacciari M., *W.'s Vienna*, pp. 59–106; Gargani A., *Science and forms of life*, pp. 107–41; Amendolagine F. and Franck G., *W.: from the 'world as a limited whole' to the 'game point of view'*, pp. 142–55; Amendolagine F., *Marginal notes on W.'s house'*, pp. 156–67; Jesi F., *W. in Kensington Gardens: the Bemerkungen über Frazer's The Golden Bough*, pp. 168–83; Schiavoni G., *Silence and random talk. Notes on W.ian criticism*, pp. 184–229.

1085. **Abelson R.**, *Can social science provide causal explanations?*, PC, 6, pp. 43–53.
Disagrees with W., P. Winch (1958) and A. R. Louch (1977) about causal explanations in psychology and the social sciences.

1086. **Almond P. C.**, *W. and religion*, S, 16, pp. 24–7.

1087. **Ambrose A.**, *The 'Yellow book' notes in relation to the 'Blue book'*, Cr, 9, pp. 3–20. Reprinted in Lazerowitz and Ambrose, 1984.

1088. **Baum W.**, *W.s Tolstojanisches Christentum*, C, 11, pp. 339–49.

1089. **Bouveresse J.**, *Le paradis de Cantor et le purgatoire de W.*, 'Critique', 33, pp. 316–51.
An examination of *L.F.M.*

1090. Bouveresse J., *L'animal cérémonial. W. et l'anthropologie*, 'Actes de la Recherche en Sciences Sociales', 16, pp. 43–54.

1091. Bruening W. H., *Aquinas and W. on God-talk*, S, 16, no. 3, pp. 1–7.

1092. Bruening W. H., *W.'s view of death*, PS(I), 25, pp. 48–68.

1093. Bruening W. H., *W.*, Washington DC, University Press of America, 1977, pp. 194.
Reviews the entire production of W. with the particular aim of establishing relations betwen *Tract.* and W.'s mature writings. Especial attention is paid to the problem of the nature of philosophy and to religion and ethics. *Review:* Hallett G. L., RM, 1979, 32, pp. 535–6.

1094. Castañeda H.-N., *El atomismo sintáctico en la filosofía posterior de W., y la naturaleza de las cuestiones filosóficas*, RevF(CR), 15, pp. 175–86.

1095. Chihara C. S., *W.'s analysis of the paradoxes in his 'Lectures on the foundations of mathematics'*, PR, 86, pp. 365–81. Reprinted in Canfield (ed.), 1986, vol. XI; in Shanker (ed.), 1986, vol. III.
An examination particularly of the discussions with the logician A. Turing recorded in *L.F.M.*

1096. Daniel, S. H., *W. on field and stream*, Au, 4, pp. 176–98.

1097. Davis D., *Limits. An essay on Yvor Winters and L.W.*, 'Poetry Nation' (Manchester), 4, pp. 21–5.

1098. Diamond C. and **White R.** (symposium), *Riddles and Anselm's riddle*, PAS(SV), 51, pp. 143–86. Diamond's essay is reprinted in Canfield (ed.), 1986, vol. XIV.
A discussion on the nature of the philosophical problems that do not seem to find a clear and unequivocal solution, with references to examples taken from W.'s later works concerning mathematics, religion and ethics.

1099. Finch H. L., *W.: the later philosophy. An exposition of the 'Philosophical investigations'*, Atlantic Highlands, N.J., Humanities Press, 1977, pp. 284.
An expository examination of some themes from *P.I.*, with some appendices that have a more historical aim (on Brouwer,

Heidegger, Buddhism, etc.). F.'s general proposition is that *P.I.* underlines a revolutionary and drastic rejection, previously heralded in *Tract.*, of the philosophical tradition derived from Cartesianism. *Reviews:* Fleming R., PInv, 1979, 2, no. 4, pp. 84-7; Phillips D.Z., PB, 1978, 19, pp. 68-72.

1100. Galliker M., *Müssen wir uns auf das Sprechen vorbereiten?: ein genetisch praktischer Ansatz der Psycholinguistik auf der Grundlage von W.*, Bern and Stuttgart, Paul Happt, 1976, pp. 202.

1101. Garavaso P., *Il fondamento unitario del pensiero di W. dal Tractatus alle Richerche Filosofiche*, V, 6, pp. 49-88.

1102. Ghins M., *La forme et le sens dans le Tractatus de W.*, RPL, 75, pp. 453-80.
Like Kant, W. defines the formal conditions of the sense of the proposition. These explain the rejection, implicit in *Tract.*, of Leibniz's principle of indiscernibles.

1103. Green J. L., *W.'s influence on philosophy of education*, 'Educational Studies', 8, pp. 1-20.

1104. Gudmunsen C., *W. and Buddhism*, London, Macmillan; New York, Harper & Row, pp. 128.
The book revolves around the thesis that there are strong analogies between the later W.'s critique of 'philosophical atomism' and the one developed by the Mādhyamika Buddhist school. *Reviews:* Canfield J. V., PR, 1980, 89, pp. 140-4; Daye D.D., PEW, 1980, 30, pp. 127-30; Drengson A.R., PInv, 1981, 4, no. 1, pp. 45-8; Streng F. J., JR, 1979, 59, pp. 238-40.

1105. Gudmunsen C., *The 'empty mind' of Professor Canfield*, P, 52, pp. 482-5.
Cf. Canfield, 1975, on 'W. and Zen'.

1106. Haikola L., *Religion as language game. A critical study with special regard to D. Z. Phillips* (Studia philosophiae religionis, 4), Lund, Gleerup, 1976, pp. 168.
After an introductory Part I, Part II sketches the main lines of W.'s theory of language, meaning and use, rules and grammar, form of life. Then, Part III considers some applications of these concepts to religious matters, discusses Phillips's ideas and

analyses some difficulties faced by the W.ian approach to the study of the nature of religion. *Review:* Sherry P., RS, 1979, 15, pp. 261-3.

1107. **Hallett G. L.**, *A companion to W.'s 'Philosophical investigations'*, Ithaca, N.Y. and London, Cornell University Press, 1976, pp. 801.

The work aims to provide an aid to reading *P.I.* and a detailed commentary of the most significant and controversial passages. After a general introduction, in which *P.I.'s* relationship to *Tract.* is briefly examined, and the general structure of the work is set out, H. groups the sections of *P.I.* consecutively under 41 heads. Each of these is given a title and introduced in a general form, then its most significant parts are analysed. An appendix on the thinkers or writers whom W. knew or read concludes the work. *Reviews:* Brown S., PQ, 1978, 28, pp. 354-5; Cordua C., 'Dialogos', 1978, 13, pp. 179-82; Ellis A., M, 88, 1979, pp. 452-4; Gill J.H., IPQ, 1978, 18, pp. 227-31; Hunter J.F.M., PR, 1978, 87, pp. 259-74; Kaminsky J., ISP, 1979, 11, pp. 234-5; Louch A., JHP, 1980, 18, pp. 240-2; Parret H., TF, 1980, 42, pp. 162-3; Phillips D.Z., PB, 1978, 19, pp. 68-9; Stroud B., Mp, 1979, 10, pp. 338-9.

1108. **Hayek F. A.**, *Remembering my cousin, L.W.*, 'Encounter', 49, no. 2, pp. 20-2.

1109. **Heil J.**, *Tractatus 4.0141*, PPR, 38, pp. 545-8.

An examination of the difficulties this section of *Tract.* poses for the understanding of the projective relationship and isomorphism between representations and states of affairs.

1110. **Heinrich R.**, *Einbildung und Darstellung. Zum Kantianismus des frühen W.*, Kastellaun and Düsseldorf, Henn, 1976, pp. 74.

Review: Steinbeck W., KS, 1978, 69, pp. 370-1.

1111. **Hintikka J.**, *Language-games*, Di, 31, pp. 225-45. Reprinted in Shanker (ed.), 1986, vol. II.

In his later work W. does not reject the semantic theory of *Tract.*, but tries to establish a relationship between reality and language through the theory of language games.

1112. **Hudson W. D.**, *W. on fundamental propositions*, SWJP, 8, pp. 7-21. Reprinted in Shanker (ed.), 1986, vol. IV.

A critical examination of the themes of *O.C.*

1113. Hughes J. A., *W. and social science. Some matters of interpretation*, 'Sociological Review', 25, pp. 721-41.

1114. Hunter J. F. M., *W. and materialism*, M, 86, pp. 514-41.

A problematical examination of the relationship between 'psychological phenomena' (thinking, remembering, etc.) and their physiological basis, with particular reference to *Z*. 608-10.

1115. Hunter J. F. M., *W. on inner processes and outward criteria*, CJP, 7, pp. 805-17. Reprinted in Canfield (ed.), 1986, vol. VII.

An examination of *P.I.* 580, on the assumption that this was the origin of many misunderstandings in the interpretation of the relationship between inner processes and outward criteria.

1116. Iglesias M. T., *Russell's introduction to W.'s Tractatus*, 'Russell', 25-28, pp. 21-38.

An examination and an historical evaluation of the differences between the version of Russell's introduction which was prepared in 1921 for the German edition of *Tract.* and the 1922 version (see entry).

1117. Kalansuriya A. D. P., *W., meaning-model and Buddhism*, Ind.PQ, 4, pp. 381-91.

1118. Kalupahana D. J., *The notion of suffering in early Buddhism compared with some reflections of early W.*, PEW, 27, pp. 423-31.

1119. Keeling L. B. and Morelli M. F., *Beyond W.ian fideism: an examination of John Hick's analysis of religious faith*, IJPR, 8, pp. 250-62.

Refers to J. Hick 'Religious faith as experiencing-as' in G. N. A. Vesey (ed.), *Talk of God*, London, Macmillan, 1968.

1120. Koenne W., *Rekursive Techniken und der Tractatus*, C, 11, pp. 289-303.

1121. Koethe J. L., *The role of criteria in W.'s later philosophy*, CJP, 7, pp. 601-22.

Present-day interpretations give an 'epistemic' version of the notion of criterion in W. They are based, however, on an erroneous understanding of the relationship between mental states and behavioural manifestations.

1122. Lamb D., *Preserving a primitive society: reflections on post-W. ian social philosophy*, 'Sociological Review' 25, pp. 689–719.

1123. Lamb D., *Hegel and W. on language and sense-certainty*, 'Clio', 7, pp. 285–301.

1124. Lazerowitz M., *The language of philosophy. Freud and W.*, Dordrecht and Boston, Mass., D. Reidel, 1976, pp. 209.
Although Freud and W. are constant points of reference in the work, only one chapter (pp. 18–43) is specifically devoted to an examination of W.'s attitude to psychoanalysis and of its metaphysical implications. *Reviews:* Arana J. R., 'Pensamiento', 1980, 36, pp. 360–1; Champlin T. S., PB, 1979, 20, pp. 32–4; Haack S., Mp, 1979, 10, pp. 340–3; Hanly C., D, 1979, 18, pp. 595–600; Lipschutz S. S., PInv, 1980, 3, no. 1, pp. 47–9; Newell R. W., P, 1979, 54, pp. 251–3; Rohatyn D., MS, 1978–9, 56, pp. 171–8.

1125. Lewis P. B., *W. on words and music*, BJA, 17, pp. 111–21. Reprinted in Shanker (ed.), 1986, vol. IV.
An examination of a number of passages from *P.G., Br.B.* and *P.I.*, with the aim of explaining what W. means by 'understanding a musical theme'.

1126. Louch A. R., *A discourse on methodology. A reply to Ernest Gellner,* PSS, 7, pp. 239–50
See Gellner, 1975, on W. and the possibility of social sciences.

1127. Luckhardt C. G., *W.: Investigations 50*, SJP, 15, pp. 81–90.
On the bases of certainty, with reference to *O.C.*

1128. Malcolm N., *Thought and knowledge*, Ithaca, N.Y. and London, Cornell University Press, 1976, pp. 218.   .
Collected essays frequently referring to W., especially in connexion with the philosophy of mind: see, in particular, the previously published *W. on the nature of mind*, pp. 133–58 (cf. Malcolm, 1970) and *Moore and W. on the sense of 'I know'*, pp. 170–98 (cf. *Essays on W.*, 1976).

1129. Malcolm N., *Memory and mind,* Ithaca and London, Cornell University Press, 1977, pp. 277.
Many explicit and implicit references to W., especially in the chapters 'The picture theory of memory' and 'The principle

of isomorphism'. Both have been reprinted in Canfield (ed.), 1986, vol. XIII.

1130. Masat Lucchetta, P., *Popper interprete di W.*, 'Sapienza', 30, pp. 300-27.

1131. Masunari T., *Was lässt sich in Bezug auf ästhetischen Wert ausdrücken und was nicht? Zur 'Ästhetik W.s'*, C, 11, pp. 315-26.

1132. Maury A., *The concepts of 'Sinn' and 'Gegenstand' in W.'s 'Tractatus'*, Amsterdam, North-Holland, 1977, pp. 176. In the first part of the work (pp. 5-93) M. examines the relationship between the notion of 'sense' and those of truth, falsehood and possibility. In the second part (pp. 93-170) he discusses the meaning of the notion of *Gegenstand,* with reference to the interpretations of Copi, 1958, Anscombe, 1959, and Stenius, 1960. In this comparison, he defends the thesis that the objects of *Tract.* also include predicates.

1133. Miller D., *The uniqueness of atomic facts in W.'s Tractatus*, T, 43, pp. 174-85. In controversy with Black, 1967, an examination of the thesis that the world cannot be divided into atomic facts in more than one way.

1134. Mohr R. D., *Family resemblance, Platonism, universals*, CJP, 7, pp. 593-600. W.'s theory of family resemblances does not affect the Platonic theory of universals, when it is correctly understood, but only ('abstractionist') theories of universals of an Aristotelian or empirical kind. See reply by Maddox, 1981.

1135. Nyíri J. C., *Musil und W. Ihr Bild vom Menschen*, C, 11, pp. 306-14.

1136. Payer P., *W.s sprachphilosophische Grundmetaphern*, C, 11, pp. 283-8.

1137. Pears D., *The relation between W.'s picture theory of propositions and Russell's theories of judgement*, PR, 86, pp. 177-96. Reprinted in *W.: sources and perspectives*, 1979; in Shanker (ed.), 1986, vol. I. Russell's 'theory of judgement', which W. implicitly criticizes, is the theory contained in a 1913 manuscript, *Theory of knowledge*, which remained unpublished (until 1984).

1138. Phillips D. L., *W. and scientific knowledge. A sociological perspective,* London, Macmillan; Totowa, N.J., Rowman & Littlefield, 1977, pp. 248. Italian translation: Bologna, Il Mulino, 1981.
This book is aimed above all at students of social sciences, offering them, through an examination of some themes taken from the later W., ideas for reflection on the foundations of their disciplines. P. dwells above all on the relationship between 'authority' and 'relativism', with frequent references to Mannheim, Kuhn, Lakatos, Polanyi, Feyerabend, and with a favourable appreciation of the interpretations of W. put forward by Winch and Toulmin. *Reviews:* Angluin D., 'British Journal of Sociology', 1978, 29, pp. 268-9; Barnes B., 'Sociological Review', 1978, 26, pp. 391-2; Buzzoni M., Ep, 1982, 5, pp. 394-7; Cebic L. B., PInv, 1979, 2, no. 2, pp. 74-7; Greenstone J. D., 'American Political Science Review', 1978, 72, pp. 1386-7; Harrison R., TD, 1979, 11, pp. 469-72; Rubinstein D., PSS, 1979, 9, pp. 341-6; Tomlinson H., 'Radical Philosophy', 1979, 22, pp. 38-40; Toulmin S., 'American Journal of Sociology', 1979, 84, pp. 996-9.

1139. Phillips D. Z., *On wanting to compare W. and Zen,* P, 52, pp. 338-43. Reprinted in Shanker (ed.), 1986, vol. IV.
A critical examination of of Canfield's thesis, 1975, according to which for both W. and Zen language and understanding are based on 'practice', or on the absence of thought.

1140. Radnitzky G., *Philosophie und Wissenschaftstheorie zwischen W. und Popper,* C, 11, pp. 249-83.

1141. Rieman F., *On linguistic skepticism in W. and Kungsun Lung,* PEW, 27, pp. 183-93.

1142. Rorty R., *W. ian philosophy and empirical psychology,* PS, 31, pp. 151-72.
The criticism made by 'W.'s followers' of the psychological explanation of behaviour is based on a justified distrust of the epistemological (Cartesian-dualistic) tradition out of which psychology was born. However, the link between psychology and this tradition no longer has a *raison d'être.*

1143. Sherry P. J., *Religion, truth and language-games,* London, Macmillan; New York, Barnes & Noble, 1977, pp. 234.

S. aims at an 'exploration' of religious language, of the notions of forms of life, of truth and the rationality of religious belief, seen in the light of W.'s later works. Only the first two chaps. (pp. 1–48) are devoted to a specific examination of W.'s theses and those of his 'followers'. The rest of the book is composed of an independent attempt to develop the information which arises out of this analysis, and to overcome the difficulties found in it. *Reviews:* Durrant M., PB, 1978, 19, pp. 72–5; Fitzpatrick J., JH, 1978, 19, pp. 333–5; Lammiman F. B., PInv, 1980, 3, no. 4, pp. 72–5; Sutherland S. R., RS, 1979, 15, pp. 121–2.

1144. Shiner R. A., *W. and the foundations of knowledge*, PAS, 78, pp. 103–24.
The activist theory of knowledge, based on the notion of 'form of life' put forward by W. in *O.C.*, is contrasted with the two classical solutions (foundationalism and coherence). Differences from Quine's theses ('Two dogmas of empiricism').

1145. Swoyer C., *Private language and skepticism*, SWJP, 8, pp. 41–50.
A reply by R.M. Lemos follows, pp. 51–2.

1146. Waismann F., *Philosophical papers*, ed. by B. McGuinness, Dordrecht and Boston, Mass., Reidel, 1976, pp. xxii, 190.
Reprints, in English translation, the pre-war articles published in 1930, 1936, 1938, 1939 (see above) and also the chapter '*Hypotheses*', not included in the English edition of *The principles of linguistic philosophy*, see 1966. A number of post-war English papers contain implicit references to the later W. In an introduction A. Quinton discusses the philosophical and human relations (sometimes painful) between Wa. and W.

1147. Waller B., *Chomsky, W. and the behaviorist perspective on language*, B, 5, pp. 43–59.

1148. White R., *W. on identity*, PAS, 78, pp. 157–74. Reprinted in Canfield (ed), 1986, vol. II.
An examination of the notion of identity in Frege (*Begriffsschrift*) which aims to clarify the philosophical importance and the role that this notion has in the construction of *Tract.*, and to explain W.'s gradual abandonment of Frege's theories.

1149. Wright E. L., *Words and intentions*, P, 52, pp. 45-62.
An examination, in the light of Grice's reduction of meaning to 'intention', of the 'confusion' which exists in W. between word-meaning and speaker's meaning when he analyses the relationship between understanding and 'continuing a series'.

1150. Wrigley M., *W.'s philosophy of mathematics*, PQ, 27, pp. 50-9. Reprinted in Shanker (ed.), 1986, vol. III.
The constructivist and finitist interpretations (cf. Dummett, 1959, Bernays, 1959, Kreisel, 1958, Kielkopf, 1970) fail to grasp the originality of W.'s thought concerning mathematics.

1151. Zimmermann J., *Zu W.s 'Über Gewissheit'. Versuch eines Überblicks*, SP, 36, pp. 226-39.

1152. Zoolalian D. E., *Augustine and W. Some remarks on the necessity of a private language*, 'Augustinian Studies', 8, pp. 25-33.

1978

1153. *Essays on Kierkegaard and W.*, ed. by R. H. Bell and R. E. Hustwit, Wooster, Ohio, College of Wooster, 1978, pp. 126.
Contributions to a symposium held at the College of Wooster in 1976 together with some replies written expressly for the volume. Of the 13 contributions those directly relating to W. are: P. Holmer, *W. and the self*; R. E. Hustwit, *Two views of the soul: Investigations, Part II, IV*, (with a response by A.J. Burgess); H. A. Nielsen, *The grammar of eternal happiness* (with a response by J. H. Whittaker); R. H. Bell, *Understanding fire-festivals and revelations* (with a reply by D. Burrell); A. D. Jensen, *Kierkegaard and W.: a shared enmity* (about their 'shared' critical attitude towards the journalistic mentality. Response by D. E. Salier). *Review:* Kellenberger J., PInv, 1978, 1, no. 4, pp. 64-6.

1154. *Over W. gesproken*, ed. by F. Boenders , Het. Baarn, Wereldvenster, 1978, pp. 109.
Conversations on aspects of W.'s thought and personality with A. Hübner, A. Janik, B. McGuinness, F. Parak, E. Anscombe, A. Kenny, G. H. von Wright, M. Black, J. Hintikka, H. Spiegelberg, N. Malcolm, J. Bouveresse.

1155. *Systèmes symboliques, science et philosophie. Travaux du Séminaire d'Epistémologie Comparative d'Aix-en-Provence E.R.A. du C.N.R.S.*, ed. by G. Granger, Paris, Éditions du C.N.R.S., 1977, pp. 308.
One section is entirely devoted to W. and contains: M. Aenishänslin, *La structure cyclique du 'Tractatus'*, pp. 243–58 (a formalization of the argumentative structure of *Tract.*); A. R. Moreno, *Le système de numérotation du 'Tractatus'*, pp. 259–82; E. Schwartz, *Remarques sur le 'sujet' selon W.*, pp. 283–303.

1156. *W. and his impact on contemporary thought*, Proceedings of the 2nd International W. Symposium, Kirchberg (Austria), 29 August to 4 September 1977, Ed. by E. Leinfellner, W. Leinfellner, H. Berghel, A. Hübner. (Schriftenreihe der W.-Gesellschaft, vol. 2.) Vienna, Hölder-Pichler-Tempsky, 1978, pp. 550; 2nd ed. 1980.
The volume is divided into four sections: 'Introduction' (pp. 25–92, dedicated to problems of a general and historical nature); 'W.'s early philosophy' (pp. 97–247); 'W.'s later philosophy of language and semantics' (pp. 253–402); 'General problems of W.'s philosophy' (pp. 407–550). 108 interventions in all.

1157. Anon, *The W. papers: current library holdings*, PInv, 3, pp. 50–3.
A list of the libraries, arranged by country, which hold a copy of W.'s papers as distributed by the Cornell University Libraries.

1158. Ackermann I. *et al.*, *W.'s fairy tale*, A, 38, pp. 159–60.
Tract. 4.014: the source of W.'s simile is identified in the collection by the Brothers Grimm.

1159. Allison D. B., *Derrida and W. Playing the game*, RP, 8, pp. 93–109.

1160. Arrington R. L., *W. and phenomenology*, PT, 22, pp. 287–300.
With reference to the essay by Ricoeur, 1967.

1161. Bachmaier P., *W. und Kant. Versuch zum Begriff des Transzendentalen*, Frankfurt and Bern, Lang, 1978, pp. 213.
Reviews: Siitonen A., PH, 1981, 14, pp. 133–4; Steinbeck W., KS, 1979, 70, pp. 519–21; Wallner F., PLA, 1980, 33, p. 269.

1162. Bachmann I., *Sagbares und Unsagbares. Die Philosophie L.W.s*, Rundfunk-Essay, 1953; in I. Bachmann, *Werke*, vol. IV, Munich and Zurich, Piper, pp. 103-27.
Text of a radio talk by the creative writer B. in which she dwells on the relation between the sayable and the unsayable in *Tract*.

1163. Bell R. H., *Understanding the fire-festivals: W. and theories in religion*, RS, 14, pp. 113-24.
The possibility of communication between different cultures, with reference to the religious element and to comments made by W. about Frazer.

1164. Bennett P. W., *W. and defining criteria*, PInv, 1, no. 4, pp. 49-60. Reprinted in Canfield (ed.), 1986, vol. VII.
The explicit definition of the concepts of 'criteria' and 'symptom', given in *Bl.B.*, pp. 24-25, conflicts with W.'s subsequent remarks about criteria in other parts of *Bl.B.*, in *P.I.* and elsewhere.

1165. Caraway C., *Is W.'s view of the relationship between certainty and knowledge consistent?*, PInv, 1, no. 4, pp. 16-22.
Appealing to passages in *O.C.*, C. argues that W.'s remarks on subjective and objective certainty establish the consistency of his views on the relation between certainty and knowledge.

1166. Clegg J. S., *Logical mysticism and the cultural setting of W.'s Tract.*, SJ, 59, pp. 29-47.
Substantial unity of logical theory and mysticism of *Tract*. Schopenhauer's influence fundamental.

1167. Danford J. W., *W. and political philosophy. A re-examination of the foundations of social science*, Chicago, Ill., University of Chicago Press, 1978, pp. 265.
A resumé of the problem of philosophical fundamentals of political thought (Plato, Aristotle, Locke, Hobbes) in the light of language criticism by W. *Reviews:* Bertman M.A., MS, 1979-80, 57, pp. 176-7; Deininger W.T., PInv, 1979, 2, no. 3, pp. 53-6; Flatham R., 'Journal of Politics', 1980, 42, pp. 336-8; Laitin D., 'American Political Science Review', 1980, 74, pp. 159-60; Moon J. D., 'Political Theory', 1980, 8, pp. 418-20; Shiner R. A., PB, 1980, 21, pp. 213-16.

1168. Davie W., *Suddenly understanding*, PInv, 1, no. 3, pp. 25-36.
An attempt to make philosophical sense of the concept of 'understanding', following the guidelines of *P.I.* 151-55, 179-84.

1169. Dilman I., *Universals: Bambrough on W.*, PAS, 79, pp. 35-58. Reprinted in Canfield (ed.), 1986, vol. V.
W. maintains that general terms do not denote any language-independent characteristic of reality. Bambrough's interpretation, 1960, appeals to objective resemblances, thus reintroducing a form of realism, which W. would have rejected.

1170. Dummett M., *Reckonings: W. on mathematics*, 'Encounter', 50, no. 3, pp. 63-8. Reprinted in Shanker (ed.), 1986, vol. III; in Canfield (ed.), 1986, vol. XI.

1171. Dummett M., *Truth and other enigmas*, London, Duckworth; Cambridge, Mass., Harvard University Press, pp. LVIII, 470.
Many of these essays contain explicit and implicit references to W. In particular: *W.'s philosophy of mathematics*, pp. 166-85 (see 1959) and *Can analytical philosophy be systematic, and ought it to be?*, pp. 437-58.

1172. Elgin C. Z., *The impossibility of saying what is shown*, SJP, 16, pp. 617-27.
The source of the distinction between saying and showing in *Tract.*, concerning logical propositions, is sought in W.'s criticism of theories like Russell's.

1173. Ellis A., *Kenny and the continuity of W.'s philosophy*, M, 87, pp. 270-5.
A critique of Kenny's interpretation, 1973, of the continuity in the development of W.'s thought from *Tract.* to his later work.

1174. Fleming N., *Seeing the soul*, P, 53, pp. 33-50.
An examination of the mind-body relationship, and that between inner processes and behaviour, in W.'s mature work.

1175. Gabriel G., *Logik als Literatur? Zur Bedeutung des Literarischen bei W.*, 'Merkur', 32, no. 4, pp. 353-62.

1176. Genova J., *A map of the P.I.*, PInv, 1, no. 1, pp. 41-55. Reprinted in Shanker (ed.), 1986, vol. II, pp. 58-73.

An attempt to provide readers of *P.I.* with a guide to its content, dividing the book into 6 main sections and giving a brief description of each.

1177. Hrachovec H., *Bilder, zweiwertige Logik und negative Tatsachen in W.s 'Tractatus'*, ZPF, 32, pp. 526–39.

1178. Hudson W. D., *Language-games and presuppositions*, P, 53, pp. 94–9.
Do language games have presuppositions? The purpose of the article is to clarify, with reference to *O.C.*, the notions of presupposition and fundamental proposition, in order to give a reply to this question.

1179. Hunter J. F. M., *A scholar's W.*, PR, 87, pp. 259–74.
A critical examination of Hallett, 1977.

1180. Hustwit R. E., *Understanding a suggestion of Professor Cavell's: Kierkegaard's religious state as a W.ian 'form of life'*, PRA, 4, pp. 329–47.

1181. Intisar-Ul-Haque, *W. on number*, IPQ, 18, pp. 33–48. Reprinted in Shanker (ed.), 1986, vol. III.
View of the nature of number in *Tract.* and in the later work, seen in its opposition to the logicism of Frege and Russell and to set theory.

1182. Kampits P., *Destruktionen, Hermeneutik und System. Neue W.Interpretationen des deutschen Sprachraumes*, PLA, 31, pp. 82–92.

1183. Kenny A. J. P., *The first person*, in C. Diamond, (ed.), *Intention and intentionality*, Brighton, Harvester, 1979, pp. 3–13. Reprinted in Kenny, 1984, pp. 77–87.

1184. Korsmeyer C., *W. and the ontological problem of art*, Pr, 59, pp. 152–61.

1185. Kreisel G., *The motto of 'Philosophical investigations' and the philosophy of proofs and rules*, GPS, 6, pp. 13–38.

1186. Kuzminski A., *Showing and saying: W.'s mystical realism*, 'Yale Review', 68, pp. 500–18.

1187. Kuzminski A., *Names, descriptions, and pictures*, RM, 32, pp. 453–70.
In parts V–VI of the article a re-interpretation and re-evaluation of W.'s picture theory of language.

1188. Lamb D., *Hegel and W. on language and sense-certainty*, 'Clio', 7, pp. 285-301.
Analogies between the two philosophers in their criticism of empiricism and of subjective idealism, and in their general conception of language.

1189. Leyvraz J.-P., *Logic and experience in W.'s later work: 'On certainty'*, MW, 11, pp. 257-69.

1190. Luckhardt C. G., *Beyond knowledge. Paradigms in W.'s later philosophy*, PPR, 39, pp. 240-52. Reprinted in Shanker (ed.), 1986, vol. III.
The notion of 'paradigm' is defined through an examination of W.'s various later work and is then applied in a discussion of certainty in *O.C.*

1191. Malcolm N., *W.'s conception of first person psychological sentences as 'expressions'*, PE, 2, pp. 59-72.

1192. Malherbe J. F., *Interprétations en conflit à propos du 'Traité' de W.*, RPL, 76, pp. 180-204.
A comparison between the interpretations of *Tract.* put forward by Russell, the Vienna Circle, and K. Popper.

1193. Malone M. E., *Is scientific observation 'seeing as'?*, PInv, 1, no. 4, pp. 23-38.
In his *Patterns of discovery*, 1969, N. R. Hanson misunderstood W.'s concept of 'seeing as', regarding it as somehow basic to all scientific observations.

1194. Mandel R., *Heidegger and W. A second Kantian revolution*, in *Hiedegger and modern philosophy. Critical essays*, edited by M. Murray, New Haven, Conn., Yale University Press, 1978, pp. 259-70.

1195. Marsonet M., *Significato e pratica sociale nel pensiero del tardo W.*, Ep.,2, pp. 371-86.

1196. Morawetz T., *W. and knowledge: the importance of 'On certainty'*, Amherst, Mass., University of Massachusetts Press, 1978, pp. 159; reissued Atlantic Highlands, N.J., Humanities Press, 1980; Brighton, Harvester Press, 1980.
An examination of the main argumentations on knowledge and certainty in *O.C.*, and on the nature of logical rules. In a concluding chapter, 'On philosophy', the problem of the nature of philosophical investigation in relation to the themes

previously dealt with is raised. *Reviews:* Beardsmore R. W.,
P, 1980, 55, pp. 130–2; Gallacher H. P., PB, 1981, 22, no. 1,
pp. 20–2; Miller R. W., ISP, 1980, 12, pp. 118–9.

1197. Parak F., *W. prigioniero a Cassino*, introduction by
D. Antiseri, Rome, Armando, 1978, pp. 69.
The recollections of a fellow-prisoner of W.'s in Cassino camp,
in Italy, after the end of the First World War.

1198. Pietra R., *Valéry, W. et la philosophie*, 'Bulletin des
Études Valéryennes', no. 20, March 1979. Republished
in *Recherches sur la philosophie et le langage* (Cahier de
Grenoble, no. 1), Grenoble, Institut de philosophie et
sociologie, 1981, pp. 57–81.

1199. Radford C., *It's on the tip of my tongue*, PInv, 1, no.
2, pp. 70–79.
A critical examination of *P.I.*, p. 231, and of W.'s non-
experiential account of remembering.

1200. Reese W. L., *Religious 'seeing as'*, RS, 14, pp. 73–87.
W.'s theory of aspects applied to the examination of the use
of metaphor in religious language.

1201. Richards G., *Conceptions of the self in W., Hume and
Buddhism*, Mo, 61, pp. 42–55.

1202. Richards G., *A W.ian approach to the philosophy of
religion. A critical evaluation of D. Z. Phillips*, JR, 58,
pp. 288–302.

1203. Ross J. J., *Rationality and common sense*, P, 53,
pp. 374–81.
Should W.'s views as expressed in *O.C.* be regarded as an endorse-
ment of 'sociologism' or are they a form of 'justificationism'?

1204. Rubinstein D., *W. and social-science*, 'Social Praxis',
5, pp. 295–322. Reprinted in Shanker (ed.), 1986, vol.
IV, pp. 290–311.

1205. Sankowski E., *W. on self-knowledge*, M, 87, pp. 256–61.
An examination of first-person psychological statements (*P.I.*
222, 246) and a critique of the interpretation put forward by
Kenny, 1973, of self-knowledge in W.

1206. Sankowski E., *Some aspects of W.'s critique of
Augustine*, ISP, 11, pp. 149–52.

1207. Shir J., *W.'s aesthetics and the theory of literature*, BJA, 18, pp. 3-11.

1208. Smith B., *Law and eschatology in W.'s early thought*, I, 21, pp. 425-41.
Ethics in the first W. seen in the light of an examination of some authors writing on the philosophy of law in Germany (A. Reinach, W. Schapp). Analogies are found in the ontological categories of *Tract.*

1209. Stripling S. R., *The picture theory of meaning. An interpretation of W.'s Tractatus logico-philosophicus*, Washington, D.C., University Press of America, 1978, pp. IX, 127.
Reviews: Balowitz V., ISP, 1983, 15, p. 122; Hustwit R.E., PRh, 1980, 13, pp. 286-9.

1210. Taylor E., *Lebenswelt und Lebensformen: Husserl and W. on the goal and method of philosophy*, HS, 1, pp. 184-200.

1211. Terricabras J.-M., *L.W. Kommentar und Interpretation*, Freiburg, Alber, 1978, pp. 745.
Reviews: Mierenfeld J., PH, 1982, 15, pp. 35-6; Wallner F., PLA, 1980, 33, pp. 273-4.

1212. Trigg R., *Thought and language*, PAS, 79, pp. 59-77.
Is it legitimate to suppose that thought might precede language-learning? Many references to W.'s opinions in *P.I.*

1213. Vander Veer G. L., *Philosophical scepticism and ordinary-language analysis*, Lawrence, Kan., Regents Press of Kansas, pp. 227.
Deals not with W. directly but with philosophical trends influenced by him, attempting to show that therapies centred on the uses of natural language have failed to clarify and disperse the doubts of classical scepticism. *Reviews:* Brown S. C., PB, 1981, 22, pp. 48-50; Grant C. K., M, 1980, 89, pp. 312-4; McArthur R. P., RM, 1981-2, 35, pp. 914-16; White A. R., PQ, 1980, 30, pp. 155-6.

1214. Verhack I., *W.'s deictic metaphysics: an uncommon reading of the Tractatus*, IPQ, 18, pp. 433-44.

1215. Wetzel C. R., *The 'Bl.B.' as an introduction to W.*, PInv, 1, no.3, pp. 37-43.

Bl.B. is especially appropriate as a help to understanding the philosophical problems that W. dealt with in *P.I.* and his way of doing philosophy.

1216. Whittaker J. H., *Language-games and forms of life unconfused*, PInv, 1, no. 4, pp. 39-48.
The original relations between the two concepts have been misinterpreted, with confusion and misunderstanding as the result.

1217. Whittaker J. H., *W. and religion: some later views of his later work*, 'Religious Studies Review', 4, pp. 188-93.

1979

1218. *Body, mind and method. Essays in honor of V. C. Aldrich*, ed. by D. F. Gustafson and B. L. Tapscott, Dordrecht, Reidel, 1979, pp. XIII, 300.
Many of the contributions refer to W., in particular: R. Rorty, *The unnaturalness of epistemology*, pp. 77-92 (W., Heidegger, Quine and others: the criticism of the Kantian-Hegelian use of the concepts of 'experience' and 'consciousness' and the task of philosophy); G. Vesey, *W. on psychological verbs*, pp. 115-27 (What do words like 'believe', 'expect', 'mean', etc. have in common? W.'s reply to this question is analysed in connection with the positions of Descartes, Locke, Brentano, Husserl); D. F. Gustafson, *'Pain', grammar and physicalism*, pp. 149-66 (Are W.'s views consistent with the truth of some recognizable form of physicalism in the philosophy of mind?); J.V. Canfield, *Calculations, reasons and causes*, pp. 179-95 (with references to *L.C.*).

1219. *El argumento del lenguaje privado*, ed. and introd. by E. Villanueva, Mexico, UNAM, Instituto de Investigaciones Filosóficas, 1979, pp. 265.
A selection and Spanish translation of writings on private language in W. including Rhees, 1954, Ayer, 1954, Cook, 1965, Ginet, 1970, Thomson, 1964, Kenny, 1971. Two unpublished writings of H. N. Castañeda are added.

1220. *Religionskritik von der Aufklärung bis zur Gegenwart. Autoren-Lexikon von Adorno bis W.*, ed. by K.-H. Weger, Freiburg, Herder, 1979, pp. 319.

Accounts of authors from various historical periods between Locke and Habermas with particular reference to their contributions to philosophy of religion. The article on W. closes the volume, for alphabetical reasons, and is written by A. Keller.

1221. *W.s geistige Erscheinung* (W., Schriften: Beiheft 3), ed. by H. J. Heringer and M. Nedo, Frankfurt, Suhrkamp, 1979, pp. 116. E.T., with a new preface by B. McGuinness: *W. and his times,* Oxford, Blackwell; Chicago, Ill., University of Chicago Press, 1982, pp. VI, 122.

In the English edition the titles of the essays are: A. Kenny, *W. on the nature of philosophy,* pp. 1–26 (particularly dedicated to the middle period of W.'s thought: much reference to unpublished material omitted from *P.G.* Reprinted in Kenny, 1984); B. McGuinness, *Freud and W.,* pp. 27–43 (an examination of W.'s references to Freud, principally those in the collection *Culture and value);* J.C. Nyíri, *W. 's later work in relation to conservatism,* pp. 44–68 (an examination of the analogies between W. and some important representatives of what N. calls 'neo-conservatism'; Dostoevsky, Spengler, P. Ernst, and others: see comments by Schulte, 1983); R. Rhees, *W. on language and ritual,* pp. 69–107 (comments on passages from *Remarks on Frazer,* related unpublished remarks); G. H. von Wright, *W. in relation to his times,* pp. 108–20 (W.'s influence on, and attitude towards, the culture of his day; reprinted in von Wright, 1982). *Reviews:* Champlin T. S., PInv, 1984, 7, no. 3, pp. 248–52; Finch H. L., PB, 1984, 25, pp. 162–4; Frohmann B., Ru, 1983, 3, pp. 71–7; Janik A., JHP, 1983, 21, pp. 419–21; Parret H., TF, 1983, 45, pp. 261–76; Szabados B., CPR, 1984, 4, pp. 31–4; Wallner F., PLA, 1981, 34, pp. 46–8.

1222. *W.: sources and perspectives,* ed. by C. G. Luckhardt, Hassocks, Harvester Press; Ithaca, N.Y., Cornell University Press, 1979, 342 pp.

Besides *R.F.* and an English translation of *Briefe an L. von Ficker* (see 'Publications of Writings by Wittgenstein'), this volume contains: F. Pascal, *W. A personal memoir,* pp. 23–60 (previously printed in 1973, reminiscences of one who was W.'s Russian teacher in the 1930s); G. H. von Wright, *The origin of W. 's Tractatus,* pp. 99–137 (reprinted with corrections, 1971); G. H. von Wright, *The origin and composition of W.'s Investigations*, pp. 138–60 (a reconstruction of the various attempts at composing the work, from 1936 onwards; a revised version is republished in von Wright, 1982); A. Janik, *W., Ficker, and 'Der Brenner'*, pp. 161–89; D. Pears, *The relation between W.'s picture theory of propositions and Russell's theories of judgment*, pp. 190–212 (reprint, 1977); P. M. S. Hacker, *Semantic holism: Frege and W.*, pp. 213–42 (the relationship between the two philosophers, in relation to Frege's thesis that 'a word has meaning only in the context to a statement'); G. P. Baker, *'Verehrung und Verkehrung': Waismann and W.*, pp. 243–85; K. Linville, *W. on 'Moore's paradox'*, pp. 286–302 (with reference to *P.I.* X); R. L. Arrington, *'Mechanism' and 'calculus': W. on Augustine's theory of ostension*, pp. 303–38. *Reviews:* Balowitz V., ISP, 1986, 18, p. 67; Cordua C., 'Dialogos', 1980, 15, pp. 204–7; Wallner F., PLA, 1980, 33, pp. 270–2; White R., PInv, 1981, 4, no. 4, pp. 79–80.

1223. *W. the Vienna Circle and critical rationalism*, Proceedings of the third international W. Symposium, Kirchberg am Wechsel, 13 to 19 August 1978, ed. by H. Berghel, A. Hübner, E. Köhler. Schriftenreihe der Wittgenstein-Gesellschaft, vol. 3. Vienna, Hölder-Pichler-Tempsky, pp. 541.
An introductory chapter contains some general historical contributions: C. Hempel, *Der Wiener Kreis – eine persönliche Perspektive* (pp. 21–6); K. Menger, *W. betreffende Seiten aus einem Buch über den Wiener Kreis*, pp. 27–9; W. Baum, *Die Weltanschauung L.W.s*, pp. 30–2; B. F. McGuinness, *W.'s 'intellectual nursery-training'*, pp. 33–40; R. H. Hurlbutt III, *W., positivism, and the possibility of social science*, pp. 60–70. The other contributions are grouped under the following headings: (1) 'Wittgenstein'; (2) 'The Vienna Circle'; (3) 'Karl Popper'; (4) 'Social theory'. The section on W. is divided into the following chapters: 'Problems of the *Tractatus*' (pp. 75–98); 'Language, meaning and metaphysics' (pp. 101–130); 'W. on perception' (pp. 133–56); 'Formal-logical problems' (pp. 159–90); 'W.'s influence on the Vienna Circle and later philosophy of science' (pp. 193–219). *Reviews:* Janik A. S, PInv, 1981, 4, no. 3, pp. 82–5; Stock W. G., PLA, 1984, 37, pp. 100–2; Wallner F., PLA, 1980, 33, pp. 267–9.

1224. Améry J., *An den Grenzen des Scharfsinns. Zu den 'Vermischten Bemerkungen' L.W.s*, 'Neue Rundschau', 90, pp. 86-95.

1225. Austin J., *Criteriology: a minimally theoretical method*, Mp, 10, pp. 1-17.
An examination of the central role played by the notion of 'criterion' (rather than that of 'use') in the later W.'s theory of meaning. A. argues against the interpretation that sees in W. a philosopher of ordinary language.

1226. Barker P., *Untangling the net metaphor*, PRA, 5, pp. 182-99.
Tract. 6.3ff on science and Newtonian mechanics.

1227. Barrett W., *The illusion of technique*, New York, Anchor, 1979, pp. XXII, 416.
B. identifies W., Heidegger, and William James as the three main leaders in western thought of a revolt against determinism, nihilism, and the supremacy of technique, and in favour of the right of humanity to aspire to liberty. *Reviews:* Ballard E. G., RM, 1978-9, 32, pp. 736-8; Borgmann A., MW, 1980, 13, pp. 458-65; Desmond W., IJP, 1979, 3, pp. 148-9; Manser A., M, 1981, 90, pp. 147-9; Neiman A., NS, 1980, 54, pp. 102-8.

1228. Barthofer A., *W. mit Maske: Dichtung und Wahrheit in Thomas Bernhards Roman 'Korrektur'*, 'Geschichte und Literatur', 23, pp. 186-207.

1229. Baum W., *L.W. und die Religion*, PJ, 86, pp. 272-99.
An examination of W.'s 'mysticism' at the time of *Tract.*, and of its complex relationship to religion.

1230. Black M., *W.'s language-games*, Di, 33, pp. 337-53. Reprinted in Shanker (ed.), 1986, vol. II.
A critical examination of the meaning that W. attributes to the notion of *Sprachspiel*, based on the observation that autonomy cannot be attributed to the various language games. In fact the latter presuppose a web of conceptual relationships which can be found throughout language as a whole.

1231. Bolton D. E., *An approach to W.'s philosophy*, London, Macmillan; Atlantic Highlands, N.J., Humanities Press, 1979, pp. 226.

The main aim of this book is to find an historical classification for W.'s work. In B.'s opinion, *Tract.* is the sign of a turning-point in a philosophical tradition whose origins go back to the 16th and 17th centuries, and which is defined (ch. II, 'Tradition and originality in the *Tract.*') with particular reference to Descartes, Newton, Berkeley, Locke. In *P.I.*, on the other hand, B. finds a drastic rejection of this tradition, to which *Tract.* also belonged, and locates a stronger link with contemporary sensitivity which is expressed in a relativism whose features are defined through a comparison with Plato's *Theaetetus* (ch. IV). *Reviews:* Bogen J., TeaP, 1981, 4, pp. 67–74; Burke T. E., M, 1982, 91, pp. 614–15; Fogelin R., PR, 1982, 91, pp. 119–21; Rosen S., RM, 1980–1, 34, pp. 780–2; Saint-Fleur J. P., 'Cahiers de Philosophie', 1981–2; pp. 183–6.

1232. Bruening W. H., *The ethics of silence*, IndPQ, 7, pp. 51–9.
A comparison between the ethics of W. and that of some trends in Zen Buddhism.

1233. Cambi F., *La recezione della filosofia del linguaggio di L. W. nell'opera di I. Bachmann*, Pisa, Giardini, 1979, pp. 37.
Examines the writings of this creative writer of the 1950s with a view to tracing the philosophical influence on her of Heidegger and W.

1234. Cameron J. M., *Bodily existence*, PACPA, 53, 59–70. Reprinted in Shanker (ed.), 1986, vol. IV, pp. 138–48.

1235. Carney J. D., *W.'s theory of names*, AJP, 57, pp. 59–68.
On the basis of an examination of *P.I.* 79, C. defines W.'s theses in relation to the traditional theory of the meaning of names, according to which these have a 'sense', where the 'sense of a name is a description synonymously correlated with it'.

1236. Cavell S., *The claim of reason. W., scepticism, morality and tragedy*, London and New York, Oxford University Press, 1979, 1982, pp. XXII, 511.
Four essays from different periods: only the first two concern W.: *W. and the concept of human knowledge* (pp. 3–125); *Scepticism and the existence of the world* (pp. 129–243). The principal problems treated are: the nature of the criteria we use to identify internal and external objects; knowledge of

other minds; how philosophy can deal with sceptical objections (frequent comparisons between W. and J. L. Austin). The remaining chapters treat the same themes but pay progressively less attention to questions of analysis. Chapter 3 concerns the foundation of morality; chapter 4 is a divagatory literary-philosophical essay which seeks to establish a point of contact between Anglo-Saxon and continental philosophy. *Reviews*: Bates S., PL, 1980, 4, pp. 266–73; De Pater W. A., TF, 1984, 46, p. 376; Ducker D., IPQ, 1981, 21, pp. 109–11; Fischer K. R., WJP, 1981, 14, pp. 228–32; Garver N., PPR, 1981, 14, pp. 562–3; Hamlyn D. W., PB, 1981, 22, pp. 186–8; Hollander J., 'Yale Review', 1980, 69, pp. 577–83; Hope V., I, 1981, 24, pp. 470–80; Hrachovec H., PLA, 1982, 35, pp. 91–2; Kenny A. J. P., TLS, 1980, no. 4021, p. 449; Lear J., 'New York Times Book Review', 1979, 84, p. 30; Louch A., Mp, 1981, 12, pp. 310–22; Mannison D. and Reinhardt L., PInv, 1982, 5, pp. 227–44; Margolis J., ISP, 1981, 13, pp. 85–8; Mounce H. O., PQ, 1981, 31, pp. 280–2; Palmer A., M, 1982, 91, pp. 292–5; Rohatyn D., MS, 1981–2, 59, pp. 63–4; Rorty R., RM, 1980–1, 34, pp. 759–74; Sessions W. L., RM, 1981, 34, pp. 601–2; Wallner F., PLA, 1982, 35, pp. 159–63; Weitz M., JP, 1981, 78, pp. 50–6.

1237. Clay M., *A conceptual index of W.'s 'On certainty'*, PInv, 2, no. 3, pp. 61–84.

1238. Diffey T. J., *On defining art*, BJA, 19, pp. 15–23.
The definition of art in Plato and W. A comparison and a critical analysis.

1239. Ebersole F. B., *The family-resemblance metaphor*, in his *Language and perception. Essays in the philosophy of language*, Washington, D.C., University Press of America, 1979, pp. 1–78.
Of the seven essays in the volume this is the one most concerned with W. It considers 'some difficulties' that E. sees in some passages of *Bl.B.* and *P.I.* dealing with the concepts of 'common properties', 'common features', and 'family resemblances'.

1240. Erde E. L., *Principia nonsensica*, PInv, 2, no. 1, pp. 24–40.
A critical analysis of different meanings attached to the concept of 'nonsense' 'in the currents stimulated by W.'.

1241. Fay T. A., *Heidegger and W. on the question of ordinary language*, PT, 23, pp. 154-59.

The great differences between the two philosophers make the attempts which have been made to bring their works closer to each other seem rather dubious.

1242. Fromm S., *W.s Erkenntnisspiele contra Kants Erkenntnislehre*, Freiburg, Alber, 1979, pp. 267.

A critical comparison of the two philosophers divided into three parts: 1. an account of the transcendental deduction in the *Critique of pure reason;* 2. an examination of W.'s philosophy of language as revealed by *P.I.;* 3. the identification of several aspects of Kant's theory of knowledge that seem incapable of meeting satisfactorily the questions posed by W. *Review*: Echternach H., PH, 1982, 15, pp. 105-6.

1243. Gargani A., *W. tra Austria e Inghilterra*, Turin, Stampatori, 1979, pp. 180.

The work brings together four essays (titles translated from the Italian): 'W. and Austrian culture'; 'The philosophical schools of Oxford and Cambridge'; 'Language analysis'; 'Philosophy as linguistic therapy and philosophy as vision'. The last two were published earlier, in 1974 and 1966 respectively. *Reviews*: Garavaso P., V, 1980, 9, pp. 217-19; Grassl W., GPS, 1981, 14, pp. 213-15.

1244. Garvey J. C., *W. and other minds*, PS(I), 26, pp. 72-95.

1245. Genova J., *W.'s later picture 'theory' of meaning*, PInv, 2, no. 1, pp. 9-23.

It is equally improper to maintain that *Tract.* picture theory is compatible with W.'s later theory of meaning (Kenny) and that this latter involves a repudiation of the former (Hacker). Both views fail to capture the complex relationship between W.'s early and late thinking.

1246. Gill J. H., *W. and metaphor*, PPR, 40, pp. 272-84.

The appeal to metaphor in W.'s method of analysis, in *Tract.*, in *P.I.*, and in *O.C.*

1247. Goodman R. B., *Schopenhauer and W. on ethics*, JHP, 17, pp. 437-47.

With particular reference to *Tract.* 6.421-6.4311.

1248. Green O. H., *W. and the possibility of a philosophical theory of emotion*, Mp, 10, pp. 256-64.

W. criticizes the theories that identify emotions with both internal feelings and external behaviour. Nevertheless, he does not exclude the possibility that a satisfactory theory of emotions may be put forward.

1249. Grewendorf G., *Is W.'s private language argument trivial?*, R, 21, pp. 149-61.

Contrary to the ruling interpretations, W.'s argument on private language is independent of the question about the private nature of our sensations.

1250. Gustafson D. F., *W. on meaning something*, PInv, 2, no. 3, pp. 18-31.

An interpretation based on *Z.* 7 and *P.I.* 666.

1251. Hacking I., *What is logic?*, JP, 76, pp. 285-319.

Part III on 'W.'s by-product theory of logic' deals with *Tract.*

1252. Hall R. L., *W. and Polanyi: the problem of privileged self-knowledge*, PT, 23, pp. 267-78.

1253. Haller R., *Die gemeinsame menschliche Handlungsweise*, ZPF, 33, pp. 521-33.

In the examination of the research on foundations in W., H. finds a number of analogies with Spengler.

1254. Haller R., *Studien zur österreichischen Philosophie. Variationen über ein Thema*, Amsterdam, Rodopi, 1979, pp. 194.

In the second half of this volume H. collects articles on various aspects of the relation between W. and contemporary Austrian thought: *L.W. and die österreichische Philosophie*, pp. 107-21 (see 1968); *Sprachkritik und Philosophie: W. und Mauthner*, pp. 123-40; *Philosophische Irrtümer und die Sprache*, pp. 141-8; *War W. ein Skeptiker?*, pp. 149-62; *W. und die 'Wiener Schule'*, pp. 163-87.

1255. Hamilton J. R., *What if there were a religious 'form of life'?*, PInv, 2, no. 3, pp. 1-17.

There can be no clear description of what the religious person does, which is available to the non-believer. Therefore, assurance of the intelligibility of religious utterances is not possible on the basis of an appeal to a religious 'form of life'.

1256. Harrison B., *An introduction to the philosophy of language*, London, Macmillan, 1979, pp. 303.

The last two chapters 'Objects and the determinateness of sense' (pp. 209-26), and 'Meaning and use' (pp. 227-58), respectively deal with *Tract.* (considered in its relation to Frege) and with W.'s later philosophy of language.

1257. Heil J., *Making things simple*, Cr, 11, pp. 3-33.
The existence of simple objects in *Tract.* constitutes a requirement which is made necessary by the picture theory of language.

1258. Helme M., *An elucidation of Tractatus 3.263*, SJP, 17, pp. 323-34.
On the meaning of primitive signs and the role of ostensive definition in *Tract.*

1259. Hülser K., *Wahrheitstheorie als Aussagentheorie. Untersuchungen zu W.s Tractatus*, Königstein, Forum Academicum, 1979, pp. 244.
A wide-ranging reconstruction of, and commentary on, *Tract.* and its theory of truth, designed to show that this is the main theme of W.'s research and that it leads to the idea of a logical language. The central chapters are devoted to the theory of the proposition, to that of truth, that of meaning, to the picture theory, and to logical truth. A final chapter examines W.'s relation to Frege and also compares him with modern German thinkers such as Habermas and Mans.

1260. Ishiguro H., *Subjects, predicates, isomorphic representation, and language games*, in *Essays in honour of J. Hintikka*, ed. by E. Saarinen *et al.*, Dordrecht, Reidel, 1979, pp. 351-64. Reprinted in Canfield (ed.), 1986, vol. 1.

1261. Jensen H., *Reid and W. on philosophy and language*, PS, 36, pp. 359-76.
An examination of a number of analogies with T. Reid on the importance of the analysis of language in philosophy, with the aim of shedding light on the sources of W.'s thought.

1262. Kielkopf C. F., *W., aposteriori necessity and logic for entailment*, Ph, 9, pp. 63-74. Reprinted in Shanker (ed.), 1986, vol. III.

1263. Klemke E. D., *Blanshard's criticism of W.'s Tractatus*, Pr, 60, pp. 305-11.

1264. Kuroda W., *Phenomenology and grammar*, AH, 8, pp. 89-107.
A comparison between Husserl (*Logical investigations*) and the later W.

1265. Lamb D., *Language and perception in Hegel and W.*, Amersham, Avebury Publishing Co., 1979; New York, St. Martin's Press, 1980, pp. 135.
L. stresses the continental character of W.'s philosophy and points out a number of analogies with Hegel, particularly in respect of the critical attitude of both philosophers to the empirical account of the relation between language and reality and of sensory realism (chs. 1-3). L. also points out the common attempt to transcend abstract distinctions between philosophical discourse on one side, and life and reality on the other (chs. 4-5). *Reviews*: Harris H. S., JHP, 1982, 20, pp. 441-5; Gerth N., PR, 1982, 91, pp. 636-40.

1266. Lee H. D. P., *W. 1929-1931*, P, 54, pp. 211-20.
The recollections of one of W.'s former pupils, taken from notes of lectures and conversations. They are only indirectly concerned with philosophical themes, but refer to various aspects of W.'s personality.

1267. Levi A. W., *The biographical sources of W.'s ethics*, Te, no. 38, pp. 63-76.
L. supports the thesis that the source of W.'s ethical positions can be connected to some passages from his biography, and particularly to a feeling of guilt which comes from his homosexuality. See the criticism of this article by Rudebush-Berg, 1979, Schwarzschild, 1979, Steinvorth, 1979, Janik, 1980. A reply by Levi in *W. once more*, Te, 40, pp. 165-73.

1268. Linville K., *W. at criticism*, SJP, 17, pp. 85-94.
W.'s philosophical method aims to bring about a change 'in the way of seeing', not a change in philosophical opinions.

1269. McKee P. L. and **Slauson W.**, *W., General terms and common resemblances*, M, 88, pp. 120-3.
Do all games have something in common (*P.I.* 66)? An examination of the difficulties.

1270. Magnanini D., *Tolstoi e W. come 'imitatori di Cristo'*, 'Sapienza', 32, pp. 89-100.

1271. Menger K., *Selected papers in logic and foundations,* *didactics, economics* (Vienna Circle Collection, 10), Dordrecht, Reidel, 1979, pp. 341.

A collection of papers, some previously published (1928–61), some not: references to W. are of an historical character and mostly concern his relations with the Vienna Circle (see esp. the Introduction). A chapter, 'W. on formulae and variables' (pp. 153–60) discusses *P.I.* 143ff. on the subject of mathematical variables.

1272. **Penco C.**, *Matematica e regole. W. interprete di Kant*, Ep, 2, pp. 123–52.

1273. **Phillips D. Z.** and **Manser A. R.**, *Alienation and the sociologizing of meaning*, PAS(SV), 53, pp. 95–133.
An examination of the sociological approach to the study of meaning making numerous critical references to W.

1274. **Pippin R. B.**, *Negation and not-being in W.'s Tractatus and Plato's Sophist*, KS, 70, pp. 179–96.

1275. **Putnam H.**, *Analyticity and apriority: beyond W. and Quine*, MWSP, 4, pp. 423–41. Reprinted in Canfield (ed.), 1986, vol. X.
The meaning and the limitations of the theory of logical necessity in Quine and W. (the latter's 'finitism' is discussed).

1276. **Reeder H. P.**, *Language and the phenomenological reduction. A reply to a W.ian objection*, MW, 12, pp. 35–46.

1277. **Roberts H. R. T.**, *The concept of 'seeing as' in W.'s philosophy of religion*, IndPQ, 7, pp. 71–82.

1278. **Rubinstein D.**, *W. and science*, PSS, 9, pp. 341–6.
On D. L. Phillips' interpretation, 1977, of W.'s account of the foundation of the social sciences.

1279. **Rudebush T.** and **Berg W. M.**, *On W. and ethics: a reply to Levi*, Te, 40, pp. 150–60. (Cf. Levi, 1979).

1280. **Savitt S. F.**, *W.'s early philosophy of mathematics*, PRA, 5, pp. 539–59. Reprinted in Shanker (ed.), 1986, vol. III.

1281. **Schwarzschild S. S.**, *W. as alienated Jew*, Te, 40, pp. 160–65.
A critical answer to the attempt by Levi, 1979, to find in W.'s biography the origins of his philosophical theories.

1282. Schwyzer H., *Concepts and objectivity*, PInv, 2, no. 2, pp. 1–8.
An evaluation of Kant's and W.'s 'objectivity thesis', considered as an attempt 'to block the movement towards scepticism'.

1283. Seidel H., *Ingeborg Bachmann und L.W.: Person und Werk L.W.s in den Erzählungen 'Das dreissigste Jahr' und 'Ein Wildermuth'*, 'Zeitschrift für deutsche Philologie', 98, pp. 267–82.

1284. Sellmann J., *The Koan: a language-game*, IndPQ, 7, pp. 1–9.
Beyond the more obvious differences there is a complementary relationship between W.'s method and the one adopted in Rinzai Zen.

1285. Slater B. H., *W.'s later logic*, P, 54, pp. 199–209.
An examination of *R.F.M.*, and an attempt to define W.'s theory on the nature of 'the law of the excluded middle' placing it in relation to the contrasting solutions given by Brouwer and Russell.

1286. Spiegelberg H., *Augustine in W.: a case study in philosophical stimulation*, JHP, 17, pp. 319–27.
A study of the influence exerted by St. Augustine on W. through an examination of the passages of W.'s writings containing references to the *Confessions*.

1287. Steinvorth U., *The ideological sources of W.'s ethics: reply to Levi*, Te, 41, pp. 166–72 (see Levi, 1979).

1288. Steinvorth U., *W., Loos und Karl Kraus*, ZPF, 33, pp. 74–89.
An examination of the Austrian cultural environment in which W.'s character was formed, and a critique of the interpretation given by Janik-Toulmin, 1973.

1289. Tennant N., *Language games and intuitionism*, Sy, 42, pp. 297–314.
T. takes as his point of departure, and tries to improve on, the 'game theoretic semantics for first order languages', which Hintikka derived from W.'s theory of language games, 1973.

1290. Tugendhat E., *Selbstbewusstsein und Selbstbestimmung. Sprachanalytische Interpretation*, Frankfurt, Suhrkamp, 1979. E.T.: *Self-consciousness and self-determination*,

Cambridge, Mass., and London, MIT Press, 1986, pp. XXXI, 339.

The volume aims to show that the traditional concept of self-consciousness, whether in the theoretical or in the practical sphere, as developed by Descartes, Kant, Fichte, and Hegel, has to be abandoned in the light of criticisms from authors such as W., Heidegger, and G. H. Mead. Two chapters devoted to W.: 'The impossibility of a private language'; 'The way out of the fly-bottle'.

1291. **Wallner F.**, *Neue Perspektiven der W.-Forschung.* Bericht vom 2. Symposium am W. Archiv in Tübingen, C, 13, pp. 121–4.

1292 **Wienpahl P.**, *Eastern Buddhism and W.'s Philosophical investigations*, 'Eastern Buddhists', 12, no. 2, pp. 22–54.

1293. **Williams C.J.F.**, *Is identity a relation?*, PAS, 80, pp. 81–100.

Contains an analysis and discussion of *Tract.* 5.53ff. on the correct way of expressing what is normally expressed by an affirmation of identity.

1294. **Williams J. C.**, *Experiencing the meaning of a word*, MW, 12, pp. 3–12.

1295. **Wolniewicz B.**, *A W.ian semantics for propositions*, in *Intention and intentionality. Essays in honour of G. E. M. Anscombe*, edited by C. Diamond and J. Teichman, Hassocks, Harvester Press, 1979, pp. 165–78. Reprinted in Canfield (ed.), 1986, vol. II.

An examination of the theoretical tenability of the notion of elementary proposition in Anscombe's interpretation, 1959, of *Tract.*

1296. **Wuchterl K.** and **Hübner A.**, *L. W. in Selbstzeugnissen und Bilddokumenten*, Reinbek, Rowohlt, 1979, pp. 156. *Reviews:* Drudis Baldrich R., AP, 1981–2, 4, pp. 226–8; Schischkoff G., PLA, 1979, 32, pp. 319–22; Wallner F., PLA, 1980, 33, pp. 274–6.

1297. **Zimmermann R.**, *W. zwischen Hermeneutik, Phänomenologie und analytischer Systematik*, PRd, 26, pp. 198–213.

An examination of recent discussions of W.'s later work (Brand, 1975, J. Zimmermann, 1975, Hottois, 1976, Birnbacher, 1974).

1980

1298. *Language, logic and philosophy*. Proceedings of the Fourth International W. Symposium, 28 August to 2 September 1979, Kirchberg am Wechsel, Austria; edited by R. Haller and W. Grassl (Schriftenreihe der Wittgenstein-Gesellschaft, Vol. 4). Vienna, Hölder-Pichler-Tempsky, 1980, pp. 617.

Only part of the volume is directly concerned with W. (pp. 171-333). This part contains 42 contributions falling under the following heads: (1) 'W.'s philosophy in its historical context'; (2) 'Logic and semantics in the Tractatus'; (3) 'W., the Vienna Circle, and the philosophy of science'; (4) 'Transcendentalism in W.'s philosophy'; (5) 'Family resemblance and universals'; (6) 'W. and the foundations of psychology'; (7) 'W.ian ethics'; (8) 'Knowledge, certainty and belief'.

1299. *Les philosophes anglo-saxons par eux-mêmes* ('Critique', 36, nos. 399-400), Paris, Minuit, 1980.

A special number containing 19 articles, many of which refer to W. In particular: G. P. Baker and P. M. S. Hacker, *W. aujourd'hui*, pp. 690-704 (republished in English in Shanker (ed.), 1986, vol. II, pp. 332-72); J. Bouveresse, *Frege, W., Dummett et la nouvelle 'Querelle du réalisme'*, pp. 881-96.

1300. Amdur S., *Toward a definitive index of W.'s (later) work: more terms for an index of 'On Certainty'*, PInv, 3, no. 1, pp. 57-9.

A pendant to the index previously published in the same review by M. Clay, 1979. In the introduction A. discusses the project of a computerized indexing of W.'s later work, including the *Nachlass*.

1301. Apel K.-O., *Towards a transformation of philosophy*, London, Routledge & Kegan Paul, 1980.

Essays selected mainly from the second volume of a larger German collection, 1973. Concerned with W. are: *W. and the problem of hermeneutic understanding*, pp. 1-45 (reprinted in Shanker (ed.), 1986, vol. IV); *The communication community as the transcendental presupposition for the social sciences*, pp. 136-79.

1302. Austin J., *W.'s solutions to the color exclusion problem*, PPR, 41, pp. 142-9. Reprinted in Shanker (ed.), 1986, vol. I.

W. proposed two incompatible solutions to the colour exclusion problem in *R.L.F.* and in *P.R.* This difference gives us an insight into the origins of his late philosophy.

1303. Baker G. P. and **Hacker P. M. S.**, *W.: understanding and meaning. An analytical commentary on the 'Philosophical investigations'*, vol. 1, Oxford, Blackwell; Chicago, Ill., Chicago University Press, 1980, pp. 692.

The work offers a detailed commentary of the first 184 sections of *P.I.* These are grouped into six chapters, according to thematic criteria: 'The Augustinian picture (§§1-27)'; 'Ostensive definition and analysis (§§27-64)'; 'Determinacy of sense (§§65-88)'; 'Philosophy (§§89-133)'; 'The general propositional form (§§134-142)'; 'Meaning and understanding (§§143-184)'. Each chapter provides a detailed exegetic analysis of the sections considered in it, followed by more general expositions of an historical or theoretical nature. In these last particular attention is reserved for the examination of relationships with the work of Frege and Russell, and for the connections between *P.I.* and W.'s other writings, including the unedited manuscripts, with the aim of sketching a picture of the development of the philosopher's thought. Subsequently republished, with minor modifications, in two parts, one exegetical, the other containing the 70 short essays on themes drawn from Part I of *P.I.* (cf. Baker and Hacker, 1983). *Reviews:* Baker J., PS(I), 1981, 28, pp. 327-32; Bell D., PQ, 1982, 32, pp. 363-73; Bogen J., TeaP, 1981, 4, pp. 67-74; Burnheim J., AJP, 1982, 60, pp. 284-6; Finch H., PB, 1981, 22, pp. 140-3; Helme H., GPS, 1981, 14, pp. 153-64; Imbert C., RIP, 1983, 37, pp. 205-6; Lachterman D.R., PRh, 1982, 15, pp. 212-14; Malcolm N., TLS, 1980, no. 4046, p.1181; Nowak R., PJ, 1982, 89, pp. 187-91; Parret H., TF, 45, pp. 277-80; Pletcher G. K., MS, 1983, 60, pp. 283-4; Radford C., M, 1982, 91, pp. 441-51; Reix A., RPL, 1983, 81, pp. 669-72; Rosen S., RM, 1981, 34, pp. 776-8; Stroud B., PR, 1983, 92, pp. 282-4; Walker R. C. S., Ph, 1986, 16, pp. 95-100; Wallner F., PLA, 1982, 35, pp. 67-72; Weitz M., ISP, 1982, 14, pp. 68-70.

1304. Barker P., *Hertz and W.*, SHPS, 11, pp. 243-256.

An examination of the influence exerted on *Tract.* by the

scientific thought of the nineteenth century, and in particular by the figures of Hertz and Boltzmann.

1305. Bartley W. W., *W. and homosexuality*, TLS, no. 4011, p. 145.

1306. Baum W., *L.W.'s world view*, R, 22, pp. 64-74.
An examination of the importance of religious experience in W.'s personality and writings. B. considers in particular the influence in this direction exerted on W.'s development by W. James, Tolstoy, St. Augustine, Kierkegaard, and others.

1307. Baxley T. F., *W.'s theory of quantification*, ILR, 11, no. 21, pp. 46-55. Reprinted in Shanker (ed.), 1986, vol. III.
Maintains against other commentators that the *Tract.* theory of quantification has to be distinguished from the theory of generalization and is truth-functional not substitutional.

1308. Beerling R. F., *Sprachspiele und Weltbilder. Reflexionen zu W.*, Freiburg, Alber, 1980, pp. 290.

1309. Bennett P. W., *W.'s theory of knowledge in 'On Certainty'*, PInv, 3, no. 4, pp. 38-46.
A critical reconstruction of the centrality for theory of knowledge (according to *O.C.*) of the notion of system.

1310. Billing H., *W.s Sprachspielkonzeption*, Bonn, Bouvier, 1980, pp. 139.
A study of the notions of grammar, sign, and rule, examining W.'s use of these terms in a number of passages from *Tract.* to W.'s last writings. *Review:* Wallner F., PLA, 1982, 35, pp. 41-3.

1311. Bouveresse M. J., *W. grammairien*, Cri, no. 403, pp. 1156-63.
Presents the themes of *P.G.* on the occasion of the French translation of that work.

1312. Braghieri Dell'Anno M., *Introduzione alla logica di W.*, Rome, La Goliardica, 1980, pp. 127.

1313. Bruening S. M., *The aesthetic imperative as categorical*, D(PST), 22, pp. 33-44.
Sartre and W. are compared on the basis of their shared thesis that ethics and aesthetics are both subject to a single categorical imperative of a Kantian type.

1314. Candlish S., *The real private language argument*, P, 55, pp. 85-94.
An examination of *P.I.* 256-271, and a critique of the interpretations given by Fogelin, 1976, and Kenny, 1973.

1315. Cavalier R. J., *L. W. 's 'Tractatus logico-philosophicus': a transcendental critique of ethics*, Washington, D.C., University Press of America, pp. XII, 238.
After an introductory chapter in which he analyses the influences of other thinkers upon *Tract.* (among others, Hertz, Kierkegaard, Schopenhauer, Tolstoy) C. stresses the 'transcendental' character of W.'s critique of language (consisting mainly in his defining the conditions for the possibility of language) and of his theory of the subject, the will and the nature of ethics. *Reviews:* Bogen J., TeaP, 1981, 4, pp. 67-74; Haist G., Au, 1982, 9, pp. 235-48.

1316. Cook J. W., *Fate of ordinary language philosophy*, PInv, 3, no. 2, pp. 1-72.
Ordinary language philosophy is seen as a reaction against (and partly as a development of) logical analysis expounded by Russell and *Tract.* See, in particular, the ch. entitled 'The flank attack: W.'s new philosophical method'.

1317. Cook J. W., *Notes on W. 's 'On Certainty'*, PInv, 3, no. 4, pp. 15-37. Reprinted in Shanker (ed.), 1986, vol. II; in Canfield (ed.), 1986, vol. VIII.
On the theory of meaning and philosophical method in *O.C.* See criticisms of this article by H. Le Roy Finch, PInv, 1981, 4, no. 3, pp. 74-7, and response by J. W. Cook, ibid., pp. 78-81.

1318. Costall A., *The limits of language: W. 's later philosophy and Skinner's behaviorism*, B, 8, pp. 123-31.

1319. Davies B., *W. on God*, P, 55, pp. 105-108.
A comment on a passage from *R. F.* concerning belief in God.

1320. Droescher H.-M., *Grundlagenstudien zur Linguistik. Wissenschaftstheoretische Untersuchungen der Sprachphilosophischen Konzeptionen Humboldts, Chomskys und W.s*, Heidelberg, Groos, 1980, pp. 596.
In the final part of the volume (pp. 345-364) D. evaluates W.'s contribution to linguistic science by his theory of language games.

1321. Faghfoury M., *Doctoral dissertations on W.*, PRA, 6, no. 1407, pp. 266-77.

1322. Fay T. A., *Two approaches to the philosophy of ordinary language: Heidegger and W.*, RCSF, 35, pp. 79-86.
The concept of language and W.'s 'therapeutic' method are set against Heidegger's position, which places a greater emphasis on the poetic and creative role of language.

1323. Frascolla P., *Il concetto di infinito nella filosofia della matematica di W.*, 'Annali della Scuola Normale Superiore di Pisa', 10, pp. 639-754.
A critical analysis of the notion of infinity in W., extending from *Tract.* to the later writings, with a discussion of the relevant literature.

1324. Frascolla P., *Il modello costruttivistico nella filosofia della matematica di W.*, RF, 71, pp. 297-306. E.T. in Shanker (ed.), 1986, vol. III.
W.'s constructivism in mathematics concerning the infinite and the theory of real numbers, seen in relation to intuitionism.

1325. Gier N. F., *W. and 'forms of life'*, PSS, 10, pp. 241-58.
G. discusses a number of widespread interpretations (including Winch, 1958 and Hunter, 1968), criticizing in particular those with a sociological or psychological tendency. G. prefers to bring out the parallel between the notion of *Lebensform* in W. and that of 'condition of the possibility of experience' in Kant.

1326. Glouberman M., *Tractatus: pluralism or monism?*, M, 89, pp. 17-36.
In *Tract.* W. wavers between two opposite theses: on the one hand, the structure of reality conditions that of language; on the other, language determines the ontological structure of the world. Between these two different solutions G. argues in favour of a 'monistic' interpretation.

1327. Gozzi G., *La distruzione del legame sociale. Da W. a Luhmann*, AA, nos. 179-80, pp. 41-61.
The discovery of a new epistemological model, which follows the abandoning of the verificationist and reductionist view, is found by G. in the passage from *Tract.* to *P.I.*, and is represented as a great transformation in scientific knowledge and in contemporary culture as a whole.

1328. Hanfling O., *Does language need rules?*, PQ, 30, pp. 193-205.
A critical examination of the role played by the notion of rule in the theory of meaning, with special reference to a number of widespread interpretations of W.

1329. Hargrove E. C., *W., Bartley, and the Glöckel school reform*, JHP, 18, pp. 453-61.
H. rejects Bartley's thesis, 1973, that W. was decisively influenced by Glöckel and the principles of the Austrian School Reform and stresses, instead, the importance for W.'s evolution of his personal experience as a teacher.

1330. Heil J., *Cognition and representation*, AJP, 58, pp. 158-68.
Analysing Armstrong's theory of knowledge H. shows how it is related to the doctrine of picturing developed in *Tract*.

1331. Hinman L. M., *Philosophy and style,* Mo, 63, pp. 512-29.
Kierkegaard and W. are cited as examples to show that a philosopher's style is integral to his philosophical position. The entire number of the review is devoted to 'Philosophy as style and literature as philosophy'.

1332. Holmer P. L., *W. 'saying' and 'showing'*, NZSTR, 22, pp. 222-35.

1333. Hornsby J., *Arm raising and arm rising*, P, 55, pp. 73-84.
A critical examination of the problem, raised in *P.I.* 622, concerning the relationship between intention and action in voluntary acts.

1334. Hunter J. F. M., *W. on language and games*, P, 55, pp. 293-302.
An examination of the analogy between uses of language and games, with the aim of clarifying the problematic notion of 'language game' (understood as an actual or possible way of using words).

1335. Hurkmans A. G. A., *De Saussure and W.*, in *Linguistic studies offered to Berthe Siertsema*, ed. by D. J. van Alkemade *et al.*, Amsterdam, Rodopi, 1980, pp. 71-84.

1336. Janik A., *Philosophical sources of W.'s ethics*, Te, 44, pp. 131-44. Reprinted in Janik, 1985.

Entering the controversy provoked by an article by Levi, 1979, J. maintains that the analysis of W.'s ethics must be reduced to its more literally philosophical aspects, and in particular to its relationship to his epistemological theses.

1337. Kimball R. H., *Private criteria and the private language argument*, SJP, 18, pp. 411-16.
An attempt to relate to W.'s private language argument Austin's distinction between performative and constative utterances.

1338. King-Farlow J., *'Common sense' and 'Certainty': earlier Moore, later Moore, and later W.*, PInv, 3, no. 2, pp. 73-85.
K.-F. distinguishes in Moore a 'dogmatic' and 'more liberal' defence of common sense and analyses in this regard W.'s comments on Moore in *O.C.*

1339. Lamb D., *Hegel from foundation to system*, The Hague, Boston, Mass. and London, Nijhoff, 1980, pp. XVIII, 234.
In an attempt to show Hegel's relevance to modern problems L. compares him with a number of authors, and in particular with W. The principal analogy between the two is said to consist in their abandoning foundational problems and opting instead for a descriptive philosophy.

1340. Lamb D., *The philosophy of praxis in Marx and W.*, PF, 11, pp. 273-98.

1341. Lapointe F. H., *L.W.: a comprehensive bibliography*, Westport, Conn., Greenwood, 1980, pp. 297.
The first part of the volume contains in alphabetical order of author the titles of books (reviews are given in each case) and doctoral dissertations. In the second part articles are listed under subject-headings. Often the same article occurs under more than one head. An author index closes the book. *Reviews:* Bogen J., TeaP, 1981, pp. 67-74; Teichman J., PInv, 1983, 6, pp. 229-34.

1342. Lenzen W., *W.s Zweifel über Wissen und Gewissheit*, GPS, 10, pp. 43-52.

1343. Marconi D., *W. e le ruote che girano a vuoto*, Ep, 3, pp. 165-84.
Reflections on the nature of philosophy and the correct method of analysis in *Tract.* and later writings of W.

1344. Masat Lucchetta P., *La presenza di pensatori russi in W.*, 'Sapienza', 33, pp. 56–78, 202–22.
The influence exerted on W., especially by Kropotkin, Tolstoy and Dostoevsky.

1345. Miller R. W., *Solipsism in the Tractatus*, JHP, 18, pp. 57–74. Reprinted in Canfield (ed.), 1986, vol. III.
M. maintains, as against other commentators, that solipsism is forced on W. by a general view of reference as based on mental representation, which is the theme of earlier sections of *Tract*. This interpretation is then applied to the treatment of the problem of mental representation and other minds in *P.I.*

1346. Monro D. H., *The sonneteer's history of philosophy*, P, 55, pp. 363–75.
A collection of 23 sonnets dedicated to 23 philosophers from Thales to W. Sonnet 24 forms a 'Coda' ('Some thought philosophy would reach an end / With W. . . . .').

1347. Morawetz T. H., *Understanding, disagreement and conceptual change*, PPR, 41, pp. 46–63.
An attempt to elicit and evaluate some insights from *O.C.* in order to clarify the ideas of 'conceptual scheme' and shared language-games as conditions of mutual understanding and even of disagreement.

1348. Morstein P. von, *Kripke, W., and the private language argument*, GPS, 11, pp. 61–74.
A critical examination of Kripke's interpretation (see 1982 and *Perspectives*, 1981) in the course of which v.M. stresses the transcendental nature of W.'s theory of language rather than its analogies with Hume's scepticism.

1349. Musgrave A., *W.ian instrumentalism*, T, 46, pp. 65–105.
W. followers (*Tract.* 6.341–6.342) have never given a good reason why we should abandon realism in favour of their view according to which scientific theories are not descriptions of reality but merely devices or instruments for analysing phenomena.

1350. Nielsen H. A., *Realism, nominalism, and W.*, PInv, 3, no. 1, pp. 21–5.
Possible uses of W.'s philosophical method in examining the opposition between realism and nominalism.

1351. Oaklander L. N. and **Miracchi S.**, *Russell, negative facts, and ontology*, PSc, 47, pp. 434-55.

An interpretation of the theory of logical atomism, negative facts and formal necessity based on Russell's lectures on 'The philosophy of logical atomism' (reprinted in *Logic and knowledge*, see 1956) and on *Tract*.

1352. Oetjens H., *W.'s Regeldiktum als Selbstkritik seiner Wahrheitstheorie im 'Tractatus'*, GPS, 10, pp. 53-63.

1353. Olmsted R., *W. and Christian truth claims*, SJT, 33, no. 2, pp. 121-32.

1354. Peterson T. D., *W. for preaching. A model for communication*, Lanham, Md., University Press of America, 1980, pp. 180.

A preacher finds in W.'s later theory of language and grammar an explanation of the failure of communication he himself had faced in his activity, and a new perspective to see how communication in preaching works.

1355. Radnitzky G., *Analytic philosophy as the confrontation between W.ians and Popper*, BSPS, 67, pp. 239-86.

1356 Rasmussen D. B., *Deely, W., and mental events*, NS, 54, pp. 60-67.

Discussing a previous article by J. Deely, R. examines W.'s theses concerning the relevance which mental states have to the determination of the meaning of words.

1357. Reeder H. P., *Husserl and W. on the 'Mental picture theory of meaning'*, HS, 3, pp. 157-67.

R. finds many analogies between the two philosophers, both being critics of the 'mental picture theory of meaning' and of the concept of 'essence'.

1358. Reguera I., *La miseria de la razón. El primer W.*, Madrid, Taurus, 1980, pp. 190.

1359. Rorty R., *Philosophy and the mirror of nature*, Princeton, N.J., Princeton University Press; Oxford, Blackwell, 1980, pp. 401.

The writings of the later W. together with those of Heidegger and of Dewey are constantly referred to by R. in his exposition of 'the anti-Cartesian and anti-Kantian revolution' – the break with traditional research into the foundations of knowledge – which R. considers to be the common aim of all three.

1360. Rose D., *Malinowski's influence on W. on the matter of use in language*, JHBS, 2, pp. 145-9.

1361. Sádaba Garay F. J., *W. y su obra*, Barcelona, Dopesa, 1980, pp. 144.

1362. Scharfstein B. A., *W.*, in his *The philosophers. Their lives and the nature of their thought*, Oxford, Blackwell, 1980, pp. 318-34.
Contains a chapter dedicated to W. as part of a general analysis of 20 philosophers from Descartes to Sartre which relates their work to, and in part explains it by, psychological features of their personalities and decisive episodes in their lives.

1363. Shiner R. A., *Foundationalism, coherentism and activism*, PInv, 3, no. 3, pp. 33-38.
A defence of the 'activist' theory of knowledge that S. finds in *O.C.* against all attempts to introduce foundationalist and coherentist epistemologies.

1364. Stromberg W. H., *W. and the nativism-empiricism controversy*, PPR, 41, pp. 127-41.
W.'s discussion of seeing aspects, as well as other theses in *P.I.* II, and in *Z*, are in large part derived from criticism of the technical vocabularies used by Gestaltists (Koehler) and empiricists (Helmholtz) in their controversy about visual perception.

1365. Thiselton A. C., *The two horizons: New Testament hermeneutics and philosophical description, with special reference to Heidegger, Bultmann, Gadamer, and W.*, Grand Rapids, Mich., Eerdmans, 1980, pp. 484.
Reviews: Brodie L., Th, 1981, 45, pp. 480-6; Macquarrie J., RS, 1980, 16, pp. 496-7; Morgan R., HJ, 1981, 22, pp. 331-3; Schneiders S. M., JR, 1982, 62, pp. 307-9.

1366. Thomson G., *W. Some personal recollections*, 'Revolutionary World', vol. 37-38-39, pp. 86-8.

1367. Thurman R. A. F., *Philosophical nonegocentrism in W. and Candrakirti in their treatment of the private language problem*, PEW, 30, pp. 321-37.

1368. Tiles M., *Kant, W. and the limits of logic*, in *History and philosophy of logic*, vol. I, ed. by I. Grattan-Guinness, Tunbridge Wells, Kent, Abacus, 1980, pp. 151-70.

Analogies with Kant in *Tract.* treatment of logic and mathematics and in its distinction between 'saying' and 'showing'.

1369. Tilghman B. R., *Aesthetic descriptions and secondary senses*, PInv, 3, no. 3, pp. 1-15.

In what sense are the notions of 'seeing as' and 'aspect perception' (*P.I.* II, 11) important for aesthetics? And to what extent can the duck-rabbit paradigm be used to understand the experiences of aspects? Comments on this article by P. Kivy, PInv, 1981, 1, no. 1, pp. 35-38, and reply by Tilghman, ibid., pp. 39-40.

1370. Vasa A., *L'ateismo religioso di L.W.*, AF, 2-3, pp. 285-313.

1371. Vollrath E., *Eine Fehlinterpretation, und was ihre Folgen sind. Zu den politischen Implikationen von K.-O. Apels W.-Interpretation,* PJ, 87, pp. 149-64.

K.-O. Apel's transcendental-hermeneutic interpretation of W., against which V. sets a logical positivist reading.

1372. Winch P., *'Eine Einstellung zur Seele'*, PAS, 81, pp. 1-15. Reprinted in Canfield (ed.), 1986, vol. XII.

An analysis and interpretation of the problem of knowledge of other minds in W., centred on the opening paragraphs of *P.I.* II, iv.

1373. Wright C., *W. on the foundations of mathematics*, London, Duckworth; Cambridge, Mass., Harvard University Press, pp. 481.

For this book Wr. recycles material used for graduate classes over a period of several years. Preserving for the most part the form there used, Wr.'s exposition provides an analytical commentary, with *R.F.M.* as its particular subject-matter, but also making frequent use of *Tract.* The work is divided into chapters, each of which is dedicated to an argument on the philosophy of mathematics, and is preceded by information on the main sections examined. An extensive thematic index facilitates analytical consultation of the work. *Reviews:* Cameron J. R., PB, 1982, 23, pp. 86-90; Diamond C., PQ, 1981, 31, pp. 352-66; Fischer A., R, 1981, 23, pp. 68-70; Gillies D.A., BJPS, 1982, 33, pp. 422-33; Kielkopf F., PSc, 1981, 48, pp. 503-5; Kitcher P., 'Isis', 1981, 72, pp. 151-2; McCarty C., GPS, 1981, 14, pp. 165-75; Roeper P.,

AJP, 1982, 60, pp. 376-9; Rosen S., RM, 1980, 34, pp. 405-7; Sluga H. D., I, 1982, 25, pp. 115-24; Steiner M., JSL, 1984, 49, pp. 415-17; Tiles M., TLS, 1980, no. 4030, p. 714.

1374. Wrigley M., *W. on inconsistency*, P, 55, pp. 471-84. Reprinted in Shanker (ed.), 1986, vol. III; in Canfield (ed.), 1986, vol. XI.
Answering C. S. Chihara's criticisms of W., 1977, Wr. attempts to show that the theses about inconsistency in *L.F.M.* are sound and can best be understood when regarded as part of a global and radical conventionalistic theory of necessity, rather than as a species of constructivism.

1981

1375. *Austrian philosophy: studies and texts*, ed. by J. K. Nyíri, Munich, Philosophie Verlag, 1981, pp. 200.
Of the essays contained three directly concern W.: A. Janik, *W.: an Austrian enigma*; R. Haller, *W. and Austrian philosophy*; F. Rossi-Landi, *Towards a marxian use of W.*

1376. *Essays in philosophical analysis*, dedicated to E. Stenius on the occasion of his 70th birthday, ed. by I. Pörn (APF 32), Helsinki, Societas Philosophica Fennica, 1981, pp. 264.
16 essays, of which those directly concerning W. are: L. Hertzberg, *Science and certainty*, pp. 60-78 (refers to W.'s remarks on scepticism in *O.C.*); M. B. Hintikka and J. Hintikka, *W.: some perspectives on the development of his thought*, pp. 79-95 (the changes, after *Tract.*, concerning the notions of showing, ostensive definitions, language game, criterion; reprinted in modified form in Hintikka and Hintikka, 1986, and in Canfield (ed.), 1986, vol. VI); A. Maury, *W. and the limits of language*, pp. 149-67 (the notion of 'limit of language' in *Tract.* is considered mainly in connection with the nature of logic and the relation between language and reality); M. Sintonen, *Stenius's picture theory and Bradley's regress*, pp. 232-47 (does Stenius's interpretation of the picture theory of *Tract.* (see 1960), according to which sentential signs as facts include properties and relations, open the way to Bradley's regress?).

1377. *Ethics. Foundations, problems and applications,*

Proceedings of the 5th International W. Symposium,
August 1980, Kirchberg am Wechsel, Austria, ed. by
E. Morscher and R. Stranzinger, (Schriftenreihe der
W.-Gesellschaft), Vienna, Hölder-Pichler-Tempsky, 1981,
pp. 525.
Only the last three sections of the volume concern W.: 'W.
on ethics' (pp. 349–371); 'W. and Kant' (pp. 375–428); 'The
philosophy of W.' (pp. 431–518).

1378. *Langage ordinaire et philosophie chez le 'second' W.*,
ed. by J.-F. Malherbe (Série Pédagogique de l'Institut de
Linguistique de Louvain, 10), Louvain-la-Neuve, Cabay,
1981, pp. 108.
Proceedings of a 'Séminaire de philosophie du langage',
1979–80. The volume includes the following contributions:
J. F. Malherbe, *La problématique des collisions entre jeux de
langage*, pp. 11–90; J. Liu, *Jeux de langage et formes de vie*,
pp. 21–9; Ndumba Y'oole L'Ifefo, *La 'grammaire' de W.*,
pp. 31–41; P.J. Welsch, *Métaphores et jeux de langage*,
pp. 43–56 (with a comparison between P. Ricoeur and W.);
Ngwey Ngond'a Ndenge, *Le normal et le pathologique dans
la thérapeutique W.ienne*, pp. 57–76; B. Stevens, *Philosopher
ou faire parler le langage lui-même*, pp. 77–99 (on
Heideggerian analysis of philosophical method).

1379. *L. W.: personal recollections*, ed. by R. Rhees, Oxford,
Blackwell, 1981. Revised ed.: *Recollections of W.*,
London and New York, Oxford University Press, 1984,
pp. X, 235.
R. Rhees, *Preface*, pp. XII–X (gives details of the contributors
to the volume and of their relations with W.); H. Wittgenstein,
My brother Ludwig. Mein Bruder Ludwig, pp. 1–25 (previously
published, see 1973; here an *Editor's note*, pp. 11–13, is added
giving some further details); F. Pascal, *W. A personal memoir*,
pp. 26–62 (reprint, see 1973); F. R. Leavis, *Memories of W.*,
pp. 63–81 (previously published in 1973; contains anecdotes,
impressions, recollections, and accounts of non-philosophical
conversations from the years just after 1929); John King,
Recollections of W., pp. 83–90 (relate to the years 1930–6);
M. O'C. Drury, *Some notes on conversations with W.*,
pp. 91–111 (already printed in 1976, see above; chiefly concern
W.'s attitude towards philosophy and towards authors such

as Dostoevsky, Tolstoy, Kierkegaard, St. Augustine); M. O'C.
Drury, *Conversations with W.*, pp. 112-186 (a longer draft,
dating from 1974, of the content of the foregoing item.
A reworking of notes taken in the years 1929-51, many on
religious themes); R. Rhees, *Postscript*, pp. 190-231 (sums up
the evidence and comments on a 'confession' written out by
W. in the 1930s and on W.'s plan to migrate to Russia in 1935).
Reviews: Diamond C., CPR, 1985, 5, pp. 377-9; Genova J.,
CPR, 1981, 1, pp. 279-80; Innis R.E., MS,, 1982-3, 60,
pp. 211-12; Largeault J., RPFE, 1982, 107, p. 75; McFetridge
I., PQ, 1984, 34, pp. 69-73; Nyíri J. K., PLA, 1982, 35,
pp. 164-7; Villanueva E., Cr, 1981, 13, pp. 86-7.

1380. *Perspectives on the philosophy of W.*, ed. by I. Block,
Oxford, Blackwell, 1981, pp. XII, 322; Cambridge, Mass.,
MIT Press, 1982.

Proceedings of a Colloquium held at London (Ontario, Canada)
to commemorate the 25th anniversary of W.'s death. I. Block,
Introduction, pp. VII-XII; K. Blackwell, *The early W. and the
middle Russell*, pp. 1-30 (relations between the two
philosophers, in particular W.'s criticisms of Russell's theory
of judgement, analysed in the light of unpublished letters and
manuscripts by Russell); M. Dummett, *Frege and W.*, pp. 31-42
(W.'s great debt to the work of Frege); H. Ishiguro, *W. and
the theory of types*, pp. 43-59 (W.'s criticisms of Russell's
theory of types, in particular in connexion with the doctrine
of 'showing' in *Tract.* Reprinted in Canfield (ed.), 1986);
B. McGuinness, *The so-called realism of W.'s Tractatus*,
pp. 60-73 (W.'s theory of meaning in *Tract.* does not really
require the ontology usually ascribed to him); D. Pears, *The
logical independence of elementary propositions*, pp. 74-84
(examines the theoretical grounds that led W. first to deny that
an elementary proposition can be contradicted by another
elementary proposition, then later to abandon this thesis);
P. M. S. Hacker, *The rise and fall of the picture theory*, pp. 85-
109 (logical atomism and picture theory in *Tract.* are closely
linked, but the logical aspects of the theory are abandoned as
time goes on. Reprinted in Shanker (ed.), 1986, and in Canfield
(ed.) 1986); E. Stenius, *The picture theory and W.'s later
attitude to it*, pp. 110-139 (it is incorrect to maintain that the
later W. rejected the picture theory, at least if the true purport
of the theory is borne in mind); A. Kenny, *W.'s early*

philosophy of mind, pp. 140–147 (an interpretation of *Tract.*
5.541–5.5423. Reprinted in Kenny, 1984 and in Canfield (ed.),
1986); G. E. M. Anscombe, *A theory of language?*, pp. 148–158
(the discussion of the examples of language-games at the
beginning of *P.I.* must not be understood as an attempt to
produce a theory of language); P. Winch, *Im Anfang war die
Tat*, pp. 159–178 (the distinction between the truth-conditions
of a proposition and the conditions for asserting that same
proposition cannot be used to explain the differences between
the earlier and the later W. Reprinted in Winch, 1987); D. Z.
Phillips, *W.'s full stop*, pp. 179–200 (on limits and possibilities
of a search for explanations and justifications in philosophy,
with particular attention to W.'s remarks on ethics and religion.
Reprinted in Canfield (ed.), 1986); P. Ziff, *Quote: Judgements
from our brain*, pp. 201–211 (critical comments on W.'s claim
that causal explanations are irrelevant to the understanding of
aesthetic reactions. Reprinted in Canfield (ed.), 1986); F. Cioffi,
W. and the fire festivals, pp. 212–237 (concerning W.'s
remarks on Frazer's *Golden Bough* and the nature of
explanation for aesthetic feelings. Reprinted in Shanker (ed.),
1986, and Canfield (ed.), 1986); S. A. Kripke, *W. on rules and
private language: an elementary exposition*, pp. 238–312 (not
included in the American edition. The 'private language
argument', as applied to inward sensations, is only a special
case of a much more general discussion concerning language
and the notion of 'following a rule'. Reprinted in Canfield (ed.),
1986; expanded in Kripke, 1982). *Reviews:* Bell D., Ru,
1983-4, 3, pp. 66–70; Burnheim J., AJP, 1982, 60, pp. 282-4;
Jones O. R., M, 1984, 93, pp. 131-4; McFetridge I., PQ, 1984,
34, pp. 69–73; Parret H., TF, 1983, 45, pp. 261–76; Stroud B.,
PR, 1984, 93, no. 1, pp. 140-3; Teichman J., PInv, 1984, 6,
pp. 229–34; Wallner F., PLA, 1984, 37, pp. 169–71; Zwicky
J., D, 1984, pp. 357–61.

1381. *Sprache und Erkenntnis als soziale Tatsache*; ed. by
R. Haller (Schriftenreihe der W.-Gesellschaft, vol. 5),
Vienna, Hölder-Pichler-Tempsky, 1981, pp. 147.

Proceedings of a symposium held in Rome in 1979. A. Gargani,
*W. und die wissenschaftliche und literarische Kultur in
Österreich*, pp. 13–22; B. McGuinness, *Der sogenannte
Realismus in W.'s 'Tractatus'*, pp. 23–34; M. Rosso,
Wahrheitsbegriffe im 'Tractatus', pp. 35–44; V. Tonini, *Eine
realistische Transformation von W.'s 'Traktat'*, pp. 45–48;

'C. Penco, *Mathematik und Interesse*, pp. 49–56; R. Haller, *Die gemeinsame menschliche Handlungsweise*, pp. 57–68; A. G. Conte, *Variationen über W.'s Regelbegriff*, pp. 69–78; D. Marconi, *W.: Die Annahme des 'anthropologischen' Standpunktes und die Aufgabe der Metaphysik*, pp. 79–83; W. Röd, *Der vorgebliche Missbrauch der Sprache in metaphysischen Aussagen (Überlegungen zu W.s metaphysischem Grunderlebnis)*, pp. 84–96; P. Garavaso, *Aporien einer Definition des Aufgabenbereiches und der Grenzen des philosophischen Wirkens in der W.schen Spekulation*, pp. 97–100; G. Frey, *Die transzendentale Deutung W.s*, pp. 101–107; F. Rossi-Landi, *W. und die Entfremdung*, pp. 108–118; E. Morscher, *Inwiefern ist die Sprache ein soziales Phänomen?*, pp. 119–124; G. Derossi, *Der Systembegriff bei W. und in der gegenwärtigen Semiotik*, pp. 125–130; P. Kampits, *Sprachspiel und Dialog. Zur Sprachdeutung L.W.s und Ferdinand Ebners*, pp. 131–140.

1382. *The autonomy of religous belief*, ed. by F. Crosson, Notre Dame, Ind. and London, University of Notre Dame Press, 1981, pp. 162.
Many of the essays making up this volume refer directly or indirectly to W.: in particular J. M. Cameron, *The idea of Christendom*, pp. 8–37; D. Z. Phillips, *Belief, change and forms of life: the confusion of externalism and internalism*, pp. 66–92; K. Nielsen, *Religion and groundless believing*, pp. 93–107; K. Sayre, *A perceptual model of belief in God*, pp. 108–127; W. P. Alston, *The Christian language-game*, pp. 128–162.

1383. *W., aesthetics and transcendental philosophy;* edited by K. S. Johannessen and T. Nordenstam (Schriftenreihe der W.-Gesellschaft, 6). Vienna, Hölder-Pichler-Tempsky, pp. 193.
Proceedings of a Symposium held at Bergen (Norway) in 1980. K. E. Tranøy, *W. and the ethics of science*, pp. 15–21; V. Rossvaer, *Philosophy as an art form*, pp. 25–31; R. Haller, *War W. ein Neokantianer?*, pp. 32–42; W. Röd, *Enthält W.s 'Tractatus' transzendentalphilosophische Ansätze?*, pp. 43–53; W. Leinfellner, *The development of transcendentalism. Kant, Schopenhauer and W.*, pp. 54–70; I. Gullvåg, *W. and Peirce*, pp. 70–85; G. Fløistad, *The concept of world in Heidegger and W.*, pp. 86–95; G. Frey, *Kunstwerk, Sprachspiel und Lebensform*, pp. 99–107; K. S. Johannessen,

Language, art and aesthetic practice, pp. 108-26; T. Nordenstam, *Intention in art*, pp. 127-35; L. Hertzberg, *Acting as representation*, pp. 136-51; L. Aagaard-Mogensen, *What's in beholders' eyes*, pp. 152-8; S. Kjørup, *W. and the philosophy of pictorial languages*, pp. 159-73; J. Meløe, *Das Bild in unserer Welt*, pp. 174-7; A. Focke, W. und die österreichische Literatur, pp. 178-88. *Reviews:* Janik A., PInv, 1985, 8, pp. 155-9; McFee, G., BJA, 1982, 22, pp. 275-8; Meuwese, W. A. T., MSc, 1982, 15, pp. 272-3; Reix A., RPL, 1983, 81, pp. 669-72; Tilghman B., JAAC, 1982, 40, p. 444.

1384. *W. to follow a rule*, edited by S. H. Holtzman and C. M. Leich, London, Routledge & Kegan Paul, 1981, pp. XIII, 250.

Proceedings of a colloquium held in Oxford in 1979. Only the first three of the nine essays collected in the volume deal directly with W.'s work. The others are rather attempts to treat and develop independently problems raised by him. C. M. Leich and S. H. Holtzman, *Introductory essay: Communal agreement and objectivity*, pp. 1-27 (on rules and understanding. A discussion of *P.I.* §§139-242); G. Baker, *Following W.: some signposts for 'Philosophical investigations'* §§*143-242)*; pp. 31-71 (reprinted in Canfield (ed.), 1986); C. Peacocke, *Reply. Rule-following: the nature of W.'s arguments*, pp. 72-95 (criticism of the former article, mainly concerning the alleged denial by W. of the possibility of a systematic semantic theory. Reprinted in Canfield (ed.), 1986); C. Wright, *Rule-following, objectivity and the theory of meaning*, pp. 99-117; G. Evans, *Reply. Semantic theory and tacit knowledge*, pp. 118-137; J. McDowell, *Non-cognitivism and rule-following*, pp. 141-162 (on following a rule and ethics. Reprinted in Canfield (ed.), 1986); S. Blackburn, *Reply. Rule-following and moral realism*, pp. 163-187; C. Taylor, *Understanding and explanation in the 'Geisteswissenschaften'*, pp. 191-210 (on possibility and foundation of social science. Reprinted in Canfield (ed.), 1986); P. Pettit, *Reply. Evaluative 'Realism' and interpretation*, pp. 211-245. *Reviews:* Baker J., PS(I), 1982-3, 29, pp. 291-296; Churchill J., Th, 1984, 48, pp. 685-690; Lewis P., PInv, 1983, 6, pp. 145-149; Parret H., TF, 1983, 45, pp. 280-288; McFetridge I., PQ, 34, pp. 69-73; Stroud B., TLS, 1982, no. 4110, p. 37.

1385. Agassi J., *Science and society. Studies in the sociology* *of science*, Boston, Mass. and London, Reidel, 1981, pp. 531.

Of the essays collected here two refer directly to W.: *Was W. really necessary?*, pp. 33–44; *Between metaphysics and methodology*, pp. 253–61. In both A. attacks an attitude towards metaphysics which he ascribes to W. and the 'W.ians'.

1386. Aidun D., *W. on grammatical propositions*, SJP, 19, pp. 141–8. Reprinted in Shanker (ed.), 1986, vol. II.

A. discusses the possibility of interpreting the notion of 'grammatical proposition' in the light of 'grammatical rule', pointing out difficulties created for such a programme by the usual definition of an analytic proposition.

1387. Anscombe G. E. M., *The collected philosophical papers*, 3 vols., Oxford, Blackwell; Minneapolis, Minnesota University Press, 1981.

Of the three volumes only the first, *From Parmenides to W.* contains essays (two in number) expressly concerned with W.: *Retractation*, pp. 108–11 (see 1965) and *The question of linguistic idealism*, pp. 112–33 (see *Essays on W.*, 1976.)

1388. Assoun P. L., *W. séduit par Freud, Freud saisi par W.*, 'Le Temps de la Réflexion', no. 2, pp. 355–83.

1389. Baker J., *Playing the language game game*, MS, 58, pp. 185–93.

The use of invented language games in W.'s philosophical analysis and in his theory of language (*P.G.*, *B.B.B.*, *P.I.*).

1390. Bambrough J. R., *Peirce, W. and systematic philosophy*, MWSP, 6, pp. 263–73.

Although there is no reference to Peirce in *P.I.*, there are numerous echoes in W. of ideas, phrases, analogies, etc., that can be found in Peirce's *Collected papers*.

1391. Baumgarten E., *W.'s conception of the 'willing subject'*, MW, 14, pp. 15–24.

Some analogies between the concept of 'willing subject' in *N.B.* and *Tract.* and the phenomenological concept of 'embodied consciousness'. Some ethical consequences of this.

1392. Bindeman S., *Heidegger and W. The poetics of silence*, Washington, D.C., University Press of America, 1981, pp. 153.

The analysis of the relation between symbolism and silence in Heidegger and W. is seen as a basis for an independent development of a 'phenomenological poetics of silence'. *Review:* Sefler G.F., ISP, 1983, 15, pp. 73-5.

1393. Botwinick A., *W. and historical understanding*, Washington, D.C., University Press of America, 1981, pp. 55.

1394. Bouveresse J., *Herméneutique et linguistique*, in *Meaning and understanding*, ed. by H. Parrett and J. Bouveresse, Berlin and New York, Walter de Gruyter, 1981, pp. 112-153.
Frequent comparisons between W. and Gadamer.

1395. Bouveresse J., *W. and the philosophy of language*, in *Contemporary philosophy: a new survey*, vol. I, *Philosophy of language*, ed. by G. Fløistad and G. H. von Wright, The Hague, Nijhoff, 1981, pp. 83-112.
An attempt to reconstruct W.'s changing views on language in the transition from *Tract.* to *P.I.*

1396. Broyles J. E., *Talk about space: W. and Newton*, PInv, 4, no. 4, pp. 45-55.
W.'s method employed to unmask 'misleading analogies generated by surface grammar', as illustrated by 'the various illusions about space that find expression in Newton's thought'.

1397. Canfield J. V., *W.: language and world*, Amherst, Mass., University of Massachusetts Press, 1981, pp. 230.
The central part of the book deals with the concept of criterion and that of grammatical truth in W.'s later writings, with particular attention to language games concerning pains, sensations, etc. Also discusses carefully the nature (whether empirical or *a priori*) of rules applied in those usages of language, and the origin of necessity of grammatical remarks. *Reviews:* Burke T. E., M, 1983, 92, pp. 633-4; Champlin T. S., PInv, 1984, 7, pp. 248-52; Coburn R. C., PR, 1984, 93, pp. 271-4; Finocchiaro M.A., 1984-5, 38, pp. 380-4; McFetridge I., PQ, 1984, 34, pp. 69-73; McNulty T. M., MS, 1983-4, 61, pp. 132; Mouloud N., RMM, 1985, 90, pp. 130-2; Mounce H. O., P, 1983, 58, pp. 124-6; Nelson J. O., RM, 1984-5, 38, pp. 380-2; Schwyzer H., CPR, 1983, 3, pp. 166-8; Zwicky J., CJP, 1985, 15, pp. 151-85.

1398. Cappio J., W. *on proper names, or: Under the circumstances*, PS, 39, pp. 87–105.

It is erroneous to suppose, as Kripke and Dummett do, that *P.I.* 79 contains a solution of the problem of meaning of proper names which is a bare improvement on the theory of Frege and Russell. A correct understanding of this passage requires a recognition of the central importance of the notion of 'the circumstances' in W.'s theory of meaning.

1399. Carney J. D., W. *'s theory of picture representation*, JAAC, 40, pp. 179–85.

1400. Chandra S., W. *and Strawson on the ascription of experiences*, PPR, 41, pp. 280–98.

A comparison between *P.I.* and Strawson's *Individuals* on the issue of sensations, private experience, other minds etc.

1401. Cheng Hsueh-Li, *Nāgārjuna, Kant and W.*, RS, 17, pp. 68–85.

After expounding the Mādhyamika philosophy of emptiness C. evaluates the later W.'s theory of language from the point of view of Nāgārjuna's criticism of metaphysics.

1402. Churchill J., W. *'s lectures on religious belief*, S, 20, no. 2, pp. 23–35; no. 3, pp. 33–9.

Examines the development of W.'s thought on religion and the problem of the 'meaning of life' from *Tract.* onwards.

1403. Clark R. G., *Problems with an 'intuitionist' example*, PInv, 4, no. 4, pp. 17–23.

In the example of continuing a numerical series, discussed in *P.I.* 135, what exactly entails the rejection of the Platonist theory of meaning?

1404. Cook J. W., *Malcolm's misunderstandings*, PInv, 4, no. 2, pp. 72–90.

Reply to a criticism by Malcolm, 1981, of a previous article by C., 1980.

1405. Diamond C., *What nonsense might be*, P, 56, pp. 5–22. Reprinted in Shanker (ed.), 1986, vol. II; in Canfield (ed.), 1986, vol. VI.

D. defines what she calls 'a natural view of nonsense', as applied to a sentence, and then contrasts it with that held by Frege and by middle and later W.

1406 Dilman I., *Studies in language and reason*, London, Macmillan, 1981, pp. 218.

Of the 11 essays included in the volume two refer directly to
W.: *W.: meaning and circumstances*, pp. 136–162 (an analysis
of W.'s thesis that words and sentences have meanings 'in the
traffic of human life'); *Bambrough: universals and family
resemblances*, pp. 163–187 (in criticising Bambrough, 1960,
D. maintains that the realistic appeal to objective similarities,
in order to justify our systems of classification, involves a
vicious circle. A final section suggests some comparisons
between W. and Plato.)

1407. Double R., *On a W.ian objection to Kripke's dualism
argument*, PRA, 7, pp. 171–81.
Can the private language argument be used against Kripke's
Cartesian dualism? A criticism of Levin's article, 1975.

1408. Findlay J. N., *Kant and the transcendental object.
A hermeneutic study*, Oxford, Oxford University Press,
pp. XXIV, 392.
In section VI (v. pp. 367–376) of the final chapter entitled 'Last
comparisons and assessments', F. discusses W., regarded as 'a
philosopher whose thought was in certain respects deeply
Kantian, both in its earlier and its later phases'.

1409. Fogelin R. J., *W. and classical scepticism*, IPQ, 21,
pp. 3–15. Reprinted in Shanker (ed.), 1986, vol. II.
W.'s central idea is that the questions of classical scepticism
may be dismissed because they lack meaning. He maintained
this position, with a remarkable continuity, through all stages
of his development, from *Tract.* to *O.C.*

1410. Frongia G., *Guida alla letteratura su W. Storia e analisi
della critica* (Pubblicazioni dell'Università di Urbino),
Urbino, Argalia, 1981, pp. 342.
The original Italian version (extending only to 1980) of the
present volume. *Reviews*: Biasutti F., V, 1982, 11, p. 521;
Ercoleo M., GM, 1982, 4, pp. 401–3; Finocchiaro M. A., RM,
1984, 38, pp. 388–90; Reguera I., RevF(Sp), 1982, pp. 115–19.

1411. Gallagher K. T., *W., Heraclitus, and 'the common'*, RM,
35, pp. 45–56.
A critical analysis of W.'s later theory of language seen as an
'ingenious and influential' attempt to dissolve the difficulty of
subjectivism and scepticism by a stress on the public character
of language.

1412. Geach P. T., *W.'s operator N*, A, 41, pp. 168-71.
The meaning and use of the N operator (*Tract.* 6.001) has often
been misunderstood; for example it has been confused with
binary joint denial. A misunderstanding connected with
operator N is also at the basis of R.J. Fogelin's criticism of W.,
1976. See reply by Fogelin in *W.'s operator N*, A, 1982, 42,
pp. 124-7. A further note by Geach: *More on W.'s operator*,
ibid., pp. 127-8.

1413. Gier N. F., *W. and phenomenology*, Albany, N.Y., State
University of New York Press, 1981, pp. XIX, 249.
Examines an alleged objective affinity between W. and authors
in the phenomenological tradition (Husserl, Heidegger, and,
more recently, Merleau-Ponty and Gadamer) and speculates on
possible influences exercised by the former two on W., traces
of which G. finds especially in the middle-period writings. To
explain how W. was alive to phenomenological problems, G.
points out the part played in his intellectual formation by
authors such as Schopenhauer, E. Spranger, G. Simmel, and
O. Spengler. *Reviews*: Brough J. B., IS, 1985, 15, pp. 165-6;
Burnheim J., AJP, 1982, 60, pp. 282-6; Hottois G., RIP, 1985,
39, p. 184; Ihde D., JBSP, 1983, 14, pp. 209-10; Innis R. E.,
RM, 1982-3, 36, pp. 449-51; Mays W., ISP, 1984, 16,
pp. 106-7; Reeder H. P., CPR, 1983, 3, pp. 118-20; Rubinstein
D., PSS, 1984, 14, pp. 82-5; Soto C. H., Cr, 1982, 14,
pp. 109-11.

1414. Gier N. F., *W. and Heidegger: a phenomenology of forms
of life*, TF, 43, pp. 269-305.
The principal analogy between W.'s *P.I.* and Heidegger's *Being
and time* resides in their common transcendental origin: both
seek to identify the formal connections of lived experience.

1415. Gill J. H., *W. and metaphor*, Washington, D.C.,
University Press of America, 1981, pp. 232.
G. sees 'an important relation between the metaphoric quality
of W.'s writings and his conception of philosophy'. In order
to develop this thesis he analyses (Part I) different kinds of
theories on metaphor, and considers (Part II) a range of
metaphorical expressions used by W. in works of different
periods. *Reviews*: Blizek W. L., JAAC, 1982, 41, pp. 111-12;
Hinman L. M., PPR, 1985, 45, pp. 465-7; Shibles W., ISP, 1984,
16, pp. 107-9.

1416. Grosholz E., *W. and the correlation of logic and arithmetic*, R, 23, pp. 31–49. Reprinted in Shanker (ed.), 1986, vol. III.

For an adequate understanding of W.'s philosophy of mathematics and his criticisms of Russell's logicism it is necessary to adopt an historical perspective and to bear in mind how mathematical problems arise and how they are dealt with.

1417. Hanfling O., *Logical positivism*, Oxford, Blackwell; New York, Columbia University Press, 1981, pp. 181.

Many references to the relation between W. and logical positivism, especially in the chapter entitled '*Tract.*, verificationism, and meaning as use', pp. 143–48.

1418. Henry P. E., *W. et la double négation,* in B. Conein *et al.* (eds.), *Matérialités discursives. Colloque*, (Nanterre, 1980), Lille, Presses universitaires de Lille, 1981, pp. 105–114.

On the nature of philosophy and the impossibility of escaping from it.

1419. High D. M., *W. on doubting and groundless believing*, 'Journal of the American Academy of Religion', 49, no. 2, pp. 294–66.

1420. Hrachovec H., *Vorbei. Heidegger, Frege. W. Vier Versuche*, Basel, Stroemfeld; Frankfurt, Roter Stern, 1981, pp. 379.

A chapter each deals with the early W. and the other two philosophers named. A fourth chapter draws some conclusions about their relation to philosophical 'tradition'. *Review*: Vetter H., PLA, 1983, 36, pp. 232–5.

1421. Hudson W. D., *The light W. sheds on religion*, MWSP, 6, pp. 275–92. Reprinted in Shanker (ed.), 1986, vol. IV; in Canfield (ed.), 1986, vol. XIV.

Drawing on writings of different periods from *N.B.* to *L.R.B.* and *O.C.*, H. finds two alternative conceptions of religion in W. distinguished by a different relationship with the limit of thinking.

1422. Huff D., *Family resemblances and rule-governed behavior*, PInv, 4, no. 3, pp. 1–23.

Opposing Bambrough's interpretation, 1960, H. connects W.'s

concept of family resemblance with those of rule and rule-governed behaviour, and with his criticism of essentialist views.

1423. Hunter J. F. M., *W. on seeing and seeing as*, PInv, 4, no. 2, pp. 33-49.
An interpretation of *P.I.*, II, xi. W.'s single aim in this chapter, says H., is to argue down the temptation to suppose that the expression 'to see as', when used assertively, records the occurrence of an event or a process.

1424. Hutcheson P., *Husserl and private language*, PPR, 42, pp. 111-18.
Is Husserl committed to some sort of private language, and as such subject to W.'s objections in *P.I.*? A critical examination of S. Cunningham's views on this point. See the reply by Cunningham, 1983, and a rejoinder by Hutcheson, 1986.

1425. Iglesias M. T., *Russell and W.: two views of ordinary language*, PS(I), 28, pp. 149-63.
Is ordinary language in order as it is? An analysis of the opposing answers given by Russell and by W. to this question may help to explain Russell's misunderstanding of *Tract.*

1426. Kass M., *A surprising consequence of the Tract.*, JPL, 10, pp. 345-7.
On the logical form of the objects in a world containing a finite number of facts.

1427. Kisro-Völker S., *Die unverantwortete Sprache. Esoterische Literatur und atheoretische Philosophie als Grenzfälle medialer Selbstreflexion. Eine Konfrontation von James Joyces Finnegans Wake and L.W.s Philosophischen Untersuchungen.* (Theorie und Geschichte der Literatur und der schönen Künste, 45). Munich, Fink, 1981, pp. 361.
W. and Joyce are found to have analogous attitudes in their respective fields of philosophy and theory of the novel: they reflect on the limits of the sayable and are aware of the difficulties of looking to a metalanguage as a tool of inquiry. On W. see especially pp. 44-56 and 116-204.

1428. Klemke E. D., *Popper's criticisms of W.'s Tract.*, MWSP, 6, pp. 239-61.
Criticisms of *Tract.* contained in *The open society* merit more

attention than has been dedicated to them until now, even if in many cases they rest on a misunderstanding of W.'s theses.

1429. Kroy M., *Early W. on death*, IndPQ, 9, pp. 239-44.
Some incoherences in the *Tract.* section on death are explained by an unresolved tension between a naturalist approach to the nature of the subject and a number of positions closer to the transcendental idealism of Husserl.

1430. Leyvraz J.-P., *Le langage quotidien comme fondement de notre liaison au monde, dans la pensée de W.*, SP, 40, pp. 17-26.

1431. Lütterfelds W., *Zur sprachanalytischen Rehabilitierung des kantischen Idealismus bei W.*, ZDP, 3, pp. 78-87.

1432. McFee G., *On the interpretation of W.*, M, 90, pp. 592-9.
A critical survey of the interpretation of the notion of a criterion given by Hacker and Baker in their different works on W. (see especially Hacker, 1972; Baker, 1974; Baker and Hacker, 1976, 1980).

1433. Mackie J. L., *Five o'clock on the sun*, A, 41, pp. 113-14.
On W.'s criticism of the analogy argument for understanding 'He has a pain' in *P.I.* 350. Comments on M.'s interpretation by Angene, 1982, and King, 1982.

1434. Maddox M., *On the compatibility of family resemblance. A rejoinder to Dr. Mohr*, D(PST), 24, pp. 9-13.
W.'s theory of family resemblances is not incompatible with Aristotle's theory of universals. A criticism of Mohr, 1977, who reaches the opposite view.

1435. Magnanini D., *Il pensiero religioso di L. W.*, Rome, La Goliardica, 1981, pp. 194.

1436. Malcolm N., *Misunderstanding W.*, PInv, 4, no. 2, pp. 61-71.
A criticism of the discussion by Cook, 1980, of W.'s position in *O.C.* as regards the notion of a 'propositional view'. See reply by Cook, 1981.

1437. Malcolm N., *W.: the relation of language to instinctive behaviour*, Swansea, University College of Swansea, 1981, pp. 26. Reprinted in PInv, 1982, 5, pp. 3-22; in Canfield (ed.), 1986, vol. VI; in Shanker (ed), 1986, vol. II.
J. R. Jones Memorial Lecture, delivered in May 1981. An

exegetical analysis of the thesis that 'language did not emerge from reasoning' (*O.C.*, 475). According to this view, M. maintains, not merely is much of the first language of a child grafted on to instinctive behaviour, but also the whole of the complex employment of language by adult speakers embodies something resembling instinct.

1438. Malherbe J.-F., *Épistémologies anglo-saxonnes*, Namur, Presse Universitaire de Namur/Presses Universitaires de France, 1981, pp. 206.
The second half of the volume is dedicated to 'Le renversement du logicisme', and chapters IV and V examine the 'first' and the 'second' W.

1439. Malherbe J.-F., *Logique et langage ordinaire dans les 'Philosophische Untersuchungen' de W.*, RPL, 79, pp. 191–210.
Continuity and change between *Tract.* and *P.I.*

1440. Martin J. A. Jr, *Collingwood and W. on the task of philosophy. An interesting convergence*, PT, 25, pp. 12–23.
Despite superficial differences M. finds in these two philosophers 'extensive similarities' which stem from 'a striking convergence of views of the basic purpose of philosophy'.

1441. Maury A., *Sources of the remarks in W.'s Zettel*, PInv, 4, no. 1, pp. 57–74.
A list correlating the remarks published in Z. with early typescripts and still earlier manuscripts, copies of which still exist in W. papers.

1442. Meynell H., *Lonergan, W. and where language hooks onto the world*, in Matthew L. Lamb (ed.), *Creativity and method. Essays in honor of B. Lonergan*, Milwaukee, Wis., Marquette University Press, 1981, pp. 368–81.

1443. Michel N., *Eine Grundlegung der Pädagogik in der Frühphilosophie L.W.s*, Frankfurt and Bern, Lang, pp. 201.
Examines the last sections of *Tract.* for their significance for the problems of education: M. thinks this is on the side of the subject rather than on that of the world, since teaching and learning are connected with the limits of what can be known.

1444. Mounce H. O., *W.'s Tractatus. An introduction*, Oxford, Blackwell; Chicago, Ill., University of Chicago Press, 1981, pp. 136. Spanish translation: Madrid, Tecnos, 1982. Expounds *Tract.* for students in 12 short chapters. *Reviews:* Bezuidenhout A., SAJP, 1982, 1, pp. 163–4; Klemke E. D., CPR, 1983, 3, pp. 187-9; Llewelyn J. E., PInv, 1983, 6, no. 2, pp. 153–6; McFetridge I., PQ, 1984, 34, pp. 69-73; Reix A., RPL, 1983, 81, pp. 670-2; Trainor P., MS, 1983, 60, p. 289.

1445. Munitz M. K., *Contemporary analytic philosophy*, New York and London, Macmillan, 1981, pp. 434.

Three central chapters are devoted to the three periods of W.'s activity: 'The limits of language', 'Verificationism', 'Language-games'.

1446. Nielsen K., *On the rationality of groundless believing*, IS, 11, pp. 215-29.

A critical examination of the views of W., Malcolm, Winch and other 'W.ians' about givings reasons for religious belief.

1447. Pareti G., *Linguaggio privato ed eventi mentali tra W. e la filosofia analitica*, RF, 72, pp. 102-37.

1448. Penco C., *Matematica e gioco linguistico. W. e la filosofia della matematica del '900*, Florence, Le Monnier, 1981, pp. XIV, 261.

The method and purpose of W.'s philosophy of mathematics (in particular his 'anthropological point of view') are contrasted with ideal representatives of the three principal foundational schools of the present day, Frege and Russell for logicism (chapter 1), Hilbert for formalism (chapter 2), Brouwer for intuitionism (chapter 3). *Review:* Cavina S., Ep, 6, 1983, pp. 165-8.

1449. Pradhan R. C., *Language and experience. An interpretation of the later philosophy of W.*, Meerut, Anu Prakashah, 1981, pp. VIII, 258.

1450. Radford C., *Life, flesh and animate behavior. A reappraisal of the argument from analogy*, PInv, 4, no. 4, pp. 56-64.

In his discussion R. refers to the problem raised in *P.I.* (281-4), whether inanimate things like plants and machines can feel, think, etc.

1451. Reguera I., *W.*, Part 1: *La filosofía y la vida*; Part 2: *La felicidad y el arte*, Teo, 11, pp. 57–77, 279–314.

1452. Resnik M. E., *Frege and analytic philosophy: facts and speculations*, MWSP, 6, pp. 83–103.
In a chapter 'Frege's influence on analytic philosophy', Russell, W., Carnap are each allotted a section.

1453. Rubinstein D., *Marx and W. Social praxis and social explanation*, London, Routledge & Kegan Paul, 1981, pp. 231.
The two philosophers have a number of theses regarding philosophy in common, mostly arising from their critical attitude to 'Cartesian dualism'. Importance of these theses for the study of social phenomena. *Reviews:* Burns S. A. M., CJP, 1985, 15, pp. 133–49; Churchill J., Th, 1983, 47, pp. 290–6; Gier N. F., CPR, 1983, 3, pp. 201–3; McHoul A. W., PSS, 1984, 14, pp. 567–72; Nelsen R. S., Et, 1983, 93, pp. 622–3; Van Schaik L., SAJP, 1983, 2, pp. 156–7.

1454. Russell B., *Letter to A. Shalom*, 'Russell', 1, p. 62.
Facsimile of a letter of 16.5.1960 in which Russell comments on an article sent him by S. entitled 'The metaphysical thinking underlying W.'s *Tract.*'. See also comments by Shalom, 1982.

1455. Sankowski E., *W. on the cognitive status of avowals*, PS(I), 28, pp. 164–75.

1456. Scruton R., *From Descartes to W. A short history of modern philosophy*, London, Routledge & Kegan Paul, 1981, pp. 298.
The chapter on W. (pp. 271–284) is included in the last (5th) part of the book ('Recent philosophy') where S. also considers Frege and 'Phenomenology and existentialism'.

1457. Skyrms B., *Tractarian nominalism*, PS, 40, pp. 199–206.
W.'s basic idea was that the ontology of the subject (traditional nominalism) and the ontology of the predicate (Platonism) were equally wrong, and that they should give way to the ontology of the assertion.

1458. Soles D. H., *Some ways of going wrong. On mistakes in 'On certainty'*, PPR, 42, pp. 555–71.
Examines the role of error in W.'s refutation of scepticism in *O.C.*

1459. Soto C. H., *El interludio fenomenológico de W*, Cr, 13, pp. 25-43.
References to phenomenology in writings of W.'s middle period. Summary in English.

1460. Svensson G., *On doubting the reality of reality. Moore and W. on sceptical doubts*, (Stockholm studies in philosophy, 8), Stockholm, Almqvist & Wiksell International, 1981, pp. 117.
The first chapter is an examination of Moore's position. The second examines some parts of *O.C.* In the third the views of the two philosophers on the possibility of eliminating scepticism are compared.

1461. Szabados B., *W. on belief*, PP, 10, pp. 24-34.

1462. Szabados B., *W. on 'mistrusting one's own belief'*, CJP, 11, pp. 603-12.
Contrary to what W. maintains in *P.I.*, in certain special contexts it is intelligible and appropriate to speak of someone as mistrusting his own belief.

1463. Temkin J., *W. on epistemic privacy*, PQ, 31, pp. 97-109.
W.'s major concern in his treatment of sensations is the complete rejection of 'epistemic privacy': the view that only I can really know if I am in pain. T. then examines this rejection contrasting it with the 'non-cognitive thesis of avowals'.

1464. Thompson M., *On a priori truth*, JP, 78, pp. 458-81.
Frequent references to the notions of analyticity and apriority in *Tract.* and later works.

1465. Vollrath E., *Eine Fehlinterpretation, und was ihre Folgen sind. Zu den politischen Implikationen von K.-O. Apels W.-Interpretationen*, PJ, 87, pp. 149-64.

1466. Ward A., *Intensionality in W.'s Tractatus*, Ki, 11, pp. 30-52.
An examination of W.'s thesis that propositions which appear to be non-extensional can be subsumed under the thesis of extensionality.

1467. Wertz S. K., *On the philosophical genesis of the term 'form of life'*, SWPS, 6, pp. 1-16.
The origin of the expression *'Lebensform'* is traced back, primarily in German philosophy, and particularly in that of

Schopenhauer. However the concept also occurs in a number
of 20th-century authors, such as Croce, Ortega and Huizinga.

1468. Worthington B. A., *Ethics and the limits of language
in W.'s Tractatus*, JHP, 19, pp. 481-96.
The conclusions of *Tract.* as regards ethics related to its theory
of language, to W.'s rejection of metaphysics, and to the
influence of Schopenhauer.

1469. Wuchterl K., *Thesen zur analytischen Religionsphilosophie*, PJ, 88, pp. 343-56.
Frequent references to W.'s philosophy of religion in the course
of an investigation of possible links between analytical
philosophy and hermeneutics.

1982

1470. *Actas do Colóquio luso-austríaco sobre L.W.* ('Revista
Portuguesa de Filosofia', 38, n. 1) Braga, Faculdade de
Filosofia, 1982, pp. 181.
Proceedings of a conference held in Lisbon in December 1980.
Contents include: B. McGuinness, *The path to the Tractatus*,
pp. 7-12; W. Leinfellner, *Is W. a transcendental philosopher?*,
pp. 13-27; H.-D. Huesgen, *Pensamento e linguagem.
Horizontes duma nova filosofia segundo L.W.*, pp. 29-43;
V. Alves de Sousa, *Redução lógica da filosofia em W.*,
pp. 45-69; R. Haller, *W. und Spengler*, pp. 71-8; M. Antunes,
O problema da certeza do último W., pp. 79-85; C. H. Silva,
A cor do indizível, ou da estética da lógica em L.W.,
pp. 87-119; A. Melo, *Sentido e desfiguração metafísica no
Tractatus de W.*, pp. 121-33; A. Marques, *Teoria da
Abbildung e heracliteanismo no Tractatus*, pp. 135-41;
I. M. C. Silva, *Reflexões sobre o valor do simbolo em W.*,
pp. 143-51; M. Lourenço, *Towards the elimination of the
concept of truth in an analytical construction,* pp. 153-69.

1471. *Idealism: past and present*, ed. by G. Vesey (Royal
Institute of Philosophy Lecture Series, 13), Cambridge and
London, Cambridge University Press, 1982, pp. 290.
Three of the articles deal with W. and his relation to idealism:
C. Wright, *Anti-realist semantics: the role of 'criteria'*,
pp. 225-248; N. Malcolm, *W. and idealism*, pp. 249-267 (a

criticism of Williams's interpretation, see *Understanding W.*, 1974. Reprinted in Canfield (ed.), 1986, vol. VIII.); D. Bolton, *Life-form and idealism*, pp. 269–284 (the later philosophy of W., being 'based in life', is incompatible with idealism).

1472. *Language and ontology*, Proceedings of the 6th international W. symposium, Kirchberg am Wechsel (Austria), 23 to 30 August 1981; ed. by W. Leinfellner, E. Kraemer, J. Schank (Schriftenreihe der W.-Gesellschaft, vol. 8), Vienna, Hölder-Pichler-Tempsky, 1982, pp. 544.
Opening address by G. E. M. Anscombe. The last three sections of the volume are devoted to the work of W.: 'W.'s early philosophy', pp. 419–461; 'W.'s late philosophy', pp. 465–503; 'W. in historical context', pp. 507–542. 26 papers in all.

1473. *Rationality and science. A memorial volume for M. Schlick in celebration of the centennial of his birth*, ed. by E.T. Gadol, Vienna and New York, Springer-Verlag, 1982, pp. 228.
Many of the contributions refer to W.'s relations with Schlick. Particularly interesting are the comments of authors who were themselves close to the activities of the Vienna Circle: A. J. Ayer, *The Vienna Circle*, pp. 36–54; H. Feigl, *Moritz Schlick: a memoir*, pp. 55–82; K. Menger, *Memories of M. Schlick*, pp. 83–103.

1474. *Schlick und Neurath. Ein Symposion*, ed. by R. Haller, ('Grazer Philosophische Studien', vols 16–17), Amsterdam, Rodopi, 1982, pp. 489.
This number of the review is devoted to the proceedings of a conference held in June 1982: many references to W., especially to his relations with Schlick, Neurath, and the Vienna Circle. Specifically dedicated to such themes are the following contributions: M. Black, *Verification revisited. A conversation*, pp. 35–47 (mentions W.'s criticisms of the verifiability principle); B. McGuinness, *W. on probability. A contribution to Vienna Circle discussions*, pp. 159–74 (W. conceived the laws of nature as hypotheses whose general form provides the basis for judgements of probability. The influence of this theory on Schlick, Neurath, Waismann and other modern philosophers of science); J. Schulte, *Bedeutung und Verifikation: Schlick, Waismann und W.*, pp. 241–253 (the influence of the early

W. on the theory of meaning of Schlick and Waismann; W.'s subsequent abandonment of the principle of verification as principal criterion of sense); A. G. Gargani, *Schlick and W. Language and experience*, pp. 347–63 (the doctrine of internal relations, the notion of meaning as use and the principle of verification are closely related in W.'s and Schlick's works during the early 1930s. Reprinted in Shanker (ed.), 1986, vol. I. Italian translation in Gargani, 1983); W. Lütterfelds, *Schlicks Theorie des Wieder-Erkennens und W.s Kritik*, pp. 399–418 (a reconstruction of W.'s criticisms of Schlick's theory of knowledge); F. Wallner, *W. und Neurath. Ein Vergleich von Intention und Denkstil*, pp. 419–23 (compares the two philosophers, dwelling principally upon the themes of the unity of science and of language, the theory of language games, the definition of metaphysics, and the role of ideological assertions).

1475. *Wien, Kundmanngasse 19. Bauplanerische, morphologische und philosophische Aspekte des W.-Hauses*, Munich, Fink, 1982, pp. 250.

Intended as an interdisciplinary analysis of the relation between aspects of W.'s philosophy and various architectural problems involved in the planning of the Kundmanngasse house. In the first part T. Sperling, *Daten, Pläne und Erläuterungen zum Haus Kmg. 19*, pp. 10–75, documents the building technically, setting out a chronology, reproducing original documents and plans, and including photographs of details, external and internal. The second part of the book assembles a number of critical articles: L. Rentschler, *Das W.-Haus. Eine morphologische Interpretation*, pp. 77–163 (sets W.'s house in relation to tendencies in Austrian architecture, particularly late baroque and neo-classical); A. Grünenwald and R. Ohme, *Das Palais Stonborough und seine Morphologie. Versuche visueller Assoziationen*, pp. 165–217; G. Gebauer, *Die Syntax des Schweigens*, pp. 219–239 (relation of W.'s architecture to the theory of form in *Tract.*); A. Grünenwald and L. Rentschler, *Methodische Ansätze für eine Interpretation der W.schen Architektur. Seminarbericht*, pp. 239–250. *Review:* Haller R. in GPS, 1984, 21, pp. 219–21.

1476. Aidun D., *W., philosophical method and aspect-seeing*, PInv, 5, pp. 106–15.

The method of grammatical investigation which W. employs

is intended to get the person who is philosophically puzzled to 'see aspects' of grammar which are puzzling, in a different light.

1477. Ambrose A., *W. on mathematical proof*, M, 91, pp. 264-72. Reprinted in Lazerowitz and Ambrose, 1984; in Shanker (ed.), 1986, vol. III.
An examination of some 'paradoxical consequences' following from W.'s thesis (*R.F.M.* and elsewhere) that, at least for some propositions, the result of a mathematical proof gets its meaning from the proof itself.

1478. Angene L. E., *Five o'clock here*, A, 42, pp. 78-9.
Mackie's remarks, 1981, on the topic of the sentence 'It's 5 o'clock on the sun' show that he has failed to understand the meaning of *P.I.* 350.

1479. Arabi O., *W.: langage et ontologie* (Bibliothèque d'histoire de la philosophie), Paris, Vrin, 1982, pp. 192.
Examines the 'two philosophies' of W., the first being viewed as a version of Frege's 'semantic realism', while the second is seen in relation to changing tendencies in 20th-century philosophy of mathematics. *Review:* Malherbe M., EP, 1985, pp. 257-8.

1480. Ard D. J., *Knowing a name*, PPR, 43, pp. 377-88.
The 'key to the whole of the *Tract.*' is found in W.'s argument about what it takes to know the meaning of a name.

1481. Ayer A. J., *Philosophy in the twentieth century*, London, Weidenfeld & Nicolson, 1982, pp. 283.
As well as many scattered references the volume contains two sections devoted to W.: 'The *Tract.* and its sequels', pp. 108-21; 'The later W.', pp. 142-57. The former considers *Tract.* in the context of the philosophy of the Vienna Circle and Popper, and describes the influence that it had on A. in the early 1930s; the latter is part of a chapter devoted also to Carnap and Ryle. *Reviews:* Teichman J., P, 1984, 59, pp. 415-17; Watson R. A., JHP, 1984, 22, pp. 490-2.

1482. Baker G. P. and **Hacker P. M. S.**, *The grammar of psychology. W.'s 'Bemerkungen über die Philosophie der Psychologie'*, 'Language and Communication', 2, pp. 227-44. Reprinted in Shanker (ed.), 1986, vol. II.

1483. Barker P., *Uncle Ludwig's book about science*,

Proceedings of the 42nd Annual Meeting of the Southwestern Philosophical Society, PTo, suppl. vol., pp. 71–8.

Analogies between W.'s concept of 'language games' and Kuhn's concept of 'exemplars'.

1484. **Basu D. K.**, *Simples on demand. A problem in the Tractatus*, Ind PQ, 10, pp. 85–92.

On the nature of simple objects and their relation to the theory of meaning.

1485. **Baum W.**, *W.: Das Christentum als einzig sicherer Weg zum Glück. Neue Quellen zur negativen Theologie im 'Tractatus'*, ZKT, 104, pp. 191–5.

Passages in *N.B.* examined to show the relations between W. and other forms of 'negative theology'.

1486. **Bernhard T.**, *W.s Neffe. Eine Freundschaft.* Frankfurt, Suhrkamp, 1982, pp. 163.

Examines in quasi-fictional form the character and literary production of Paul W., a younger cousin (hence 'nephew') of W., who died in 1979. Some references to his relations with 'the' W.

1487. **Billing H.**, *Privatsprachenargument und Selbstbewusstseinstheorie*, C, 16, pp. 60–4.

1488. **Bouveresse M. J.**, *La philosophie peut-elle être systématique?*, SP, 41, pp. 9–38.

W. and modern debates on the function of philosophy and the possibility of system in it.

1489. **Bouwsma O. K.**, *Toward a new sensibility*, ed. by J. L. Craft and R. E. Hustwit, Lincoln, Neb., University of Nebraska Press, 1982, pp. XIX, 277.

12 essays, mostly unpublished at the time of B.'s death. Directly concerning W. are: *A new sensibility*, pp. 1–4; *Conceptual vs. factual investigations*, pp. 5–16; *A difference between Ryle and W.*, pp. 17–32. The first two essays are part of a paper, written in 1968, stimulated by discussions with graduate students in a seminar on *P.I.* The third was already published in 1972.

1490. **Brenner W.**, *W.'s color-grammar*, SJP, 20, pp. 289–98.

Reconstructs *R.C.* in the light of passages drawn from other writings.

1491. Carl W., *Sinn und Bedeutung. Studien zu Frege und W.* (Philosophie, 7), Frankfurt a.M., Athenäum/VVA, 1982, pp. 233.

C. analyses a number of works by the two authors, seeing them as part of the development of semantic theories bridging the 19th and 20th centuries. Chapters 1–3 cover Frege, while chapters 4–6 discuss the 'philosophy of language' of *Tract.* emphasizing (pp. 145–168) its divergences from Frege and Russell. *Reviews:* Mohanty J. N., RM, 1984, 38, pp. 116–17; Schmit R., ZPF, 1986, 40, pp. 146–9; Schulte J., PRd, 1984, 31, pp. 60–74.

1492. Carlson J. W., *W. and philosophy of religion. An application of emergence themes*, in *History of philosophy in the making*, edited by Linus J. Thro, Washington, D.C., University Press of America, 1982, pp. 255–73.

1493. Cheng Hsueh-Li, *Zen, W. and neo-orthodox theology. The problem of communicating truth in Zen Buddhism*, RS, 18, pp. 133–49.

1494. Chihara C. S., *The wright-wing defense of W.'s philosophy of logic*, PR, 91, pp. 99–108. Reprinted in Canfield (ed.), 1986, vol. XI.

A critical discussion of the interpretation and defence of W.'s views on logical consistency given by C. Wright, 1980.

1495. Conway G. D., *W. on foundations*, PT, 26, pp. 332–44.

W.'s philosophy compared with that of Heidegger and Nishida.

1496. Coyne M. U., *Eye, 'I', and mine. The self of W.'s Tractatus*, SJP, 20, pp. 313–23. Reprinted in Canfield (ed.), 1986, vol. III.

Analyses the notion of metaphysical subject to interpret *Tract.* 5.6 and the possible 'coincidence of solipsism with realism'.

1497. Davies B., *Scarlet O'Hara. A portrait restored*, P, 57, pp. 402–7.

Examines the critical comment in *L.R.B.* on remarks by Fr. C. O'Hara on the relation between science and religion.

1498. De Monticelli R., *Dottrine dell'intelligenza: Saggio su Frege e W.*; introduction by M. Dummett, Bari, De Donato, 1982, pp. XXX, 213.

An examination of the different doctrines concerning language and 'thoughts' (*Gedanken*) by Frege in his theory of propositions and by W. in his picture theory. This last is reconstructed, using *inter alia* examples of representation by graphic, pictorial, and musical means, and its general philosophical implications are discussed. *Reviews:* Negri A., AA, 1983, no.197-8, pp. 133-42; Penco C., Ep, 1983, 6, pp. 360-3.

1499. Eagleton T., *W.'s friends,* 'New Left Review', no.135, pp. 64-90.

A speculative reconstruction, based on published sources, of W.'s relations with various representatives of the culture of the left: the classical scholar G. Thomson, P. Sraffa, N. Bachtin. References also to, and comparisons with, various authors such as Derrida, Adorno, Gramsci, etc.

1500. Edwards J. C., *Ethics without philosophy. W. and the moral life.* Gainesville, Fla., University Presses of Florida, 1982, pp. 271.

Without aspiring to exegetical precision (as E. himself acknowledges), but rather through 'an assemblage of reminders', the book tries to identify 'the spirit of W.'s thought', both in its earlier and in its later period. This is located in W.'s doctrine of the showing-saying relation, and in his 'mute appeals' to the mystical, e.g. in 'the fundamental significance of silence' in philosophy. *Reviews:* Coyne M. U., IPQ, 1984, 24, pp. 198-201; Drengson A. R., CJP, 1985, 15, pp. 111-31; Janik A., JHP, 1985, 23, pp. 602-4; MacLean A. C., P, 1987, 62, pp. 247-9; Malherbe M., EP, 1985, pp. 556-7; Mounce H. O., CPR, 1984, 4, pp. 101-2; Pletcher G. K., MS, 1984-5, 62, pp. 56-7; Taylor A., RM, 1983-4, 37, pp. 626-7; Whittaker J., PInv, 1985, 8, pp. 323-7.

1501. Fischer H. R., *Wahrheit, grammatischer Satz und Lebensform. Der epistemologische Aspekt in W.s Privatsprachenargumentation,* C, 16, pp. 65-74.

An interpretation of *P.I.* 245-52 showing that 'I know that I am in pain' is grammatical in character and that grammatical propositions are transcendental.

1502. Fleischacker S., *Religious questions: Kafka and W. on giving grounds,* S, 21, pp. 3-18.

Stylistic and literary analogies, especially between *The Castle* and *O.C.,* show that the two authors have similar attitudes

towards moral and religious questions and that both are aware
of the limits of language in answering them.

1503. Gallagher K. T., *W., Augustine and language*, NS, 56,
pp. 462–70.
A reconstruction of St. Augustine's theory of language designed
to show that W.'s interpretation thereof at the beginning of
P.I. is vitiated by grave misunderstandings and by a simplistic
view of how words acquire meaning.

1504. Gargani A., *Freud, W., Musil*, Milan, Shakespeare &
Company, 1982, pp. 127.

1505. Gier N. F., *W., intentionality, and behaviorism*, Mp,
13, pp. 46–64.
Contrary to the view of commentators such as Chihara and
Fodor, W. cannot be considered a behaviourist in the classical
sense given the allowance he makes for intentionality and
anti-reductionism.

1506. Goddard L. and **Judge B.**, *The metaphysics of W.'s
Tractatus* ('Australasian Journal of Philosophy',
Monograph Series, n. 1), Bundoora (Victoria), Australasian
Association of Philosophy, 1982, pp. 72.
An interpretation of propositions 1–2.062 with the aim
of clarifying the ontology of *Tract.* W.'s objects, according
to G. and J., are not material objects, objects of acquaintance
(in Russell's sense), simple ideas, or sense data. Their nature
can better be understood by comparing them with objects
of geometry (ch. 2) or with elementary particles of contemporary physics. If so interpreted, the metaphysics of
Tract. will appear rather coherent, and closer to the Kant–
Husserl–Meinong tradition than to the British constructive
atomism. *Reviews:* Block I., D, 1984, 23, pp. 361–4; Bogen J.,
CPR, 1984, 4, pp. 147–9; Finch H. L., PB, 1983, 24,
pp. 158–9.

1507. Godwin W., *Analysis and the identity of indiscernibles*,
A, 42, pp. 80–2.
There is an incoherence at the heart of *Tract.* arising from
certain requirements of its theory of analysis on the one hand,
and from its rejection (5.5302) of the principle of the identity
of indiscernibles on the other.

1508. Goodman R. B., *W. and ethics*, Mp, 13, pp. 138–48.

W.'s pre-1930 views on ethics re-examined in the light of *O.C.* and compared with the views of Kant and Kierkegaard.

1509. Haack R., *W.'s pragmatism*, APQ, 19, pp. 163–71.
Many similarities between W.'s later work and some characteristically pragmatist views derive from a common 'naturalist' view of meaning. Nevertheless W.'s naturalism is descriptive, whereas the pragmatists' naturalism is explanatory. W.'s descriptivism is at the root of many of the difficulties in his conception of meaning.

1510. Hanfling O., *On the meaning and use of 'I know'*, PInv, 5, pp. 190–204.
Dissenting from other interpretations H. finds a theoretical ambivalence in W.'s criticisms of Moore in *O.C.*: H. traces this back to W.'s view of the relation between the philosophical and the ordinary use of 'I know'. Criticisms of this article by Cook, 1985.

1511. Hausmann L., *W. in Austria as an elementary-school teacher*, 'Encounter', 58, n. 4, pp. 16–25.
English translation of an account partially published in German in 1970. The author, a retired Austrian schoolteacher, gathered information and testimony from inhabitants of the area where W. was an elementary schoolteacher between 1920 and 1926. E. C. Hargrove, the translator, briefly presents the material, casting doubt, *inter alia*, on theses and assertions of W. W. Bartley (see 1973) concerning the same period. A reply by Bartley and a rejoinder by Hargrove, ibid., 1982, nos 3–4, pp. 111–12.

1512. Hedengren P., *Henslee on method and other minds*, SWPS, 8, pp. 9–15.
A reply to Henslee's article, 1982.

1513. Henslee D., *Methods and other minds*, SWPS, 8, pp. 1–8.
A criticism of the interpretation given by Chihara and Fodor (1965) toW.'s treatment of the problem of other minds. See a reply to this article by Hedengren, 1982.

1514. Hunts C., *W.'s seeing-as and a theory of art*, Au, 9, pp. 157–72.

1515. Janik A., *On W.'s relationship to Schopenhauer*, in *Zeit der Ernte-Studien zum Stand der Schopenhauer-Forschung*, ed. by W. Schirmacher, Stuttgart, Bad Cannstatt, Frommann, 1982, pp. 447.

1516. Jeet B., *W.'s use of 'grammatical'*, Ind PQ, 10, pp. 55-63.
Grammatical analysis as a tool of philosophical inquiry in the later W.

1517. Kalin M., *Time and multiplicity in the 'Tractatus'*, SJP, 20, pp. 337-57.
Attempts to bring together the *Tract.* treatment of metaphysical themes (especially death) and of linguistic ones by examining the notions of time and of multiplicity.

1518. Kerr F., *Russell vs Lawrence and for W.*, 'New Blackfriars', 63, pp. 430-40.

1519. Kerr F., *W. and theological studies*, 'New Blackfriars', 63, pp. 500-8.

1520. King J., *Five o'clock on the sun: a reply to J. L. Mackie*, A, 42, p. 77.
Mackie's explanation of 'It's 5 o'clock on the sun', 1981, misses the point made in *P.I.* 350.

1521. Kreuzer F. and **Haller R.**, *Grenzen der Sprache - Grenzen der Welt. W., der Wiener Kreis und die Folgen*, Vienna, Deuticke, 1982, pp. 123.
The first part of the volume (pp. 7-79) gives the text of an interview between K. (a politician and television personality) and H. It gives a brief account of W.'s intellectual personality, relating him above all to Austrian philosophy and to the Vienna Circle. The remainder of the volume is devoted to Schlick, Neurath, and Hahn, *Review:* Stock W. G., PLA, 1984, 37, pp. 288-90.

1522. Kripke S. A., *W. on rules and private language. An elementary exposition*, Oxford, Blackwell, 1982, pp. X, 150. Italian translation: Turin, Boringhieri, 1984.
The 'private language argument' reflects only a particular aspect of a much more general view about language held by W., and has primarily to be explained in terms of the problem of 'following a rule'. In dealing with this problem W. faced a 'paradox' (see ch. 2) which is connected with the fact that we follow rules as we do, without reason and justification. To this 'paradox' W. gave a reply that, in a Humean sense, could be called a 'sceptical solution' (see ch. 3) which in part he applied also to the problem of 'other minds' (see 'Postscript',

pp. 114–145). *Reviews:* Abbott B., 'Language', 1984, 60, pp. 646-9; Anscombe G. E. M., CJP, 1985, 15, pp. 103-9; Anscombe G. E. M., Et, 1985, 95, pp. 342-52; Bogen J., CPR, 1983, 3, pp. 284-6; Churchill J., Th, 1985, 49, pp. 481-5; Diamond C., PB, 1983, 24, no. 2, pp. 96-8; Dilman I., PInv, 1985, 8, pp. 295-305; Eldridge R., RM, 1983-4, 37, pp. 859-60: Engel P., RPFE, 1983, 108, pp. 496-9; Feldman F., PPR, 1985-6, 46, pp. 683-7; Gellner E. A., 'American Scholar', 1984, 53, p. 243; Horwich P., PSc, 1984, 51, pp. 163-71; Hyslop A., AJP, 1984, 62, pp. 193-4; Joos E., LTP, 1985, 41, pp. 257-9; Kerr F., JH, 1985, 26, pp. 466-70; Kreisel G., CPR, 1983, 3, pp. 287-9; Landesman C., JCP, 1986, 12, pp. 349-59; Loar B., N, 1985, 19, pp. 273-80; Oliveri G., Pa, 1984, 2, pp. 523-40; Parret H., TF, 1983, 45, pp. 288-90; Peacocke C. M., PR, 1984, 93, pp. 263-71; Scruton R., M, 1984, 93, pp. 592-602; Strawson P. F., TLS, 1983, no. 4167, pp. 123-4; Vermaak M., SAJP, 1984, 3, pp. 38-40; Winch P., PQ, 1983, 33, pp. 398-404.

1523. Kroy M., *Les paradoxes phénoménologiques de la mort*, RMM, 87, pp. 531-50.

Some reference is made to remarks in *Tract.* on death and their relation to phenomenology.

1524. Lear J., *Leaving the world alone*, JP, 79, pp. 382-403. Dissenting from Dummett's conventionalist account of W.'s views on logical necessity, 1959, L. relates W.'s views on the validity of the law of the excluded middle to his 'non-revisionary' approach to philosophy and to his theory of meaning.

1525. Leinfellner W., *La filosofia di W. è trascendentale?* Pa, 1, pp. 21-32.

1526. Long P., *Formal relations*, PQ, 32, pp. 151-61. In the course of a study of the distinction between internal and external relations L. discusses the thesis (attributed to *Tract.*) that 'a fact is a complex'.

1527. Lütterfelds W., *Bin ich nur öffentliche Person?*, Königstein/Ts., Forum Academicum, 1982, pp. 135. Discusses E. Tugendhat's (see 1979) use of W.'s analytic method to criticize Fichte's views on self-consciousness (*Selbstbewusstsein*). Themes touched on include the relation between public and private, solipsism, and the identity of the subject.

1528. Lyas C. A., *Herbert Marcuse's criticism of 'linguistic' philosophy*, PInv, 5, pp. 166–89.

Marcuse's criticisms of W. and other linguistic philosophers in *One-dimensional man* (see 1961) reveal a fundamental misunderstanding of their intentions and philosophical views.

1529. Malherbe J. F., *Athéisme scientiste et métaphysique de la représentation*, RTL, 13, pp. 31–48.

Critical reconstruction of W.'s attitude towards metaphysics in *Tract*. Also draws on later writings.

1530. McCarthy G., *Newman and W.: the problem of certainty*, ITQ, 49, pp. 98–120.

Discusses, inconclusively, the reference to J. H. Newman in *O.C.*

1531. McDowell J., *Criteria, defeasibility and knowledge*, 'Proceedings of the British Academy', 68, pp. 455–79.

Exegetical and critical commentary from an epistemological point of view of the notion of 'criterion' in W.'s later writings. Relation to the notion of 'symptom' and application to problems in the philosophy of mind.

1532. Meynell H., *Doubts about W.'s influence*, P, 57, pp. 251–9.

Criticizes conventionalist and relativist accounts (e.g. those by D.Z. Phillips and D. Bloor) of parts of *O.C.*

1533. Napoli E., *La contraddizione di W.*, Teor, 2, no. 2, pp. 57–84.

1534. Nielsen K., *An introduction to the philosophy of religion*, London, Macmillan; New York, St. Martin's Press, 1982, pp. 218.

The central parts of the book incorporate in a modified form writings already published: *The challenge of W.*, see 1973; *W.ian fideism*, see 1967. N. reconstructs 'W.ian fideism' and compares it critically with his own ideas on the philosophy of religion.

1535. Nowak R., *Neuere W.-Literatur*, PRd, 29, pp. 196–226.

Surveys recent literature on W. and attempts to place it in the context of present-day discussion.

1536. Nyíri J. K., *Neues von W. Würdiges und Fragwürdiges in den jüngsten Veröffentlichungen*, PLA, 35, pp. 164–74.

1537. Peacocke C., *Critical study: W. and experience*, PQ, 32, pp. 162-70. Reprinted in Canfield (ed.), 1986, vol. XIII. (See Foot, 1983.)

1538. Radnitzky G., *Entre W. et Popper. Philosophie analytique et théorie de la science*, AP, 45, pp. 3-62.
First a reconstruction of Popper's criticisms of W.'s legacy to the Vienna Circle and logical empiricism; then an analysis of the opposition of 'W.'s later followers' to Popper's philosophy of science.

1539. Ring M. K., *Sensations and kinaesthetic knowledge*, PRA, 8, no. 1485, pp. 111-68.
An analysis and development of the criticisms moved by W. among others against the psycho-physiological theory of kinaesthesis.

1540. Rorty R., *Consequences of pragmatism*, Minneapolis, University of Minnesota; Brighton, Harvester Press, 1982, pp. 237.
Two previously published articles in this volume refer specifically to W.: *Keeping philosophy pure,* pp. 19-36 (on the nature of philosophy and philosophical method); *Cavell on skepticism,* pp. 176-190 (a criticism of Cavell, 1979).

1541. Roy P. K., *'The mystical' in the philosophy of W.*, Ind PQ, 10, pp. 263-76.

1542. Schachter J. P., *The private language passages*, CJP, 12, pp. 479-94.
Is W.'s thesis *(P.I.* 243ff.) that a logically private language is impossible one premiss of an argument against solipsism? A reconstruction of W.'s reply both to 'Sceptics' and to 'Realists'.

1543. Schulte J., *Coro e legge. Il 'metodo morfologico' in Goethe e Wittgenstein*, Int, 2, pp. 99-124. German version in GPS, 21, 1984, pp. 1-32. Examines some analogies between Goethe's concept of morphology and the later W.'s theory and practice of philosophical method.

1544. Schulte J., *Seguire una regola. Nuovi studi su W.*, 'Lingua e Stile', 17, pp. 497-512.
Discusses the various accounts of what it is 'to follow a rule' as given by Kripke, 1982, and others.

1545. Shalom A., *Reply to Russell's letter of 16 May 1960*, 'Russell', 2, no. 2, pp. 45-51.
An imaginary letter to Russell commenting on a previous correspondence (in the 1960s) about *Tract.* See Russell, 1981.

1546. Snow N. E., *Some comments on Luckhardt's interpretation of empirical propositions as paradigms*, PPR, 43, pp. 259-63.
Luckhardt's attempt, 1978, to draw a strict parallel between what W. in *O.C.* calls 'truisms', and what other writers call 'paradigms', forces the former into too narrow a role.

1547. Soto C. H., *El Tractatus desde la perspectiva de las Investigaciones filosóficas*, ReF(Mex), 15, pp. 193-209.
The criticisms of psychologism in *P.I.* are traced back to *Tract.*

1548. Spiegelberg H., *W. calls his philosophy 'phenomenology': one more supplement to 'The puzzle of W.'s Phänomenologie'*, JBSP, 13, pp. 296-9.
A further use of the term 'phenomenology' by W. around the year 1930 not considered in a previous article, 1969, throws new light on W.'s relation to Schlick and the Vienna Circle.

1549. Stevenson L., *The metaphysics of experience*, Oxford, Clarendon Press, 1982, pp. 137.
S. wishes to revive a Kantian philosophy that will seek the 'necessary conditions for experience', using 'many ideas from the mainstream of contemporary analytical philosophy', and from W. in particular.

1550. Stevenson L., *W.'s transcendental deduction and Kant's private language argument*, KS, 73, pp. 321-37.
The theory of rules and that of judgement in the later W. provide a form of objectivity for knowledge and enable us to avoid solipsism: thus they give us a standpoint from which we can review the Kantian synthesis and transcendental deduction.

1551. Tominaga T. T., *Taoist and W.ian mysticism*, JCP, 9, pp. 269-89.

1552. Visser H., *W.'s debt to Mach's popular scientific lectures* M, 91, pp. 102-5.
Philosophy of physics in *Tract.* was directly and strongly influenced by Mach, especially in connection with matters like chronometry, geometry, space and time, physical principles.

1553. von Wright G. H., *Wittgenstein*, Oxford, Blackwell; Minneapolis, Minn., University of Minnesota Press, 1982, pp. 218. German translation: Frankfurt, Suhrkamp, 1986.

French translation: Mauvezin, Trans-Europ-Repress, 1986.
Italian translation: Bologna, Il Mulino, 1983.
A collection of articles previously published, often with considerable modification: *Introduction*, pp. 1-11 (gives previously unpublished information on the state of W.'s. *Nachlass* and on the criteria employed in its publication); *L. W. A biographical sketch*, pp. 13-34 (a slightly modified reprint of the version published in 1955); *The W. papers*, pp. 35-62 (a reprint of von Wright, 1970, with more considerable modifications); *The origin of the 'Tractatus'*, pp. 63-109 (a thoroughly revised and expanded version of the edition of 1972. Some major changes regarding the first publication of *Tract.* in England); *The origin and composition of the 'Philosophical investigations'*, pp. 111-136 (revision of an essay published in 1979); *W. on probability*, pp. 137-162 (already published in 1969; substantial revisions in section 5); *W. on certainty*, pp. 163-182 (see von Wright, 1973. Reprinted in Canfield (ed.), 1986, vol. VIII.); *Modal logic and the Tractatus*, pp. 183-200 (incorporates some sections of an early published paper; reprinted in Canfield (ed.), 1986, vol. II); *W. in relation to his times*, pp. 201-216 (already published in 1979). *Reviews:* Engel P., RPFE, 1984, 109, pp. 132-3; Finch H., PB, 1984, 25, no. 3, pp. 162-4; Kerr F., HJ, 1985, 26, pp. 466-70; McFetridge I., PQ, 1984, 34, pp. 69-73; Morawetz T., ISP, 1986, 18, pp. 110-11

1554. Waismann F., *Lectures on the philosophy of mathematics*, edited with an Introduction by W. Grassl (Studien zur österreichischen Philosophie, vol. IV), Amsterdam, Rodopi, 1982, pp. 167.

This volume, which brings together some of Wa.'s writings on the philosophy of mathematics which were presented as lectures in Oxford during the 1950s, includes also, as an Appendix (pp. 157-67), a fragment of the German text of a lecture given by Wa. in September 1930, in Königsberg, at the Second Conference on Theory of Knowledge in the Exact Sciences (see Frank *et al.*, 1930, and Hann *et al.*, 1931), where he spoke after Carnap, Heyting, von Neumann. The lecture, which had the title *Über das Wesen der Mathematik: der Standpunkt W.s*, expounded W.'s viewpoint on mathematics and is an elaboration of remarks made by W. in conversations with Wa. and Schlick (see *W. V. C.*). In the introductory chapter, *F. Waismann on the foundations of mathematics*, pp. 3-25,

Grassl explains the nature of this text and analyses other aspects of the relation between Wa. and W. An English translation of the fragment of the lecture is included in Shanker (ed.), 1986, vol. III.

1555. Westphal J., *Brown*, I, 25, pp. 417–33.
In an attempt to solve some puzzles raised in *R.C.* about the grammar of language referring to colours, We. offers 'a real definition of brown from which the puzzle propositions follow logically'.

1556. Westphal J., *Is W.'s Goethe Stock's Goethe?*, M, 91, pp. 430–1.
Some statements in G. Stock's review of *R.C.* previously published in the same journal, 1980, rest on misunderstandings of Goethe's theory of colours and of W.'s relation with it.

1557. Wolniewicz B., *A formal ontology of situations*, SL, 4, pp. 381–414.
A 'W.ian' semantic theory based on an ontology of 'elementary situations'.

1558. Worthington B. A., *An aspect of W.'s development*, Ep, 5, pp. 161–7.

1559. Worthington B. A., *Language and the self in W.'s Tractatus*, PS(I), 29, pp. 148–56.
Tract. 5.6–5.641 and 6.4–7 interpreted in the light of analogies with Schopenhauer.

1560. Wright C., *Strict finitism*, Sy, 51, pp. 203–82.
Dummett's objections to the coherence of strict finitism and to W.'s later philosophy of mathematics 'are ill-taken'.

1561. Zwicky J., *W. and the logic of inference*, D, 21, pp. 671–92.

1983

1562. *Epistemology and philosophy of science*, Proceedings of the 7th International W. Symposium (Kirchberg am Wechsel, August 1982), ed. by P. Weingartner and J. Czermak (Schriftenreihe der W.-Gesellschaft, vol. 9). Vienna, Hölder-Pichler-Tempsky, 1983, pp. 573.

Only the third part is devoted to W.: it consists of the following sections: *Wittgenstein*, pp. 425-475; *Problems of epistemology and philosophy of science in W.*, pp. 479-518; *W. and his relation to contemporary philosophy*, pp. 519-555; *W.'s relation to religion and metaphysics*, pp. 559-570; 29 essays in all.

1563. *L. Wittgenstein*, ed. by J. Hintikka, Sy, 56, nos. 2-3, pp. 119-388.

This special number of the periodical contains the proceedings of a conference held at Florida State University in April 1982 and sponsored by the Austrian Institute of New York. It contains the following items: H. Sluga, *Subjectivity in the 'Tractatus'*, pp. 123-39 (reprinted in Canfield (ed.), 1986); R. J. Fogelin, *W. on identity*, pp. 141-54; J. Hintikka and M. B. Hintikka, *Some remarks on (W.ian) logical form*, pp. 155-70 (republished in Hintikka and Hintikka, 1986, and in Canfield (ed.), 1986); A. Maury, *Reality and logical form*, pp. 171-80; R. L. Arrington, *Representation in W.'s 'Tractatus' and middle writings*, pp. 181-98; L. Wiesenthal, *Visual space from the perspective of possible-worlds semantics*, pp. 199-238; D. F. Gottlieb, *W.'s critique of the 'Tractatus' view of rules*, pp. 239-51 (reprinted in Canfield (ed.), 1986); B. B. Wavell, *W.'s doctrine of use*, pp. 253-64; W. D. Goldfarb, *I want you to bring me a slab. Remarks on the opening sections of the 'Philosophical investigations'*, pp. 265-82 (reprinted in Canfield (ed.), 1986); R. M. Dancy, *Alien concepts*, pp. 283-300 (on the notion of 'essentially different concepts', reprinted in Canfield (ed.), 1986); M. Gilbert, *On the question whether language has a social nature. Some aspects of Winch and others on W.*, pp. 301-18; C. G. Luckhardt, *W. and behaviorism*, pp. 319-38; K. K. Obermeier, *W. on language and artificial intelligence. The Chinese-room thought experiment revisited*, pp. 339-49; P. Ziff, *Remarks on W.'s 'Remarks on the foundations of mathematics'*, pp. 351-61 (reprinted in Canfield (ed.), 1986); C. J. B. MacMillan, *'On certainty' and indoctrination*, pp. 363-72; C. Black, *Obvious knowledge*, pp. 373-85 (on certain kinds of self-knowledge).

1564. *L.W. e la cultura contemporanea*, ed. by A. Gargani, Ravenna, Longo, 1983, pp. 127.

Proceedings of an international conference at the Biblioteca Classense in Ravenna, 26-27 April 1982. G. Kothanek, *La cultura viennese ai tempi di W.*, pp. 9-12; A. Gargani, *Filosofia come analisi e forme del sapere*, pp. 12-22; B. McGuinness, *W. e Freud*, pp. 23-37; J. Schulte, *W. e la Gestaltpsychologie*, pp. 39-48; A. Hübner, *Critica del linguaggio in W. e sviluppo delle scienze naturali*, pp. 49-58; F. Bianco, *Gadamer e W.*, pp. 59-65; E. Melandri, *W. e la psicologia come scienza umana*, pp. 67-92; R. Egidi, *Il significato di 'probabilità' nel W. intermedio*, pp. 93-99; E. Picardi, *W. e la teoria del significato*, pp. 101-107; M. Sbisà, *Come non essere W.ni*, pp. 109-115; G. Di Giacomo, *La nozione di 'uso' e la funzione della filosofia in W.*, pp. 117-127.

1565. *W. Momenti di una critica del sapere*, ed. by R. Egidi, Naples, Guida, 1983, pp. 117.

Contributions: A. Gargani, *W. e la cultura austriaca*, pp. 11-35; A. G. Conte, *Paradigmi d'analisi della regola in W.*, pp. 37-82; R. Egidi, *Intenzione e ipotesi in W.*, pp. 83-114 (deals with middle-period writings). *Reviews:* Ercoleo M., GM, 1984, 6, pp. 266-7; Genesini P., 'Bollettino Filosofico', 1983, 17, p. 87; Hohenegger H., Ca, 1983, pp. 181-5; Micheletti M., RFN, 1984, 76, pp. 507-8.

1566. *W. Sein Leben in Bildern und Texten*, ed. by M. Nedo and M. Ranchetti; introduction by B. F. McGuinness. Frankfurt, Suhrkamp, 1983, pp. XI, 394.

A pictorial reconstruction of important phases in W.'s life. It is divided into 16 chapters, moving from infancy to death. The illustrations (photographs, drawings, reproductions of letters and documents, etc.) are accompanied by brief texts drawn from W.'s correspondence or manuscripts, designed to explain or comment more or less directly on the illustrations. The introduction by McG., pp. I-XV, offers a framework within which to view the mass of material assembled in the volume and dwells particularly on W.'s family background and intellectual formation. An appendix 'Chronik und Werk', pp. 352-62, gives a brief chronology of W.'s life. *Reviews:* Brems-Van Belle G., TF, 1984, 46, pp. 668-9; Haller R., 'Camera Austria', 1984, 14, p. 79; Wallner F., PLA, 1985, 38, pp. 36-40.

1567. Archer D. J., *Küng, W. and God*, ITQ, 50, pp. 239-49.

1568. Armengaud, F., *Moore et W.: 'Je crois que/Je sais que -'*, in Parrett, H. (ed.), *On believing*, Berlin, De Gruyter, 1983, pp. 31-47.

1569. Baker G. P. and **Hacker P. M. S.**, *An analytical commentary on W.'s 'Philosophical investigations'*, Oxford, Blackwell, 1983, pp. XXV, 322.
Contains the exegetic part of the *Commentary* on the first 184 sections of *P.I.* already published in 1980.

1570. Baker G. P. and **Hacker P. M. S.**, *W. Meaning and understanding. Essays on the 'Philosophical investigations'*, Oxford, Blackwell, 1983, pp. 400.
Contains 70 brief essays (already published in 1980) on themes drawn from the first 184 sections of *P.I.*.

1571. Bayen B., *Writers, Lichtenberg and W.*, 'La Nouvelle Revue Française', no. 364, pp. 91-8.

1572. Bearsley P., *Augustine and W. on language*, P, 58, pp. 229-36.
Although W. is wrong in his judgement that Augustine's conception of language is simple and ingenuous, none the less his own position is remote from Augustine's and not reconcilable with it, contrary to the view of Kenny (see *Understanding W.*, 1974).

1573. Bloor D., *W. A social theory of knowledge*, New York, Columbia University Press; London, Macmillan, 1983, pp. 213.
W.'s later philosophy has a strong 'sociological' and 'naturalistic' character, in the sense that it 'stresses the priority of society over the individual', emphasising at the same time the basic function of actual forms of life. This aspect has not always been appreciated (for example in Winch's interpretation, 1959) but, if properly understood, and with some adjustments, can be developed into a systematic 'sociology of knowledge'. *Reviews:* Burnheim J., AJP, 1985, 63, pp. 241-3; Cooke V. M., IPQ, 1985, 25, pp. 329-30; Hacking I., 'Social Studies of Science', 1984, 14, pp. 469-76; Marshall S. E., CPR, 1985, 5, pp. 96-8; Mounce H. O., BJPS, 1985, 36, pp. 344-6; Schiller B.-M., JHP, 1986, 24, pp. 137-9; Sharrock W. W. and Anderson R. J., HS, 1984, 7, pp. 375-86; Sullivan D., Et, 1985-6, 16, p. 216.

1574. Brecher R., *Karl Barth: W.ian theologian manqué*, HJ, 24, pp. 290-300.
In a contribution to recent debates about the theologian

K. Barth, B. dwells in particular on the problem of the relationship of philosophical analysis to theology. He points out some 'parallels, if not direct connections', between Barth and 'approaches stemming from the work of the later W.'.

1575. Burkhardt A., *Bedeutung und Begriff. Die Fragwürdigkeit des W.schen Methodologie-Konzepts*, ZPF, 37, pp. 68-87.
Criticizes the method of analysis and theory of meaning of the later W. on the grounds that they are based on the uses of ordinary language and hence not applicable to the language of philosophy and science.

1576. Canfield J. V., *Discovering essence*, in *Knowledge and mind: philosophical essays*, ed. by C. Ginet and S. Shoemaker, New York, Oxford University Press, 1983, pp. 105-29. Reprinted in Canfield (ed.), 1986, vol. VII.
Criticizing Kripke's realist theory of kind terms, C. shows how W.'s view of criteria yields a viable account of the discovery of essence, both in everyday and scientific discourse.

1577. Carruthers P., *On concept and object*, T, 49 (part 1), pp. 49-86.
C. starts with a critical discussion of the notion of incompleteness of an expression in Frege – then opposes to it an interpretation (divergent from that of Stenius, 1960) of the picture theory, names, predicates and relational expressions in *Tract*.

1578. Cavina S., *La ricerca della salute. Osservazioni su L. W.*, Ep, 6, pp. 81-8.

1579. Champlin T. S., *The elusiveness of meaning*, PInv, 6, pp. 276-300.
After a review of several 'language-games' played with the word 'meaning', C. discusses some passages on meaning from W., Ryle and other modern philosophers.

1580. Churchill J., *The coherence of the concept 'language-game'*, PInv, 6, pp. 239-58.
Dissenting from other authors who have considered the concept of 'language game' ambiguous, vague, incomplete or descriptively false, C. distinguishes three closely related main senses of the term that he considers both coherent and useful for the philosophical investigation of language.

1581. Churchill J., *W.'s adaptation of Schopenhauer*, SJP, 21, pp. 489-501.

W. does not make a passive use of terms and problems derived from Schopenhauer (will, happiness, the riddle of life, the sense of the world, and so on) but adapts and transforms them in the light of his own philosophy which is centred on the problem of the limits of language.

1582. Cook J. W., *Magic, witchcraft and science*, PInv, 6, pp. 2-36. Reprinted in Canfield (ed.), 1986, vol. XIII.

Are we entitled to judge as true or false the myths and magical practices of primitive peoples? A discussion of the contrasting replies given to this question by Evans-Pritchard ('the objectivist view') on one side, and by W. and Winch ('the emotivist view') on the other.

1583. Cunningham S., *Husserl and private languages. A response to Hutcheson*, PPR, 44, pp. 103-11.

See Hutcheson, 1981, on the relationship between W.'s private language argument and the phenomenological reductions of Husserl. See also the subsequent reply by Hutcheson, 1986.

1584. Drury M. O'C., *Letters to a student of philosophy*, parts 1-2, edited with an Introduction by D. Lee, PInv, 6, pp. 81-102, 159-174.

15 'letters' written by D. in 1954 and addressed to his own son, who was at the time less than two years old. In fact a series of reflexions on religious and ethical problems, and on the power of philosophy to answer them. Many references to W. 'I want in these letters', says D., in the first of them, 'to try and help your thinking about these matters in the same way that W. helped me.' In the introduction (pp. 76-81) Lee gives an account of the relations between Drury and W., and gives an interpretation of what the 'letters' are intended to show.

1585. Easton S. M., *Humanist Marxism and W.ian social philosophy*, Manchester, Manchester University Press, 1983, pp. 148.

An elucidation and defence of 'the central tenets of humanist Marxism' via an examination of some of W.'s ideas about the function of language and the relevance of philosophy for practical and political life. In his desire to show that the two philosophers exhibit 'some fundamental similarities' E. criticizes both the anti-humanist and scientistic interpretations imposed on Marx by many Marxists and also the exclusively analytic interpretation of W. given in Anglo-Saxon philosophy. *Review:* Burnheim J., AJP, 1985, 63, pp. 243-4.

1586. Finch H. LeRoy, *W.'s long journey. Logical ideal to human norm*, IPQ, 23, pp. 3-11.

A brief sketch of W.'s itinerary from an ideal of simplicity derived from logical language to the search for concrete norms immanent in a (Tolstoyan) rejection of metaphysical complications.

1587. Foot P., *Peacocke on W. and experience*, PQ, 33, pp. 187-91. Reprinted in Canfield (ed.), 1986, vol. XIII.

Peacocke's interpretation, 1982, of W.'s treatment of some problems connected with experience and imagination. *R.P.P.* is considered 'in places misleading and in places definitely wrong'.

1588. Forbes G., *Scepticism and semantic knowledge*, PAS, 84, pp. 223-37.

An analysis of the 'sceptical paradox' which Kripke, 1982, extracts from the sections of *P.I.* preceding 243, after which F. examines and defends the 'dispositionalist response' to the sceptical problem raised by Kripke.

1589. Frongia G., *W.: regole e sistema*, (Collana di filosofia, 8), Milan, Angeli, 1983, pp. 268.

Both in *Tract.* and later works the concept of 'system' plays a central role in the explanation of the function of linguistic rules (chs. 1-2), of the nature of logical necessity (ch. 3), of mathematics (ch. 4) and of scientific procedure (ch. 5). What W. rejected in his late work was the fundamental position of *Tract.* according to which logically simple propositions were logically independent; what he maintained was the idea (in some sense transcendental) of the constitutive function of some basic formal rules of language (deep grammar). In the last chapter the problem of formal connections between different systems of rules is discussed. *Reviews:* Calcaterra R.M., Pa, 1985, 3, pp. 322-6; Engel P., RPFE, 1985, 110, pp. 50-2; Ercoleo M., GM, 1986, pp. 399-400; Hohenegger H., Ca, 1983, nos 1-2, pp. 177-80; Mangilli A., V, 1977, 16, pp. 191-3; Micheletti M., RFN, 1984, 76, pp. 495-7; Rainone A., Ep, 1984, 7, pp. 318-21.

1590. Goldstein L., *W. and the logico-semantical paradoxes*, R, 25, pp. 137-53. Reprinted in Canfield (ed.), 1986, vol. XI. A reconstruction of the development of W.'s treatment of the logico-semantical paradoxes, starting from *Tract.*, in an attempt to show the consistency of the solution ultimately adopted in later works.

1591. Graff E., *W.'s 'world-picture' in 'On certainty'*, Ki, 13, pp. 21-37. Examines W.'s fully mature attitude towards philosophy by means of ananalysis of the notion of 'world-picture' in *O.C.*

1592. Gutting G., *Religious belief and religious skepticism*, Notre Dame, Ind., University of Notre Dame, 1983, pp. 192. In ch. 1 ('The W.ian approach') an analysis of the 'dissolution' of the problem concerning the justification of religious beliefs.

1593. Hatab L. J. and **Brenner W.**, *Heidegger and W. on language and mystery*, ISP, 15, no. 3, pp. 25-43. Some important analogies between the two philosophers especially as regards their conception of language, their aesthetics, and their shared critical attitude towards the role of science in modern society.

1594. Hekman S., *From epistemology to ontology. Gadamer's hermeneutics and W.ian social science*, HS, 6, pp. 205-24.

1595. Hinman L. M., *Can a form of life be wrong?*, P, 58, pp. 339-51. In showing the ways in which it is possible to say that a form of life, in W.'s sense, is wrong, H. notes some similarities between W., Quine and Gadamer.

1596. Hoering W., *Zufall und Notwendigkeit in W.'s 'Tractatus'*, E, 19, pp. 217-23. Reprinted in *Methodology, epistemology and philosophy of science*, ed. by C. G. Hempel, H. Putnam, and W. K. Essler, Dordrecht, Reidel, 1985. Where does W. place the laws of science when he distinguishes (in *Tract.*) between logical truths and contingent truths?

1597. Hottois G., *Heidegger et W. Deux formes de la hantise contemporaine du langage*, IJP, 4, pp. 125-30.

Heidegger and W. react similarly to the hegemony of scientific knowledge.

1598. Kellemberger J., *W. and truth in incompatible religious traditions*, SR, 12, pp. 167–81.

1599. Küng G., *The difficulty with the well-formedness of ontological statements*, To, 2, pp. 111–19.
Compares the positions of Russell, W., Carnap, Tarski, and Lesniewski.

1600. Kurtzman H. S., *Modern conceptions of memory*, PPR, 44, pp. 1–19.
In an 'Historical survey' including British empiricism, Wundtians, and behaviourists, a section is also dedicated to 'W. and his successors'.

1601. Leich C. M., *Creation and discovery: W. on conceptual change*, in *The need for interpretation. Contemporary conceptions of the philosopher's task*, ed. by S. Mitchell and M. Rosen, London, Athlone Press; Atlantic Highlands, N.J., Humanities Press, 1983, pp. 33–53.
An interpretation of and commentary on W.'s thesis that the progress of mathematics involves continual conceptual change.

1602. Leilich J., *Die Autonomie der Sprache: ein Grundgedanke W.s*, Munich, Profil Verlag, 1983, pp. 179.
The thesis of the autonomy of language, round which L. develops his interpretation of the later W., rests on the fact that outside our language-games there can be no justification of our utterances. Reality, detached from language, can provide no such criterion (see also ch. 2 'Philosophie, logische Form und Tiefengrammatik'). This thesis, according to L., provides two strategies against relativism.

1603. Lennard S. H. C., *Architecture as autobiography: the meaning of W.'s architecture*, 'Humanist', 43, 25–30.

1604. Lescourret M.-A., *Vers une grammaire de la certitude*, Cri, 39, pp. 764–73.
Examines *inter alia* Bouveresse's reading of the later W.

1605. McEvoy J., *St. Augustine's account of time and W.'s criticisms*, RM, 37, pp. 547–78.
St. Augustine's conception of time is reconstructed in the light of *Conf.* xi and considering W.'s criticism in *P.I.* Particular

attention to problems of measurement, relations between space
and time and irreversibility of time.

1606. Magee B., *Schopenhauer's influence on W.*, in his *The philosophy of Schopenhauer,* Oxford, New York, Oxford University Press, 1983, pp. 286-315.

1607. Martin D. M., *An index for W.'s 'On certainty'*, PRA, 9, no. 1555, microform publication.
An index of more than 800 entries often indicating the context in which they occur.

1608. Nyíri J. K., *Ludwig Wittgenstein*, Budapest, Kossuth Kiadó, 1983, pp. 115.

1609. Parrini P., *Empirismo logico e convenzionalismo,* Milan, F. Angeli, 1983, pp. 118.
In a reappraisal of the Kantian and Neo-Kantian elements in neopositivism P. examines W. along with other founders of this school.

1610. Porpora D. V., *On the post-W.ian critique of the concept of action in sociology,* JTSB, 13, pp. 129-46.

1611. Rasmussen D. B., *Rorty, W. and the nature of intentionality,* PACPA, 57, pp. 152-62.

1612. Read S., *Quine's private language,* R, 25, pp. 49-57.
Quine's thesis about indeterminacy of translation and of meaning is compared with W.'s private language argument.

1613. Ring M., *Baker and Hacker on section one of the 'Philosophical investigations'*, PInv, 6, pp. 259-75.
Baker and Hacker, 1980, have misinterpreted W.'s intention and achievement in his criticism of Augustine's picture of language. For a reply to this article, see Siemens, 1986.

1614. Romanos G., *Quine and analytic philosophy,* Cambridge, Mass., MIT Press, 1983, pp. XVII-227.
In this attempt to determine Quine's place in the history of thought particular attention is paid both to the earlier and to the later W., associated with Carnap and others as representing the more Kantian wing of the philosophy of language.

1615. Rundle B., *Family resemblance and explanations of meaning,* C, 17, pp. 53-63.
By closely examining some examples drawn from W., R.

attempts to show that the notion of 'family resemblance' is hardly coherent and in any case inadequate to explain the meaning of words unless supplemented by semantic definitions.

1616. Schatzki T. R., *The prescription is description: W.'s view of the human sciences*, in *The need for interpretation. Contemporary conceptions of the philosopher's task*, ed. by S. Mitchell and M. Rosen, London, Athlone Press; Atlantic Highlands, N.J., Humanities Press, 1983, pp. 118–140.

In what ways is the type of understanding that, according to W., philosophy should seek through a descriptive method similar to the type of understanding sought by human science? An interpretation and evaluation dissenting from those proposed by Winch, 1958.

1617. Schoen E. L., *W. and Aristotle on knowledge from perception*, SJP, 21, pp. 435–51.

On private language and the role of sensation in linguistic learning (*P.I.* 244–6). Some analogies with Aristotle's *Metaphysics* and *Posterior analytics*.

1618. Schulte J., *W. and conservatism*, R, 25, pp. 69–80. Reprinted in Shanker (ed.), 1986, vol. IV.

A critical commentary on Nyíri's thesis (see *Essays on W.*, 1976): W.'s writings and his theoretical attitude do not reveal a conservative position in the sense maintained by N.

1619. Schweidler V., *W.s Philosophiebegriff*, Freiburg, Alber, 1983, pp. 188.

The unity of W.'s thought must be sought in his attitude towards philosophy, the aim he ascribes to philosophical reflection, the method of inquiry he himself uses, and the relation he finds between philosophy and life. *Reviews:* Hemel U., Bi, 1984, pp. 454–5; Hemel U., TP, 1985, 60, p. 118; Wallner F., GPS, 1986, 27, pp. 214–22; Wimmer R., PJ, 1985, 92, pp. 415–25.

1620. Schwyzer H., *How are concepts of objects possible?*, KS, 74, pp. 22–44.

W.'s notion of language game (see mainly pp. 40ff.) provides us with a solution to the problem (which in Kant's doctrine of schematism remains unsolved) of how concepts of objects are possible.

1621. Shiner R. A., *Canfield, Cavell and criteria*, D, 22, pp. 253-72. Reprinted in Canfield (ed.), 1986, vol. VII.
A comparison and critical evaluation of the views of Canfield, 1981, and Cavell, 1979, on the notion of criterion in W.

1622. Slater H., *W.'s aesthetics*, BJA, 23, pp. 34-7.
Did W. take an 'objectivist' or 'subjectivist' position in his remarks on aesthetics?

1623. Soames S., *Generality, truth functions, and expressive capacity in the Tractatus*, PR, 92, pp. 573-89. Reprinted in Canfield (ed.), 1986, vol. II.
Are propositions expressible in the predicate calculus constructible from elementary propositions by successive applications of a single truth functional operation? S. shows that a lacuna, pointed out by Fogelin, 1976, in the logical symbolism of *Tract.*, regarding this question can be filled without disturbing the central doctrine of W.

1624. Stock G., *Meaning, truth and negation*, PAS, 84, pp. 251-263.
S. considers negation and negative description by reference to what W. says about it in *Tract.* and *P.R.*

1625. Stroud B., *W.'s philosophy of mind*, in G. Fløistad (ed.), *Contemporary philosophy. A new survey*, vol. IV, The Hague, Nijhoff, 1983, pp. 319-41. Reprinted in Canfield (ed.), 1986, vol. IX.

1626. Thiele S., *Die Verwicklungen im Denken W.s*, Freiburg, Alber, 1983, pp. 342.
T. aims to show that there is continuity between various phases in W.'s thought, but that there are no grounds to ascribe a transcendental position to him. *Tract.* (according to T.) exhibits what Kant would have considered a dogmatic and pre-critical way of thinking. The later writings show signs of an attempt to resolve 'the entanglements' of the first work (in particular the contradictions of the picture theory and the difficulties in the theory of negation): still, W. is led into yet further entanglements, this time connected with his exaggerated behaviourism and his anthropological conventionalism. *Reviews:* Sokolowski R., RM, 1984-5, 38, pp. 408-411; Wallner F., GPS, 1986, 27, pp. 214-222; Wimmer R., PJ, 1985, 92, pp. 415-425.

1627. Tilghman B., *Seeing and seeing-as in W.'s Tractatus*, PInv, 6, pp. 116-34.
A reconstruction of the treatment of the problem of perception in early W., in the light of *Tract.* 5.5423, followed by an examination of the criticisms of that treatment implicit in *P.I.*

1628. Tominaga T. T., *Ch'an, Taoism, and W.*, JCP, 10, pp. 127-45.

1629. Valent I., *La forma del linguaggio. Studio sul Tractatus-logico-philosophicus,* Collana della Facoltà di Lettere e Filosofia dell'Università di Venezia, Abano Terme, Francisci, 1983, pp. 324.
The 'general form of a proposition' is considered central for the understanding of *Tract.* and of the theoretical dilemmas arising from that work. *Review:* Lambert J., RPFE, 1985, 175, pp. 347-8.

1630. Wallner F., *Die Grenzen der Sprache und der Erkenntnis. Analysen an und im Anschluss an W.s Philosophie*, (Philosophica, vol. 1), Vienna, Braumüller, 1983, pp. XIII, 306.
A volume devoted principally to *Tract.* and in particular to the relation between language and world, the picture theory, the philosophy of logic, the contrast between the normativity of logic and that of ethics, the difference between the position of *Tract.* and that of the Vienna Circle and of Carnap especially, and W.'s attitude towards transcendentalism. Some points of continuity with the later W. are mentioned. *Review:* Lütterfelds W., C, 1985, 19, pp. 102-4.

1631. Wallner F., *Eine Neubesinnung auf W.'s Philosophie*, in *Wahrheit und Wirklichkeit*, ed. by P. Kampits, G. Pöltner and H. Vetter, Berlin, Duncker & Humblot, 1983, pp. 193-210.

1632. Wallner F., *W.s philosophisches Lebenswerk als Einheit* (Philosophica, vol. 2), Vienna, Braumüller, 1983, pp. 96.
A brief introduction designed to show the unity and novelty of W.'s philosophical method. The central chapters are devoted to the relation between W. and the Vienna Circle. *Review:* Lütterfelds W., C, 1985, 19, pp. 102-4.

1633. Walsh W. H., *Rétrospective sur la philosophie linguistique*, AP, 46, no. 3, pp. 353-84.

Evaluates the contribution of the later W., placing him historically in the context of Moore, Ryle, and Austin, with whom he is compared.

1634. Weinert F., *Ways of criticizing metaphysics. Kant and W*, KS, 74, pp. 412–36.

1635. Weitz M., *Making sense of the Tractatus*, MWSP, 8, pp. 477–506.
Re-examines the distinctions in *Tract.* between sense and nonsense and saying and showing, and gives an interpretation of the nature of the propositions of the work itself.

1636. Whittaker J. H., *Tractatus 6.4312: immortality and the riddle of life*, PInv, 6, pp. 37–48.
Critical reconstruction of W.'s attitude towards religion in the light of *Tract.* 6.4312. The closing sections of that work are not mere appendages but conclusions deeply related to everything that precedes.

1637. Willett-Shoptaw C., *A deconstruction of W.*, Au, 10, pp. 75–81.
A critical examination of the problem of meaning in *P.I.* designed to bring out the indeterminacy of the contexts within which a linguistic item is employed. See also M. Green's comments on this article, ibid., pp. 82–5.

1638. Williams M., *W. on representation, privileged objects, and private languages*, CJP, 13, pp. 57–78.

1639. Winch P., *Facts and super-facts*, PQ, 33, pp. 398–404.
A critical analysis of Kripke, 1982, centred on the connection between the private language argument and W.'s treatment of the 'following a rule' problem. Reprinted in modified form in Winch, 1987.

1984

1640. *Aesthetics*, Proceedings of the 8th International W. Symposium (Kirchberg am Wechsel, 15–21 August 1983), Part I, ed. by R. Haller (Schriftenreihe der W.-Gesellschaft, vol. 10/1), Vienna, Hölder-Pichler-Tempsky, 1984, pp. 262.

Of the six sections into which the contributions are divided
only two are specifically dedicated to W.: 'Aesthetics in W.',
pp. 17–53; 'Contributions to W.'s philosophy', pp. 211–260.
20 essays in all.

1641. *Essays on W.'s later philosophy*, ed. by C. Wright
('Synthese', 58, n. 3), Dordrecht and Boston, Mass.,
Reidel, 1984, pp. 286–481.

S. Blackburn, *The individual strikes back*, pp. 281–301 (on
Kripke's treatment of the rule-following problem and
scepticism. See Kripke, 1982); M. Budd, *W. on meaning,
interpretations and rules*, pp. 303–323 (on *P.I.* 138ff.);
J. McDowell, *W. on following a rule*, pp. 325–363; C.
Peacocke, *Colour concepts and colour experience*,
pp. 365–381; C. Wright, *Second thoughts about criteria*,
pp. 384–405, reprinted in his *Realism, meaning and truth*,
Oxford, Blackwell, 1987); G. P. Baker and P. M. S. Hacker, *On
misunderstanding W.: Kripke's private language argument*,
pp. 407–450 (a criticism of Kripke, 1982, reprinted in Canfield
(ed.), 1986, vol. X. See also Baker and Hacker, 1984);
P. Carruthers, *Baker and Hacker's W.*, pp. 451–479 (a criticism
of the conception of W.'s philosophy as presented in Baker
and Hacker, 1980).

1642. *Philosophy and life. Essays on J. Wisdom*, ed. by
I. Dilman, The Hague, Nijhoff, 1984, pp. 345.

Some of the 15 essays in this volume deal with aspects of the
relation between Wisdom and W. In particular R. Bambrough,
Discipline and discipleship, pp. 201–17, looks at this relation
in the context of a general discussion of the interaction between
teacher and pupil in a discipline such as philosophy.
J. Nammour, *Generality and the importance of the particular
case*, pp. 241–70, deals with the problem of universals and
family resemblances in W. and criticizes the interpretation
given by Bambrough, 1960.

1643. *Philosophy of religion*, Proceedings of the 8th
International W. Symposium (Kirchberg am Wechsel,
15–21 August 1983), Part II, ed. by W.L. Gombocz
(Schriftenreihe der W.-Gesellschaft, vol. 10/2), Vienna,
Hölder-Pichler-Tempsky, 1984, pp. 252.

The introductory part of this volume contains in German, with
an English translation, a 'Preface' by W. L. Gombocz and an

'Opening address' by J. M. Bochenski. Contributions to the 'symposium' are divided into six sections: 'Foundations and methods of philosophy of religion', pp. 37–69; 'Epistemology of belief, faith and religion', pp. 73–117; 'Philosophical theology and proofs for God's existence', pp. 121–150; 'Religion, philosophy of religion, and W.', pp. 153–176; 'Religion and (religious) practice', pp. 179–204; 'Religion, science, world models', pp. 207–250.

1644. Anderson R. J. and **Sharrock W. W.**, *Under the influence*, P, 59, pp. 385–8.
Criticizes the conventionalist interpretation of W. given by Meynell, 1982. Passages from W. quoted in support of this interpretation could equally well be read in other ways.

1645. Anderson R. J., Hughes J. A., Sharrock W. W., *W. and comparative sociology*, I, 27, pp. 268–76.
Interprets and defends the theses of W. in *R.F.*, regarding causal explanation of beliefs and actions and the connection between science and magic.

1646. Anscombe G. E. M., *W. on rules and private language*. Et, 95, pp. 342–52.
A critical examination of passages in Kripke's book, 1982, and of his sceptical interpretation of W. on rule-following and private language.

1647. Armstrong B. F. Jr, *W. on private languages. It takes two to talk*, PInv, 7, pp. 46–62. Reprinted in Canfield (ed.), 1986, vol. IX.
Contesting a number of other interpretations of W.'s private language argument, A. maintains that that argument rules out the possibility both of contingently unshareable languages (Robinson Crusoe case) and of essentially unshareable languages.

1648. Arregui J. V., *Acción y sentido en W.*, Barañain (Pamplona), EUNSA, 1984, pp. 260.

1649. Baker G. P. and **Hacker P. M. S.**, *Language, sense and nonsense. A critical investigation into modern theories of language*, Oxford, Blackwell, 1984, pp. 389.
B. and H. attempt to identify and assess what they consider an essential element in many modern theories of language: 'the conception of language as a calculus of rules for the use of

symbols'. Frequently they find that W.'s *Tract.* is one of the sources of inspiration for this conception of language: see especially ch. 1 'Historical bearings', pp. 39–46. *Reviews:* Bogen J., I, 1985, 28, pp. 467–82; Eldridger R., PInv, 1986, 9, pp. 229–44; Engel P., RPFE, 1985, 175, pp. 46–9; Heal J., M, 1985, 94, p. 307; Stevenson L., P, 1985, 60, pp. 270–2.

1650. Baker G. P. and **Hacker P. M. S.**, *Scepticism, rules and language*, Oxford, Blackwell, 1984, pp. XIII, 140.
The book contains three different essays linked by related exegetical and theoretical problems: *On misunderstanding W.: Kripke's private language argument*, pp. 1–55 (already published in *Essays on W.'s later philosophy*, 1984); *The illusions of rule-scepticism*, pp. 56–97; *Rule-scepticism and the harmony between language and reality*, pp. 98–136. In the first essay B. and H. criticize Kripke's, 1982, sceptical interpretation of *P.I.*, §§193–242, maintaining that not only does it give an unfaithful representation of W.'s thought, but also it leads to some absurd conclusions about language and knowledge of other minds. In the second essay they try to explain the theoretical reasons for which rule-scepticism has become very attractive to present-day philosophers. In the final essay they clarify the conceptual connections of meaning with the use and with the explanations of expressions. *Reviews:* Craig E., PQ, 1985, 35, pp. 212–14; Diamond C., PB, 1985, 26, pp. 26–9; Eldridge R.. PInv, 1986, 9, pp. 229–44; Engel P., RPFE, 1985, 175, pp. 45–6; Heal J., M, 1985, 94, pp. 307–10; Summerfield D. M., Et, 1985–6, 66, pp. 671–2.

1651. Baker L. R., *On the very idea of a form of life*, I, 27, pp. 277–89.
An alternative proposal for an interpretation of the notion of 'form of life' based on a critical examination of current literature (Kripke, Putnam, Rorty, *et al.*).

1652. Bell R. H., *W.'s anthropology. Self-understanding and understanding other cultures*, PInv, 7, pp. 295–312.
How can we come to understand the depth of certain practices in the lives of persons who hold beliefs and customs different from our own? Examines W.'s reply, partly in the light of theses maintained by the anthropologist C. Geertz.

1653. Benvenuto S., *Tra W. e Freud*, in his *La strategia freudiana. Le teorie freudiane della sessualità rilette attraverse W. e Lacan*, Naples, Liguori, 1984, pp. 21–60.

1654. Blackburn S., *Spreading the word: grounding in the philosophy of language*, Oxford, Clarendon Press, 1984, pp. 368.
Many references to W., especially in the chapter 'How is meaning possible', pp. 69-109.

1655. Bouveresse J., *W. critique de Frazer*, RePL, 4, pp. 165-184.

1656. Bramann J. K., *W.'s Tractatus and the modern arts*, Rochester, N.Y., Adler, 1984, pp. 224.

1657. Burkhardt A., *W.'s 'Wörterbuch für Volksschule' from a linguistic and philosophical viewpoint*, 'Muttersprache. Zeitschrift der Deutschen Sprache', 95, nos 1-2, pp. 30-41.

1658. Caraway C., *Criteria and circumstances*, SJP, 22, pp. 307-16.
Criteria are neither logically sufficient conditions nor the normal sort of inductive evidence provided by symptoms. One of the keys to understanding W.'s conception is to recognize that 'circumstances' provide the necessary background for the use of psychological terms.

1659. Cascardi A. J., *Remembering*, RM, 38, pp. 275-302.
Proposes a non-mentalist and non-psychological model of memory, employing some aspects of W.'s philosophy of mind connected with the notions of 'following a rule' and 'going on'.

1660. Cherry C., *Knowing the past*, PInv, 7, pp. 265-80.
In *R.F.*, and other later works W. shows 'an essentially historical interest' in his concern with how we perceive ourselves as standing to the past.

1661. Churchill J., *W. on the phenomena of belief*, IJPR, 16, pp. 139-52.
Assesses the importance of W.'s contribution to understanding the nature of religious belief and to resolving the dilemma between the cognitivist and the non-cognitivist approach.

1662. Cioffi F., *When do empirical methods bypass 'the problems which trouble us'?*, in *Philosophy and literature*, ed. by A. P. Griffiths, Cambridge and London, Cambridge University Press (supplement to 'Philosophy', 53, 1983) pp. 155-172. Reprinted in Canfield (ed.), 53, 1986, vol. V.

W.'s criticisms of Freud and Frazer (see especially first part of the paper) raise problems of great importance about the nature of the explanation of human behaviour in the social sciences.

1663. Cook D. J., *Hegel, Marx and W.*, PSC, 10, no. 2, pp. 49-74.
Analyses the profound differences between the three authors as regards their theories of language, of society and of dialectic.

1664. Cox C. H. and **Cox J. H.**, *W.'s vision*, New York, Libra Publishers, 1984, pp. VII, 68.

1665. Deitz S. M. and **Arrington R. L.**, *W.'s language-games and the call to cognition*, B, 12, no. 2, pp. 1-14.
Assesses the importance that the late W.'s theory of language might have for a behaviourist approach to the problems of knowledge. See criticisms by Lamal, 1985, and Morris, 1985.

1666. Diamond C., *What does a concept script do?*, PQ, 34, pp. 343-68.
What is the relation between the idea of a logically adequate system of notation in W. (*Tract.*) and in Frege, and what are their views on the appropriate method in philosophy? In what sense, as Geach maintains (see *Essays on W.*, 1976), are the roots of W.'s doctrines about saying and showing to be found in Frege's work?

1667. Dilman I., *Quine on ontology, necessity and experience: a philosophical critique*, Albany, N.Y., State University of New York Press; London, Macmillan, 1984, pp. 138.
The contrasts between Quine and the later W. are brought out, especially in the last two chapters: 'Are there universals?' and 'Are there logical truths?'.

1668. Dunlop C. E. M., *W. on sensation and 'seeing-as'*, Sy, 60, pp. 349-67.
Re-examines W.'s private language argument with particular attention to the theses of *P.I.* Part II on 'seeing-as' and the theory of aspects.

1669. Eschbach A., *Karl Bühler. Symbolic concepts and their relationship to the later philosophy of W.*, 'Zeitschrift für Semiotik', 6, pp. 397-420.

1670. Faghfoury M. and **Armour L.**, *W.'s philosophy and religious insight*, SJP, 22, pp. 33-47.

The originality of W.'s treatment of what in his early writings and in the *Tract.* he called 'mystical', and of what in his later work he called value-judgement.

1671. Ferber R., *Der Grundgedanke des 'Tractatus' als Metamorphose des obersten Grundsatzes der 'Kritik der reinen Vernunft'*, KS, 74, pp. 460-8.

Some analogies between what W. (*Tract.* 4.0312) calls his 'fundamental thought' and what Kant in the *Critique of pure reason* calls 'the highest principle of *a priori* synthetic judgements'. *Tract.* uses some of the principles of critical philosophy in its analysis of language.

1672. Findlay J. N., *W.: a critique*, London and Boston, Mass., Routledge & Kegan Paul, 1984, pp. 262.

W.'s thought, whether in his first or in his second period, is so original and so systematic that it can only be appreciated by comparing it with the classics of philosophy, particularly with Kant. In this spirit, after two chapters devoted to examining 'the context of W.'s thought' (Brentano, Meinong, Husserl, Russell, Frege, Moore) F. proceeds to a critical examination, in as many chapters, of *Tract.*, *B.B.B.*, *R.F.M.*, *P.I. Reviews:* Bacharach M., M, 1987, 96, pp. 423-7; Llewelyn J., I, 1986, 29, pp. 363-76; Manser A., PB, 1986, 27, no. 2, pp. 38-41; Williams M., CPR, 1986, 6, pp. 273-5.

1673. Frascolla L., *W. e il principio del terzo escluso*, RF, 75, pp. 293-309.

1674. Frongia G., *W. trent'anni dopo*, 'Nuovi Argomenti', no. 10, pp. 64-79.

Examines W.'s reception in Italy and the changes his image has undergone in the thirty years since the publication of the first Italian translation of *Tract.*, 1954.

1675. Gallagher K. T., *'Meaning' and 'mental process'. Some demurrals to W.*, Th, 48, pp. 249-73.

Critical examination of W.'s theory of language, principally in the light of *P.I.*

1676. Garver N., *Die Lebensform in W.s 'Philosophischen Untersuchungen'*, GPS, 21, pp. 33-54.

Is the notion of 'forms of life' in *P.I.* applicable only to forms of human behaviour connected with the ability to master a language, or does it also explain other phenomena to be found in nature (such as, e.g., the behaviour of animals)? See Haller's reply, 1984, to this article.

1677. Garver N., *Neither knowing nor not knowing*, PInv, 7, pp. 206-24.
An analysis of and commentary on W.'s remark that 'it cannot be said of me that I *know* that I am in pain' (*P.I.*, 246). Some analogies between W. and Kant's anti-sceptical position in his treatment of the antinomies of pure reason.

1678. Geller J. L., *W. on the 'charm' of psychoanalysis*, PRA, 10, pp. 57-65.
Examines W.'s remarks on psychoanalysis in *C.F.*, and proceeds to compare them with Freud's theses regarding the attitudes of an analytic patient.

1679. Graham G., *Mystery and mumbo-jumbo*, PInv, 7, pp. 281-94.
In discussing the nature and the consequences of contradiction in religious belief, G. refers critically to W's views on this matter.

1680. Grattan-Guinness I., *Notes on the fate of logicism from 'Principia mathematica' to Gödel's incompletability theorem*, HPL, 5, pp. 67-78.
In a rapid survey of the development of logicism G.-G. discusses *inter alia* the influence of *Tract.*, particularly as revealed in the second edition of *Principia mathematica* (see especially pp. 70ff.).

1681. Gustafson D. F., *W. and a causal view of intentional action*, PInv, 7, pp. 225-43.
Contradicting a number of interpreters G. maintains that some remarks of the later W. on the topics of action, behaviour, voluntary action, intention, etc. are compatible with at least one type of causal theory of intentional action.

1682. Hacking I., *W. rules*, 'Social Studies of Science', 14, pp. 469-76.
On Bloor's interpretation of W., see 1983, and on the possibility of a social theory of knowledge.

1683. Hagberg G., *Art and the unsayable: Langer's tractarian aesthetics*, BJA, 24, pp. 325-340.
Langer's explanation of the expressive power of art, 1949, rests on the assimilation of art to the theory of language of *Tract.*

1684. Haller R., *Lebensform oder Lebensformen?*, GPS, 21, pp. 55-63.
A critical examination of the interpretation of *'Lebensform'* ('form of life') given by Garver in 1984. Reprinted in Haller, 1986.

1685. Haller R., *Was W. a neopositivist?*, in *Journées internationales sur le 'Cercle de Vienne'* (1983) ('Fundamenta Scientiae', 1984, 5), Oxford, Pergamon, 1984, pp. 271-83. Reprinted in Haller, 1986; in Shanker (ed.), 1986, vol. I.

1686. Hambourger R., *Moore's paradox and epistemic justification*, PRA, 10, pp. 1-12.
Discusses Moore's paradox about belief and W.'s solution of it. Finally proposes a solution of H.'s own, based on an analysis of the uses of 'I believe that . . .'.

1687. Hanfling O., *What does the private language argument prove?*, PQ, 34, pp. 468-81.
Dissenting from other interpreters of the private language argument (*P.I.* 258) H. finds it centred on the relation between the use of the sign 'S' discussed by W. and the straightforward uses of language.

1688. Iglesias T., *Russell's 'Theory of knowledge' and W.'s earliest writings*, Sy, 60, pp. 285-332.
The theory about 'constituents' and 'forms' of propositions espoused by Russell in *Theory of Knowledge*, 1913, is rejected by W. less explicitly in *N.B.*, more obviously in *Tract.*

1689. Kenny A., *The legacy of W.*, Oxford, Blackwell, 1984, pp. XV, 150.
A collection of essays all, save the fifth, previously published. Only the first four are devoted to the study of W.'s own thought, while the remainder endeavour rather to develop some of his ideas on different subjects. In particular, the last three attempt to show 'the damaging effect of the unconscious Cartesianism', criticised by W., in three different writers such as Teilhard de Chardin, R. L. Gregory, N. Chomsky. *W.'s early philosophy of mind*, pp. 1-9 (already published in *Perspectives on the philosophy of W.*, 1981); *The ghost of the Tractatus*, pp. 10-23 (already published in *Understanding W.*, 1974); *From the big typescript to the 'Philosophical grammar'*,

pp. 24-37 (already published in *Essays on W.*, 1976); *W. on the nature of philosophy*, pp. 38-60 (already published in *W. and his times*, see *W.s geistige Erscheinung*, 1979); *Intentionality: Aquinas and W.*, pp. 61-76; *The first person*, pp. 77-87 (on Anscombe's criticism of the Cartesian self); *Names and indirect speech*, pp. 88-105 (on *oratio obliqua*, taking account of W.'s ideas on proper names); *Teilhard de Chardin's 'The phenomenon of man'*, pp. 106-124; *The homunculus fallacy*, pp. 125-36; *Language and the mind*, pp. 137-47. *Reviews:* Arrington R. L., B, 1986, 14, pp. 61-4; Budd M., JP, 1987, 84, pp. 42-5; Frohmann B., Mp, 1986, 17, pp. 183-8; Genova J., CPR, 1986, 6, pp. 161-3; Long P., PQ, 1986, 36, pp. 306-8; Rashid D., PInv, 1986, 9, pp. 245-53; Summerfield D. M., Et, 1985-6, 16, pp. 450-1.

1690. Kurthen M., *Der Schmerz als medizinisches und philosophisches Problem. Anmerkungen zur Spätphilosophie L.W.s und zur Leib-Seele-Frage*, Würzburg. Königshausen & Neumann, 1984, pp. 104.

1691. Lazerowitz M. and **Ambrose A.**, *Essays in the unknown W.*, New York, Prometheus Books, 1984, pp. 233.

In this series of essays L. and A. seek to identify a number of profound insights which W., because of his 'iconoclastic' attitude towards conventional philosophy, never developed adequately. The chapter titles are: *Introduction: W.'s iconoclastic breakthrough*, pp. 11-14; *W.'s philosophical odyssey*, pp. 15-29; *Necessity and philosophy*, pp. 30-62; *Commanding a clear view of philosophy*, pp. 63-77; *Bouwsma's paradox*, pp. 78-94; *The fly-bottle*, pp. 95-108; *Sic et non*, pp. 109-120; *Two paradoxical statements*, pp. 121-126; *The 'Yellow Book' notes in relation to the 'Blue Book'*, pp. 127-138 (a reprint, see Ambrose, 1977); *W. and linguistic solipsism*, pp. 139-149; *Reason and the senses*, pp. 150-160; *Being and existence*, pp. 161-166; *Mathematical generalizations and counterexamples*, pp. 167-181; *W. on mathematical proof*, pp. 182-192 (previously published, see Ambrose, 1982); *Is philosophy of mathematics 'an idleness in mathematics'?*, pp. 193-216; *Infinite power*, pp. 217-224; *The philosopher and daydreaming*, pp. 225-233. *Reviews:* Cooke V. M., IPQ, 1985, 25, pp. 433-4; Gerrard S., Et, 1985-6, 16, p. 451.

1692. Lear J., *The disappearing 'We' (part I)*, PAS(SV), 58, pp. 219-42.

Dissenting from the interpretation of Kripke, 1982, L. attempts to cast W. as a post-Kantian rather than as a neo-Humean, showing that his anti-sceptical argument shares some features with Kant's transcendental argument. See reply by Stroud, 1984.

1693. Lütterfelds W., *'Etwas sehen als'. W.s 'Bemerkungen über die Philosophie der Psychologie', §1-§33)*, AZP, 9, no. 3, pp. 41-60.

1694. McGinn C., *Consciousness of other minds*, PAS(SV), 58, pp. 119-137.
In the second part of the paper a discussion of Kripke's interpretation, 1982, of W. on other minds.

1695. McGinn C., *W. on meaning. An interpretation and evaluation* (Aristotelian Society Series, vol. 1), Oxford, Blackwell, 1984, pp. XIV-202.
McG. proposes (ch. 1) an interpretation on W.'s views on meaning, understanding and rules, which leads him to some conclusions that he contrasts (ch. 2) with those reached by Kripke, 1982, concerning the 'sceptical solution' of the rule-following problem. Finally he offers some assessment both of the theoretical value of W.'s thesis (ch. 3) and of Kripke's arguments (ch. 4). *Reviews:* Carruthers P., PB, 1986, 27, pp. 36-8; Coady C. A. J., P, 1987, 62, pp. 103-6; Hart K., AJP, 1986, 64, pp. 362-4; Heal J., PQ, 1986, 36, pp. 412-19; Rashid D., PInv, 1986, 9, pp. 245-53.

1696. McGinn M., *Kripke on W.'s sceptical problem*, R, 26, pp. 19-31.
McG. examines Kripke's explanation of 'W.'s sceptical solution to a sceptical paradox' about private language and understanding (see Kripke, 1982). Then she opposes her own interpretation of the subject to Kripke's.

1697. Maddy P., *How the causal theorist follows a rule*, MWSP, 9, pp. 457-78.
An attempt to apply what M. considers to be W.'s rule-following argument, to 'any semantic theory that involves a causal theory of reference'.

1698. Marconi D., *W. on contradiction and the philosophy of paraconsistent logic*, HPQ, 1, pp. 333-52.

Defends W.'s views on contradiction and inconsistency in logic
and mathematics, as expressed in his writings after *Tract.*,
against critics such as Chihara, and compares those views with
aspects of 'paraconsistent logic'.

1699. **Margolis J.**, *W. and natural languages: an alternative
to rationalist and empiricist theories*, in his *Culture and
cultural entities. Toward a new unity of science*,
Dordrecht, Reidel, 1984, pp. XIII, 170.

1700. **Marini S.**, *La 'Conferenza sull'etica' di L.W.*, RFN, 76,
pp. 122-34.

1701. **Markus G.**, *The paradigm of language: W., Lévi-Strauss,
Gadamer*, in *The structural allegory*, ed. by J. Fekete,
Minneapolis, University of Minnesota Press, 1984,
pp. 104-29.

1702. **Martin D.**, *'On certainty' and religious belief*, RS, 20,
pp. 593-613.
Examines some themes in *O.C.* of possible importance for
philosophy of religion and weighs them against some
fundamental presuppositions of a Christian faith.

1703. **Moser P. K.**, *Justified doubt without certainty*, PPQ,
65, pp. 87-103.
W.'s thesis that 'the game of doubt presupposes certainty' (*O.C.*
115) is wrong.

1704. **Mulligan K.**, **Simons P.**, **Smith B.**, *Truth-makers*, PPR,
44, pp. 287-321.
Examines the isomorphism theory of *Tract.* in the context of
a wider study of the theory of truth in Russell, Tarski and
others.

1705. **Nielsen K.**, *On mucking around about God: some
methodological animadversions*, IJPR, 16, pp. 111-122.
Contains a criticism of 'W.ian fideism'.

1706. **Nielsen K.**, *W.ian moralism, ethnomethodology and
moral ideology*, Ind PQ, 11, pp. 189-99.

1707. **Nyíri J. C.** and **McGuinness B. F.**, Introduction to Karl
Wittgenstein's *Politico-economic writings*, ed. by
J. C. Nyíri (Viennese Heritage, vol. 1), Amsterdam,
Philadelphia, John Benjamins, 1984, pp. I-XL.

A presentation of the figure of Karl Wittgenstein (the philosopher's father) in the social and economic context of Austria in the second half of the nineteenth century, where he found full scope for his capacities as a financial and industrial *entrepreneur*. Particular attention is devoted to the family atmosphere among the W.s and to their social and cultural relations. The volume contains an annotated re-publication of Karl W.'s newspaper articles and lectures (previously published privately in 1913), which cover the period from 1888 to 1905. A summary of them in English is provided.

1708. Oliveri G., *Le 'Ricerche' di W. nella lettura di S. Kripke*, Pa, 1, pp. 523–40.

1709. Palmer A., *A meeting of minds*, M, 93, pp. 398–409.
Examines parallels between Frege (*Posthumous writings*) and W. (*O.C.*) regarding the problems of the learning and the understanding of language.

1710. Pareti G., *A proposito del concetto di 'Annahme'*, RF, 75, pp. 431–56.
The notion of *Annahme* ('supposition') in W. compared with that in Frege, Russell, Meinong and others.

1711. Rainone A., *Verificazionismo, proposizionalismo, essenzialità. Note su W. e Carnap*, Phy, 26, pp. 517–32.

1712. Reeder H. P., *Language and experience. Descriptions of living language in Husserl and W.*, Lanham and London, Center for Advanced Research in Phenomenology, University Press of America, 1984, pp. XII, 213.
R.'s intention is to contribute, through an analysis of some aspects of the theories of the two thinkers, to a 'closer dialogue between Continental and analytic philosophy'. Chs. 2–3 are devoted to a comparative reconstruction of the relation between 'public and private aspects of language' in W. and in Husserl; chs. 3–4 to an analysis and evaluation of their descriptive methods in philosophy, considered as mutually complementary. *Review:* Ihde D., JBSP, 1986, 17, pp. 204–5.

1713. Screen D. P., *Realism and grammar*, SJP, 22, pp. 523–534.
Many of the principles taken to be definitory of realism are what W. called 'grammatical remarks', in the sense that they

call attention to certain features of the grammar of truth and of related concepts, and express rules for the use of these concepts.

1714. Shanker S. G., *Sceptical confusions about rule-following*, M, 93, pp. 423–9. Reprinted in Shanker (ed.), 1986, vol. II.

A critical examination of Kripke's sceptical interpretation of W.'s concepts of rule-following and understanding, 1982.

1715. Shanker S. G., *W.'s solution of the 'hermeneutic problem'*, C, 18, no. 44, pp. 50–61. Reprinted in Shanker (ed.), 1986, vol. IV.

W.'s *reductio ad absurdum* of the arguments of the sceptic provides material for the solution of the sceptical dilemmas posed by Quine and Apel. Kripke's interpretation, 1982, is again criticized.

1716. Siitonen A., *Tractatus, schön und gut*, GPS, 21, pp. 65–87.

The notions of 'good' and 'beautiful' in *Tract.* are analysed in the context of its theory of 'sense'. Two principal meanings of the term 'nonsensical' are then identified.

1717. Staten H., *W. and Derrida*, Oxford, Blackwell; Lincoln, Neb., University of Nebraska Press, 1984, pp. XVIII, 182.

S. finds fundamental analogies between the writings of the later W. and the earlier Derrida (particularly in D.'s writings on Aristotle and Husserl). What unites the two philosophers (according to S.) is a 'deconstruction' of the boundary between literary and philosophical discourse, which is based on a similar conception of the functioning of language, on a parallel stress on 'grammar' (as distinct from object-talk), and on criticism of the classic philosophical concept of form. *Reviews:* Fischer M., PL, 1986, 10, pp. 93–7; Hart K., AJP, 1986, 64, pp. 362–4; Llewelyn J., PB, 1986, 27, pp. 154–6.

1718. Stroud B., *The allure of idealism: the disappearing 'we'* (part II), PAS (SV), 58, pp. 243–58.

Reply to Lear, 1984, on the distinction and relation between subjective conditions of thought and objective validity. The parallel between Kant and W., stated by Lear, is discussed in the second part of the paper.

1719. Tilghman B. R., *But is it art?*, Oxford, Blackwell, 1984, pp. 163.

The subject of the book is whether it is possible to formulate a philosophical definition or theory of art. T. draws on his own writings on W. and constantly refers to W.'s philosophy. In particular chs. 2-5 examine a number of criticisms of traditional theories of aesthetics which have been attributed to W. T. shows that these are based on misunderstandings of W.'s thought. Finally chs. 6-7 contain an extensive analysis of W.'s ideas about seeing-as and aspect perception, experiencing the meaning of a word, secondary sense, etc.

1720. Tymoczko T., *Gödel, W. and the nature of mathematical knowledge*, PSA, 2, pp. 449–468. Comments by P. Benacerraf, ibid., pp. 475–85.

1721. Wang H., *W.'s and other mathematical philosophies*, Mo, 67, pp. 18–28.
In the context of a general discussion of the relations between philosophy and mathematics Wa. examines some passages of *N.B.* and *Tract.* on this point and looks at the relation W. had to Russell, Ramsey, Frege, Gödel, *et al.*

1722. Wójcicki R., *R. Suszko's situational semantics*, SL, 43, pp. 232–40.
Examines some analogies between the situational semantics of the Polish logician, R. Suszko, and W.

1723. Wright C., *Kripke's account of the argument against private language*, JP, 81, pp. 759–78.
Criticizes the 'sceptical' interpretation of Kripke, 1982, especially as regards the private-language argument (*P.I.* 243ff.) and the rule following considerations.

1724. Young J., *W., Kant, Schopenhauer and critical philosophy*, T, 50, pp. 73–105.
Compares the three philosophers, especially as regards their views on ethics, aesthetics, religion, nature, and the tasks of philosophy.

1985

1725. *Moritz Schlick*, ed. by B. McGuinness (Sy, 64, no. 3), pp. 271–422.
Many scattered references in this special number, but also two

essays particularly concerned with W.: B. McGuinness, *W. and the Vienna Circle*, pp. 351-8 (an examination of W.'s account of propositions and of the verification principle, in the period 1929-31, designed to show the continuity between W.'s early and later philosophy); A. Quinton, *Schlick before W.*, pp. 389-410 (Q. contests the interpretation according to which Schlick was completely under the philosophical influence of W. in the period 1927-36 and shows that the origins of Schlick's later ideas are already to be found in his *General theory of knowledge*, 1918).

1726. *Philosophie, Wissenschaft, Aufklärung: Beiträge zur Geschichte und Wirkung des Wiener Kreises*, ed. by H.-J. Dahms, Berlin, De Gruyter, 1985, pp. XI, 418.
18 essays on the origins and development through the 1930s of the Vienna Circle, particular attention being paid to the contributions and personalities of W., Neurath, Reichenbach, Zilsel, and Carnap.

1727. *Philosophy of mind – Philosophy of psychology.* Proceedings of the 9th International W. Symposium (Kirchberg am Wechsel, 19-26 August 1984), ed. by R. M. Chisholm, J. C. Marek, J. T. Blackmore, A. Hübner (Schriftenreihe der W.-Gesellschaft, vol. 11), Vienna, Hölder-Pichler-Tempsky, 1985, pp. 662.
After an 'Opening address' by R. M. Chisholm, the contributions are distributed in 13 distinct sections; only 4 contain writings directly concerning W.: 'W. and the philosophy of mind', pp. 387-429; 'W.'s early philosophy', pp. 433-473; 'W.'s late philosophy', pp. 477-533; 'Logic and the philosophy of language', pp. 577-600. 33 essays in all.

1728. *Sprachspiel und Methode. Zum Stand des Wittgenstein-Diskussion*, ed. by D. Birnbacher and A. Burkhardt (Grundlagen der Kommunikation: Bibliotheksausgabe), Berlin and New York, de Gruyter, pp. XVI, 211.

1729. *Studies in the philosophy of J. N. Findlay*, ed. by R. S. Cohen, R. M. Martin, M. Westphal, Albany, N.Y., State University of New York Press, 1985, pp. XV, 478.
The volume contains numerous references to W., especially in two contributions by Findlay himself: *My life: 1903-1973*, pp. 1-51; *My encounters with W.*, pp. 52-69 (previously

published, see 1972) and in an essay by R. Plant, *Findlay and W.*, pp. 70–112.

1730. *The philosophy of language*, ed. by A. P. Martinich, New York and Oxford, Oxford University Press, 1985, pp. 492. In the seventh and last part of this volume, entitled 'Private languages', three classic essays on this theme are republished: A. J. Ayer, *Can there be a private language?*, pp. 453–60 (see 1954); J. Cook, *W. on privacy*, pp. 461–78 (see 1965); S. Kripke, *On rules and private language*, pp. 479–92 (see 1982, abstracts).

1731. *Wittgenstein*, a special number of Ma, 8, pp. 119–65. It contains the following articles: A. R. Moreno, *A propósito da noção de 'estética' em W.*, pp. 119–46 M. Helen and M. Lazerowitz, *A new consideration of the positivist criterion*, pp. 147–50; J. N. Kaufmann, *Critique w.ienne de la théorie de la mesure*, pp. 151–70; F. Latraverse, *Remarques sur W. et la question de la convention*, pp. 171–84; J.-C. Dumoncel, *Esquisse d'une théorie w.ienne du dialogue et de la conversation*, pp. 185–212; B. Stevens, *W. dans l'économie de l'histoire de l'être*, pp. 213–31; R. Vallée, *Jeux de langage, signification non-littérale et théorie de la conversation*, pp. 233–43; J. Laberge, *L'idée de preuve chez W. Remarques sur son 'finitisme'*, pp. 245–56; E. Villanueva, *Causalidad y datos sensibles en la filosofía de la percepción*, pp. 257–65.

1732. *W. and contemporary philosophy*, ed. by B. F. McGuinness and A. G. Gargani ('Teoria', vol. 5, no. 2), Pisa, ETS, 1985, pp. 237. Contains the following essays: G. P. Baker and P. M. S. Hacker, *W. and the Vienna Circle. The exaltation and deposition of ostensive definition*, pp. 5–33 (reprinted in Shanker (ed.), 1986); D. Birnbacher, *W. und die 'Verhexung unseres Verstandes durch die Mittel unserer Sprache'*, pp. 35–60; A. Gargani, *Internal relations, syntax and use in W.'s philosophical analysis*, pp. 61–71 (chiefly concerned with W.'s middle period); N. Garver, *W.'s dualism*, pp. 73–95 (influence of Frege's dualism on *Tract.* and *P.I.*); R. Haller, *War W. von Spengler beeinflusst?*, pp. 97–112 (W. owes his descriptive method in philosophy to Spengler (reprinted in Haller, 1986)); W. Künne, *Sinn(losigkeit) in 'Über Gewissheit'*, pp. 113–133; B. F. McGuinness, *Language and reality in the Tractatus*, pp. 135–144 (against the realistic interpretation of *Tract.*); K. Mulligan, *'Wie die Sachen sich zueinander verhalten' inside and outside the Tractatus*, pp. 145-174 (the contrast between W. and Husserl on objects and relations); D. Pears, *The emergence of W.'s local atomism*, pp. 175-186 (a comparison with Russell's theory on names and propositions); J. Schulte, *Es regnet, aber ich glaube es nicht*, pp. 187-204 (W. discusses Moore's paradox to criticize a Fregean theory of assertion); P. M. Simons, *The old problem of complex and fact*, pp. 205-225 (centred on an interpretation of *Tract.* 3.24); B. Smith, *Weininger und W.*, pp. 227-237 (will, happiness and ethics in *N.B.* and *Tract.*).

1733. Anderson T., *W. and Nāgārjuna's paradox*, PEW, 35, pp. 157-69.

Nāgārjuna's appeal to silence is reminiscent of the *Tract.*'s own paradox, that of a philosophy which negates itself in its quest for the absolute.

1734. Ayer A. J., *Wittgenstein*, London, Weidenfeld & Nicolson; New York, Random House, 1985, pp. 155. French translation: Paris, Seghers, 1986; Italian translation: Bari, Laterza, 1986.

An introductory book designed to appeal 'to a reader who did not already have considerable training in philosophy', but also intended to be 'of some interest to professional philosophers'. After an introductory 'Biographical sketch' A. takes into account, in different short chapters, the main works and subjects treated by W.: 'The *Tractatus*', 'The period of transition', 'The Brown book', 'The foundations of mathematics', 'Philosophical investigations', 'On magic and religion', 'The philosophy of psychology', 'Knowledge and certainty'. In a final chapter he analyses 'W.'s influence' on Moore, Russell, the Vienna Circle, A. himself, and numerous other British philosophers. *Reviews:* Budd M., M, 1986, 95, pp. 389-92; Moulder J., SAJP, 1987, 6, pp. 36-8; Rashid D., PInv, 1986, 9, pp. 320-3; Stock G., PB, 1986, 27, pp. 96-8.

1735. Baker G. P. and **Hacker P. M. S.**, *W.: rules, grammar and necessity. An analytical commentary on the 'Philosophical investigations'*, vol. 2, Oxford, Blackwell, 1985, pp. VI, 352.

Continues from vol. 1 of their commentary (see 1980). Vol. 2 covers sections 143-242 of *P.I.* As before, the mainly exegetical sections are interspersed with essays containing general exposition and theoretical matter. Constant reference is made to the *Nachlass*, both to support interpretations suggested and also to reconstruct the genesis of the work. An introductory chapter analyses the differences between successive versions of the work and brings out the importance of the writings on the philosophy of mathematics for the 1937 draft. The titles of the essays are: 'Rules and grammar', pp. 34-64; 'Accord with a rule', pp. 81-106; 'Following rules, mastery of techniques and practices', pp. 154-181; 'Agreement in definitions, judgements and forms of life', pp. 229-251; 'Grammar and necessity', pp. 263-347. *Reviews:* Budd M., PB, 1987, 28, pp. 21-4.

1736. Baum W., *Ludwig Wittgenstein*, Berlin, Colloquium-Verlag, 1985, pp. 94.

Reviews: Diané C., BJA, 1986, 26, pp. 286-8; Swiggers P., TF, 1987, 49, pp. 119-20.

1737. Best D., *Feeling and reason in the arts*, London, George Allen & Unwin, 1985, pp. 200.

Many references to W.'s philosophy of language and its significance for aesthetics.

1738. Bilodeau R., *Attribution d'états mentaux et justification de l'action*, D, 24, pp. 639-53.

A critical examination of A. R. Louch's attempt (in *Explanation and human action*) to apply certain theses drawn from W.'s philosophy of mind and philosophy of action in an examination of the normative aspects of the social sciences. The attribution of relativism to W. is particularly contested.

1739. Botwinick A., *W., scepticism and political participation. An essay in the epistemology of democratic theory*, Lanham, University Press of America, 1985, pp. 42.

A study of problems of political participation in the light of various classical theories of democracy. As well as the classical authors (Hobbes and Kant) and the moderns (from Rawls to Rorty) B. also examines the contribution that the later thought of W. can make to the understanding of fundamental aspects of social and political phenomena.

1740. Bouveresse J., *W. face à la psychanalyse*, 'Austriaca', 11, no. 21, pp. 49–61.

1741. Bramann J. K., *W.'s Tractatus and the modern arts*, Rochester, N.Y., Adler, 1985, pp. 203.
An interdisciplinary presentation of the links between analytic philosophy and certain trends in modern art. Six different themes from *Tract.* are examined in as many chapters and set in relation to the work of 29 artists, writers, film-makers, etc., who include Kafka, Marinetti, Chaplin, and Rimbaud. *Review:* Collinson D., BJA, 1986, 26, pp. 286–8.

1742. Brockhaus R. R., *On pulling up the ladder. Tractatus 6.54*, IS, 15, pp. 249–70.
What is the function of the propositions considered senseless in *Tract.*? What problems arise in connexion with solipsism? B. attempts to answer these questions by a reading of Schopenhauer.

1743. Brose K., *Sprachspiel und Kindersprache. Studien zu W.s 'Philosophische Untersuchungen'*, Frankfurt and New York, Campus-Verlag, 1985, pp. 336.
Examines some themes of W.'s relative to the learning of language, the problem of meaning, and that of grammatical rules, with a view in particular to their implications for educational theory and practice.

1744. Brose K., *The limits and possibilities of the language-game*, R, 27, pp. 121–32.
On the systematic structure of *P.I.*

1745. Brunner H., *Vom Nutzen des Scheiterns: eine literaturwissenschaftliche Interpretation von L. W.s Philosophischen Untersuchungen*, Bonn, Frankfurt, New York, Lang, 1985, pp. 266.

1746. Cacciari M., *Intérieur et expérience. Notes sur Loos, Roth et Wittgenstein*, Cri, 41, pp. 106–18.

1747. Carruthers P., *Ruling-out realism*, Ph, 15, pp. 61–78.
There is a crucial lacuna in the argument for anti-realism in the theory of meaning, as presented by Dummett and Wright. This lacuna can only be filled by the rule-following considerations of the later W.

1748. Churchill J., *W. on faith and wisdom*, SJP, 23, pp. 413–30.

In spite of their enormous influence on contemporary thought, the link between W.'s views in religion (both in *Tract.* and in later work) and his broader philosophy of language is neither as close nor as systematic as many have supposed.

1749. **Cianfrone P.**, *Motivi fregeani nella semantica del Tract.*, RStF, 40, pp. 309-25.

1750. **Cockburn D.**, *The mind, the brain and the face*, P, 60, pp. 477-93.

In his own examination of the relations between mind and body, C. refers frequently to W. and his approach to the problem of our knowledge of other minds.

1751. **Collinson D.**, *Ethics and aesthetics are one*, BJA, 25, pp. 266-272.

An examination of *N.B.*, *Tract.*, and *L.E.* designed to show the close connexion between ethics and aesthetics in the early philosophy of W. and the relation of that philosophy to some contemporary tendencies in aesthetics.

1752. **Connolly J. M.**, *Gadamer and the author's authority: a language-game approach*, JAAC, 44, pp. 271-8.

The hermeneutic rejection of the idea that understanding is ever finished or complete can be buttressed by W.'s later conception of language and meaning; and Gadamer's point about literary criticism can be restated in W.ian terms.

1753. **Cook J. W.**, *The metaphysics of W.'s 'On certainty'*, PInv, 8, pp. 81-119.

In sharp divergence from some schools of interpretation C. finds in *O.C.* two quite different kinds of theory, neither of which is sound or provides an adequate answer to philosophical scepticism.

1754. **Cook J. W.**, *Hanfling on Moore*, PInv, 8, pp. 287-94.

Hanfling's defence of Moore's use of 'I know', 1982, in the context of his anti-sceptical argument criticised in *O.C.*, rests on some misunderstandings of Moore's thesis and intentions.

1755. **Cooper W. E.**, *Is art a form of life?*, D, 24, pp. 443-53.

A critical examination of the thesis, maintained by R. Wollheim in *Art and its objects* (1980), according to which 'art is, in W.'s sense, a form of life'. Also an attempt to clarify how far the 'mysterious notion' of form of life can aid us to understand the nature of art.

1756. Curtis B., *W. and philosophy for children*, 'Thinking', 5, no. 4, pp. 10-19.

1757. De Monticelli R., *Immagini dell'anima. Per una lettura dei testi W.ni sulla filosofia della psicologia*, Teor, 5, no. 1, pp. 47-76.

1758. Eckert D., *Philosophie als Krankheit und Therapie. Marginalien zu Freud und W.*, 'Austriaca', 11, no. 21, pp. 63-67.

1759. Eldridge R., *The normal and the normative: W.'s legacy, Kripke and Cavell*, PPR, 46, pp. 555-75.
A critical examination of W.'s search for justification and of the interpretations of Kripke, 1982, and Cavell, 1979. What kinds of questions about justification, if any, can be settled by appeals to what is normal within a form of life?

1760. Engel P., *Comprendre un langage et suivre une règle*, Phi, 8, pp. 45-64.

1761. Ercoleo M., *W.: dalla logica assoluta alla prassi*, GM, 7, pp. 103-77.

1762. Fontaine-De Visscher L., *W. Le langage à la racine de la question philosophique*, RPL, 83, pp. 559-83.
Method and task of philosophy in *Tract.* and in later writings.

1763. Frongia G., *L'etica in W.*, in *Studi di etica*, Rome, Edizioni dell'Ateneo, 1985, pp. 161-93.
The central importance of ethics in W.'s thought is shown by means of a reinterpretation of his theory of the subject, of the will, and of happiness in *Tract.* and in his writings of the early 1930's.

1764. Gargani A., *Lo stupore e il caso*, Bari, Laterza, 1985, pp. XV, 193.
In a *tour d'horizon* of modern culture, covering figures like Einstein, Kakfa, Musil, I. Bachmann, G. also republishes 4 essays devoted to W.: *Freud e W.*, pp. 117-135; *Schlick e W.: linguaggio ed esperienza*, pp. 137-156; *W. e gli atti intenzionali*, pp. 157-172 (reprinted also in Shanker (ed.), 1986); *Linguaggio e forme di vita nel secondo W.*, pp. 173-188.

1765. Goldfarb W., *Kripke on W. on rules*, JP, 82, pp. 471-88.
A critical examination of Kripke's 'sceptical' interpretation of

W., 1982. G. raises objections, in particular, to the distinction between the treatment of 'public language' and the argument about 'private language' that Kripke draws in reconstructing W.'s position.

1766. Goldstein I., *Communication and mental events*, APQ, 22, pp. 331-8.
A discussion of the problems raised by W.'s arguments about private language and knowledge of other minds. Outlining his own solution G. rejects what he calls the solution of 'radical W.ians', according to which 'communication about sensations and other private events is impossible'.

1767. Griffin N., *Russell's multiple relation theory of judgment*, PS, 47, pp. 214-47.
The first part of the article is an examination of the nature, origin and history (1906-13) of the multiple relation theory of judgement. The second part (pp. 226-44) analyses W.'s criticisms of that theory, during Russell's writing of *Theory of knowledge* (1913, published 1984), criticisms that led Russell to abandon that work.

1768. Griffin N., *W.'s criticism of Russell's theory of judgment*, Ru, 5, pp. 132-45.
An analysis of the nature of Russell's epistemic foundations in *Theory of knowledge* (1913), in the attempt to explain why he came, as a result of criticism from W., to consider his own ideas unsatisfactory and to leave the book unfinished.

1769. Hanfling O., *Was W. a sceptic?*, PInv, 8, pp. 1-16.
A critical examination of Kripke's interpretation, 1982, according to which 'there can be no such thing as meaning anything by any word': the attribution to W. of 'a new form of scepticism' and that of solipsism rests on a deep misunderstanding of his writings and intentions.

1770. Hannings G., *W. on the grammar of mathematics*, SAJP, 4, pp. 115-26.

1771. Hintikka J. and **Hintikka M. B.**, *Ludwig looks at the Necker cube. The problem of 'seeing as' as a clue to W.'s philosophy*, APF, 38, pp. 36-48.

1772. Hoffman P., *Kripke on private language*, PS, 47, pp. 23-8.
The 'sceptical solution' to the sceptical paradox that Kripke,

1982, attributes to W. is 'a dismal failure' and cannot do the work of distinguishing between a private and a public language. See criticisms by Rudebusch, 1986.

1773. Hunter J. F. M., *Understanding W. Studies of 'Philosophical investigations'*, Edinburgh, Edinburgh University Press, 1985, pp. XIII, 248.

27 short chapters reviewing main themes of *P.I.* in the same order as they arise in the work. H. wishes to respect W.'s own method of inquiry and views on philosophical analysis. The central chapters deal with: the private language, private objects, knowledge of other minds, behaviourism, etc. *Reviews:* Baker L. R., CPR, 1986, 6, pp. 69–71; Champlin T. S., PB, 1986, 27, pp. 219–21; Fogelin R., M, 1987, 96, pp. 418–21; Gomm R. M., PInv, 1987, 10, pp. 271–5; Hinton J. M., P, 1987, 62, pp. 111–13.

1774. Incandela J. M., *The appropriation of W.'s work by philosophers of religion. Towards a re-evaluation and an end*, RS, 21, pp. 457–74.

1775. Jacquette D., *Wittgenstein on Frege's 'Urteilstrich'*, ILR, 16, pp. 79–82.

1776. Janik A., *Essays on W. and Weininger*, (Studien zur österreichischen Philosophie, vol. 9), Amsterdam, Rodopi, 1985, pp. 161.

A collection of essays, only some of which had been previously published: *In place of an introduction: writing 'W.'s Vienna'*, pp. 5–25 (on the genesis of the volume published in 1973 by J. and Toulmin); *Schopenhauer and the early W.*, pp. 26–47 (already published, 1966); *How not to write Austrian intellectual history again*, pp. 48–63 (on the relationship between philosophy, history and social science, as considered in the other essays); *W. and Weininger*, pp. 64–73 (about W. as 'lifelong reader of Weininger'); *Philosophical sources of W.'s ethics*, pp. 74–95 (already published, 1980); *Writing about Weininger*, pp. 96–115; *Nyíri on the conservatism of W.'s later philosophy*, pp. 116–135 (criticism of Nyíri's 'conservative' interpretation of *P.I.*); *W., Marx and sociology*, pp. 136–157. *Review:* Zwicky J., CPR, 1986, 6, pp. 386–8.

1777. Kampits P., *L.W.: Wege und Umwege zu seinem Denken*, Graz, Vienna, Cologne, Verlag Styria, 1985, pp. 223.

Intended as a popular introduction with an Austrian slant.
Review: Swiggers P., TF, 1987, 49, pp. 121-2.

1778. Kimmel L., *Sense and sensibility*, PInv, 8, pp. 199-207.
A 'view from the bridge' of W.'s and Bouwsma's shared view
of philosophy, its task and its method.

1779. Klapwijk J., *Philosophien im Widerstreit. Zur
Philosophie von Dilthey, Heidegger, James, W. und
Marcuse*, Riehen/Schweiz, Immanuel-Verlag, 1985,
pp. 93. (A translation from the Dutch.)

1780. Lamal P. A., *A response to call to cognition: comments
on Deitz and Arrington*, B, 13, pp. 147-9.
Is W.'s philosophy compatible with a behaviourist standpoint?
A commentary on, and criticism of Deitz and Arrington, 1984.

1781. Latraverse F., *Les études w.iennes au Canada. État de
la recherche, 1970-1984*, 'Philosophiques', 12,
pp. 197-209.

1782. Lazerowitz M. and **Ambrose A.**, *Necessity and
language*, London, Croom-Helm, 1985, pp. 252.
Many of the essays in this collection contain references of one
kind or another to W. In particular: M. Lazerowitz, *Necessity
and language*, pp. 5-37 (already published in *Philosophy and
language*, Ambrose and Lazerowitz (eds.), 1972); A. Ambrose,
Factual, mathematical and metaphysical inventories,
pp. 38-61 (also included in her *Essays in analysis*, see 1966);
A. Ambrose and M. Lazerowitz, *Assuming the logically
impossible*, pp. 69-79; A. Ambrose, *Mathematical generality*,
pp. 101-120 (already published in *Philosophy and language*,
Ambrose and Lazerowitz (eds.), 1972); A. Ambrose and
M. Lazerowitz, *On making a philosophical problem
disappear*, pp. 241-248.

1783. Lennox S., *Bachmann and W.*, 'Modern Austrian
Literature', 18, nos 3-4, pp. 239-59.
W.'s influence (together with that of Heidegger) on the
formation and writings of this Austrian writer.

1784. Lugg A., *Was W. a conservative thinker?*, SJP, 23,
pp. 465-74.
A criticism of interpretations such as those of D. Bloor, 1983,
and Nyíri, 1982, of W.'s thinking and personality.

1785. McFee G., *How to be an idealist*, IS, 15, pp. 41–53.
In an attempt to show 'what would be meant by being an idealist for the 80s' McF. uses some ideas from Collingwood's later work and from W. to sketch a transcendental idealistic point of view.

1786. McGuinness B., *Ornament und Askese in der Denkweise W.s*, in *Ornament und Askese im Zeitgeist des Wien der Jahrhundertwende*, ed. by A. Pfabigan, Vienna, Brandstätter, 1985, pp. 275–285.
Part of the proceedings of a symposium held in Vienna in 1985. McG. attempts to show that W.'s austerity in aesthetic matters is his own form of ornament. Analogies are found in the moral sphere.

1787. Majer U., *Hertz, W. und der Wiener Kreis*, in Dahms H.-J. (ed.), *Philosophie, Wissenschaft, Aufklärung. Beiträge zur Geschichte und Wirkung des Wiener Kreises*, Berlin and New York, De Gruyter, 1985.

1788. Malone M. E., *There is in W.'s work no argument and no conclusion*, PInv, 8, pp. 174–88.
The title reproduces a sentence of Bouwsma's which should serve as a guide for every correct interpretation of, or comment on the writings of, the later W. since it captures an essential aspect of his method. Other 'W.ian philosophers' who do not sufficiently heed this advice are criticized.

1789. Marshall J. D., *W. on rules: implications for authority and discipline in education*, JPE, 19, pp. 3–11.

1790. Moore A. W., *Set theory, Skolem's paradox and the Tractatus*, A, 45, pp. 13–20.
Some light is thrown on the nature of the debate between relativists and non-relativists by the analogies between the paradox of *Tract.* (its propositions are by its own lights nonsense) and the paradox raised by the Löwenheim-Skolem theorem.

1791. Moore A. W., *Transcendental idealism in W., and theories of meaning*, PQ, 35, 134–55.
Taking as his starting-point B. Williams's thesis (see *Understanding W.*, 1974) that in *Tract.* and in W.'s later work there is a common element of transcendental idealism, M. draws out the implications this has for a philosophical theory of meaning.

1792. Morris E. K., *W.'s language-games and the call to cognition*, B, 13, pp. 137–46.
Examines and comments on an article on language-games by Deitz and Arrington, see 1984.

1793. Moser P. K., *Does uncertainty require certainty?*, LA, 28, pp. 83–91.

1794. Moser P. K. and **Flannery K.**, *Kripke and W.: intention without paradox*, HJ, 26, pp. 310–18.
Critical discussion of the thesis (ascribed to *O.C.*) that doubt presupposes some other thing as certain.

1795. Munz P., *Our knowledge of the growth of knowledge. Popper or W.?*, London and Boston, Mass., Routledge & Kegan Paul, pp. 353.
Popper and W., according to M., are ideal types of the two opposed conceptions of science characteristic of late positivism: those of evolutionary epistemology and of sociological explanation of the growth of knowledge respectively. Discussing this opposition and drawing on other contemporary authors, such as Kuhn, M. criticizes the 'absolute relativism' that he finds in W. and argues in favour of the evolutionary approach.

1796. Nielsen K., *On finding one's feet in philosophy: from W. to Marx*, Mp, 16, pp. 1–11.

1797. Perissinotto L., *W. Linguaggio, soggetto, mondo*, (Collana della Facoltà di Lettere e Filosofia dell'Università di Venezia, vol. 16), Abano Terme, Francisci, 1985, pp. 220.

1798. Rao A. P., *W.: a second look*, JICPR, 2, pp. 127–43; 3, pp. 129–65.

1799. Rentsch T., *Heidegger und W. Existential- und Sprachanalysen zu den Grundlagen philosophischer Anthropologie*, Stuttgart, Klett-Cotta, 1985, pp. 343.
An attempt to compare and to lead to convergence the two philosophical approaches of the analytic school and of continental phenomenology by means of an examination of Heidegger and of the later W. R. claims that the two have in common a rejection of any ontology supposed pre-existent to human operations and the attempt to understand. This

common element is a valid starting-point for a 'philosophical anthropology'.

1800. Ricketts T. G., *Frege, the Tractatus, and the logocentric predicament*, N, 19, pp. 3–15.

W.'s *Tract.* is, in large measure, a response to some tensions in Frege's conception of logic, due in particular to his attempt to deal with issues raised by the 'logocentric predicament': in order to give an account of logic, we must presuppose and employ logic.

1801. Sádaba Garay F. J., *Lenguaje, magia, metafísica. El otro W.*, Madrid, Libertarias, 1985, pp. 192.

1802. Sauvé D., *L'argument du langage privé*, D, 24, pp. 3–31.

The private language argument turns on whether it is possible to refer to sensations outside the framework provided by a common language.

1803. Sharrock W. W. and **Anderson R. J.**, *Criticizing forms of life*, P, 60, pp. 394–400.

A critical examination of the thesis attributed to W. and/or P. Winch, according to which a form of life cannot possibly be criticized from the outside, cannot be considered wrong, etc.

1804. Sherry D., *A concordance for W.'s 'Remarks on the foundations of mathematics'*, HPL, 6, pp. 211–13.

Intended to facilitate consultation of *R.F.M.* and comparison of the two editions (1956 and 1983).

1805. Stenhouse D., *Active philosophy in education: paradigms and language games*, London, Allen & Unwin, 1985, pp. 229.

Discusses the possibility of applying W.'s concept of a language-game to educational philosophy and to practice in various areas, extending from the learning of language to that of mathematics.

1806. Stock G., *Negation. Bradley and W.*, P, 60, pp. 465–76.

An examination of the theory of negation in Bradley's *Principles of logic*, and a comparison with W.'s views on negation as they developed between *Tract.* and *P.R.*

1807. Strasser K., *Konrad Bayer und L.W.: zwei Formen eines Denkens*, C, 19, no. 46, pp. 84–96.

1808. Strawson P. F., *Scepticism and naturalism: some varieties*, London, Methuen, 1985, pp. 95.

Much exegesis and discussion of the later philosophy of W.,
especially in the section 'Hume and W.', pp. 14–21, and in
chap. 4, 'The matter of meaning'. S. associates W. with Hume
since he considers him 'the most powerful latter-day exponent'
of a form of 'naturalism' closely related to that of Hume, which
provides an effective reply to the problems posed by classical
scepticism.

1809. Strube W., *Über drei Methoden der sprachanalytischen
Ästhetik*, C, 19, pp. 39–52.
Examines three distinct approaches to aesthetics, all based on
the analysis of linguistic usage, one being that of W..

1810. Voltolini A., *W.: analisi come terapia e analisi come
mitologia*, RF, 76, pp. 435–463.

1811. Wiesenthal L., *Visual space from the perspective of
possible world semantics* (part II), Sy, 64, pp. 241–70.
For the first part of this article, see *L.W.*, Hintikka (ed.), 1983.
The aim of the article is 'to study, in the framework of visual
space, concepts of reference and meaning in modal logic'. The
'semantical basis of visual space', laid down in part I, takes the
form of an interpretation of W.'s studies of visual space in *P.R.*,
206.

1812. Williams M., *W.'s rejection of scientific psychology*,
JTSB, 15, pp. 203–23.

1813. Worthington B., *Miti del linguaggio. Un'interpretazione del pensiero di W.*, Genoa, Tilgher, 1985,
pp. 108.

1814. Wünsche K., *Der Volksschullehrer L.W., mit neuen
Dokumenten und Briefen aus den Jahren 1919–1926*,
Frankfurt, Suhrkamp, 1985, pp. 357.
An assembly of documents, testimony from former pupils, and
letters illuminating W.'s life in the Teachers' Training College
and in the villages where he taught (1919–1926), held together
by a running commentary by Wü. Emphasis is laid on the
struggle and self-abnegation involved in W.'s renunciation of
wealth and privilege and on the moral and religious aims of
his pedagogical work. Bartley's interpretation of this phase of
W.'s life is contested. A *Nachwort* (pp. 289–91) lays more
emphasis on the importance of these years as an attempt to

lead the life of a saint than on the lessons that may have formed
W.'s later philosophy. Part 3 (pp. 295–341) contains letters,
mostly from W. to Ludwig Hänsel.

1986

1815. *From Bolzano to W. The tradition of Austrian
philosophy*, ed. by J. C. Nyíri (Schriftenreihe der
W.-Gesellschaft, vol. 12/2) Vienna, Hölder-Pichler-
Tempsky, 1986, pp. 200.
The volume contains 19 papers based on talks delivered at the
'Seminar on Austrian philosophy' organized on the occasion
of the 10th International W. Symposium (1985). A number of
these papers contain references to W., especially as regards his
relation to Austrian culture of the 19th century,but only two
are specifically devoted to this theme: E. Morscher,
*Propositions and states of affairs in Austrian philosophy
before W.*, pp. 75–85; A. G. Gargani, *Ethics and the rejection
of philosophical theorizing in W. and in Austrian culture*,
1986, pp. 183–94.

1816. *International bibliography of Austrian philosophy*, ed.
by W. L. Gombocz, R. Haller, N. Henrichs, Amsterdam,
Rodopi, 1986, pp. 98.
This publication provides, on an annual basis, information on
the writings of Austrian philosophers and on the literature
about them. The period covered in this first volume is 1974–5.
The name W. (see 'Namenregister', p. 98) attracts the largest
number of references.

1817. *Le Cercle de Vienne – Doctrines et controverses*, ed. by
J. Sebestik and A. Soulez, Paris, Librairie des Méridiens-
Klincksieck, 1986, pp. 313.
The volume contains 16 contributions to a conference held in
Paris in 1983 on the theme of the Vienna Circle. Many
references to W., particularly in: R. Haller, *W., était-il néo-
positiviste?*; B. McGuinness, *Langage et réalité dans le Tract.*

1818. *L. Wittgenstein*, ed. by J.-P. Cometti, Marseille, Sud-Revue
Littéraire, 1986, pp. 266.
Contents of this special issue of the review 'Sud' dedicated to
W.: J. Bouveresse, *Le 'paradoxe de W.' ou comment peut-on*

suivre une règle, pp. 11-55; J.-P. Cometti, *'Adagio cantabile'*.
Esthétique et philosophie, pp. 56-73; A. Gargani, *Techniques
descriptives et procédures constructives: Schönberg-W.*,
pp. 74-121; G.-G. Granger, *'Bild' et 'Gleichnis'*. *Remarques
sur le style philosophique de W.*, pp. 122-134; B. McGuinness,
Freud et W., pp. 135-55; M. Meyer, *W. et Valéry. Deux figures
de la modernité*, pp. 156-72; G. H. von Wright, *W. et son
temps*, pp. 173-88; J.-P. Cometti, *La maison de la
Kundmanngasse*, pp. 189-95. At the end of the volume a
French translation of letters by W. to Engelmann, Ficker and
B. Russell. *Chronologie* and selected bibliography by J.-P.
Cometti.

1819. *L. Wittgenstein. Critical assessments*, ed. by S. G.
Shanker, 4 vols., London, Croom-Helm, 1986.
104 essays on W., most reprinted without substantial
modification. Thematic arrangement within volumes, each of
which is provided with an introduction. A fifth volume (see
V. A. Shanker and S. G. Shanker, 1986) is a bibliography. The
titles of the volumes are: Vol. 1: *From the 'Notebooks' to
'Philosophical grammar'. The construction and dismantling
of the 'Tractatus'*, pp. 351; Vol. 2: *From 'Philosophical
investigations' to 'On certainty'. W.'s later philosophy*,
pp. 372; Vol. 3: *From the 'Tractatus' to 'Remarks on the
foundations of mathematics'. W. on the philosophy of
mathematics*, pp. 412; Vol. 4: *From theology to sociology. W.'s
impact on contemporary thought*, pp. 465.

1820. *Philosophy in Britain today*, ed. by S. G. Shanker,
London, Croom-Helm, pp. 311.
Essays in which various authors sum up the state of British
philosophy: the two most directly concerning W. are: G. Baker,
philosophía: εἰκὼν καὶ εἶδος; pp. 1-57; E. Gellner, *Three
contemporary styles of philosophy*, pp. 98-117.

1821. *The philosophy of W. A fifteen volume collection*, edited
with an introduction by J. V. Canfield. New York and
London, Garland, 1986.
Photographic reproduction of articles and sections of books
on W. from 1923 to the date of publication, arranged by subject
and then chronologically, intended to give a panorama of
critical discussion. Includes some little known titles. 278 items
in all. The editor provides an introduction to each volume. The

volume titles are: *The early philosophy – language as picture; Logic and ontology; 'My world and its value'; The later philosophy – views and reviews; Method and essence; Meaning; Criteria; Knowing, naming, certainty, and idealism; The private language argument; Logical necessity and rules; Philosophy of mathematics; Persons; Psychology and conceptual relativity; Aesthetics, ethics, and religion; Elective affinities.*

1822. *The tasks of contemporary philosophy*, ed. by W. Leinfellner, F. M. Wuketits, Proceedings of the 10th International W. Symposium, (August 1985), (Schriftenreihe der W.-Gesellschaft vol. 12/1), Vienna, Hölder-Pichler-Tempsky, pp. 565.

The final part (pp. 441–559) is devoted to W.'s philosophy and divided into the following sections: 'W.'s Tract.'; 'W.'s transitional period'; 'Language games'; 'W.ian semantics'; 'Kripke's W.ian analysis' (see 1982); 'W. in historical context' (comparisons with Kant, Hegel, Kierkegaard, Marx).

1823. Andronico M., *Descrivere e immaginare nel secondo W.*, F, 37, pp. 3–44.

1824. Armstrong D. M., *The nature of possibility*, CJP, 16, pp. 575–594.

In the course of developing his own 'combinatorial theory of possibility' A. acknowledges his debt to a classical exposition of this idea given in *Tract*. 3.4.

1825. Barker A. W., *Nestroy and W.: some thoughts on the motto to the 'Philosophical investigations'*, 'German Life and Letters', 39, no. 2, pp. 161–7.

1826. Bender K., *Sur la notion de simple selon W.*, LTP, 42, pp. 57–60.

1827. Bering K., *Die Rolle der Kunst in der Philosophie L. W.s. Impulse für die Kunstgeschichte?*, Essen, Verlag Die Blaue Eule, 1986, pp. 103.

1828. Botwinick A., *W. and scepticism: an essay on the unity of W.'s thought*, PRA, 12, pp. 163–76.

The distinction between saying and showing is the key to the unity of W.'s philosophy and also the answer to scepticism.

1829. Bouwsma O. K., *W.: conversations, 1949–1951*, ed. by

J. L. Craft and R. E. Hustwit, Indianapolis, Ind., Hackett, 1986, pp. XXXII, 78.
Notes taken by B. of conversations with W. during three different periods: July–August 1949 (Cornell); October 1949 (Smith College); August 1950–January 1951 (Oxford). Posthumous, but edited and typed by B. before his death. An introduction by the later editors presents the figure of B. and explains what sort of notes these are.

1830. **Brown D.**, *W. against the 'W.ians'. A reply to Kenneth Surin on the Divine Trinity*, 'Modern Theology', 2, pp. 257–76.
W.'s philosophy is compatible with a number of Christian dogmas (the Incarnation, the Trinity, etc.).

1831. **Broyles J. E.**, *W. on personal identity: some second thoughts*, PInv, 9, pp. 56–65.
A critical account of the way in which W. tackles the problem of personal identity. In some passages of *Bl.B.*, W. has not completely succeeded in freeing his account of personal identity from the legacy of traditional dualism.

1832. **Budd M.**, *W. on sensuous experiences*, in *Mind, causation and action*, ed. by L. Stevenson, R. Squires, J. Haldane, Oxford and New York, Blackwell, 1986, pp. 64–85 (also in PQ, 36 (1986), pp. 174–95).
An examination of W.'s negative and positive views on the self-ascription of sensation and on their connections with problems of rule-following and private language. W. fails to take into account the causal role of sensations in producing behaviour.

1833. **Caraway C.**, *Criteria and conceptual change in W.'s later philosophy*, N, 17, pp. 162–171.
In criticizing the radically conventionalist interpretation of W., C. concentrates in particular on the notions of 'criterion' and 'symptom' and on the problem of the formation and change of concepts.

1834. **Chauviré C.**, *Comprendre la musique chez W.*, Cri, 42, no. 475, pp. 1159–1181.

1835. **Coates P.**, *Kripke's sceptical paradox: normativeness and meaning*, M, 95, pp. 77–80.
Presents and discusses Kripke's interpretation of W. and, in particular, the 'dispositional account of meaning' (see Kripke, 1982).

1836. Cooke V. M., *W. and religion*, 'Thought', 61, pp. 348-59.
For W. religion is closely connected with the ethical and mystical. Some analogies with Kierkegaard.

1837. Coughlan M. J., *W.ian philosophy and religious belief*, Mp, 17, pp. 230-40.

1838. Covell C., *The redefinition of conservatism: politics and doctrine*, New York, St. Martin's Press, 1986, pp. XII, 267.
The figure of W. and those of two 'W.ians' (J. Casey and J. Scruton) are made central to a general analysis of the features of modern 'conservative' thought, with a view to redefining the notion of 'conservatism'.

1839. De Martelaere P., *W., critique de Moore. De la certitude sans savoir*, RPL, 84, pp. 208-28.

1840. Eldridge R., *Problems and prospects of W.ian aesthetics*, JAAC, 45, pp. 251-61.
A number of influential philosophers of art, influenced by W., have argued that all attempts to define art are either deeply mistaken or impossibly confused. But there are difficulties in W.ian aesthetics that can be overcome through a 'W.ian phenomenology of art'.

1841. Gert B., *W.'s private language arguments*, Sy, 68, pp. 409-39.
W.'s attack on private language contains two arguments, one proving that a private language is impossible, the other that it bears no relationship to our ordinary language. An evaluation of the philosophical importance of W.'s achievement.

1842. Gill J. H., *Metaphor and language acquisition: a view from the West Pole*, SJP, 24, pp. 219-33.
W.'s notion of 'family resemblances' 'can be used to cast a great deal of light on how metaphorical speech actually works'.

1843. Glannon W., *What literary theory misses in W.*, PL, 10, pp. 263-72.

1844. Goldstein L., *The development of W.'s views on contradiction*, HPL, 7, pp. 43-56.
W. maintains both in *Tract.* and later, though for different reasons, that contradictions are not false propositions but have a status of their own.

1845. Goodman R. B., *How a thing is said and heard: W. and Kierkegaard*, HPQ, 3, pp. 335-53.
Comparison of W. and Kierkegaard as regards the limits of communication through language and the higher form of communication implicit in ethics and religion.

1846. Hacker P. M. S., *Insight and illusion, themes in the philosophy of W.*, rev. ed., Oxford, Clarendon Press, 1986, pp. 341.
A radical revision of the edition published in 1972 (see entry). Six out of 11 chapters are rewritten, and some of the others are significantly reworked. In a new preface H. explains the reasons for these far-reaching changes. The reformulations particularly affect the semantic theory of *Tract.*, W.'s relations with Frege and Russell; a number of themes connected with W.'s writings from the 1930s; the later semantic theory and in particular the role of the notion of criterion; the private language argument. The affinity of W. with Kant summed up in the first edition by the sub-title 'The metaphysics of experience', vanishes in this new edition.

1847. Haller R., *Fragen zu W. und Aufsätze zur österreichischen Philosophie* (Studien zur österreichischen Philosophie, vol. 10) Amsterdam, Rodopi; Atlantic Highlands, N.J., Humanities Press, 1986, pp. 254.
The volume is divided into four parts: the first deals with the question, 'Is there an Austrian philosophy?'; the second is devoted to the Vienna Circle; the third is entitled 'Fragen zu W.': here H. reprints articles with the following titles, 'Was W. a neo-Kantian?', 'Was W. influenced by Spengler?', 'Was W. a neo-positivist?' (see 1984), 'Form of life or forms of life?' (see 1984); the fourth part analyses the evolution of Austrian philosophy in the last fifty years. *Review:* Swiggers P., TF, 1987, 49, p. 122.

1848. Harris J. F., *Language, language-games and ostensive definition*, Sy, 69, pp. 41-9.
Differences and similarities in the theory of language in *Tract.* and in *P.I.*.

1849. Harrison B., *Frege and the picture theory: a reply to G. Stock*, PInv, 9, pp. 134-9.

An answer to criticisms by Stock, 1986, of H.'s interpretation of the picture theory in *Tract.*, see 1979.

1850. Heal J., *W., Kripke and meaning*, PQ, 36, pp. 412-19.
A critical examination of Kripke, 1982, and McGinn, 1984.

1851. High D. M., *On thinking more crazily than philosophers: W., knowledge and religious beliefs*, IJPR, 19, pp. 161-175.
The account of belief, knowledge and certainty and the relations between these concepts in *O.C.* serves to render more intelligible W.'s account of religious beliefs in earlier writings.

1852. Hintikka M. B. and **Hintikka J.**, *Investigating W.*, Oxford, Blackwell, 1986, pp. XIX, 326.
H. and H. examine certain aspects of W.'s thought over different periods, with frequent use of previous publications of their own and frequent reference to the *Nachlass*. Chs. 2-5 are dedicated principally to the nature of objects, to the picture theory, to the problem of colour - incompatibility and to logical form in *Tract.* Chs. 6-8 attempt an historical explanation of changes of opinion in W.'s 'transition period', while chs. 9-11 deal above all with the notions of language-game, private experience and private language in the writings subsequent to 1936.

1853. Hochberg H., *Causality and generality in the 'Treatise' and 'Tractatus'*, 'Hume Studies', 12, pp. 1-17.
A comparison with Hume based on an interpretation of *Tract.* 5.135-5.1361, 6.37, where W. rejects the existence of a causal connection (or relation or nexus).

1854. Hutcheson P., *Husserl's alleged private language*, PPR, 47, pp. 133-6.
A reply to Cunningham, 1983. On the relationship between W.'s private language argument and the phenomenological reductions of Husserl.

1855. Jones K., *Is W. a conservative philosopher?*, PInv, 9, pp. 274-87.
Light is thrown on this question by considering W.'s rejection of all philosophical doctrines and his views on meaning and linguistic community, with their implications for the problem of linguistic change.

1856. Joubert J.-M., *Ce qu'est un miracle selon L. W.*, 'Revue Thomiste', 86, pp. 115-26.

1857. Kannisto H., *Thoughts and their subject. A study of W.'s 'Tractatus'* (APF 40), Helsinki, Societas Philosophica Fennica, 1986, pp. 184.

The chief aim of the book is 'to challenge the picture of the early W. as mainly a logician with a strong bent towards the sciences', and to present him 'as more a metaphysician and an epistemologist, or even a fantast of a sort', locating his *Tract.* in the philosophical context of Frege and Russell, and stressing the Kantian roots of his answers. K advances some hypotheses about the presence of psychological considerations in the *Tract.*; proposes some interpretations of the controversial *Tract.* 5.542, and of the distinction between the empirical and metaphysical subject; finally K. analyses W.'s solution of the 'transcendental' problem of defining the conditions that make the meaningful use of language possible.

1858. Kerr F., *Theology after W.*, Oxford, Blackwell, 1986, pp. XII, 202.

The purpose of the book is to show the relevance of W.'s later writings for theology. In parts 1 and 2 it analyses W.'s criticism of the picture of the self as an autonomous and rational consciousness and considers his attitude toward the idealism-realism dilemma. In part 3 ('Theology without the mental ego') the book points out the impact that W.'s theory of the self, in conjunction with some other overtly theological topics in his later writings, can have on modern discussion in the philosophy of religion.

1859. Krebs V. J., *Objectivity and meaning: W. on following rules*, PInv, 9, pp. 177-86.

Leich's and Holtzman's account and criticism of W. (see *W. to follow a rule*, 1981) involve a misrepresentation of his position about the relation between communal agreement and objectivity in meaning and language.

1860. Laurence C. W., *Chuang Tzu and W. on world-making*, JCP, 13, pp. 383-91.

1861. Llewelyn J., *Following and not following W.*, I, 29, pp. 363-76.

A critical review of the different interpretations given by

McGinn, 1984, Findlay, 1984, and Kripke, 1982, of W.'s views on rules, private language, solipsism, and knowledge of other minds.

1862. López de Santa María Delgado P., *Introducción a W.: sujeto, mente y conducta*, Barcelona, Herder, 1986, pp. 269.

1863. McDonough R. M., *The argument of the 'Tractatus': its relevance to contemporary theories of logic, language, mind and philosophical truth*, Albany, N.Y., State University of New York Press, pp. XII, 311.
Central to *Tract.* is the thesis that logical constants are not representative and that the propositions of logic are tautologies. From this thesis the first four chapters derive the fundamental aspects of the picture theory and the ontology of *Tract.* It is also shown what relation these parts of the work have to the philosophy of logic and logical atomism of Russell. In the remaining chapters McD. examines the relations sketched in *Tract.* between propositional sign and thought, also the saying-showing distinction and the function of silence and of the mystical in communication. *Review:* Cooke V. M., IPQ, 1986, 26, pp. 403–4.

1864. Maddy P., *Mathematical alchemy*, BJPS, 37, pp. 279–314.
A critical examination of W.'s anti-realism in the philosophy of mathematics and of its connexion with his theses about criteria, rule following, etc.

1865. Malcolm N., *Nothing is hidden: W.'s criticism of his early thought*, Oxford, Blackwell, 1986, pp. XII, 252.
Rejecting some contrary interpretations, M. regards *P.I.* as 'an assault upon the fundamental conceptions' of *Tract.* and sees in the two works 'a dramatic conflict between two radically different philosophical outlooks'. From this point of view he takes into account the following topics in as many chapters: 'The form of the world'; 'Language and objects'; 'The elements of reality'; 'Thoughts'; 'Whether a proposition shows its sense'; 'Two kinds of logical analysis'; 'The inner process analysis'; 'Language as expressive behaviour'; 'Following a rule'; 'Mind and brain'; 'Certainty'. Especially in the first eight chapters M. contrasts the *Tract.* with W.'s later thoughts. In ch. 11, referring to the last notebooks, M. compares the views of W. and

Descartes on certainty. *Reviews:* Carruthers P., PQ, 1987, 37, pp. 328-31; Hacker P.M.S., PInv, 1987, 10, pp. 142-50; Mulhall S., M, 1987, 96, pp. 113-16.

1866. Marini S., *La presenza di Kierkegaard nel pensiero di W.*, RFN, 78, pp. 211-226.

1867. Mounce H. O., *Following a rule*, PInv, 9, pp. 187-98. Criticizes both the 'sceptical interpretation' by Kripke of W.'s private language argument, see 1982, and the 'refutation' of that interpretation by Baker and Hacker, 1984, which 'reveals confusions as great as those they attribute to Kripke'. See also: G. P. Baker and P. M. S. Hacker, *Reply to Mr. Mounce*, ibid., pp. 199-204.

1868. Mulligan K. and **Smith B.**, *A Husserlian theory of indexicality*, GPS, 28, pp. 133-63. The account of Husserl's 'theory of indexicality' in *Logical investigations* is contrasted with parallel ideas in Frege and W. (see pp. 143ff.).

1869. Nicolet D., *W.: à la recherche du livre*, SP, 43, pp. 191-200.

1870. Nielsen K., *La longue marche à travers les institutions: de W. à Marx*, 'Philosophiques', 13, pp. 113-29. Presidential Address before the 28th Congrès de l'Association Canadienne de Philosophie (1984). W.'s influence on present-day philosophers (on N. himself, Rorty, and others).

1871. Nyíri J. C., *Gefühl und Gefüge. Studien zum Entstehen der Philosophie W.s* (Studien zur österreichischen Philosophie, 11), Amsterdam, Rodopi, 1986, pp. 207.

1872. Pateman T., *W.ian aesthetics*, BJA, 26, pp. 172-5. Discusses Best's views, 1985, on aesthetics and the later W.

1873. Peterson D., *W.'s 'Grundgedanke' and the independence thesis*, PInv, 9, pp. 315-19. Once a short missing argument is supplied, the logical independence thesis can be seen as a consequence of the 'fundamental thought' (*Tract.* 4.0312), according to which logical constants are not representatives.

1874. Phillips D. Z., *Belief, change and forms of life*, London, Macmillan; Atlantic Highlands, N.J., Humanities Press, 1986, pp. 138.

A republication in amplified and reorganized form of articles partly published before (cf. in particular Phillips, 1979, and *Perspectives*, 1981). According to P., W.'s ideas about language, his notion of form of life, and his philosophical method, when these are correctly understood, are a fundamental contribution to the understanding of the character of religious belief, particularly in its relation to cultural changes in society.

1875. Portmann F., *Glaubenlose Religion und Glaubensreligion*, C, 20, pp. 69–78.
Imaginary dialogue between W. and an unnamed interlocutor on religious belief, criteria, etc.

1876. Portmann F., *Religion und Vernunft: eine Rekonstruktion von W.s Religionsphilosophie*, SP, 45, pp. 127–151.

1877. Rigal E., *Variations W.iennes sur le thème 'Sinn und Bedeutung'*, Phi, 11, pp. 74–92.

1878. Rudebusch G., *Hoffman on Krikpe's W.*, PRA, 12, pp. 177–82.
Does Kripke's W., 1982, fail in his solution to the 'sceptical paradox'? Reply to Hoffman, 1985.

1879. Schulte J., *Erlebnis und Ausdruck. W.'s Philosophie der Psychologie*, Munich, Philosophia Verlag, 1986, pp. 176.
A study based on W.'s manuscript production in the years 1945-9, showing how his interest turned to systematic analysis of psychological concepts and to detailed criticism of Gestalt psychology. The intimate connexions between 'inner' experience, instinctive expression, and mastery of a technique have implications for aesthetics and the philosophy of meaning, but W. need not and does not countenance the construction of a folk psychology, or a theory of any kind, as a basis for the use of psychological concepts.

1880. Senchuk D. M., *Privacy regained*, PInv, 9, pp. 18–35.
S. aims to 're-establish the distinction between public and private phenomena', a distinction challenged by 'more or less W.ians' (Malcolm, Donagan, Ryle) and by W. himself.

1881. Shanker V. A. and Shanker S. G., *A W. bibliography*, vol. 5 of *L.W.: Critical assessments*, 1986, pp. 361.
The fullest bibliography published to date. Covers publications up to the start of 1985. 6000 titles (books, articles, reviews)

arranged alphabetically by author. Subject index at the end of
the volume. An initial section (pp. 1–21) republishes G. H. von
Wright, *The W. papers*, 1970.

1882. Sharrock W. W. and **Anderson R. J.**, *Margaret
Gilbert on the social nature of language*, Sy, 68,
pp. 553–8.
M. Gilbert (see article in *L. W.*, Hintikka (ed.), 1983) in order
to show the possibility of a language-using castaway, has
adopted a standard argument (the Crusoe case) that begs the
central question that was at issue for W.

1883. Shusterman R., *W. and critical reasoning*, PPR, 47,
pp. 91–110.
W.'s contribution to aesthetics is not solely negative (as
supplying the meta-theory which invalidates all theory), but
contains also some important points on the nature of aesthetic
concepts and reasoning and on the source of aesthetic
appreciation.

1884. Siemens R. L., *Merrill Ring on Baker and Hacker*, PInv,
9, pp. 216–24.
M. Ring's criticism, 1983, of the interpretation that Baker and
Hacker, 1980, give of *P.I.* 1, on Augustine's picture of language,
involves some misunderstandings of W. See also M. Ring, *Reply
to Siemens*, ibid., pp. 225–8.

1885. Simons P., *Tractatus mereologico-philosophicus?*, GPS,
28, pp. 165–86.
The philosophies of the late Brentano and the early W. can
be brought closer by means of a reinterpretation of the theory
of states of affairs and propositions in *Tract.*

1886. Smith M. A., *Peacocke on red and red*, Sy, 68,
pp. 559–76.
A criticism of Peacocke's interpretation of W. on colour
concepts and colour experience, see 1984. Reply by Peacocke,
ibid., pp. 577–80.

1887. Somerville J., *Moore's conception of common sense*,
PPR, 47, pp. 233–53.
What did Moore mean by 'common sense' and what is its
importance for philosophy? W.'s criticisms of Moore's appeal
to common sense in philosophy actually help us to answer
these questions.

1888. Stegmüller W., *Kripkes Deutung der Spätphilosophie W.s*, Stuttgart, Kröner, pp. VII, 136.

1889. Stock G., *The picture theory and assertion*, PInv, 9, pp. 129-33.
A close analysis of the picture theory and of the notion of proposition and assertion in *Tract.* shows that W. at the time had no more sympathy for a Fregean view of thinking and judgement than he manifests in *P.I.* See a comment on this article, by Harrison, 1986.

1890. Stroud-Drinkwater C., *Seeing and following some rules*, Di, 40, pp. 4-18.

1891. Suter R., *Saul W.'s sceptical paradox,* PRA, 12, pp. 183-93.
Discussion and criticism of Kripke, 1982. The 'sceptical paradox' is here called 'Saul W.'s' because it 'is neither W.'s nor Kripke's'.

1892. Tait W. W., *W. and the 'skeptical paradoxes'*, JP, 83, pp. 475-88.
Contrary to Kripke's interpretation, 1982, W. intended no sceptical paradoxes or sceptical solutions. Rather, he was attempting to clarify confusions which underlie the appearance of paradox.

1893. Tarca L., *Il linguaggio sub specie aeterni* (Collana della Facoltà di Lettere e Filosofia dell'Università di Venezia), Abano Terme, Francisci, 1986, pp. 436.

1894. Temkin J., *A private language argument*, SJP, 24, pp. 109-21.
In part 1 T. offers an interpretation of the private language argument 'which is independent of the considerations about verification and the reliability of memory which seem to be involved in *P.I.* 258-70. In part 2 he considers and discusses the views of Fogelin, 1976, and Kripke, 1982, on these matters.

1895. Tomasini A., *W. y argumentos trascendentales*, Rev F, 19, pp. 89-100.

1896. Vohra A., *W.'s Philosophy of mind*, London, Croom-Helm, 1986, pp. 160.
A summary account of the main themes of the philosophy of mind dealt with by the later W.: self-consciousness, private

language, scepticism, knowledge of other minds, etc. *Review:* Cockburn D., CPR, 1987, 7, pp. 39-41.

1897. Wang H., *Beyond analytic philosophy. Doing justice to what we know*, Cambridge, Mass., and London, M.I.T. Press, 1986, pp. XII, 276.
A critical examination of the contribution of a number of analytical philosophers, including Russell, Carnap and other members of the Vienna Circle, and Quine. Many scattered references to W. but also a chapter devoted to him (pp. 75-100), which reviews the structure of *Tract.* and its influence on Russell and also discusses W.'s attitude towards philosophy.

1898. Westphal J., *White*, M, 95, pp. 311-28.
'Why is it that something can be transparent green but not transparent white?' (*R.C.* I, 19). We. proposes a reply to W.'s puzzle question and concludes that the distinction between logic and science, which W. sets up, is a false one. See the comments of Gilbert, 1987, on this article.

1899. White A. R., *Common sense: Moore and W.*, RIP, 40, pp. 313-30.
Re-examines the thesis advanced against Moore by W. in *O.C.* Contrary to appearances, the views of the two philosophers are not completely incompatible.

1900. Wuchterl K., *Neuerscheinungen zu W.*, AZP, 11, no. 2, pp. 49-58.

1987

1901. *Logic, philosophy of science and epistemology*, Proceedings of the 11th International W. Symposium (1986), edited by P. Weingartner and G. Schurz (Schriftenreihe der W.-Gesellschaft, vol. 13), Vienna, Hölder-Pichler-Tempsky, 1987, pp. 430.
Sections include: 1. W.: his contribution to epistemology and philosophy of science; 2. language and epistemology; epistemological standpoints; 3. philosophy of mathematics; 4. methodological problems of scientific disciplines; 5. theories of scientific progress.

1902. *Meaning and the growth of understanding. W.'s significance for developmental psychology*, ed. by M. Chapman and R. A. Dixon, Berlin, New York, London, Springer, 1986, pp. 236.

A collection of essays addressed to 'developmental psychologists and scientists in allied disciplines' introducing them to a number of themes in W.'s philosophy relevant to 'developmental theory, method and substantive research'. M. Chapman and R. A. Dixon, *Introduction: W. and developmental psychology*, pp. 1–10; K. Brose, *Pedagogical elements in W.'s late work 'On certainty'*, pp. 11–22; J. Russell, *Rule-following, mental models and the developmental view*, pp. 23–48; R. A. Dixon, *W., contextualism and developmental psychology*, pp. 49–67; J. Brandtstädter, *On certainty and universality in human development: developmental psychology between apriorism and empiricism*, pp. 69–84; J. Coulter, *Recognition in W. and contemporary thought*, pp. 85–102; M. Chapman, *Inner processes and outward criteria: W.'s importance for psychology*, pp. 103–27; J. Margolis, *W.'s 'forms of life': a cultural template for psychology*, pp. 129–49; E. Rosch, *W. and categorization research in cognitive psychology*, pp. 151–66; C. J. Patterson, *W., psychology and the problem of individuality*, pp. 167–85; D. Bullock, *Socializing the theory of intellectual development*, pp. 187–218; R. Harré, *Grammar, psychology and moral rights*, pp. 219–30. Subject index.

1903. *Wittgenstein*, a special number of TF, 49, pp. 3–81.

This special number of TF contains the following articles: P. Winch, *W.: picture and representation*, pp. 3–20 (also published in his *Trying to make sense*, 1987. Text of a lecture give at Leuven in 1986. On the role of pictures in the life of a religious believer); H. De Dijn, *W.: betekenis en chaos*, pp. 21–40 (pp. 40-1, summary in English: *W.: meaning and chaos*); H. Boukema, *Familiegelijkenissen: W. als criticus en erfgenaam van Frege*, pp. 42–69 (pp. 69–70, summary in German); P. Swiggers, *W., Kripke, Chomsky: geen regel van drie*, pp. 71–80.

1904. Aldrich V. C., *Kripke on W. on regulation*, P, 62, pp. 375–93.

Kripke, 1982, gives an erroneous interpretation of passages in *P.I.* regarding the private language argument, thereby showing that he has failed to understand the aim of W.'s analysis. The reason for this 'failure' lies in 'his (traditional and essentialist) belief that psychological states are first subjectively encountered in a first-person way'.

1905. Bar-On A. Z., *W's concept of knowledge*, GPS, 29, pp. 63-75.

1906. Bell D., *The art of judgement*, M, 96, pp. 221-244.
An inquiry based on the Kantian doctrine of judgement, but making frequent reference to W., especially in the last section, 'A W.ian postscript', where B. insists on the character, both Kantian and at the same time W.ian, of his own conclusions.

1907. Bouveresse J., *La force de la règle. W. et l'invention de la nécessité*, Paris, Les Éditions de Minuit, 1987, pp. 175.

1908. Bradley R. D., *W.'s tractarian essentialism*, AJP, 67, pp. 43-55.
An interpretation of the theory of simple objects and internal properties in *Tract.*, which sees W. as committed to a form of 'atomistic essentialism': internal properties determine but are not identical with the combinations into which simple objects enter. The implications of this theory for the picture theory and metaphysics of *Tract.*

1909. Bradley R. D., *Tractatus 2.022-2.023*, CJP, 17, pp. 349-59.
In *Tract.* 2.022-2.023 W. is envisaging a multitude of possible worlds, having a common form. But did W. also maintain, as Ramsey, 1923, and other commentators believe, that the same set of simple objects is to be found in each of these possible worlds, and that the form which all worlds have in common is to be identified with this single set of objects?

1910. Brenner W. H., *'Brownish-yellow' and 'reddish-green'*, PInv, 10, pp. 200-11.
Westphal, 1982, and others criticize W. for not approaching the analysis of colours in a scientific or experimental way: all such criticisms are rooted in the same error. B. defends W.'s 'grammatical approach' which grounds incompatibility of colours in a linguistic convention.

1911. Brose K., *W. als Sprachphilosoph und Pädagoge. Grundlagen zu einer Philosophie der Kindersprache*, Frankfurt, Campus Verlag, 1987, pp. 260.

1912. Budd M., *W. on seeing aspects*, M, 96, pp. 1-17.
In numerous places in W.'s later writings we find examples of
what can be called 'noticing an aspect'. The philosophical
importance of the concept of noticing an aspect is due to its
location at a crucial point in our concept of the mind.

1913. Burnyeat M. F., *W. and Augustine 'De magistro'*, PAS,
61, pp. 1-24.
Examines St. Augustine's *De magistro*, partly with the aim of
clarifying the passage from *Confessions* (I. viii. 13) that W.
quotes at the beginning of *P.I.* St. A.'s views on the learning
of language are much more sophisticated than at first appears
in *P.I.* and show some analogies with W.'s own.

1914. Curtis B., *The language-game of morality*, PInv, 10,
pp. 31-53.
The importance that W.'s notion of a language-game ('a rule-
powered social practice, involving the use of words') could
have for moral philosophy. Rules of morality can be
understood as rules of a family of language-games: that of
imperatives. W. leaves a sketch of such a model in his mature
writings: C. seeks to complete it.

1915. Descombes V., *Philosophie analytique versus
philosophie continentale*, Cri, 43, no. 478, pp. 240-54.
Discusses two supposedly antithetical philosophies and takes
W. as typical of one of them.

1916. Dilman I., *Love and human separateness*, Oxford and
New York, Blackwell, 1987, pp. 169.
Ch. 2 of this vol., 'W. on "the existence of other people"'
(pp. 27-35), deals with W.'s idea of human person. What W.
calls 'an attitude towards a soul' constitutes the logical root
of our understanding and is a prototype of a way of thinking.

1917. Eldridge R., *Hypotheses, criterial claims and
perspicuous representations: W.'s 'Remarks on Frazer's
"The golden bough"'*, PInv, 10, pp. 226-45.
W. criticises Frazer for attempting to explain social practices
and social phenomena in terms of beliefs based on hypotheses
about natural phenomena.

1918. Eldridge R., *Problems and prospects of W.ian aesthetics*,
JAAC, 1987, 45, pp. 251-61.

1919. Fischer H. R., *Sprache und Lebensform. W. über Freud und die Geisteskrankheit*, Frankfurt, Athenäum, 1987, pp. 357.

1920. Gilbert P., *Westphal and W. on white*, M, 96, pp. 399–403.

'Why is it that something can be transparent green but not transparent white?' (*R.C.* I, 19). The answer given by Westphal, 1986, is unsatisfactory as a response to W.'s question.

1921. Harris N. G. E., *W. and Searle's assertion fallacy*, PInv, 10, pp. 134–41.

In *Speech acts*, 1969, J. R. Searle alleged that W. has committed an 'assertion fallacy', which consists in 'confusing the conditions for the performance of the speech act of assertion with the analysis of the meaning of particular words occurring in certain assertions'. H. seeks to acquit W. of this charge.

1922. Henderson D. K., *Winch and the constraints on interpretation: versions of the principle of charity*, SJP, 25, pp. 153–73.

Discussing the problem of the interpretation of other cultures, H. criticizes the solutions proposed by Winch in *The idea of social science*, see 1958, and identifies the 'W.ian roots of his strategy'.

1923. Hilmy S., *The later W. The emergence of a new philosophical method*, Oxford and New York, Blackwell, 1987, pp. 340.

The volume examines the emergence of W.'s 'method' or approach to philosophy in his later writings. In the introductory chapter H. discusses the importance and the limits of the use of W.'s *Nachlass*, the relation between W.'s style and method, the significance of some sections of the manuscript for the subject matter. In the last chapters H. faces some more general implications such as: 'W.ian relativism and the dynamic view of language' (ch. 5); 'Metaphysics and W.'s struggle against the intellectual currents of our times' (ch. 6). Much of the volume is composed of notes referring to and discussing the W.ian corpus.

1924. Hunter J. F. M., *Some thinking about thinking*, PInv, 10, pp. 118–33.

An interpretation and discussion of a remark by W. that the

concept of 'thinking' might be conceived as 'formed on the model of a kind of imaginary auxiliary activity' (*Z.* 106).

1925. James M., *W.*, in his *Reflections and elaborations upon Kantian aesthetics*, Uppsala, Uppsala University, 1987, pp. 93–105.

1926. Mackenzie I., *W. and aesthetic responses*, PL, 11, pp. 92–103.

A critical discussion of the thesis attributed to W. (*B.B.B.*, *L.C.*), according to which aesthetic responses are not causal responses and are not open to experimental revision.

1927. McLaughlin P., *W. and moral knowledge*, DR, 105, pp. 12–22.

1928. Marconi D., *L'eredità di W.*, Bari, Laterza, 1987, pp. 171.

1929. Moore A. W., *Beauty in the transcendental idealism of Kant and W.*, BJA, 27, pp. 129–37.

The *Tract.* expresses a form of transcendental idealism which has many aspects in common with that of Kant, but also permits the solution of a number of paradoxes that in Kant remain unresolved, in particular regarding the distinction between how things are and how they are in themselves, and also aesthetics and its connection with ethics.

1930. Niedermair K., *W.s Tractatus und die Selbstbezüglichkeit der Sprache*, Frankfurt, Bern, New York, Paris, Lang, 1987, pp. 223.

N. proposes an interpretation of what he considers an ambivalent and paradoxical element in *Tract.*: the self-referential use of language to provide a foundation for its own sense and to exercise an autoregulative function. In the first two parts the book examines the possibility of a formal theory establishing conditions for the sense of statements and compares the solutions of W., Russell, and Carnap. In the third part the contrast in *Tract.* between 'saying' and 'showing' is considered and Stenius's interpretation, see 1960, is criticized.

1931. Pears D., *The false prison. A study of the development of W.'s philosophy*, vol. 1, Oxford and New York, Oxford University Press, 1987, pp. 202.

The first of two vols. in which P. proposes to give a summary of W.'s philosophical development from *N.B.* to his most mature works. This vol. is divided into two parts, the first giving a 'wide-angle view' of the entire plan of the work, bringing out the Kantian critical framework within which W. carried out his inquiries and other elements of continuity between the 'early' and the 'later' system. The second part examines the early system; central chapters are: 'Logical atomism', 'The basic realism of the *Tract.*', 'Sentences as pictures', 'Solipsism'.

1932. Perszyk K., *Tractatus 5.54–5.5422*, Ph, 17, pp. 111–26.
The common interpretations of W.'s treatment of sentences which purport to express 'propositional attitudes' ('A believes that p') are mistaken. W.'s intention is in fact to dismiss them as nonsense, that is, as non-genuine propositions attempting to say what can only be shown. The relation of this solution with Russell's theory of judgement.

1933. Sayers B., *W., relativism and the strong thesis in sociology*, PSS, 17, pp. 133–45.

1934. Seabright P., *Explaining cultural divergence: a W.ian paradox*, JP, 84, pp. 11–27.
Some influential interpretations of W.'s approach to our use of language and concept of 'form of life' have the consequence of ruling out completely the possibility of social science. Such a conclusion, although it might appear to be supported by a superficial reading of W., is an untenable one, both in fact and as interpretation.

1935. Shanker S. G., *W. and the turning-point in the philosophy of mathematics*, London, Croom Helm; Albany, N.Y., SUNY Press, 1987, pp. 358.
S.'s aim is 'to establish the outlines for a fresh approach to W.'s remarks on the philosophy of mathematics' by concentrating on the material of the early 1930s, as found in *P.R.* and *P.G.* He unmasks the fallacies underlying some prevailing interpretations (Dummett and others) tending to represent W. as involved in an anti-realist attack on the foundations of mathematics, or committed to a 'full-blooded conventionalism' (see ch. 7) or to a 'radical constructivism'. The tendency of W.'s inquiries must much rather be sought in his anti-metaphysical criticism of the foundations of mathematics and in his attacks on meta-mathematics and on Hilbert's programme (see ch. 6).

1936. Stromberg W., *W.: theoretical psychology and the* *classification of psychological concepts*, PInv, 10, pp. 11–30.

Critics have to date overlooked an important aspect of the writings of the later W., namely his attempt to give a taxonomy of psychological concepts. An attentive examination of *Z.*, *P.I.*, and *R.P.P.* gives evidence 'that a novel and critical view of theoretical psychology was emerging in W.'s work'.

1937. Tilghman B. R., *The moral dimension of the P.I.*, PInv, 10, pp. 99–117.

The 'moral dimension of the *P.I.*' (connected with the distinction in *Tract.* between what can be said and what we must be silent about) has largely been overlooked. In this regard W.'s concern with language and psychology may be considered, in a sense, propaedeutic.

1938. Werhane P. H., *The constitutive nature of rules*, SJP, 25, pp. 239–54.

A criticism of the interpretation given by Temkin, 1986, and others of W., on language (the 'community views'): W. maintains that rules, not the social practices of a community, are the 'bedrock' of language and human activities, and that it is the notion of a rule, not that of a community, that precludes the possibility of a private language.

1939. Westphal J., *Colour: some philosophical problems from W.*, (Aristotelian Society Series, vol. 7), Oxford, Blackwell, 1987, pp. 117.

A collection of writings in part already published, 1986. Its aim is to give an explication of a number of 'puzzling propositions' that W. discusses in *R.C.* but to which he nowhere gives specific answers. In the introduction We. stresses the philosophical significance of these puzzles and explains his 'method for solving' them. In the central chapters he discusses problems connected with the colours white, brown, grey, red, green. Then he devotes the last chapters to 'Refutation of physicalism', 'Impossible colours and the interpretation of colour space', 'Simple sensations, science and the subject'.

1940. Wider K., *Hell and private language argument: Sartre and W. on self-consciousness, the body, and others*, JBSP, 18, pp. 120–32.

Although W. deals with linguistic issues and Sartre (*Being and nothingness*) with metaphysical ones, there is much that is common in their discussions. Both reject the analogical argument for our knowledge of other minds, and so avoid the scepticism that arises from the Cartesian analysis of consciousness.

1941. Winch P., *Trying to make sense*, Oxford, Blackwell, 1987, pp. 213.

This volume contains two articles on W. previously published in *Perspectives*, 1981 and as a review of Kripke, 1982 and others here published for the first time. Among them: *Language, thought and world in W.'s Tractatus*, pp. 3–17; *W.: picture and representation*, pp. 64–80 (on the relation between 'pictures' and religious belief).

1942. Wolgast E., *Whether certainty is a form of life*, PQ, 37, pp. 151–65.

Examines the diverging views of Moore and of W. in *O.C.* on the nature of 'truisms' and on the origin (neither empirical nor *a priori*) of their certainty.

REVIEWS OF WITTGENSTEIN'S OWN WRITINGS

A few early reviews of Wittgenstein's own writings as they were published are included in Part II, being significant contributions to the literature on him. A selection of the remaining reviews (often also highly interesting) is given below.

Notebooks 1914-16

1943. Anon, TLS, 11 Aug. 1961, p. 528. Bernstein R. J., RM, 15, 1961, p. 197. Black M., M, 73, 1964, pp. 132-41. Bouveresse J., Cri, 28, 1972, pp. 441-59. Copi I. M., JP, 60, 1963, pp. 764-8. Iglesias T., PS(I), 28, 1981, pp. 317-27. Riverso E., RSF, 15, 1962, p. 252. Schwerin A., SAJP, 1, 1982, pp. 42-3. Trinchero M., RF, 55, 1964, pp. 495-7. Weiler G., PB, 2, 1961, pp. 16-18. Wienpahl P.D., I, 12, 1969, pp. 287-316.

Prototractatus

1944. Anon, TLS, 17 Sept. 1971, p. 1111. Burnheim J., AJP, 50, 1972, pp. 80-1. Devaux P., RIP, 26, 1972, pp. 573-5. Hart W. D., JP, 70, 1973, no. 1, pp. 19-24. Newell R. W., P, 48, pp. 97-9. Rhees R., PR, 82, 1973, pp. 530-1. Winch P., PB, 13, 1972, no. 1, pp. 36-8. Wolf M., PS(I), 21, pp. 284-5. Wolter A. B., RM, 25, 1971-2, pp. 575-6.

Tractatus logico-philosophicus

1945. Anon, 'Scientific American', 207, no. 3, Sept. 1962, p. 274. Anon, TLS, 19 Jan. 1962, p. 45. Bastable J. D., PS(I), XI, 1961–2, pp. 327–8. Bernstein R. J., RM,15, 1962, p. 681. Blanché R., RPFE, 86, 1961, p.521. Chastaing M., RPFE, 93, 1968, pp. 133–5. Conte A. G., RF, 53, 1962, p. 92. Eichner H., D, 1, 1962, pp. 212–16. Gadamer H. G., PRd, 11, 1963, pp. 41–5. Geach P. T., PR, 72, 1963, pp. 264–5. Gianquinto A., RaF, 4, 1955, pp. 245–8. Grize J. B., RTP, 11, 1961, pp. 293–4. Henschen-Dahlquist A.-M., JSL, 29, 1964, p. 134. Jacob A., EP, 16, 1961, p. 477. Jarvis J., JP, 59, 1962, pp. 332–5. MacGregor G., Pr, 43, 1962, p. 559. Narveson A., D, 3, 1964, pp. 273–83. Plochmann G. K., MS, 40, 1962–3, pp. 65–7. Pöggeler O., PL, 15, 1962, pp. 304–7. Trinchero M., RF, 55, 1964, pp. 495–7. Urmson J. O., M, 72, 1963, pp. 298–300. Weiler G., PB, 1962, no. 3, p. 25.

Vermischte Bemerkungen. Culture and value

1946. Beardsmore R. W., BJA, 22, 1982, pp. 172–4. Burns S. A. M., D, 21, 1982, pp. 178–81. Canfield J. V., CPR, 3, 1983, pp. 205–7. Hallett G., G, 60, 1979, pp. 396–7. Hertzberg L., PInv, 5, 1982, pp. 154–62. Long P., PQ, 29, 1979, pp. 81–3. Nyíri J. K., PLA, 35, 1982, pp. 167–9. Tilley T. W., TS, 42, 1981, pp. 706–7. Todd D. D., PRh, 15, 1982, pp. 70–3. Villanueva E., Cr, 14, 1982, pp. 93–6.

Philosophische Bemerkungen. Philosophical remarks

1947. Anon, TLS, 9 Dec. 1965, p. 1163. Blanché R., RPFE, 96, 1971, pp. 253–4. Carlson J., MS, 54, 1977, pp. 423–4. Hampshire S., 'New Statesman', 71, 4 Feb.

1966, pp. 163–4. Largeault J., AP, 40, 1977, pp. 153–5.
Lucchese I., RSF, 30, 1977, no. 1, pp. 123–4. Malcolm N.,
PR, 76, 1967, pp. 220–9. Riverso E., RIP, 21, 1967,
pp. 508–21. Sluga H. D., BJPS, 17, 1966–7, pp. 339–41.
Stenius E., PQ, 16, 1966, pp. 371–2. Stock G., PQ, 26,
1976, pp. 178–80. von Morstein P., 'Die Welt: Der
Literatur', 2, no. 9, 29 April 1965, p. 216. Weiler G., AJP,
43, 1965, pp. 412–15. White A. R., Mp, 8, 1977, pp. 72–4.

Philosophische Grammatik. Philosophical grammar

1948. Baker G. P. and Hacker P. M. S., M, 85, 1976, pp. 269–94.
Bouveresse J., Cri, 36, 1980, pp. 1156–63. Goldstein L.,
PQ, 25, 1975, pp. 280–1. King-Farlow J., Mp, 7, 1976,
pp. 265–75. Miller R. W., PR, 86, 1977, pp. 520–44.
Stenius E., PQ, 21, 1971, pp. 376–7. Todd D. D., PRh,
8, 1975, pp. 260–2.

Bemerkungen über Frazers 'The Golden Bough'. Remarks on Frazer's 'The golden bough'

1949. Jarvie I. C., PSS, 13, 1983, pp. 117–18. Lescourret M.-A.,
Cri, 39, 1983, pp. 764–73. Reix A., RPL, 81, 1983,
pp. 668–9.

The blue and brown books

1950. Anon, TLS, 16 Jan. 1959, p. 37. Ayer A. J., 'Spectator',
14 Nov. 1958, p. 654. Bouwsma O. K., JP, 58, 1961,
pp. 141–62. Deledalle G., EP, 14, 1959, pp. 107–8.
Delpech L. J., EP, 20, 1965, pp. 562–3. Garver N., PPR,
21, 1960–1, pp. 576–7. Hampshire S., 'New Statesman',
56, 1958, pp. 228–9. Kreisel G., BJPS, 11, 1960–1,
pp. 238–51. Lorenzen P., PRd, 7, 1959, p. 160. Newman
J. R., 'Scientific American', 201, 1959, pp. 149–158.
Pole D., P, 34, 1969, pp. 367–8. Strawson P. F.,

PQ, 10, 1960, pp. 371-2. Warnock G. J., M, 69, 1960, pp. 283-4. Wienpahl P., I, 15, 1972, pp. 267-319, 434-57. Zuurdeeg W. F., JR, 40, 1960, pp. 54-5.

Notes for lectures on 'private experience' and 'sense data'

1951. Reix A., RPL, 81, 1983, pp. 668-9.

Bemerkungen über die Grundlagen der Mathematik. Remarks on the foundations of mathematics

1952. Ambrose A., PPR, 18, 1957, pp. 262-5. Ayer A. J., 'The Spectator', March 1957, pp. 319-20. Berry G. D. W., PF, 16, 1958-9, pp. 73-5. Collins J., MS, 35, 1957-8, pp. 147-50. Colombo G., 'Month', 18, 1957, pp. 356-8. Engel P., RPFE, 109, 1986, pp. 128-31. Fleming R., PInv, 3, no. 1, 1980, pp. 44-6. Goodstein R. L., M, 66, 1957, pp. 549-53. Hadot P., Cri, 15, 1959, no. 150, pp. 972-83. Kreisel G., BJPS, 9, 1958, pp. 135-58. Lewis C. J., 'Thought', 32, 1957, pp. 446-8. McBrien V. O., NS, 32, 1958, pp. 269-71. Penco C., Ep, 2, 1979, pp. 436-9. Rawlins F. I. G., 'Nature', 180, 1957, pp. 399-400. Shalom A., EP, 12, 1957, p. 433. Stegmüller W., PRd, 13, 1965-6, pp. 138-52.

Philosophische Untersuchungen. Philosophical investigations

1953. Ambrose A., PPR, 15, 1954, pp. 111-15. Anon, TLS, 28 Aug. 1953. Barone F., GCFI, 33, 1954, pp. 109-17. Barone F., F, 4, pp. 680-91. Blanché R., RPFE, 96, 1971, p. 124. Burnheim J., PS(I), 4, 1954, pp. 114-15. Collins J., 'Thought', 29, 1954, pp. 287-9. Colombo G., 'Month', 18, 1957, pp. 356-8. Copeland J. W., PF, 12, 1954, p. 112. Davie I., DR, 72, 1954, pp. 119-22.

Deledalle G., EP, 14, 1959, pp. 107-8. Findlay J. N., P, 30, 1955, pp. 173-9. Hall R., PQ, 17, 1967, pp. 362-3. Hamilton R., 'The Month', 11, 1954, pp. 116-17. Hampshire S., 'Spectator', 190, 1953, p. 682. Heinemann F. H., 'The Hibbert Journal', 52, 1953, pp. 89-90. Hutten E. H., BJPS, 4, 1953, pp. 258-60. Lübbe H., KS, 52, 1960-1, pp. 220-43. Nakhnikian G., PSc, 12, 1954, pp. 253-4. Nolet Y., RPL, 66, 1968, pp. 132-3. Rawlins F. I. G., 'Nature', 180, 1957, pp. 399-400. Scholz H., PRd, 1, 1953, pp. 193-7. Workman A. J., Pr, 36, 1955, pp. 292-3.

Zettel

1954. Bernstein J. R., RM, 22, 1968, p. 158. Gustafson D. F., P, 43, 1968, pp. 161-4. Llewelyn J. E., PQ, 18, 1968, pp. 176-7. Louch A. R., JHP, 6, 1968, pp. 98-100. Morick H., IPQ, 9, 1969, pp. 151-2. Novielli V., F, 20, 1969, pp. 643-5. Teichman J., PInv, 6, 1983, pp. 229-34. Vesey G. N. A., PR, 77, 1968, pp. 350-5. Warnock M., 'Listener', 78, 13 July 1967, p. 55. Winch P., PB, 9, no. 2, 1968, pp. 27-30.

Bemerkungen über die Philosophie der Psychologie. Remarks on the philosophy of psychology

1955. Baker G. P. and Hacker P. M. S., Language and Communication, 2, 1982, pp. 227-42 (repr. in S. G. Shanker (ed.), 1986, vol. II). Diamond C., PR, 93, 1984, pp. 458-62. Harré R., IPS, 17, 1985, pp. 118-19. Hunter J. F. M., CPR, 1, 1981, pp. 130-6. Mounce H. O., M, 91, 1982, pp. 603-9. Nyíri J. K., PLA, 35, 1982, pp. 169-72. Peacocke C., PQ, 32, 1982, pp. 162-70. Yudkin M., PInv, 4, no. 4, 1981, pp. 65-7. Zekauskas J., Et, 93, 1982-3, pp. 606-8.

Letzte Schriften über die Philosophie der Psychologie.
Last writings on the philosophy of psychology

1956. DeAngelis W. J., PInv, 7, 1984, pp. 322-30. Engel P.,
RPFE, 109, 1984, pp. 131-2. Harré R., ISP, 19, 1987,
pp. 104-6. Kerr F., HJ, 26, 1985, pp. 466-70.

Über Gewissheit. On certainty

1957. Brusin D., Ph, 4, 1974, pp. 573-82. Dilman I., P, 46,
1971, pp. 162-8. Llewelyn J. E., PQ, 21, 1971, pp. 80-2.
Palmer A., M, 81, 1972, pp. 453-7. White A. R., PB, 11,
1970, no. 2, pp. 30-2. Zimmermann J., SP, 36, 1976,
pp. 226-39.

Bemerkungen über die Farben. Remarks on colour

1958. Candlish S., AJP, 57, 1979, pp. 198-9. Fanelli V., RFN,
74, 1982, pp. 680-8. Gale R., RM, 33, 1980, pp. 653-4.
Goodman N., JP, 75, 1978, pp. 503-4. Hallett G., G, 59,
1978, pp. 433-4. Harrison B., P, 53, 1978, pp. 564-6.
Louch A., JHP, 18, 1980, pp. 240-2. Mounce H. O., PQ,
30, 1980, pp. 159-61. Parret H., TF, 42, 1980, pp. 160-4.
Shoemaker S., ISP, 11, 1979, pp. 184-5. Stock G., M, 89,
1980, pp. 448-51. Yudkin M., PR, 90, 1981, pp. 118-20.

Wittgenstein und der Wiener Kreis.
Wittgenstein and the Vienna Circle

1959. Eichner H., D, 7, 1968-9, pp. 494-5. Goodstein R. L.,
PB, 10, no. 1, 1969, pp. 27-8. Hacker P. M. S., PR, 90,
1981, pp. 444-8. Hallett G., IPQ, 20, 1980, pp. 241-2.
Nolet Y., RPL, 66, 1968, pp. 333-4. Trainor P., MS, 59,
1981-2, pp. 143-6.

Wittgenstein's lectures. Cambridge 1930-2

1960. Collins J., MS, 59, 1982, pp. 223-4. Greisch J., AP, 45, 1982, pp. 325-7. Hacker P. M. S., PR, 90, 1981, pp. 444-8. Hunter J. F. M., CJP, 14, 1984, pp. 153-65. Mayberry T. C. PInv, 4, no. 1, 1981, pp. 41-4. Morawetz T. H., ISP, 14, 1982, pp. 111-13. Villanueva E., Cr, 14, 1982, pp. 127-9. Wolff R. P., PS(I), 28, 1981, pp. 352-3. Wuchterl K., AZP, 11, no. 2, 1986, pp. 57-8.

Wittgenstein's lectures. Cambridge 1932-5

1961. Collins J., MS, 59, 1982, pp. 223-4. Greisch J., AP, 45, 1982, pp. 325-7. Hacker P. M. S., PR, 90, 1981, pp. 444-8. Hunter J., CJP, 14, 1984, pp. 153-65. Mayberry T. C., PInv, 4, no. 1, 1981, pp. 41-4. Morawetz T. H., ISP, 14, 1982, pp. 111-13. Wallner F., PLA, 35, 1982, pp. 266-8. Wolff R. P., PS(I), 28, 1981, pp. 352-3.

Lectures and conversations on aesthetics, psychology and religious belief

1962. Anon, TLS, no. 3375, 3 Nov. 1966, p. 1006. Barrett, C., AP, 28, 1965, pp. 5-22. Beardsley M. C., JAAC, 26, 1967-8, pp. 554-7. Bilsky M., PInv, 2, 1979, pp. 69-72. Bouveresse J., Cri, 28, 1972, pp. 441-59. Collins J., MS, 44, 1966-7, pp. 421-3. Engel S. M., D, 7, 1968-9, pp. 108-21. Flew A., 'Spectator', 16 Sept. 1966, p. 355. Frongia G., GCFI, 50, 1971, pp. 120-30. Gargani A. G., RCSF, 23, 1968, pp. 475-7. Griffiths L., M, 79, 1970, pp. 464-6. Hepburn R. W., PB, 8, no. 1, 1967, pp. 29-31. Hofstadter A., JVI, 3, 1969, pp. 63-71. Lescourret M.-A., Cri, 39, 1983, pp. 764-73. Morick H., IPQ, 8, 1968, pp. 651-3. Shalom A., D, 6, 1967-8, pp. 103-13. Wollheim R., 'New Statesman', 72, 1966, pp. 367-8.

Lectures on the foundations of mathematics

1963. Bouveresse J., Cri, 33, 1977, pp. 316-51. Brenner W., PM, 12, 1975, pp. 153-4. Canfield J. V., CJP, 11, 1981, pp. 333-56. Coope Ch., PB, 20, 1979, pp. 1-8. Goldstein L., PQ, 27, 1977, pp. 370-1. Gunter P. A. Y., JHP, 17, 1979, pp. 361-3. Klemke E. D., Ph, 12, 1982-3, pp. 431-4. Morrison P. G., PFR, 37, 1976-7, pp. 584-6.

Letters to Russell, Keynes and Moore

1964. Bell, D., Ru, 15, 1974, pp. 26-8. Edwards J. C., PR, 85, 1976, pp. 271-4. Goldstein L., PQ, 25, 1975, pp. 279-80. Griffin N., AJP, 53, 1975, p. 102.

Briefe an L. von Ficker

1965. Garavaso P., 'Verifiche', S, 1976, pp. 332-6. Titze H., PLA, 23, 1970, pp. 344-8.

Engelmann: Letters from Wittgenstein

1966. Anon, TLS, 12 Sept. 1968, p. 1024. Frongia G., GCFI, 50, 1971, pp. 511-17. Keyt D., D, 8, 1969-70, pp. 128-31. Trinchero M., RF, 59, 1968, pp. 243-4.

Letters to C. K. Ogden

1967. Hallett G., HJ, 15, 1974, pp. 347-8. Stenius E., PQ, 25, 1975, pp. 62-8. Wolf M., PS(I),22, pp. 275-6.

INDEX OF SUBJECTS

General

Biographical contributions, memoirs, testimony, etc., 111, 149, 152, 153, 154, 158, 159, 166, 189, 195, 205, 216, 221, 226, 229, 282, 283, 325, 328, 342, 370, 395, 410, 486, 547, 572, 582, 720, 787, 787, 801, 820, 851, 876, 881, 882, 890, 903, 914, 966, 979, 1027, 1108, 1156, 1197, 1266, 1267, 1222, 1279, 1281, 1305, 1329, 1366, 1379, 1473, 1511, 1553, 1566, 1603, 1707, 1729, 1814, 1818

Bibliographical contributions, 548, 642, 654, 744, 932, 967, 1321, 1341, 1410, 1781, 1816, 1881

The *Nachlass* and its publication, 149, 150, 226, 251, 254, 389, 568, 698, 818, 1027, 1087, 1157, 1291, 1300, 1441, 1553, 1566, 1689, 1691, 1923

Notes of Wittgenstein's lectures and conversation, 205, 283, 486, 496, 497, 734, 787, 1027, 1222, 1173, 1379, 1554, 1829

General and introductory works, 151, 170, 242, 247, 265, 341, 450, 452, 490, 507, 549, 570, 644, 654, 657, 669, 681, 692, 695, 703, 717, 729, 763, 771, 778, 789, 792, 804, 866, 877, 910, 972, 1011, 1017, 1027, 1028, 1034, 1049, 1060, 1156, 1231, 1361, 1362, 1479, 1608, 1632, 1734, 1736, 1777, 1819, 1821, 1846, 1931

The relation between different phases in Wittgenstein's thought, 168, 172, 294, 295, 297, 354, 355, 423, 450, 452, 507, 521, 533, 557, 594, 633, 643, 654, 677, 678, 690, 729, 776, 792, 810, 857, 870, 876, 877, 898, 910, 958, 990, 1025, 1034,

Wittgenstein and modern philosophy
(see also Index of thinkers referred to)

Relations with earlier philosophical traditions
(see also Index of thinkers referred to)

Writings prior to and preparatory for Tractatus

Tractatus logico-philosophicus

287, 306, 347, 369, 432, 437, 471, 474, 487, 605, 642, 706, 710, 771, 862, 910, 943, 1055, 1132, 1172, 1251, 1298, 1351, 1561, 1563, 1596, 1630, 1800, 1806, 1844, 1852, 1863

The foundations of mathematics, 4, 16, 28, 30, 33, 41, 59, 69, 90, 306, 432, 471, 485, 642, 771, 1120, 1280, 1298, 1323, 1373, 1721, 1901

Foundations of empirical science (induction, causality, the laws of physics, etc.), 30, 35, 47, 55, 67, 81, 82, 90, 123, 139, 182, 326, 432, 642, 862, 1226, 1298, 1474, 1538, 1552, 1553, 1562, 1564, 1596, 1853, 1901

Mysticism and the limits of sense; the saying–showing distinction, 4, 134, 165, 170, 178, 249, 306, 318, 321, 345, 416, 432, 451, 461, 519, 575, 651, 704, 731, 766, 780, 856, 886, 915, 946, 988, 995, 1007, 1030, 1037, 1045, 1051, 1077, 1166, 1186, 1220, 1232, 1376, 1392, 1421, 1468, 1500, 1541, 1551, 1581, 1635, 1636, 1666, 1670, 1716, 1742, 1790, 1828, 1836, 1857, 1863, 1930, 1937

The subject and solipsism, 4, 60, 62, 63, 64, 65, 119, 126, 151, 190, 260, 279, 293, 306, 381, 418, 432, 436, 437, 519, 532, 564, 575, 630, 740, 764, 789, 790, 804, 825, 910, 982, 1012, 1028, 1034, 1155, 1345, 1380, 1391, 1429, 1443, 1457, 1496, 1559, 1563, 1581, 1689, 1691, 1742, 1857, 1931, 1932

The nature of ethics and particular ethical problems, 52, 127, 131, 186, 191, 235, 241, 306, 432, 461, 519, 563, 632, 884, 886, 956, 1232, 1267, 1313, 1315, 1336, 1377, 1391, 1402, 1429, 1443, 1468, 1500, 1508, 1517, 1523, 1559, 1562, 1581, 1630, 1636, 1716, 1724, 1732, 1748, 1751, 1763, 1776, 1815, 1836, 1845, 1851, 1929

Metaphysics, 30, 44, 45, 55, 65, 66, 68, 71, 76, 79, 140, 173, 190, 212, 241, 305, 429, 432, 762, 995, 1214, 1326, 1418, 1454, 1468, 1506, 1517, 1529, 1562, 1634, 1815, 1857, 1908

Philosophical method, 4, 34, 50, 56, 57, 65, 67, 68, 71, 75, 79, 96, 106, 129, 131, 139, 173, 190, 306, 369, 428, 432, 633, 642, 771, 911, 969, 1027, 1246, 1332, 1336, 1381, 1418,

Subjects treated in writings
subsequent to Tractatus

Theory of language, 103, 107, 201, 214, 225, 289, 299, 322, 327, 337, 375, 383, 423, 468, 472, 517, 566, 567, 602, 609, 702, 757, 765, 797, 826, 858, 1062, 1066, 1303, 1335, 1380, 1381, 1384, 1411, 1437, 1563, 1572, 1593, 1613, 1647, 1649, 1665, 1675, 1689, 1690, 1731, 1735, 1743, 1752, 1850, 1855, 1923

Meaning, use, proper names, ostensive definition, etc., 87, 110, 210, 217, 250, 268, 285, 289, 322, 337, 423, 458, 525, 541, 557, 643, 686, 701, 714, 721, 767, 771, 789, 796, 823, 913, 917, 989, 1028, 1050, 1111, 1149, 1222, 1225, 1235, 1245, 1256, 1273, 1303, 1328, 1334, 1356, 1357, 1376, 1380, 1384, 1397, 1398, 1403, 1406, 1471, 1503, 1524, 1563, 1564, 1572, 1575, 1579, 1589, 1615, 1617, 1637, 1641, 1650, 1654, 1675, 1689, 1695, 1709, 1719, 1722, 1732, 1735, 1743, 1752, 1769, 1791, 1822, 1835, 1848, 1859, 1884, 1903, 1913, 1921

Understanding, meaning, learning, mastering practices, etc., 525, 683, 767, 1079, 1149, 1168, 1212, 1250, 1294, 1303, 1347, 1356, 1384, 1563, 1579, 1617, 1695, 1709, 1760, 1884, 1913

Language games, 211, 269, 319, 327, 349, 361, 362, 423, 445, 448, 509, 531, 571, 580, 587, 602, 624, 635, 667, 733, 798, 811, 821, 833, 839, 871, 887, 902, 957, 978, 1027, 1111, 1178, 1216, 1230, 1260, 1289, 1303, 1334, 1347, 1376, 1378, 1381, 1382, 1383, 1389, 1563, 1579, 1580, 1620, 1665, 1728, 1731, 1743, 1744, 1792, 1805, 1822, 1848, 1852, 1914

Rules and grammar, 87, 233, 282, 289, 299, 301, 320, 329, 331, 445, 468, 496, 531, 642, 686, 712, 908, 922, 998, 1027, 1185, 1218, 1303, 1310, 1328, 1378, 1380, 1381, 1384, 1386, 1397, 1422, 1501, 1516, 1522, 1544, 1546, 1550, 1563, 1565, 1589, 1602, 1639, 1641, 1646, 1650, 1659, 1695, 1713, 1714, 1717, 1723, 1732, 1735, 1743, 1748, 1760, 1765, 1770, 1789, 1818, 1832, 1859, 1861, 1864, 1865, 1867, 1890. 1902, 1903, 1904, 1907, 1910, 1938

Family resemblances and common names, the problem of the universals, 280, 336, 387, 396, 420, 463, 469, 478, 496, 540, 571, 578, 589, 595, 611, 620, 622, 628, 635, 638, 642, 684, 721,

Philosophy as therapy, the method and nature of philosophy, 84,
91, 100, 114, 120, 121, 163, 184, 194, 198, 199, 214, 225,
235, 238, 248, 259, 260, 269, 285, 296, 297, 317, 373, 379,
383, 384, 411, 417, 465, 472, 496, 511, 521, 523, 533, 567,
584, 617, 653, 705, 715, 729, 758, 771, 789, 792, 816, 817,
819, 854, 857, 894, 897, 898, 899, 919, 945, 949, 1043, 1056,
1171, 1196, 1213, 1221, 1236, 1243, 1246, 1254, 1261, 1268,
1303, 1316, 1317, 1322, 1331, 1336, 1343, 1365, 1378, 1380,
1381, 1385, 1389, 1390, 1415, 1440, 1476, 1488, 1528, 1540,
1549, 1550, 1564, 1584, 1602, 1619, 1642, 1663, 1689, 1690,
1691, 1701, 1712, 1717, 1724, 1727, 1728, 1732, 1744, 1758,
1762, 1778, 1782, 1788, 1810, 1818, 1820, 1865, 1874, 1886,
1923, 1928

The influence of Wittgenstein on other disciplines

Linguistics, 217, 517, 542, 624, 797, 826, 864, 911, 913, 1015,
1100, 1147, 1320, 1335, 1381, 1384, 1491, 1649, 1657

Literature and literary theory, art criticism, 499, 722, 772, 912,
1032, 1053, 1228, 1233, 1283, 1331, 1383, 1427, 1656, 1719,
1741, 1745, 1752, 1755, 1827, 1834, 1843

Architecture, 720, 966, 1475, 1603, 1818

Political thought, 1371, 1585, 1739, 1776

Theory and philosophy of history, 1393, 1601, 1660, 1731, 1776,
1784, 1855, 1874

Educational theory, 395, 828, 914, 1103, 1329, 1443, 1511,
1642, 1657, 1743, 1756, 1789, 1805, 1814, 1902, 1911, 1913

Social sciences and social anthropology, 299, 368, 459, 488, 556,
724, 785, 827, 887, 965, 985, 1031, 1042, 1085, 1090, 1113,
1122, 1138, 1163, 1167, 1195, 1204, 1223, 1273, 1301, 1384,
1385, 1453, 1563, 1573, 1582, 1585, 1594, 1610, 1616, 1645,
1652, 1662, 1663, 1706, 1738, 1739, 1776, 1874, 1901, 1902,
1917, 1922, 1933, 1934

· Psychology and psychoanalysis (see also Freud in Index of
thinkers referred to), 433, 441, 699, 789, 856, 1010, 1040,
1124, 1298, 1318, 1364, 1505, 1539, 1563, 1564, 1600, 1653,
1678, 1740, 1757, 1780, 1812, 1879, 1902, 1919, 1936

INDEX OF THINKERS
REFERRED TO IN
THE LITERATURE

References to authors of items as such are listed in that Index.

INDEX OF AUTHORS
OF ITEMS

Roman figures represent an author's items, or contributions to items, in the Guide. Italic figures represent other authors' discussions of such contributions or items. References to an author in respect of writings not in the Guide may be found in the Index of Thinkers Referred To. Reviews listed as such are not indexed, save for reviews of writings by Wittgenstein.